*Pluralism & Progressives*

Arthur Mann, Advisory Editor in American History

# PLURALISM  PROGRESSIVES

Hull House and the New Immigrants, 1890–1919

## Rivka Shpak Lissak

University of Chicago Press
Chicago & London

RIVKA SHPAK LISSAK is a lecturer in American history at Tel Aviv University.

The University of Chicago Press, Chicago 60637
The University of Chicago Press, Ltd., London

98 97 96 95 94 93 92 91 90 89      5 4 3 2 1
Library of Congress Cataloging-in-Publication Data

Lissak, Rivka Shpak
    Pluralism & progressives: Hull House and the new immigrants,
1890–1919 / Rivka S. Lissak.
        p.    cm.
    Bibliography: p.
    Includes index.
    ISBN 0-226-48502-1 (alk. paper)
    1. Hull House (Chicago, Ill.) 2. Social work with immigrants—
United States. 3. Pluralism (Social sciences)—United States.
4. Ethnicity—United States.  I. Title.  II. Title: Pluralism and
progressives.
HV4196.C4L57      1989
362.84′009773′11—dc20                                        89-32973
                                                                  CIP

To my children

**Boaz and Michal**

# CONTENTS

# ACKNOWLEDGMENTS

My study of the Hull House group began under the supervision of Professor Arthur G.Goren, while I was working on my Ph.D. dissertation at the Hebrew University, Jerusalem. I am glad to acknowledge his sympathetic support and advice. I also greatly appreciate the sympathetic support and advice of Professor Arthur Mann of the University of Chicago. The encouragement and comments of these two professors were very important in completing this manuscript.

The research reported here received financial support from the American Research Fellowship Program through the United States–Israel Educational Foundation and the History Department at Tel Aviv University.

The sympathetic help of the librarians of the Interlibrary Loan at Tel Aviv University and of the curators and archivists of the archives in the United States used for this research should also be acknowledged.

# DEFINITION OF TERMS

The terms dealt with in this study will be based on the following definitions.

*Acculturation or cultural assimilation*—acquisition of the culture of the dominant group

*Social assimilation*—disappearance of group identity through changes in the habits and customs of persons and groups

*Structural assimilation*—disappearance of group identity through nondifferential association and exogamy

*Adjustment*—partial acquisition of the culture of the dominant group and partial social assimilation through participation in the economic, educational, and political systems

# INTRODUCTION

## THE MYTH OF JANE ADDAMS
## AND HULL HOUSE

The settlement house movement was established around the end of the nineteenth century in the slums of America's cities, by groups of men and women drawn from the upper middle class. The movement, which was an integral part of a comprehensive reform movement called progressivism, sought to help the working class cope with the problems created by industrialization, urbanization, and immigration. The Progressive movement had a general common ideological denominator, but it was not a unified, coherent movement. Rather, it was a combination of several groups, each concentrating on one or two problems. The two major components within progressivism were the movements for political and social reform. Although the settlement house workers were involved in both these areas, they were more active in the demand for social reform.

Living in the slums among those they wished to rescue, settlement workers soon realized that the working class consisted mostly of immigrants. They found that the newest arrivals, who came from eastern and southern Europe, apart from their problems as industrial workers, had the additional problem of social and cultural adjustment to the American environment. This new reality obliged settlement workers to formulate views on the nature of American nationalism and culture, on the place "new immigrants" and their cultures should occupy in American society, and on the kind of assimilation policy appropriate to the settlement workers' vision of America.

Indeed, the trauma of national disunity caused by the Civil War, along with the huge immigration from eastern and southern Europe that had begun after the 1880s, led native-born Americans to a reassessment of what was called the American Idea in its relation to nationalism, nationality (later called ethnicity), and culture during the Progressive period. Many of them regarded this "new immigration" as the principal cause of their social, economic, and political problems. A most striking aspect of the "immigrant problem" was the tendency to interpret socioeconomic problems in terms of cultural conflict. Native-born Americans attributed the situation to the differences in character, culture, and traditions between them and the "new immigrants." Above all, they were worried about the tendency apparent among "new immigrants" to

1

segregate themselves in ethnic-cultural enclaves, thus perpetuating diversity and the segmentation of American society.

By the middle of the nineteenth century it was widely accepted in America that the nation had a cosmopolitan origin and that the unifying element of American nationalism for the time being was neither a common past, nor common blood, but the American Idea. Unlike European nations, Americans were not united by the conventional attributes of nationalism, but by political homogeneity: a common commitment to the idea of democracy. This was the belief that America was the land of equality, freedom, and brotherhood, whose democratic form of government was equally receptive to all members of the human race, without discrimination on national or religious grounds.

The American Idea was revealed in the prerequisites for admission to the United States, in the interpretation of democracy, and in the components of American unity. Equality involved the recognition that all human beings were born equal and worthy of joining the American nation as well as sharing the same rights and privileges of citizenship. This implied also a confidence in the equal capacity of every human being for change, adaptation, and adjustment to the new environment. Freedom consisted of the individual's right to individuality, namely, to be different. Freedom of variation or diversity was not desirable for its own sake, but as a means of securing the right of the individual to self-realization and self-fulfillment in a democratic society. Nevertheless, freedom of variation applied to individuals, not groups or cultures. The right and freedom of association were derived from the right of the individual to form associations, not from the right of groups to form distinct organizations. The motto of American nationalism—*E Pluribus Unum*—stresses the ideal of unity that will arise out of diversity. Persistent diversity was not an ideal Americans aspired to but a temporary, inevitable situation to be dealt with in a democratic and humane manner. It described a condition rather than a permanent norm or theory. The ideal was brotherhood, amalgamation, harmony, and like-mindedness. The most striking feature of the American people was the quest for unity. Americans believed that common blood was not necessary to create unity, but they did not consider permanent group diversity to be desirable for American nationalism or culture. On the other hand, there was a general view that racial and cultural amalgamation would create a better nationality type and national culture. In this way Americans dealt with the tension between unity and diversity.[1]

In other words, everyone was considered capable of becoming American by adopting the American Idea, adapting to the American type, and swearing allegiance to America. However, newcomers were welcomed as individuals, not as groups, and were expected to renounce allegiance to their country of origin. The United States government rejected proposals to allot or sell land to groups of Irish and German newcomers as such, upon this same principle. Americans believed that out of the cosmopolitan or heterogeneous composition of the American people, in due time, a homogeneous nation and culture would emerge as a result of the influence of American institutions and the blending of different individual traits.[2]

While Americans agreed on the distinct features of Americanism, they disagreed on the source of the cultural influences by which it was to be shaped. Two ethnic concepts claimed to be the sources of America's present and future greatness: the cosmopolitan and the Anglo-Saxon. The proponents of the Anglo-Saxon theory believed that the strengths of the American system lay in the dominant influence of the English political tradition and culture during the colonial period. They had confidence in the peculiar capacity of the Anglo-Saxon race and culture to absorb individuals of different origins and their cultural influences, and remain basically unchanged. This capacity was the result of the dominant qualities of the Anglo-Saxon race and culture, which had already been proved by the survival of Anglo-Saxon traits in England, in spite of the mixed nature of the English people. Cosmopolitans on the other hand proclaimed that the source of America's greatness lay in its cosmopolitan origins, in its being a melting pot composed of European nationalities and cultures, rather than the English alone.[3]

The controversy on the nature of American nationalism and culture at the turn of the century focused on three issues: heredity as against environmentalism, the individual as against the group, and unity as against diversity.

The earliest expression of the controversy was a change in the basic assumptions of the Anglo-Saxon concept of nationalism and culture. The so-called immigrant situation undermined the confidence of many of the concept's adherents in the capacity of every human being to adapt to the Anglo-American model and in the dominant influence of the Anglo-American culture in the face of large-scale immigration. Their commitment to environmentalism and equality was shaken by heredity theories and racial determinism, and many came to believe that democracy and the culture by which it was bred were dependent upon racial origins. On this issue, the proponents of the Anglo-Saxon theory split into two groups: those who adopted theories of heredity, and those who wavered between ethnocentrism and environmentalism. In any case the latter group became convinced of the need to strengthen environmental influences through compulsory acculturation. In 1894 the first group organized the Immigration Restriction League, and the second established during the first decade of the twentieth century voluntary organizations that merged in 1915 into the Americanization movement.[4]

The Immigration Restriction League was organized by the so-called aristocracy of New England. The league challenged the underlying assumptions on which the American consensus was established. These New England Brahmins became convinced that a nation's achievements were dependent upon the quality and purity of its race. The Anglo-Saxon race, they stated, had the capacity to assimilate kindred races, without losing its special genius. It was, however, incapable of assimilating those races rated lowest in the racial and cultural scale. Native-born Americans of this ''aristocracy'' believed that they were faced with the danger of degradation of the Anglo-American race and the decline of American democracy and culture. The league campaigned for restriction of immigration as the only way to stop the invasion of degraded nationalities that threatened the ability of America to fulfill its ''manifest destiny'' as the stronghold of democracy.[5]

The Anglo-American assimilationists, or Americanizers, shared the racists' view that America owed its greatness to its Anglo-Saxon origin. For them the character of the American nation and its culture had been already formed, and newcomers were welcomed only on condition that they repudiate their national affiliation, language, and culture immediately on arrival and adapt themselves to the Anglo-American type and culture. They believed the American national character and cultural and political achievement could be preserved through compulsory acculturation. Gradually, they grew more and more concerned about the ''immigrant situation,'' and finally turned, under the impact of the First World War, to the restriction of immigration.[6]

The cosmopolitan view, opposed to the Americanizers' vision of America, was dramatized in 1908 by Israel Zangwill in his play *The Melting Pot*. The use of the melting pot as a symbol was new, although the ideas it represented had their origins in the dawn of independence. The idea behind the melting pot, that Americans and newcomers would be blended and shaped into a new nation with a new national character and a new culture, was rejected by most native-born Americans and by immigrant leaders.[7]

Cultural pluralism, a new concept of American nationalism and culture, emerged in the second decade of the twentieth century. It represented the response of ''new immigrants'' to the prevailing concepts on these issues, and their own perception of the place they and their cultures should occupy in American society. The theory of cultural pluralism emerged in Jewish circles as a solution to the Jewish struggle for survival in the modern world. Other groups in America solved their problem of survival in the same way. The theory or ideology of cultural pluralism was formulated in 1915 by Horace M. Kallen in response to Edward A. Ross's book *The Old World in the New*. Though it influenced the thinking of some native-born American intellectuals such as Randolph S. Bourne and the brothers Norman and Hutchins Hapgood, cultural pluralism was not accepted among American intellectuals and liberals before the late 1930s.[8]

The settlement house movement never reached a consensus on the place ''new immigrants'' and their cultures should occupy in American society. The two main attitudes were represented by Robert A. Woods of South End House in Boston and Jane Addams of Hull House in Chicago.[9]

Robert A. Woods was a representative of the mainstream middle-class Anglo-American assimilationist view. He considered ''new immigrants'' a menace to the homogeneity, national solidarity, and inherent nature of the Anglo-American civilization. The situation was already critical because the nation had been flooded with non-Anglo-Saxon immigrants from the eighteenth century on. The Anglo-American group, therefore, had to direct the nation's resources toward the dissolving of ethnic enclaves through geographical distribution and acculturation of individual newcomers. He was convinced of the superiority of the native spirit of the Anglo-American race and civilization. His view was ethnocentric despite defining the differences between Anglo-Americans and "new immigrants" in terms of social and cultural backwardness rather than race inferiority. However, in 1911, becoming convinced that this process was very slow and would take generations, he joined the Immigration Restriction League. He became convinced that the only way to put an end to the continuous recreation of ethnic-cultural enclaves and to ensure the effectiveness of distribution and acculturation efforts was through restriction of immigration.

He suggested a two-stage program to deal with the situation in America. The first consisted of blending all immigrant groups into one, through social and racial mingling, at the same time acculturating them to the Anglo-American model. He assigned to the Anglo-American element in American society the role of acculturators. Keeping its separate social and racial identity, this elite should serve as the priests of American society. Woods was reconciled to the inevitable second stage in which the Anglo-American element would become mingled with the rest. He was determined, however, to ensure the predominance of Anglo-American civilization in the cosmopolitanized American nation. For the time being he advocated acculturation without assimilation, or cultural assimilation without structural assimilation.[10]

Among her contemporaries, Jane Addams and her settlement house in Chicago, Hull House, occupied a special place because of her devotion to the poor "new immigrants" and their plight, as it was envisioned by the public. Her contemporaries held her in reverence and her creation, Hull House, as the model institution where newcomers were understood and helped. She was chosen in polls held by the most widely read magazines as the most popular woman in the country in the years before World War I and was the subject of numerous articles, poems, and journalistic interviews.[11] She was known as "Saint Jane" as early as the mid-1890s. Professor Earl Barness, in an address before an audience at the University of Chicago, suggested that she be canonized. Journalists called her "the Good Angel of Hull House," "the only saint America has produced," "Joan of Arc" of America, and even "the Madonna." Hull House was "a Mecca toward which . . . thousands of pilgrims, rich and poor, bend their reverent steps."[12]

The myth of the unique kind of relationship Jane Addams established with both individual newcomers and with their leaders was especially cultivated by the Hull House group and by other settlement workers. Addams herself encouraged the image of her unique position as "neighbor" and "interpreter."[13] The role of Hull House in the neighborhood was described in terms of reconstruction of the old country village relationship.

> Instinctively therefore they sought protection and fellowship in the larger households of the patriarchs, in tribal clans and village communities. The neighborhood was felt to have an equal claim with the family upon the settlement household located within the city wilderness. . . . As they had been wont to exchange their experiences with each other in their old country . . . so they exchanged them with her and she with them.[14]

According to the myth Hull House was the place not only where immigrants were treated as equals, but also where their cultures were respected and cultivated. For generations of native-born Americans, Addams and the Hull House group served as a symbol of the more sympathetic attitude toward immigrants and their cultures. They were considered advocates of ethnic diversity and of the preservation and cultivation of immigrant cultures. In Hull House immigrants were encouraged to be proud of their ethnic identity—newcomers were criticized for changing their names to American-sounding ones—and respect was shown for their cultures and traditions. Under Addams's inspiration, it was stated, Hull House became an immigrant institution, where newcomers were "properly approached and developed along the lines of their traditions and ideals." Addams was the "defender" of the newcomers' right to "self-expression." She viewed with deep sympathy the cultural heritage of immigrants and encouraged them to preserve their national holidays and customs, their dress, their crafts, and their folklore.[15]

The Hull House concept of the role immigrants and their cultures should occupy in American society was developed through fruitful cooperation between Hull House leaders and a group of university professors. At the turn of the century, there was a reciprocal relationship between settlements and universities. Settlements considered themselves posts of socioeconomic investigation in the slums, aimed at ameliorating social ills. The universities' concern with research and the training of their students on one hand, and with the improvement of society on the other, explains their involvement, especially that of sociologists, in settlement work. The University of Chicago Settlement in the stockyard district and the Northwestern University Settlement on the North Side are only two of numerous examples of university involvement in sponsoring settlements and in their activity.[16] Unlike these two settlements, Hull House was not formally affiliated with any university. Nevertheless, it maintained a close relationship with the University of Chicago, and a number of University of Chicago professors or their wives served on its board of trustees.[17] During its early years, university professors used to lecture at Hull House on a wide range of topics. This study, however, will focus not on Hull House's involvement in the amelioration of social conditions, but rather on its leaders' views and policies regarding various aspects of the education and sociocultural assimilation of "new immigrants" from eastern and southern Europe.

Hull House residents involved in this aspect of the house work included Jane Addams, Grace and Edith Abbott, and Sophonisba P. Breckinridge, along with other settlement workers such as Mary E. McDowell and educators such as Ella Flagg Young. This group was closely connected with several University of Chicago professors: John Dewey, both before and after he taught at the University of Chicago; George H. Mead of the Department of Philosophy; and William I. Thomas of the Department of Sociology. Professor Herbert A. Miller of Olivet College also became attached to this group during 1911, the year he spent at the University of Chicago. These two groups were part of the Chicago Liberal Progressive caucus, and their interaction resulted in the formulation of a common approach toward the assimilation of newcomers into American society. Despite differences of opinion, which no doubt existed, Hull House's experiments and experiences with "new immigrants" influenced the theories developed by these academics in the fields of education, sociology, and social psychology in the context of modern urban societies. The views of the Hull House group were in turn influenced by these theories, as is revealed in their writings on immigrant issues, and the theories were converted into ethnic-cultural policies.[18] The Liberal Progressive concept of immigrant assimilation into American society was thus shaped through experiments, research, and intercourse by these two groups. It was based on a wide consensus on sociocultural matters created by an underlying common world view, namely, the ideas of evolutionary progress and sociohumanitarian democracy, the American Liberal tradition, and some aspects of the philosophies of Felix Adler and William James.

The Liberal Progressive concept of assimilation, which was molded in the intellectual climate of the Progressive Age, was therefore an attempt to present a humanistic and democratic alternative to what Liberal Progressives considered to be the Americanizers' inhuman and undemocratic concept of assimilation. This Liberal concept of assimilation was scientifically articulated by William I. Thomas in *Old World Traits Transplanted,* edited and published in 1921 by Robert E. Park and Herbert A. Miller.[19]

Discarding Anglo-American racism as an alternative totally unacceptable to Liberal Progressives, historians have been divided on the exact location of the Progressives' position on assimilation within the spectrum of views held by different groups in American society at that time. Their views were identified by various historians as falling within the range between Anglo-American conformity, cosmopolitanism (or the melting pot), and cultural pluralism.[20] Jane Addams, who represented the Liberal Progressive view, became the object of a controversy concerning the views of Liberal Progressives as to the role that immigrants and their cultures should occupy in American society. John Higham describes Addams's views as "a new version of the cosmopolitan ideal of American nationality—a version emphasizing cultural accretion rather than racial blending." The concept of immigrants' contributions, he stated, "represented a modification of the melting pot tradition rather than a break from it."[21] Robert A. Carlson was of the opinion that Jane Addams was a "humanitarian Americanizer," rather than a proponent of a modified melting pot tradition. She "expected that their [the humanitarian Americanizers'] patience would pay off in the eventual disappearance of the cultures of the immigrants." In his view, Addams was as committed as other Americanizers to "secure a homogeneous America" based on "Anglo-Saxonism, a middle class society, republicanism, and God's true religion."[22] Mark Krug rejected this notion.

> Addams did not want to Anglo-Saxonize or Americanize the immigrants. On the contrary, long before sociologists like Horace Kallen coined the phrase, she embraced cultural pluralism as the desired basic concept pertaining to the American society. . . . She truly believed in the theory that constituted an amalgamation of the concepts of the melting pot and cultural pluralism and was convinced that American democracy . . . would emerge richer and stronger because of the contributions of the various immigrant groups.[23]

Other historians shared Krug's view that the settlement movement in general, and Hull House in particular, developed "an early form of pluralism."[24] Granted the confusion of the meaning of both the melting pot idea and cultural pluralism, this view seems closer to John Higham's interpretation than to Carlson's.

While there is agreement among scholars that John Dewey was another representative of Liberal Progressive views, there is a similar controversy regarding his views on the role that immigrants and their cultures should play in American society. The so-called revisionists interpreted Dewey as attempting to homogenize ethnic differences and destroy ethnic cultures, while the opposing group proclaimed him a cultural pluralist.[25]

Milton M. Gordon expressed this dilemma concerning John Dewey's views, asking, "Was there anything more than the melting pot idea in this view of America by one of its foremost philosophers? It would be hard to say, although Dewey's appreciation of the cultural values in Americans' various heritages is clear enough."[26]

From these differences it seems that the key to understanding Addams's views and, through them, those of the Liberal Progressives is to examine her attitude toward ethnic-cultural persistence. Addams, like John Dewey and others, actually expressed two seemingly contradictory views simultaneously: she spoke of mutual esteem and respect of variety and in favor of cross-fertilization. Did this mean the perpetuation of ethnic-cultural uniqueness and the cultivation of distinct immigrant cultures through cultural institutions, or the gradual elimination of ethnic-cultural segregation after the absorption of immigrants and their contributions into a common fund through cross-fertilization? And above all, did the immigrant ethnic cultures have a permanent place in American life? The unresolved tension between unity and diversity in Addams's writings raises the question whether her pluralism was real or a matter of expediency and mere rhetoric.

The major concern of this study is to understand the Liberal Progressive concept of assimilation and American nationalism and culture by examining the views and policies of Jane Addams and the Hull House group, against the background of the views of John Dewey and William I. Thomas. It analyzes the Hull House idea of community, its underlying world views, its views on assimilation policies, and its concept of American nationalism and culture. I shall also endeavor to reveal the response of the immigrant communities and their leaders to the Hull House ideology and policies. In brief, I shall consider here the realities behind the myth created around this most influential woman.

# PART ONE

## LIBERAL PROGRESSIVES AND ASSIMILATION

# ONE

# THE HULL HOUSE IDEA OF COMMUNITY

Jane Addams represented a Liberal trend—historians have called it social, humanitarian, or advanced progressivism—in the Progressive movement. The uniqueness of the Liberal wing was in its more comprehensive interpretation of democracy, dictated by humanitarianism as a universal moral ethic, and by the laws of social evolutionary progress. The social thinking of Jane Addams represented an effort to reconcile the Progressive quest for a unified, efficient society with the widest happiness for the individual, based upon the tradition of Liberal humanitarianism. The mission to implement this idea of society was entrusted to the enlightened upper middle class. This concept of the role of an elite of merit and virtue in society represented a transitional stage between the old concept of a deferential society and the meritocratic concept of the so-called corporate liberal state.

Jane Addams envisioned a "harmonized-holist" society that would combine individual freedom and social harmony. She did not challenge the basic structure of society: her solution to the crisis of American society and democracy was not radical social change. She shared the Progressive consensus that the ways of dealing with these problems were to destroy the party political machines, to extend the functions of government, and to strengthen its control by a merit system and various devices in the name of "the people." She tried to reconcile the ideal of political democracy, which was an American consensus, with the reality of an emerging urban society divided along class lines, by suggesting new measures within the existing conceptual framework to secure its flexibility and endurance. Her program was to recreate a sense of community through communication between classes, social reform, and the cultivation of common values, ideas, and norms of behavior. All classes should unify for stabilization of the sociopolitical order and abandon class consciousness and narrow interests for the common welfare.[1]

Addams's idea of community was greatly influenced by the idea of the evolutionary progress of societies, the universal moral code as articulated by Felix Adler, the social and educational philosophy of John Dewey, and the pragmatism of William James. She shared the Liberal Progressive belief that

13

human civilization and the human race were advancing forward and upwards. Societies, as well as species in the biological world, were evolving through an evolutionary process from simple to complex forms, from class-oriented to universally oriented societies. This process coincided with a "spiritual evolution" of mankind, an idea developed by Felix Adler. He believed that humanity was "forging its way toward the ethical perfection of mankind" as part of the general "orientation toward the ethically perfect society." Thus "the object of social reformation shall not be a mere change in condition under which men live, but a change in human nature itself."[2]

The culmination of the two evolutionary processes was the establishment of a democratic society. This represented the highest form of social evolution created by the highest form of a universal moral code. The Western world and especially the United States, the birthplace of modern democracy, were advancing steadily towards the realization of the goals of democracy. These were humanitarianism, equal opportunities, and universal brotherhood. Human civilization was progressing towards greater awareness of human suffering and greater concern for the welfare of all human beings. Competition, the law of the jungle, was in the process of being replaced by ethical law, and men were advancing towards understanding cooperation, love, and harmony.[3]

Addams's social thinking had much in common with the social philosophy of John Dewey. Both shared an idea of community based upon the assumption that human beings are "social creatures." They sought to resolve the tension between individual freedom and society, between unity and diversity. Dewey believed that every social organism needs to unify and coordinate its components to secure order and efficient organization. This is even more indispensable in a democracy. A democracy needs a wide consensus for its very survival because of the principle of equal participation. Every individual in a democracy should share "aims, beliefs, aspirations, knowledge—a common understanding—like mindedness."[4]

By the same token the very existence of a democracy lies in the breaking down of cultural and ethnic barriers, and the unification and harmonizing of the social organism along common cultural lines. Since "isolation makes for rigidity and formal institutionalization of life," democracy means not only freer interaction between social groups but also readjustment. "By breaking down of those barriers of class, race and national territory . . . each individual gets an opportunity to escape from the limitation of the social group . . . and to come into living contact with the broader environment."[5]

Dewey asserted that the functioning of a democratic society depends on first, "how numerous and varied are the interests which are consciously shared," and second, "how full and free is the interplay with other forms of association." He defined the first of these criteria as "the extent in which the interests of a group are shared by all its members." As G. H. Bantock has pointed out, this view revealed "strong equalizing tendencies in the direction of sameness" in its "asserted need for an increased community of experience open to all." The second criterion seemed to point to a counterdirection by its insistence upon maximum "interplay with other forms of association." Yet the two actually complemented each other. The first demanded like-mindedness, and the second stated the need for desegregation and elimination of differences through communication and sharing. Community, communication, and consensus were "the sacred trinity" upon which Jane Addams's and John Dewey's democracy was based.[6]

Addams identified the crisis of American society as its failure to adapt its institutions to the economic and social changes created by urbanization, industrialization, and immigration. These changes included the segmentation of the social organism along class lines, the emergence of an underprivileged working class suffering from a lack of equal opportunities in all spheres of life, and the social and personal disorganization in the slums of America's big cities. The result was class conflict, social antagonism, and a general disintegration of moral codes and social norms. In the slums the family and local community were being weakened, while there was an increase in what Addams termed "individualization," a process that threatened the main values, the social order, and even the continued existence of the society.[7]

Her solution to these problems was "to make the entire social organism democratic, to extend democracy beyond its political expression . . . The cure for the ills of Democracy is more democracy." She raised the need of "entering upon the second phase of democracy" by adopting a more comprehensive concept, a combination of sociohumanitarian and political democracy. Political equality had no meaning without social democracy and became self-destructive in a democratic form of government. Social democracy meant social harmony, brotherhood, and understanding.[8] This was essentially a moral question, the application of a universal moral code to industrial and social life. It was impossible "to establish a higher political life" in a society divided "into rich and poor; into favored . . . and into unfavored," characterized by "over-accumulation at one end of society and destitution at the other." She hoped that members of society would "later perceive the larger solidarity which includes labor and capital, and act upon the notion of universal kinship . . . [and that] all good citizens, capitalist and proletarian would act . . . upon an ethical sense so strong that it would easily override . . . class prejudices."[9] In a situation where "class interests become the governing and motive power" Addams sought to restore harmony and brotherhood by breaking down the barriers and recreating lines of communication between members of all classes. Understanding was the key for the second stage in the democratization of society, namely, better socioeconomic and educational opportunities for the lower classes.

Addams based the demand for a wider concept of democracy upon the assumption of the "solidarity of the human race" and upon the interdependence of the different components of society: "Without the advance and improvement of the Whole," she stated, "no man can hope for any lasting improvement in his own moral or material condition."[10] She advocated recognition of the principle of mutual dependence of all strata of society for personal well-being and for the common good. This principle was suggested as an alternative to both the traditional American competitive, individualistic philosophy and the socialist concept of class conflict as the only way to advance and improve the conditions of the lower classes.

No democracy could survive nor make any progress while large numbers of its constituency were denied the minimum standards of living and culture. Good and honest government in a democracy could only be pursued by intelligent, self-supporting, and independent citizens. This meant government intervention for the sake of the underprivileged, namely, taking the needs of all components of society into consideration by securing better opportunities for the working class through social welfare, education, and labor legislation. Bettering the conditions of the lower classes was not an act of charity or an expression of the generosity of the well-to-do towards the less fortunate members of society, but a matter of self-interest on the part of the well-to-do, which served the common interest of the whole society. In short, social democracy was an inevitable stage in the evolution and progress of society towards full democracy, in accord with the Liberal humanitarian concept that held that the individual's happiness and right to opportunity was in his own and in society's best interests and was, besides, a moral obligation determined by the universal moral code, as developed by Felix Adler.[11]

Yet Addams maintained that social democracy should not be interpreted merely in terms of class and industrial relations between the higher and lower classes, but should be applied to the relations between individuals from different classes. Addams's conclusion was that "we are thus brought to a conception of Democracy not merely as a sentiment which desires the well-being of all men, but as that which affords a rule of living as well as a test of faith." Treating all human beings with dignity, respect, and sympathy was an expression of the democratic principle of the equality of all men. Such an attitude was indispensable for the reconstruction of the sense of community.[12] She was greatly influenced by the insistence on the "democratic respect for the sacredness of individuality" which was emphasized in the philosophy of William James. In his essay "On a Certain Blindness in Human Beings," he criticized the highly educated classes for their disregard of the feelings of people different from themselves. He pointed to the "stupidity and injustice of our opinions, so far as they deal with the significance of alien lives. Hence the falsity of our judgements, so far as they presume to decide in an absolute way on the value of the other persons'

16

conditions or ideals.'' James called for a democratic evaluation of other people's lives: ''wherever a process of life communicates an eagerness to him who lives it, there the life becomes genuinely significant . . . there is 'importance' in the only real and positive sense in which importance ever anywhere can be.''[13] Respect and toleration represented in James's view the ancient American doctrine of live and let live.

Another major problem that prevented reestablishing a sense of community was the social and personal disorganization in the slums, which threatened the coherence of the whole community and the continued existence of democracy. A harmonized social organism demanded that the members of the different classes share common goals and sentiments. These could be achieved by supplementing the primary agencies of society with secondary ones to strengthen social solidarity. This involved tackling the symptoms of disorganization in the slums, such as atomization, family disintegration, juvenile delinquency, and the decline of parental authority. Jane Addams therefore sought to restore the community and the family as the major traditional agencies of society, and to develop the public schools into supporting instruments of social cohesion. However, she also asserted the need for a major community institution to serve as a clearinghouse and as a source of leadership, to give direction to the other agencies, and this was the settlement house.[14]

The major role in curing the ills of American democracy was entrusted, Addams believed, to the ''better element'' in American society. The ''better element'' was a synonym for a group of the educated and enlightened, for the most part upper middle class in origin. This elite felt it had civic, humanitarian, and moral responsibilities to mediate between the upper and lower classes, create mutual understanding and sympathy, and secure through social reforms the stability and progress needed for social order. They hoped to achieve these objectives by voluntary work in social settlements, by lobbying through civic voluntary organizations for better civic and social legislation, and by contributions of money to maintain the settlements and other civic and social projects. The issue was leadership. Their major role as they saw it was to provide political leadership on municipal, state, and federal levels in their efforts to adapt American institutions to the socioeconomic changes caused by urbanization, industrialization, and immigration. The claim for leadership of this Liberal Progressive group was made in the name of the so-called middle class (in reality upper middle class), of which they considered themselves true representatives. This was the Liberal Progressive interpretation of leadership in a democracy as compared with the aristocratic concept of the leadership of the upper classes in less democratic societies.

The underlying assumption was that merit and virtue were criteria for eligibility for public service, both voluntary and governmental. It was not only the civic, humanitarian, and moral responsibility of the ''better element'' to serve, but also its legitimate right to play a leading role in society, since society deserved the best services it could get. This argument was used to undermine the legitimacy of the "democratically elected" but corrupt politicians in the bitter struggle for power and control between the political machines and upper-middle-class Progressives.[15] As Charles Nagel, former secretary of commerce and labor, argued in an address to the 1916 annual meeting of the Immigrants' Protective League, a Liberal Progressive agency, Liberal Progressives "could not admit that a proprietary class, once created, can continue by right of inheritance. They have got to earn it generation by generation . . . They have got to deserve the control if they are going to have it . . . no race should predominate except in so far as it has virtue and ability." Julian W. Mack, the president of the league, confirmed in his response to the address that Nagel's "conception of Americanization expresses, I believe, the underlying thought in the work of this League."[16]

By "merit and virtue" Jane Addams referred to intellectual competency and personal qualities. Merit meant personal capacity proved by university education, successful business enterprise, or a career in the professions. Virtue was interpreted as the pursuit of altruistic objectives for the common good of the entire society rather than of a narrow class or group or the pursuit of personal materialistic or political gains. This so-called altruistic approach to public service was influenced by the Protestant tradition and Puritan ethic of service, which was given universal articulation by Felix Adler. However, the combination of "merit and virtue" for eligibility for public service limited leadership to the members of the wealthy and leisured classes—to those who had the means to develop their personal and intellectual capacities through a long period of education, who had been socialized according to the so-called universal ethic, and who could afford to dedicate their life to social service without any wish for material compensation or personal gain.[17]

The concept of "merit and virtue" was an integral part of a more comprehensive Progressive notion that a wide foundation of common interest united all components of society and that the middle class was the best interpreter and true representative of the common interest of society. Since the middle class occupied a middle position in the social structure between the upper class with its big-business interest and the lower classes with the voting power, it served as an equilibrator, a counterbalance between the upper and lower narrow class interests. Its well-to-do members were believed to be less easily corrupted by graft and did not need to depend on the public for their subsistence while serving the public. Also, having no big-business interests, they seemed less likely to utilize public positions for business interests. The middle class was thus in a position to consider the interests and needs of all the components of society in the most disinterested way.[18]

Such an approach justified assigning a passive role to both the upper and the lower classes in the leadership of the nation, as representatives of narrow class or group interests. Moreover, the assumption that a wide foundation of common interest united society denied the legitimacy of class or group interests, although it recognized the legitimate needs of the members of all classes. The members of the lower classes were especially ill equipped for leadership because they lacked the middle-class qualities that enabled one to look beyond narrow and selfish personal, class, or group interests to the good of the whole society. The attitude towards the upper class was, however, more ambivalent, since the borders between the upper middle class and the upper class were more vaguely defined, the former being well-to-do and socially connected with the latter.[19]

This perception of the role of the middle class proved that Liberal Progressives continued to think of American society in terms of a middle-class or even a frontier classless society. Even though most of them were urban upper middle class, they still saw themselves as representatives of a rural middle-class society, namely, of "the people," although this type of society was vanishing. This was understandable for people who grew up during the transition from a rural to an urban society but were still imbued with the egalitarian principles and democratic tradition of rural middle-class society. Their self-image lagged behind their social status. The meaning of "the people" in Progressive terminology should therefore be interpreted in this context.

The idea of the leading role of the "better element" in American society was the Progressive interpretation of the traditional concept of a "deferential society," in which the "helpless" and ignorant lower classes acknowledged the qualifications of the elite and accepted its hegemony in society. In a democratic society the elite should be recruited from what Progressives termed the middle class rather than from the upper class.

Granted the dominant role of the "better element" in American society, the settlement movement considered itself to be the leaven in the dough. Jane Addams believed that persons were "chosen" for leadership by their moral eligibility and/or through a lifetime of dedication to serve society. The ultimate test was to live in the slums and to sacrifice private life and happiness for a life of discipline and total dedication to the ideal of American democracy. The settlement idea developed a new way of life which came to be called secular saintliness.[20]

Addams interpreted the settlement idea as the response of men and women drawn from the enlightened upper middle class, and representatives of the middle class, to the crisis of American society. The early settlement idea was an expression of the subjective necessity of the members of the upper middle class to serve, and the objective necessity of the lower classes to be served and led. Addams pointed to the "fast-growing number of cultivated young people who have had the advantages of college and have no recognized outlet for their active faculties," against a situation of people "without leisure or energy for anything but the gain of subsistence. The working class live side by side, many of them without knowledge of each other, without fellowship, without local tradition or public spirit, without social organization of any kind. . . . The chaos is as great as it would be were they working in huge factories without foreman or superintendent.'' This idea of the ''mutual need'' of both an enlightened elite and the ''helpless masses'' was Addams's rationalization of the voluntarism embodied in the settlement ideology. Both the need to serve and the need to be served were recognized as socially legitimate and useful.[21]

Implicit in this justification of the need for social settlements was the notion that the role of the educated upper middle class was to lead while that of the uneducated lower classes was to be passively led. Indeed, the idea that the lower classes were dependent upon the leadership abilities of the educated upper middle class gradually received more emphasis than the thesis of ''mutual need.'' Thus the concepts of merit and virtue and middle-class origins served to rationalize and justify leadership by the upper middle class.

The idea of community and the role of the so-called better element drawn from the upper middle class had direct implications for the sociocultural composition of the residents and staff of social settlements and for their policies, especially in view of the passive role assigned to the lower classes. Studies of the socioeconomic composition of settlement workers prove that the typical settlement worker was a middle-class, or upper-middle-class, white Anglo-Saxon Protestant. This elitism was determined both by the movement's concept of the nature of the working class and by the voluntarism embodied in the settlement idea. Its emphasis on service without material compensation in its earlier years, like its professionalization in later years, made it impossible for members of the lower classes to become settlement workers in any meaningful number.[22] Moreover, the role of the so-called better element was a crucial component in the settlement program. The members of the middle class had the mission to be mediators and brokers between the upper and lower classes. In addition persons of education and refinement were to serve as a source of cultural inspiration and emulation to the lower classes. The dependence of the social settlement for contributions and lobbying on persons and voluntary organizations of upper-middle- and upper-class origin further reinforced its elitist nature. This elitism was also determined by the predominance of upper-middle-class women in the settlement staff and later in the profession of social work. Since upper-middle-class women had little chance of finding employment, the settlement movement gave them jobs and work that put meaning in their lives, rather than providing them with a living.[23]

The female majority in the settlement staff greatly prejudiced its chances of playing a leading role in working-class neighborhoods. Being part of a male-oriented conservative society, the male working class found it beneath its dignity to be directed by women. This contributed to the failure of men's clubs at Hull House, as well as in settlement houses throughout the country.[24]

The demand for efficiency, expertise, and disinterestedness as qualifications for social work, which grew within the settlement movement as an integral part of the quest for efficiency, professionalism, and impartiality in the administration of public affairs of the Progressive movement, created a crisis in the settlement movement. This demand contradicted one of the basic tenets of the settlement idea, namely, voluntarism and a lifetime commitment without material compensation. Gradually, as social work became a profession and the idea of living in the slums lost its impetus, the payroll lists expanded while the volunteer lists diminished. Yet the social composition of the staff remained predominantly upper middle class because of the educational qualifications and expenses involved in training for social work. The Chicago School of Civics and Philanthropy established in 1903 to train social workers demanded, during its early years, a college education or an "exceptional experience or ability in social work together with a good general education . . . and introductory courses in sociology, civics and political economy or the reading of standard books on these subjects." The entrance requirements were somewhat lowered during the First World War, and the school demanded only "a general education equivalent to that of a good secondary school, and in addition, either . . . a considerable part of a college or university course, or . . . ability in practical work . . . and . . . evidence of good character." The tuition and other expenses involved in taking one or two years of training in social work amounted to an average of $400 to $500 a year. The average annual income of unskilled workers at the time was $500 a year, so that it was no wonder that the students and the professional social workers were mostly upper- or middle-class native-born Americans.[25]

The settlement movement's policies, derived from Jane Addams's idea of community, were to improve the living and working conditions of the working classes, to uplift them culturally, and to create a sense of community through the inculcation of a new value system. Hull House, like other settlements, carried out systematic studies of the socioeconomic, educational, and environmental conditions of the working class and then tried out solutions on an experimental basis as part of the settlement services. Its workers formulated legislative proposals and lobbied for the establishment of municipal, state, and federal agencies to deal with the designated problems. They also supported unions in their struggle for recognition, collective bargaining, and better wages and working conditions. Settlement workers rejected violence in industrial relations and sought to bring workers and employers to negotiate, rejecting any notion of class conflict. Jane Addams played a considerable role in the effort to overcome class antagonism and to establish industrial relations on a basis of understanding and cooperation.[26]

Hull House, as one of the leading settlements, undertook to establish and maintain educational and cultural enterprises for the working class and to introduce it to the treasures of civilization. In doing so settlement workers challenged the nineteenth-century assumption that the poor lacked the intellectual capacities needed for education and enjoyment of the gifts of civilization. They argued instead that workers deserved an opportunity to share the achievements of education and culture and that these in turn were socially uplifting. They sought to refine the personality of working-class people by inculcating them with the "better element's" cultural values and value system, hoping to create in them an idea of community that would purify civic and political institutions. Felix Adler's Ethical Culture School served as a model upon which settlements developed their programs, in their efforts to instill and internalize what they considered Progressive and universal moral ideals. They aimed not only to redeem the working class's "spiritual poverty" but also to wipe out class ideology and behavior and to involve members of the working class in solving along Progressive lines the problems confronted by American society for the common welfare."[27]

The settlement cultural and educational programs were designed to reshape the attitudes and ways of thinking of members of the working class. This did not necessarily imply a change of their social affiliation. Yet these programs, together with the grants and scholarships awarded to the most qualified club members, opened for the more ambitious and talented members of the working class an avenue for higher education and mobility into the middle class. This avenue, however, was open only to a minority.

The settlement sought to restore the sense of community by unifying the social organism and creating a well-integrated and harmonized society. Its aims were to bridge the gap that urbanization and industrialization had created between the poor and the rich and to develop the settlement house as a major mediator and as an agency of social leadership. Its members claimed that they had come to live among the working people in settlement houses and share the lives of poor. Actually they sought in this way to reduce the mutual suspicion and ignorance of one class towards the other and create personal contacts with members of the working class. Settlement leaders believed it was possible to deal with social gaps through communication and brotherhood and by improving the conditions of the poor, thus replacing antagonism by cooperation, sympathy, and understanding. Settlement leaders had great confidence in the power of individual inspiration through friendly relations between the well-to-do and the less fortunate members of society, which would bind the different classes in friendship and solidarity, while the model of middle-class self-discipline and self-restraint would make industrial relations less violent.[28]

The settlement ideology and its policies were in fact designed to perpetuate the existing social order. The idea that society should be administered by an elite of merit, virtue, and middle-class qualities was translated into a policy aimed at disarming the workers of their class consciousness and hostility towards the well-to-do, through personal contact, social services, and cultural indoctrination. The educational opportunities afforded by the settlements were taken by the most capable and ambitious members of the working class, who thereby advanced into the middle class. This mobility of the "better element" of the working class deprived that class of its potential leadership, thus leaving it without able leaders and perpetuating its helplessness.

The settlement ideology assigned the working class a passive role in American society. This becomes evident from the rejection of class consciousness and class interest, from the treatment of the members of the working class as individuals who have certain common needs but not a distinct interest, and from the inculcation of the concept of common interest, with the educated middle class as its true representative. Social uplifting through introducing the members of the working class to "high culture" and instilling in them a "universal ethical value system" and Progressive ideology, called "education for good citizenship," was not intended to encourage the masses' active participation in civic life. Given that eligibility for public service was conditioned by class, merit, and virtue, the members of the working class were trained to support the upper-middle-class Progressive leaders in their reform programs, upon the principle of a deferential society. The settlement workers supported the organization of workers into unions for the improvement of their working and living conditions. Their desire, however, to replace class conflict by cooperation, and their program for social legislation were intended to counteract the development of a distinct working-class political or cultural identity. The settlements sought to destroy barriers of class and race, to dissolve tensions, and to unify the social organism under the direction and leadership of the "better element." Social welfare and labor legislation sponsored by enlightened representatives of the upper middle class were designed to reduce the importance and indispensability of the unions. It was hoped to reduce them to a secondary role and transfer most of their functions to governmental agencies controlled by the upper middle class upon the principle of a merit system. Significantly, settlement workers were very critical about the lack of merit and virtue of union leaders, and their narrow class vision of industrial relations. Union leaders, on the other hand, supported only a limited labor legislation program in the form of "protective legislation" directed at women and child labor. They were willing to cooperate with Progressives on these issues, but they were determined to preserve the unions' major role in industrial relations, without the intervention of reformers or governmental agencies.[29]

While the settlement movement had been established in response to the problems of the working class, Jane Addams and other settlement leaders gradually became aware of the growing predominance of "new immigrants" from southern and eastern Europe in the slums of America's big cities.

Settlement workers thus came face to face with the dilemma of immigrant assimilation into American society and were compelled to develop their own views of the role these newcomers and their cultures should play in America. In the following chapters we shall see how the settlement movement's perception of the working class's passive role in society, as well as their idea of community and culture, were applied to the role of immigrants as a whole.

# TWO

## THE HULL HOUSE CONCEPT
## OF IMMIGRANT ASSIMILATION

The emergence of self-contained immigrant subcommunities characterized by "institutional completeness," with their own sense of community and an ethnic identity, was another factor that reinforced the divisions within American society.[1] This created the need to reconsider the relevance of the existing Hull House idea of community in the light of two questions: in what direction was American society developing, and what was a democratic solution to ethnic identity.

Examining the forces at work in the slums, the Hull House group became convinced that, although the tendencies towards ethnic segregation seemed stronger than the forces leading towards the unification of American society according to their idea of community, the unifying forces would in the long run predominate. Indeed, the group came to see the dissolution of immigrant subcommittees and the loosening of ethnic affiliation and identity as necessary for the survival of American democracy. However, the assimilation of newcomers was to take place in accord with Hull House residents' idea of political and social democracy—an expression of the "consent of the governed," namely, the wishes of the newcomers. Therefore, flexibility was required in achieving the group's goals.

The concept of assimilation of the Hull House circle was articulated in sociological terms by William I. Thomas in his study *Old World Traits Transplanted*. He pointed out that "assimilation is thus as inevitable as it is desirable; it is impossible for the immigrants we receive to remain permanently in separate groups. . . . We can delay or hasten this development. We cannot stop it. . . . And this is the completely democratic process, for we cannot have a political democracy unless we have a social democracy also."[2] This last phrase was an echo of Jane Addam's definition of social democracy. Democracy involved accepting newcomers as equals. "We must make the immigrants a working part in our system of life, ideals and political as well as economic, or lose the character of our culture." Politically this meant equal participation, while socially it meant structural assimilation. For Thomas as for Addams social democracy meant eliminating social, national, and cultural barriers among newcomers and between them and native-born Americans.

Social democracy would include free intercourse and communication, without discrimination or prejudice, racial blending through the incorporation of newcomers into primary groups—the cliques, clubs, and institutions of the host society—and intermarriage. Thomas interpreted the Hull House idea of community in sociological terms, stating that a community could survive in so far as its members "have a body of common memories sufficient to enable them to understand each other," or what is called by psychologists "apperception mass." In other words, American society could "assimilate the immigrants only if their attitudes and values, their ideas on the conduct of life, are brought into harmony with our own." This meant that "they cannot be intelligent citizens unless they 'get the hang' of American ways of thinking as well as doing." The process of assimilation required that newcomers would share the "American apperception mass," namely, "a fund of knowledge, experience, sentiments, and ideals common to the whole community."[3]

At the same time Thomas admitted that "different races and nationalities, as wholes, represent different apperception masses." Thus the immigrant could adopt the American "apperception mass" only if a certain identity of experiences and memories existed between the immigrant and American heritages. "The new experience derives its significance from the character and interpretation of previous experiences . . . in the process of learning, a new fact has a meaning and makes an appeal if it is identified with some previous experience, something that is already known and felt." Examining the differences between the immigrant and American heritages and apperception masses, Thomas concluded that they "do not differ profoundly . . . immigrant heritages usually differ but slightly from ours, probably not more than ours differ from those of our more conservative grandfathers."[4]

Thomas was expressing the Liberal Progressive consensus as proclaimed in 1912 by the committee on assimilation of the National Conference of Charities and Correction, in which Hull House residents were influential members: "It is . . . true that our literature and language, our laws and religion, have received their ideas, forms, and their very spirit, from the same primitive sources from which these newer immigrants derive their own lives. Upon this common ground the bridge between old and new traditions could gradually be built."[5]

If no essential differences existed between the American apperception mass and the immigrants', the only problem from the viewpoint of democracy was "the consent of the governed." Since America was not a nation unified by a common history or by common blood, the criterion for consent was the adoption of the American Idea. Thus Hull House residents interpreted the very decision to come to the New World as a rejection of the Old, and as implicit assent to the ideals and traditions that shaped American society—that is, the American Idea. The belief that newcomers were motivated by the high ideals

America stood for, rather than by economic considerations, distinguished the Hull House group from nativists and Americanizers.[6]

Thomas expressed another Liberal Progressive consensus when he assumed that "every country is an area of cultural characterization" with "the right to preserve these values." He reconciled the seeming discrepancy between the principle of equal participation and the idea that every country had the right to incorporate immigrants "without losing the character of its culture," arguing that as newcomers should be accepted as equals into the economic, social, and political life so their cultural contributions should also be incorporated into American civilization. The principle of equal participation in the cultural sphere was preserved by "the fact that they bring valuable additions to our culture."[7] In the absence of essential cultural differences, no contradiction existed.

Another aspect of this discrepancy was the right of the individual newcomer to be different and to preserve his cultural identity, as opposed to the idea that every country had the right to incorporate immigrants without losing the character of its culture. Edith Abbott and Sophonisba P. Breckinridge, members of the Hull House group and the teaching staff of the University of Chicago, argued that immigrants could preserve their languages, customs, and traditions, if they so wished, within the family circle: "the children and parents may speak Polish, Hungarian, Russian or Yiddish, but these same children are to be trained for a civic life that has grown out of American experience and Anglo-Saxon tradition."[8] Thomas again expressed the Hull House circle view, arguing that individuals were entitled to preserve their "sentimental memories . . . and we should let them remain unmolested in the region of personal life."[9]

Liberal Progressives therefore interpreted the American tradition of diversity in terms of the right of the individual—rather than of the ethnic group—to be different, since the right of association (for example, for religious purposes) was an individual prerogative rather than the right of a group to segregate itself along ethnic lines. Newcomers were not required to renounce their languages and cultures upon arrival and adopt the English language and American ways immediately. There were entitled to establish immigrant ethnic and cultural organizations and agencies. Nevertheless, Liberal Progressives considered these only temporary measures till the newcomers became adjusted to the American environment.[10]

Living in the slums enabled Hull House residents to watch the two forces of segregation and assimilation at work in immigrant neighborhoods. One set of forces contributed to the emergence of immigrant subcommittees and to further ethnic segmentation of American society, with the prospect of ethnic persistence. The other set of forces was leading to the dissolution of ethnic segregation and the unification of American society. The Hull House circle was confident that the second set of forces would in the long run predominate.

In Thomas's words, this process could be delayed or hastened, but not stopped.[11]

Jane Addams and the Hull House group actually developed a theory that was later known as the Chicago School of Sociology theory of "natural areas." According to their theory ethnic persistence was contradictory to the very nature of the American economic system as a mobile and distributing factor. Since mobility was a motive of paramount importance in American life, the ethnic group could not survive as a dominant reference group. Americanization was considered a necessary condition for mobility. As one settlement worker wrote in a Hull House publication, "The greatest need of the Ghetto is its annihilation. The forces working for good in it are such as are tending to exterminate it. Some of the brightest minds are leaving the community as they advance in the professional circle, taking prominent positions as lawyers, physicians, and in the daily press, as well as in business." Moving to middle-class neighborhoods, these immigrants mingled with a cosmopolitan middle class. In the cosmopolitan environment the process of acculturation and structural assimilation was completed. The role of Hull House was clear: to accelerate this process by advancing the most capable and ambitious members of the immigrant neighborhoods. "The most vaunted educational work in the settlements amounts often to the stimulation mentally of a select few who are, in a sense, of the academic type of mind, and who easily and quickly respond to the academic methods employed" (by the Hull House college extension courses).[12]

The same process of ethnic disintegration was taking place among the newcomers who remained working class. Industrial interests were becoming a stronger social factor than ethnic interests. Workingmen of different origins were forced by social and economic circumstances to live and struggle together. "The United Mine Workers of America is taking men of a score of nationalities—English speaking and Slav, men of widely different creeds, languages, and customs, and of varying powers of industrial competition— and is welding them into an industrial brotherhood . . . While the rest of the country talks of assimilation as if we were a huge digestive apparatus, the man with whom the immigrant has come most sharply into competition has been forced into fraternal relations with him." This process proved that the socioeconomic interests and Americanization of the members of the working class were much stronger than their ethnic-cultural bonds. This was especially true in those ethnic groups where employers and employees came into direct conflict. The inevitable result was, therefore, the creation of an acculturated American working class composed of people of different origins. Unions would replace *landsmanshaften,* mutual benefit societies, and national fraternal organizations as forms of socioeconomic and cultural organization in immigrant neighborhoods.[13]

Ethnic solidarity was a temporary condition, to be replaced first by social mobility, or by industrial solidarity and Americanization, and second by social and structural assimilation. The final stage was the disappearance of ethnic affiliation and the emergence of a harmonized society.

Thomas used sociological arguments to prove that ethnic persistence had no chance in America and that assimilation was inevitable because of the very nature of American society and of ethnic groups. He noted three conditions for the perpetuation of ethnic identity and segregation: "the ability to perpetuate in the new generations the traditional memories of the group without loss; the ability to create values superior to those of America, and the maintenance of separation in order not to sink to the cultural level of America; or an ineradicable prejudice on one or both sides." These conditions, Thomas stated, did not exist in America. Immigrant groups from Europe did not represent different races. They could be "classified on the basis of language and custom" only. Language was the chief sign and instrument of their separate identity. In spite of their efforts to the contrary, "all immigrant groups are losing, even too completely and rapidly their languages." Moreover, the American experience had proved that voluntary isolation usually pauperized the cultures of segregated groups. "In a world characterized by individualization of function, values must be secured from wherever they exist in the whole world." And finally, the history of the Jews in America had shown that "prejudice and discrimination may be put aside as not serious enough in America to affect the persistence of immigrant groups."[14]

In the event, the emergence of ethnic subcommunities characterized by institutional completeness (residential segregation, preservation of traditional familial roles, creation of an ethnic sense of community, and the formation of social welfare, cultural, and educational agencies) seemed to contradict the Liberal Progressive belief in inevitable assimilation. They reconciled the reality of ethnicity and their interpretation of the assimilation forces at work in the slums by arguing that the former represented a temporary stage in the adjustment of newcomers to the new environment. Unlike most Americanizers, Liberal Progressives perceived the process of transformation from one culture to another as gradual. "The influence of an age old culture is sloughed off very slowly, and spiritual or emotional adaptation to a new culture took just as slowly." Till the immigrant learned to function within a new environment, he needed the "consciousness of kind" that his ethnic milieu gave him. Hull House residents understood and respected the immigrants' need to be temporarily segregated among their own people and to recreate an ethnically and culturally familiar milieu. Jane Addams criticized native-born Americans for expecting newcomers to assimilate completely within fewer years than was humanly possible. The immigrant had to overcome his sense of alienation and the lack of a sense of community, and to adjust himself daily to an industrial-urban society and a different civilization. To do this he needed the familiar milieu to endow him with a feeling of belonging in his new environment.[15]

Furthermore, the effects of too rapid assimilation were disastrous to individuals, to the family, and to American society. The role of the family in preserving the personal integrity of adults and the importance of parental authority as a bulwark against juvenile delinquency, especially given the negative effects of the children's rapid and superficial assimilation in comparison to their parents—all this indicated that temporary segregation and gradual assimilation were urgently needed.[16]

Thomas interpreted this Hull House tenet in sociological terms explaining that the organization of the immigrant community was "necessary as a regulative measure." He emphasized "the evident value of these immigrant organizations during the period of adjustment." Despite their shortcomings, immigrant communities and immigrant organizations aided the process of Americanization. "The immigrant is not a highly individualized person. He has been accustomed to live in a small, intimate, face to face group, and his conduct has been determined by the group. Naturally he needed the assistance of such a group for a time in America, and naturally this group is composed of his own people." Also, the immigrant community represented the newcomers' need for dignity, recognition, and economic security, as a safeguard against personal disorganization and as a means of developing a sense of belonging and a sense of responsibility to society. This was true in the short run. Preserving ethnic segregation beyond the period of adjustment was considered an undesirable perpetuation of the division of American society along ethnic lines. Liberal Progressives treated ethnic institutions such as the foreign press according to this approach.[17]

The Hull House assimilation policy recognized the need of newcomers for their ethnic-cultural community and that such a community was indispensable, although its dissolution was desirable and indeed inevitable. Consequently, it envisaged a two-stage process of assimilation: temporary segregation followed by the disintegration of the ethnic community. During the period of temporary segregation newcomers should become acquainted with the American environment by acquiring competence to function successfully within the economic and political systems. This acquaintance consisted of learning the English language, understanding American political institutions, and learning the economic and social system. This represented a policy of partial acculturation, or Americanization without social assimilation, namely, living within the ethnic community while creating some economic and political ties beyond ethnic borders.[18] Jane Addams expressed her feelings on this policy, stating that "Americanism was then regarded as a great cultural task and we eagerly sought to invent new instruments and methods with which to undertake it."[19] Another condition for successful assimilation was the creation of a sense of identification with the new homeland. The Hull House group believed that this should be done by creating a sense of continuity between past and present, between the old and new environment. Addams suggested that instead of the then current assumption that "past experience and traditions have no value, and that a new sentiment must be put into aliens by some external process," the emotional attachment of newcomers to their new homeland be built upon the assumption of continuity.[20] This was a tenet of Hull House belief: "we believed that America could be best understood by the immigrants if we ourselves, Americans, made some sort of connection with their past history and experiences."[21] Thomas again articulated this idea in sociological terms, stating the importance of a certain identity of experiences and memories between immigrants and Americans for assimilation "because the process of learning a new fact has a meaning and makes appeal only if it is identified with some previous experience."[22]

Addams insisted that emotional attachment or a sense of community should be inculcated by "bringing together of the past with the present" and not by rejecting immigrants' past experiences and national traditions. Instead of a "feeble attempt to boast of Anglo-Saxon achievement," she suggested stressing the universalism of the American idea of nationalism, and the longing for freedom, liberty, and equality as common ideals in the struggles for independence of Americans, Poles, Greeks, and others. Americans should learn the history of the yearning for freedom and democracy of European people, while teaching American history and civics to newcomers. The most serious fault in the attitude of Americans toward immigrant past loyalties was, in her, opinion, their "lack of a more cosmopolitan standard" of appreciation. The issue was the transformation of identity. If, she believed, the immigrants were not forced to choose between two loyalties in becoming Americans, they would not lose their self-respect. This would make it much easier for them to start feeling American, to build their personal attachment to the community, and as a result they would become an integral part of American society.[23]

Thomas justified Hull House methods as "a wise policy of assimilation that does not destroy the attitudes and memories that are there, but builds on them." The psychology of assimilation was to build a bridge between the past and the present. Naturally the success of this method depended upon the attitude of the public towards newcomers, namely, "on how we treat them—our attitude towards their heritages." Assimilation was a function of an attitude of toleration and respect, and a democracy could survive insofar as the members of society respected each other and what they represented. Furthermore, from the practical point of view Thomas argued that "we should know by this time that under tolerance, peculiar values—such as language and religion—are only means to a fuller life; under oppression, they become the object of life." If no attempts would be made to enforce American culture upon them, Thomas went on to say, newcomers would develop no resistence towards its gradual adoption, and the process of assimilation would be completed within three generations.[24]

To strengthen the feeling of continuity, Jane Addams lobbied for a change in the Naturalization Act. In March 1912 she suggested eliminating the clause that demanded that immigrants forswear allegiance to their native land before they swore allegiance to the United States. She believed that such a demand was not only strategically wrong but also a degrading and inhuman act. Allegiance to one's mother country was a natural human feeling, and there was doubt whether those who were willing to estrange themselves from their past were doing so out of sincere motives. It was the "better element" who "refuse to forget the tie of allegiance to the land of their birth." A demand to forswear allegiance to their old country made it difficult for immigrants to identify with their new country. Addams felt that giving legitimation to feelings towards their land of birth would ease the process of integration into American society. "Might not a partial allegiance to their newly adopted country be better than none at all?" she asked. Thomas expressed these very ideas, arguing that "to cherish the memories of the former home, and wish to preserve some signs identifying them with their past . . . is a natural sentiment."[25]

The Hull House circle sought to recognize and legitimize newcomers' national feelings in order to neutralize the potentially disruptive effect of their emotional attachment to their homeland. Most newcomers belonged to the oppressed nationalities in Europe who resisted pressures towards rapid acculturation. Grace Abbott, a Hull House resident and director of the Immigrants' Protective League, considered that this was a natural response to generations of national oppression in Europe. If their national attachment to their homeland was given legitimation, immigrants would gradually turn their attention to matters of more vital interest in their lives in America.[26] Sophonisba P. Breckinridge, another Hull House resident and the secretary of the Immigrants' Protective League, believed that after European nationalities were liberated, the very societies that stimulated national feelings would "be used to establish a variety of contacts and to develop among foreign born a wider interest in the United States and its problems."[27]

Furthermore, the identification of immigrants with the struggle of their countries for independence was compatible with the traditional American support for the freedom of oppressed nations. By the same token, Addams and the Hull House group expressed sympathy towards Italian, Greek, and Armenian nationalism. They were guests of honor in the national holiday celebrations organized by immigrant national societies at Hull House. Addams was chair of a committee of American women that in December 1916 organized a conference of the oppressed or dependent nationalities of Europe, with their representatives in the United States. The conference was sponsored by Hull House, and other Hull House residents, such as Grace Abbott, were also active in it.[28]

Jane Addams and the Hull House group gave legitimation to a situation of dual loyalties, assuming that disloyalty to the United States arose only when there was a disharmony, or conflict, between two incompatible ideas. Since the national goals of immigrants almost without exception (the problem of German loyalty during the war) reinforced rather than contradicted immigrants' commitment to the American tradition, rarely did such danger arise.

The efforts to stimulate assimilation by inculcating a sense of continuity also included gradually changing newcomers' norms and patterns of behavior through the creation of an inner correlation between the old and new customs and ways of doing things. While rejecting an accelerated adaptation to new patterns of behavior, the Hull House group was committed to the assumption that changes in newcomers' patterns of behavior were inevitable. Every social and political environment developed the norms adapted to its needs. Therefore, "information . . . should be given to newcomers, with reference, for example, to the change in the legal relationship within the family group, the new responsibilities of the husband and father, and the rights of wife and children . . . instruction regarding sanitary and hygienic practices . . . food and clothing." This should be done in a "friendly" manner, by "cooperation," and without "didactic superiority." "The settlement idea included the preservation of the dignity and self-esteem of the immigrant, while attempting to modify his habits." The Hull House group developed a "procedure based on sound pedagogy" to help newcomers to adopt the American pattern of behavior and ways of doing things. This included "starting from the known and familiar and leading to the new and unaccustomed." Thus S. P. Breckinridge stated that "not enough care was taken to make Old World habits . . . the starting point of instruction of American" ones. She suggested, for example, starting any exposition of American foods, utensils, and diets to immigrant wives by inviting every wife to prepare some of her Old World cooking first. Thus no sense of antagonism between old and new ways would arise. It was this effort to create a connection between past and present experiences that constituted the unique contribution of the Hull House group to the problem of immigrant adjustment.[29]

Hull House thus aimed at creating a favorable atmosphere for the emotional and cultural transformation of newcomers without arousing antagonism between their past and present ethnic-cultural identity. As Jane Addams pointed out, "It would be a foolish and unwarrantable expenditure of force to oppose or antagonize any individual or set of people."[30] The underlying assumption was that much more could be achieved through expressions of sympathy, respect, and understanding.

# THREE

# THE ROLE OF THE SETTLEMENT IN THE ASSIMILATION OF "NEW IMMIGRANTS"

The concept of assimilation developed by the Hull House circle shaped the role of the settlement in the slums. The Hull House group adapted its programs to the reality of ethnic segregation, to the need of preparing both the immigrant and the American public for the successful assimilation of immigrants, and to the eventual unification of American society.

Hull House leaders sought to play a leading role in the preparation of new immigrants from southern and eastern Europe for successful assimilation. The major problem was to reconcile the newcomers' need for temporary segregation in their own ethnic environment with the need to prepare them for assimilation. Hull House leaders accepted initial residential segregation alongside formal and informal association of newcomers as inevitable. They were totally opposed, however, to the institutionalization of the immigrant subcommunity, that is, the perpetuation of ethnic identity through the educational segregation of the younger generation and the formation of segregated welfare agencies and cultural institutions.

In their attempt to become the leading force in the neighborhood, Hull House residents needed to identify the internal and external forces pressing ethnic communities toward the perpetuation of ethnicity. Internal forces, they argued, included unscrupulous lower-middle-class immigrant leaders and politicians, businessmen, religious leaders, and the Old World intelligentsia. For each of these groups, the preservation of an immigrant identity and ethnic segregation were at least in part a matter of self-interest. External factors included the political bosses, along with political machines whose leaders relied on the manipulation of the immigrant vote through cooperation with unscrupulous lower-middle-class leaders. According to settlement house leaders, both the ignorance of the immigrants and the attitude of contempt and disrespect towards "new immigrants" prevailing among native-born Americans made it easier for these immigrant leaders and bosses to accomplish their objectives.

To neutralize those forces perpetuating ethnicity, an alternative framework of welfare agencies under municipal, state, and federal or settlement control had to be created, and native-born Americans had to be educated to change their attitude towards "new immigrants." This could not be done without the cooperation of the immigrant middle-class leadership.

Hull House residents gradually came to realize that many of the members of the emerging immigrant middle class did not respond to Americanization and social mobility as expected. While a small fraction became alienated from their communities of origin and severed ethnic ties in an effort to join the American mainstream, most of the immigrant middle class remained in the immigrant subcommunity, and many rose to leadership positions. For them, Americanization and social mobility allowed them to become cultural brokers between their groups and the larger American society.

The process by which Hull House leaders came to terms with the problem of persistent subcommunities was gradual. Their attitudes towards the immigrant enclaves evolved in three periods: 1889 to 1892, 1892 to 1907, and 1907 to 1919. These periods correspond roughly to the three stages during which immigrant subcommunities developed institutional completeness: the religious agencies were followed by the formation of secular agencies and organizations and finally by the emergence of ethnic organizations on citywide, state, and national levels. Each stage was characterized by a different type of leader. The earliest leaders were traditional religious types, while the local and national secular leaders included members of the lower middle class and of the emerging immigrant middle class.

The first stage of community development was characterized by the creation of the religious parish. Unlike the Protestant parish, the immigrant parish, whether Catholic, Greek Orthodox, or Jewish, was a national as well as a religious entity. Immigrant groups from eastern and southern Europe such as Poles, Greeks, and Jews, deprived for centuries of formal national or political status, considered their churches and synagogues to embody their national identity and organization. This pattern was strengthened in most immigrant groups in the American environment. The parish and the Jewish *qehilah* were national-religious communities through which ethnic identity and culture were preserved via educational, cultural, and welfare agencies. The recognition of the close correlation between religion and national-cultural identity led the religious leaders to become advocates of ethnic persistence and to support institutional completeness within the immigrant subcommunity. The nonreligious tasks of the parish and the *qehilah* were attended to by lower-middle-class leaders as members of the parish's agencies, and by ethnic parochial schools and Talmud Torahs (Jewish religious schools). These latter institutions represented community efforts to maintain a segregated educational system for the transmission of traditional ideas, values, and customs to the younger generation through the teaching of the history, geography, literature, and languages of the homeland.[1]

The second stage of community development was characterized by the establishment of secular institutions and organizations outside the control of the church or synagogue in order to attain ethnic self-sufficiency. These included mutual benefit societies and *landsmanshaften* as well as social and cultural agencies such as theaters, literary and dramatic societies, and the foreign-language press.[2] The mutual benefit societies and *landsmanshaften* were established generally by lower-middle-class leaders. These immigrant small businessmen controlled the group economy, which consisted of small commercial enterprises, banks, employment agencies, saloons, and restaurants in the immigrant neighborhood. The cultural agencies were formed by the Old World intelligentsia, a small circle who played a large role in the ethnic education system and in *landsmanshaften* and mutual benefit societies.

The achievement of self-sufficiency through institutional completeness did require the introduction of American management methods, efficiency, and expertise within ethnic institutions. At the same time, this third stage required the establishment of new agencies, such as hospitals, clinics, nurseries, Hebrew and Sunday schools, and community centers. This stage also involved the formation of federated welfare agencies and city, state, and national fraternal orders. A new type of leadership emerged, composed of the "better element" among immigrants. They were recruited from the emerging immigrant middle class, professionals and businessmen who had received some or all of their education in America. These second-generation leaders were Americanized and economically successful, thus being in a position to expand beyond the narrow boundaries of the immigrant neighborhood economy. Their economic, political, and civic ties transcended slum and ethnic boundaries and bound them to American economic, professional, and political organizations. Their experiences put them in a position to adapt immigrant community agencies to "American" methods, and thereby to serve as cultural brokers.[3]

Hull House policies developed during these three stages as its leaders adopted new means to fit the changing situation in the immigrant neighborhoods. Throughout they avoided direct confrontation with the immigrant communities as such, focusing instead on ethnic leaders, the educational system, and the development of activities at Hull House.

During the early stage of development of the immigrant community, Hull House residents failed to assess accurately the significance of religious leadership in "immigrant colonies." Assuming similarities between immigrant and Portestant parishes, settlement house workers failed to grasp the nationalistic character of the immigrant parish, in which religion was as much an expression of ethnic as religious identity. They further underestimated the role of religious leaders as heads of an immigrant community rather than merely of a religious entity. While Hull House leaders recognized residential segregation and religious affiliation as key aspects of immigrant adaptation, they nonetheless persisted in treating immigrants as a helpless mass, a flock without a shepherd.[4] Despite these misconceptions, Hull House members applied to the immigrant situation the same principles they worked out to deal with the problems of the working class and the segmentation of American society. Hull House residents sought to accept newcomers as equals both politically and socially, to educate and socialize them according to the values and norms of American society, to elevate them culturally, to deal with their problems of social and personal disorganization, to create lines of communication among newcomers and between them and native-born Americans, and thus to reunify the social organism.[5]

The settlement sought to become the center of neighborhood life and a source of inspiration to and influence on all the inhabitants. As the Hull House charter stated, the settlement was "to provide a center for a higher civic and social life; to institute and maintain educational and philanthropic enterprises." Hull House leaders wished to become the major agency of social reorganization and cultural adjustment in the immigrant neighborhood. In time, the settlement's sociocultural and educational programs as well as its clubs were to replace the immigrant's informal meeting places—the saloon, the Greek coffeehouse and the Jewish restaurant—as well as the formal immigrant associations such as *landsmanshaften* and mutual benefit societies. For this purpose the settlement house created a whole framework of secondary agencies to meet the welfare, educational, and sociocultural needs of newcomers.[6]

In the process of educating and socializing newcomers, "new immigrants" were treated as individuals with certain common problems, rather than as groups having distinct cultural identities and interests. Hull House organized ethnically mixed clubs and initiated cultural and educational programs "along American lines" in its efforts to introduce newcomers to American civilization and inculcate them with the proper ideas, sentiments, and norms of behavior that the settlement workers considered indispensable for the unification of the social organism and the restoration of social harmony.[7] In the context of this assimilationist focus, Hull House leaders evinced concern about the parochial schools and Talmud Torahs, which they regarded as religious institutions representing a restrictive and conservative view of education. They considered the public school to be the only appropriate educational system capable of socializing and educating immigrant children and, through them, the immigrant family.[8]

By the second stage around the turn of the century, Hull House leaders became aware that immigrant communities were moving towards institutional completeness rather than dissolution. They increasingly realized that ethnic religious, welfare, educational, and sociocultural institutions represented an effort to establish a segregated community in which ethnic identity and culture could be preserved and cultivated.[9] Finally, they realized that bilingual parochial schools in immigrant neighborhoods were not just religious schools, but rather represented efforts by immigrants to preserve their distinctive identity through social and institutional segregation and the cultivation of their language and culture. Parochial schools were initiated by religious leaders to ensure the loyalty of the younger generation to the church of their fathers. But because prayers in ethnic churches were recited in the native language, rather than in Latin, the preservation of ethnic identity was also an important objective of the system, one not at first appreciated by the settlement workers. This objective was reinforced by teaching the history, geography, and literature of the homeland.[10]

Recognizing the importance of "consciousness of kind" for newcomers confronted with a foreign environment, and understanding that the process of assimilation was gradual, Hull House leaders accepted ethnic segregation as a temporary stage in the process of assimilation. They were, however, uncompromisingly opposed to the perpetuation of ethnicity through permanent institutions such as parochial schools.[11] To settlement residents it appeared that immigrant leaders were taking advantage of newcomers' temporary need for a familiar environment in order to perpetuate ethnic segregation beyond the time needed for adjustment to American society. They became convinced that small businessmen, in particular, had developed a comprehensive network of immigrant economic agencies—in order to assume the role of mediators between the immigrant and the American economic system. The economic dependence of the immigrant community on the brokerage of small businessmen was, then, viewed as a means of controlling a community and its agencies as well as creating political dependence. Lower-middle-class leaders could thus turn any immigrant enclave into a political interest group which would become bound to ward bosses and political machines.

Hull House residents clearly considered these immigrant leaders as obstacles to the implementation of their own objectives in the ethnic neighborhoods and to the objectives of the Progressive movement as a whole. The real villains were the immigrant lower-middle-class leaders, not only perpetuating ethnicity but also supplanting the settlement workers and Progressives who wished to create communication between newcomers and Americans and serve as cultural brokers, as well as threatening their chances to reform the political system. By obstructing communication between the new working-class immigrants and the middle and upper classes, these immigrant leaders also perpetuated the segmentation of society. They thus were seen as the major obstacle in the way of solving the crisis of American society.

In the context of Hull House leaders' perception of lower-middle-class immigrants' leadership, the settlement reevaluated its policies. While no dramatic changes occurred in the movement's objectives, Hull House leaders for the first time formulated ethnic policies and programs designed to counter the perpetuation of ethnicity. Their policies included fighting the supposedly unscrupulous lower-middle-class leaders and their political allies, the bosses and the party machines. Hull House leaders sought to release the immigrant masses from the hold of these two groups by means of social reform, establishing an alternative framework of disinterested and more efficient welfare and employment agencies and postal banks to replace the services provided by ethnic bosses and agencies. Thus they hoped to eliminate the circumstances that enabled immigrant businessmen and bosses to control the immigrant vote, by rendering their services obsolete.[12]

Hull House residents also became involved in the general efforts of civic organizations to eliminate the bilingual school system, first through indirect legislation, then through state supervision (see chapter 4). Finally, Hull House leaders developed a policy of "segregation within integration" to cope simultaneously with the temporary need of newcomers for their Old World milieu and the long-term need for their assimilation. The idea behind this policy was that even during the early years in America, when newcomers felt most secure within their own cultural milieu, they should not be totally segregated, so as not to come under the influence and control of those leaders with a selfish interest in the permanent perpetuation of ethnic difference. The alternative was partial segregation within American settlements and neighborhood centers where newcomers had opportunities to meet their countrymen and socialize along ethnic lines without being entirely cut off from the new environment. Hull House leaders believed that events held under American auspices would gradually expose newcomers to American influences. To this end, Hull House established ethnically mixed clubs, promoted American cultural events, initiated "ethnic receptions" and ethnic clubs, and founded a labor museum (see below).

When the immigrant subcommunity reached its third stage of development and achieved institutional completeness along with the gradual Americanization of its agencies through a new Americanized middle-class leadership, Hull House leaders anticipated an inevitable clash between the latter and the lower-middle-class counterpart. This clash was inevitable only if settlement house residents were right that the lower-middle-class and the Americanized middle-class immigrants disagreed in their definition of a favorable pattern of immigrant adjustment to American society.[13] Hull House leaders had become convinced that middle-class ethnic leaders sought to serve as cultural brokers between the members of the ethnic community and American society; that they sought gradually to eliminate ethnic and cultural barriers, first on an intergroup basis and then through free communication between individuals; and that they would finally bring about the dissolution of the immigrant subcommunity.[14] In the resulting struggle for control over immigrant adjustment to the American environment, Hull House leaders anticipated that ward bosses and party machines would support the lower-middle-class leaders, while Progressive Americans would support middle-class leaders. Only the victory of the latter could pave the way to better communication and cooperation between immigrant subcommunities and settlements and allow the integration of second- and third-generation immigrants into the American mainstream.

From this perspective Hull House leaders saw no contradiction between the role the immigrant middle-class leaders performed in their subcommunities, and the settlement's own system of socialization and acculturation through autonomous welfare, educational, and cultural agencies. They took it for granted that the Americanized members of the middle class shared their values, ideas, and sentiments as well as their ways of doing things. Interpreting the role of these immigrant leaders as cultural brokers, they expected them to cooperate with settlement leaders in the gradual transference of newcomers and their children from ethnically segregated institutions to Hull House and other American agencies (see chapter 5).[15]

In 1907–8 Hull House leaders elaborated their "segregation within integration" assimilation policies. These included inviting immigrant national societies, mutual benefit societies, and literary clubs to use the Hull House facilities at low rates, and elaborating the house club system to attract immigrants and thus further its assimilation policies.

The Hull House group also decided to try to implement its policy of "segregation within integration" in the public school system. This would involve introducing ethnic studies into public schools as a temporary expedient and as a way of eliminating the bilingual schools, as immigrant children transferred into public schools. Their success in obtaining ethnic studies in the Chicago public high schools' curriculum by 1912 resulted from the cooperation between themselves and immigrant middle-class leaders, to the dismay of both immigrant religious leaders and American-born nativists. (see chapter 4).

Hull House "segregation within integration" represented one aspect of its overall assimilation policies. Another manifestation of Hull House's assimilation policy was the "college culture" program, which introduced immigrants to Western and particularly American culture. Through settlement-based classes teachers sought to inculcate American values by teaching literature, art, and music as a way of refining the personality of the working class, thus helping newcomers to adapt to American civilization.[16]

In many ways Hull House programs resembled those offered by immigrant community centers. The essential difference was that the ethnic policies at Hull House represented only one stage in its long-term goal of achieving assimilation, while in immigrant community centers ethnic programs represented a way of life, the most desirable pattern of immigrant integration into American society. Furthermore, Hull House ethnic programs comprised only a secondary component of its overall program, while in immigrant community centers ethnic programs were primary. The ethnic features of Hull House programs were thus a vehicle for the creation of the conditions necessary for cultural transformation, that is, the disintegration and dissolution of ethnic segregation, and incorporation of newcomers into the general society upon equal terms.

This intermittent and temporary character of ethnic segregation at Hull House was emphasized by Victor Yarros, a Hull House resident. "Some elements do not mix and cause trouble to teachers and directors . . . There is no idyllic harmony in our neighborhood and the classes may have to be segregated for a time to avoid friction and waste of effort."[17] Nonetheless, the introduction of ethnic elements into the settlement's cultural programs reflected a genuine attempt to attract newcomers to Hull House. They were meant to serve as expressions of respect and appreciation towards immigrants' cultural heritages, and to recognize the legitimacy of their national pride. As Jane Addams explained in 1904, "The principle which is at the foundation of the work is the effort to reach . . . these foreigners by appealing to their national instincts."[18]

The third element that lay at the heart of Hull House ethnic policy was, in her words, "to build a bridge between European and American experiences in such a wise as to give them both more meaning and a sense of relation."[19] Aware of the psychological and cultural barriers that made it difficult for most newcomers, youngsters and adults, to mingle in ethnically mixed social groups along American lines, Hull House hosted ethnic receptions and ethnic clubs. Beginning in the early 1890s, Hull House leaders invited French, Bohemians, Germans, and Italians to segregated meetings at which cultural programs were performed. The most successful receptions, and the only ones that lasted till 1900, were those of the Italians. They included Italian music, plays, and literature along with lectures on the political situation in Italy and the history of its struggle for unification and independence.[20] Starting in 1906–7, Hull House also invited Italians to celebrate the annual Mardi Gras, as the Irish community was invited to celebrate St. Patrick's Cotillion.[21]

The production of several ancient Greek plays, such as Sophocles' *Ajax* and *Electra,* through cooperation between Hull House and leaders of the Greek colony during 1899, 1903, and 1905 reflected the same ethnic policy. In 1906, a Greek-American meeting sponsored by Hull House and local community leaders included lectures on Greek civilization, on the struggle of Greece for independence, and on Turkish atrocities. The entertainment at these meetings included Greek folk songs and dances.[22]

Another initiative attached to Hull House's ethnic programs was the opening of the Labor Museum in 1901. One of its objectives was to demonstrate to native-born Americans and to immigrant children the signifi-

cance of immigrants' cultural resources. Exhibitions of immigrant craftsmanship were accompanied by demonstrations of their methods of production in
the various ethnic traditions.[23]

The ethnic receptions, celebrations, and demonstrations were organized to
attract newcomers to Hull House upon an individual basis. Hull House leaders
hoped that through these activities immigrants would become acquainted with
settlement residents and would be persuaded to participate in other programs.
Hull House's intention, then, was social and cultural assimilation on the
individual level, which could be accomplished most effectively by incorporating "new immigrants" into its existing club system. This goal was evident
in the composition of the permanent adult clubs, which were ethnically
mixed, including native-born Americans, Germans, Irish, and some Scandi-
navians, and were conducted upon the American middle-class club model. Its
programs included cultural events such as lectures and readings in American
and west European literature, principles of American democracy, current
politics of reform, and so forth.[24]

An intermediate stage existed from 1892 to 1906 as Hull House formed
ethnic clubs, namely, separate clubs for specific immigrant groups. The first
ethnic clubs were designated for Italian youngsters who did not feel at ease in
ethnically mixed clubs. Still, their programs were conducted along "American lines."[25]

The third stage in the development of Hull House assimilation policies
emerged in 1907–8 as a result of residents' growing understanding of
immigrant cultures and communities. This year marked the full and final
articulation of the "segregation within integration" programs of the settlement leaders.

By 1900 it was clear that Hull House had failed to attract "new immigrant"
adults to ethnic receptions and to adult clubs upon an individual basis. The
only surviving ethnic reception, the Italian, was actually a meeting of the
personal friends of Mastro-Valerio, the only Italian resident at Hull House at
that time and editor of *La Tribuna*, an Italian radical newspaper. It was the
regular meetings of two Italian clubs at Hull House and the success of the
Greek-American meeting in 1906 that convinced Hull House leaders to
change their tactics. From that point on they encouraged immigrant mutual
benefit societies, *landsmanshaften*, literary and dramatic clubs, charity
organizations, and national orders to hold their regular meetings at Hull
House, by offering low rental rates for their rooms. Considering the sacrifices
involved in raising money for immigrant community centers from poorly paid
lower-class immigrants, the Hull House offer to open its facilities to
immigrant societies and organizations on reasonable terms must have been
very tempting. Table 1 shows the increasing number of independent ethnic
societies and groups that rented Hull House facilities and the declining
number of Hull House's own ethnic programs in the years 1892–1916. It was

hoped that sociocultural activities organized by immigrant societies would be transferred to Hull House and other American settlements and that direct lines of communication would thus be opened between settlement workers and "new immigrants," and among individuals of different ethnic groups. Within American institutions every ethnic group could be both segregated and exposed to other groups as well as to native-born Americans, thus being in a sufficiently secure position to create contacts with members of other groups. Indeed, some Hull House leaders hoped thus to bring about the closing of ethnically segregated immigrant community halls and centers.[26] Hull House also served as a model for the establishment, with similar intentions, of community centers and field houses by the City of Chicago and other cities throughout the country.

Hull House leaders also came to believe that immigrant children could be attracted most easily through the introduction of ethnic cultural programs. During 1906–7 an experimental club composed of east European Jewish

Table 1 Ethnic Club and Society Activities and Hull House Ethnic Receptions

| Years | Hull House ethnic receptions | Ethnic societies and clubs (renting Hull House rooms and halls) |
|---|---|---|
| 1892 | Italians, Germans | |
| 1897 | Italians, Germans, Bohemians | Eldorado (east European Jewish club) Italian Band |
| 1900 | Italians | Italian Band |
| 1903/4 | (Greek play) | Dante Alighieri Society |
| 1905 | (Greek play) | Italian Band |
| 1906/7 | Greek-American meeting | Bruno Gordano Club Italian Band |
| 1910 | | Bruno Gordano Club 6 Greek societies 1 Russian society 2 Italian societies |
| 1913 | | 6 Greek societies 2 Russian societies 1 Italian society 1 German society |
| 1916 | | 6 Greek societies 3 Russian societies 2 Italian societies 1 east European Jewish Society |

Sources: *Hull House Bulletin*, no. 12 (1899): 9–10, no. 1 (1903/4): 15–16, no. 1 (1905/6): 3–4, 23; *Hull House Year Book*, 1906/7, 37; 1910, 25, 32; 1921, 12–13, 34; 1929, 13, 15–16.

youngsters performed two plays on Biblical themes before the Hull House clientele (the stories of Joseph and his brothers, and Queen Esther), while experimental classes were taught on Irish and Italian history at the Hull House Boys' Club.[27] As a result of the success of these activities, in 1907–9 Hull House leaders reevaluated their ethnic clubs policy and added a third type of club. The original Hull House club was ethnically mixed and its activities conducted along "American lines." The second type of club had a single ethnic composition, but its activities were conducted along American lines, as in the ethnically mixed clubs. The third type not only had a single ethnic composition but also conducted its activities along both ethnic and American lines and was aimed at those youngsters who were not attracted to the other two types.[28] Hull House still intended to transfer immigrant youngsters to ethnically mixed clubs after this period of temporary segregation. This is indicated by the greater number of ethnically mixed clubs (see table 2) as well as by the policy regarding the children's clubs. These latter, formed for the immigrants' children who had been born in America or who had arrived when very young and who were naturally more exposed to American influences, were only ethnically mixed. Through these clubs immigrant children were educated, socialized, and integrated into American culture.[29]

The Hull House club system served as a laboratory for democracy and social and cultural assimilation. The ethnically mixed clubs were meeting

Table 2  Types of Hull House Clubs for youngsters

| Year | Ethnically segregated, American activities | Ethnically segregated, American and ethnic activities | Ethnically mixed | Total |
|---|---|---|---|---|
| 1892 | 1 Italian | | 0 | 1 |
| 1897 | 2 Italian<br>1 Bohemian | | 0 | 3 |
| 1903/4 | 1 Italian | 2 Italian | 0 | 3 |
| 1906/7 | 2 Jewish | 2 Italian | 5 | 9 |
| 1910 | 1 Jewish | 2 Italian | 6 | 9 |
| 1913 | 3 Jewish<br>1 Polish<br>1 Italian | 1 Jewish literary club<br><br>1 Italian | 4 | 11 |
| 1916 | 2 Jewish<br>1 Italian | 2 Italian<br>1 Polish | 3 | 9 |

Source: *Hull House Year Book*, 1906/7, 21–23, 41–43; 1910, 20, 44–47; 1913, 17–22, 41–42; 1916, 26–30, 39–41.

Note: The proportion between the different types of clubs indicates also that most of Hull House's clientele preferred ethnically mixed clubs. The implications of this situation are discussed in chapter 7.

places for otherwise segregated children and inculcated tolerance and respect for differences as a product of coexistence. They taught that the preconditions for democracy were the breaking down of national and cultural differences and the unification of American society on the basis of common interests, ideas, feelings, and norms of behavior, as opposed to segregation and preservation of ethnic identity.[30] As John Dewey said, "The work of such an institution as Hull House has been primarily . . . being a social clearing-house . . . bringing people together, of doing away with barriers of caste, or class, or race, or type of experience that keep people from real communion with each other."[31] The Hull House club system was also an agency for socialization. The underlying assumption was that traits ordinarily considered racial were really cultural and that by modifying cultural traits through educational means the causes of supposedly racial friction could be removed. This actually meant the Americanization of newcomers. Thus in the two types of ethnic clubs the character and habits of thought and behavior were gradually modified by introducing immigrant youngsters to an American environment and the American way of doing things. Hull House was in fact inculcating a middle-class concept of character, defined by Theodore Roosevelt as the embodiment of American civilization: "character involves those qualities essential for moral efficiency: resolution, courage, energy, self-control, fearlessness, taking the initiative, assumption of responsibility, just regard for the rights of others, and (finally) common sense."[32] These American traits reflected the individualistically oriented type of personality cultivated at Hull House. There the concept of personality was totally in contrast with the peer-group mentality characteristic of rural peasant societies (see chapter 7). This concept broke up group solidarity and encouraged individual newcomers to prefer self-realization through mobility and the severing of group ties.[33]

Hull House's cultural policies reflected the same assimilatory aims as the club policies. The ethnic-cultural programs were of casual or occasional nature, and some of them were experimental. Since Hull House leaders opposed preserving and cultivating immigrant cultures for their own sakes, they made no attempt to devise systematic programs to teach immigrant children the languages and cultures of their ancestors. Evidence of this policy could be seen in the content of the various cultural activities in the fields of drama, art, and music, and literary programs sponsored by Hull House.

A full 60 percent of the plays performed by the Hull House Players, the institute's dramatic association during the years 1899 to 1939, were written by native-born Americans, 30 percent of the plays were written by English playwrights, and the remaining 10 percent were written by west European playwrights, some of them Irish. During the Players' long career, it performed only two plays—in 1906–7 and in 1916—that had anything to do with immigrants, though hardly with their cultures. One, written by a young

Russian Jewish girl, dealt with the adjustment problems of the east European Jewish community in the Hull House neighborhood, and the other was Zangwill's *The Melting Pot,* which dealt with the blending of all newcomers into Americans. All the ethnic plays presented in foreign languages on the Hull House stage were initiated and performed by immigrant literary and dramatic clubs who rented the Hull House theater hall for that purpose.[34] Similarly, the programs of the music and art departments were mainly designed to introduce immigrants to Western and American art and music.[35] Hull House art and music departments did not undertake as their major task to record and cultivate ethnic art and ethnic music. Such enterprises were sponsored occasionally when a Russian song, and some hymns sung by a Jewish cantor, were recorded or an exhibition of ethnic crafts was held at the Labor Museum.[36]

Hull House concerts, held every Sunday afternoon, were performed by musicians from every part of the city and the Hull House children's choir. The repertoire consisted mostly of west European and American music and only occasionally folk music, and "the number of people . . . caring for the best music was not large."[37] The Hull House art gallery and loan exhibitions were also intended to acquaint working people with the best art. The pictures in the art gallery were loaned by well-to-do Chicago collectors and included English, American, and west European paintings. As Addams has recorded, "The pictures were some of the best that Chicago could afford, several by Corot, Watts, and Davis. European country scenes, sea views, and Dutch interiors bring forth many pleasant reminiscences."[38]

The schools of music and art were designed to teach a limited number of immigrant children.[39] They aimed at fostering the talents and skills of immigrant children as individuals. Jane Addams spoke of "the amount of talent and ability which goes to waste in the crowded districts." She deplored the lack of "provision made to ascertain what the individual child is best adapted for, and to see to it that he is educated along these lines." Hull House developed the musical, artistic, and dramatic talents of immigrant children by introducing them to Western and American art, music, and drama, and teaching them the skills needed to participate.[40] She urged, "Utilizing their genuine qualities in digging out their intellectual gold, in discovering the genius and developing the latent talent—whether it be for music, painting, or any other . . . it would open to us a vast store-house of unused material"[41]

The literature presented in the clubs and public lectures also indicates the cultural orientation of Hull House. The children's clubs acquainted children with Snow White, Puss-in-Boots, William Tell, King John, and Wat Tyler and with American stories about the frontier, stories that were to supplant their parents' Old World stories. Immigrant youngsters were introduced to modern philosophy, through Royce's "Aspects of Modern Philosophy," to Herbert Spencer, Plato, and social psychology. They became acquainted with Dante, Browning, Shakespeare, Ibsen, Shaw, Galsworthy, and George Eliot.[42]

The institute's college extension courses introduced newcomers to Western-American culture and created opportunities for individual immigrants to gain higher education in the professions or to develop their intellectual talents to prepare them to gain higher education. The most popular courses were in English and American literature, languages, history, mathematics, drawing, and painting. Courses were also given in biology, physiology, industrial history, sociology, social philosophy, and even electricity. These courses were taught by members of the University of Chicago faculty, and credit was given to pupils who met the requirements. Hull House encouraged talented immigrant youngsters to gain higher education, by arranging grants and scholarships. Those who were able to take advantage of the opportunities owed their personal success to what they acquired at Hull House, as well as to the financial aid. It is significant that, as a result of this cultural assimilation and social mobility, many of these became alienated to varying degrees from their ethnic groups. Alex Elson and Philip Davis are typical examples (see chapter 7).[43]

Even the modern languages taught as part of the extension courses reflected the Hull House cultural orientation. The Languages Department did not include the languages of the groups living in the neighborhood, such as Hebrew, Yiddish, modern Greek, or Russian, but rather those considered an integral part of the genteel tradition—German, French, and Italian.[44]

Hull House gradually changed its cultural policy, during the first decade of the twentieth century, shifting the emphasis from the so-called college culture to sports, dancing, playing games, and crafts: in 1902 Hull House had thirty-two educational courses and nine manual and craft course; by 1905 the proportion was nine to twenty-three.[45] This was an effort to adapt its programs to the changing ethnic composition of the neighborhood, in particular to the predominance of Italians of peasant background. Nonetheless, Hull House continued to introduce those Italian children who aspired to an education to the "college culture." At the same time, Hull House continued its policy of socialization, making determined efforts to inculcate Italians with American, namely middle-class, norms of behavior, as reflected in the rules fixed for dancing parties, playrooms, and other activities, as well as the cooking and housekeeping clubs.[46]

In short, Hull House was not an immigrant institution in the sense that it represented a pluralist cultural view of society. It was, rather, an American institute that sought to integrate individual newcomers of different backgrounds into a cosmopolitan, America-oriented society by breaking down ethnic barriers and ending segregation. As a result, immigrant children and youngsters who were ethnically oriented did not usually attend Hull House. Those who came were attracted by its American programs rather than by its ethnic-cultural ones. They came to Hull House to become Americanized, in their efforts to break ethnic ties and assimilate into the American mainstream.

# FOUR

## HULL HOUSE, THE EDUCATION OF IMMIGRANT CHILDREN, AND ETHNIC STUDIES

The same considerations that shaped the ethnic-cultural policy at Hull House also determined the Hull House circle's ethnic policy for the public school system. This Liberal Progressive group in Chicago sought to implement its idea of assimilation in the public school system and revealed flexibility in adopting new methods to achieve these objectives, namely, the teaching of ethnic studies in public schools.

The Liberal Progressives' view of the public school's role in socializing and educating immigrant children as future citizens in the American democracy arose from the idea of community and immigrant assimilation, which we have examined in the preceding chapters. John Dewey explained the implications of this idea for education:"'society exists through the transmission . . . this transmission occurs by means of communication of habits of doing, thinking, feeling from the older to the younger."[1] However, "the existence in the United States of a combination of different groups with different traditional customs" had "forced the demand for an educational institution which shall provide something like a homogeneous and balanced environment for the young. Only in this way can the centrifugal forces set up by juxtaposition of different groups within one and the same political unit be counteracted."[2]

Examination of the views expressed by Jane Addams and Hull House in the parochial versus public school controversy, and the introduction of "ethnic studies" into the public school curriculum in Chicago revealed what the Liberal Progressive position was on the education of immigrant children as far as assimilation and the preservation of ethnic identity and culture were concerned. The Hull House leaders totally rejected the parochial school system as a socializer and educator of immigrant children and instead sought to transfer immigrant children to public schools. In particular, the main thrust of their campaign against the parochial system at the turn of the century was directed against the bilingual schools, namely, the ethnic parochial schools in immigrant neighborhoods. They believed that these combined the most objectionable features of the parochial system: the ethnic segregation of immigrant children in separate schools, a curriculum designed to serve their ethnic orientation, the absence in the schools of a Progressive concept of education, and a poorly qualified staff. They also criticized the physical conditions of the schools as being far worse than those of the public schools.

Hull House was particularly concerned by the parochial school's institutional segregation of immigrant children, which was inconsistent with the Progressives' idea of democracy, and its autocratic world view and norms of behavior. Dewey expressed this concern in the controversy of 1915 over a bill providing for the division of the Illinois school system into "general" and "vocational" schools. He accused the Roman Catholic church, which supported the bill, of having "a better and stronger claim for a divided apportionment of school funds and school control than have industrial interests," claiming "that the bill in question puts our Catholic fellow citizens in a still better position to urge a still further division." He feared that if the precedent of separation was established, "what sound reasons can be urged against further administrative segregations on behalf of profound religious convictions? And if there are communities where Poles or Germans predominate or form a considerable fraction of the community, why should not another splitting occur to care for their special needs?" He insisted that "the unity of the public-school system is the best guarantee we possess of a unifying agency to deal successfully with the diversified heterogeneity of our population." He was also opposed to the division of the school system into "general" and "vocational" because it would intensify "the increasing tendency toward stratification of classes in this country."[3]

The Hull House group shared Dewey's conviction that the public school was much better fitted than the parochial school for the task of educating and socializing immigrant children to live in a democratic society. Jane Addams praised the public schools as "a socializing and harmonizing factor" in the neighborhoods inhabited by the foreign born. For her the ultimate objective of the public school was "to modify the character and conduct of the individual . . . and to lead the immigrant child, who will in turn lead his family, and bring them with him into the brotherhood for which they are longing." Ella Flagg Young, one of the pillars of the Chicago public school system and a Liberal Progressive, added that "the free public school has made the child of foreign parents strive to take on the habits of thought that would identify him with the people whose ancestors were merged into this social and political society at an earlier date than were his." Furthermore, she maintained that "the differences growing out of the social customs of the many nations into which long ago the races had divided have been brought into the public school to be minimized, obliterated, homogenized in the process of unification." She praised the public school for its role "in creating a sentiment favorable to oneness, to Americanism . . . The comradeship in experience developed by the democratic spirit pervading the methods in instruction and discipline, is a more positive factor in the sympathetic appreciation existing between members of different religious and social organizations than the association in private or denominational schools can ever be."[4]

The bililngual schools in the "new immigrant" neighborhoods not only suffered from all the shortcomings of the parochial system but greatly aggravated them. The curriculum with its emphasis on the teaching of foreign languages and cultures was designed to preserve and cultivate the ethnic identity of its pupils, instead of seeking to help the children adjust to the American environment.[5]

As Edith Abbott and S. P. Breckinridge pointed out, "the churches in the foreign neighborhoods, as a means of self-preservation . . . attempt to maintain the national language through the parochial schools . . . the foreign born . . . tend to segregate themselves in separate national . . . schools where . . . the speech, the ideals, and to some extent the manner of life of the mother country are zealously preserved and guarded."[6] In these schools the study of the English language and American history, geography, literature, and civics was secondary to foreign studies. Breckinridge and the Abbott sisters claimed that these features of the bilingual schools created "a problem of adaptation both difficult and complex." They insisted that "the child who leaves the parochial school must be fitted into an American community life in which the mastery of the English tongue is not merely a necessary tool but the only medium through which he may share the most valuable products of American civilization."[7]

As we have seen, the Hull House group, unlike most native-born Americans, did not demand that the immigrant repudiate his language and culture and adopt the English language and American ways immediately on arrival. However, although they acknowledged the right of immigrant parents to transmit their languages and traditions to their children, they pointed out that these children should still "be trained for a civic life that has grown out of American experience and Anglo-Saxon tradition."[8] Finally, they argued that the teachers who taught the English language and American subjects in the bilingual schools had "a limited knowledge of the English language" and "comparatively few speak it fluently." They were therefore unfitted for the task of transmitting American values to immigrant children. Most of them were also unfamiliar with the social and industrial conditions in the country.[9] The lack of professional qualifications of the teachers and the intolerable physical conditions of these schools, whose standards were considered far below those of the public schools,[10] were included in the criticism of the east European Jewish private school, the *cheder.* Hull House residents approved the efforts of Americanized German Jews to eliminate the traditional *cheder.* They criticized "these Talmud schools" for their poor facilities, but their major concern was that "young boys ruin their eyesight over Hebrew characters, distort their minds with rabbinical casuistry, . . . and defer the hopes of American citizenship by the substitution of Judisch for English."[11] In short, the Hull House group regarded the bilingual schools "as an educational and social misfortune."[12]

The policy of Jane Addams and the Hull House group towards the bilingual school system evolved in three stages: first they sought to eliminate the system through indirect legislation, then to change its very nature through state supervision, and finally to eradicate it altogether by introducing ethnic studies into the public school curriculum.

As early as the 1890s, Hull House was involved in a controversy with Father Dunne of the Italian Catholic parish in its neighborhood, over the education of Italian children. Hull House initiated a campaign to establish an additional public school in the neighborhood in opposition to the priest's desire to establish a parochial school to meet the educational needs of the Italian children in the area. The provisions of the compulsory education law and the child labor law, which were strongly supported by Hull House, were also aimed against the bilingual parochial schools. Under pressure from the Catholic church in Illinois, the compulsory education law of 1893 had omitted the old provision that compulsory regulations could be met by attendance at schools offering instruction in English. Similarly, the words "in English" had been omitted from the child labor law of 1903, which included the requirement that children leaving school to go to work should be able to speak, read, and write in English. The Hull House group demanded that these provisions be reintroduced. Since Hull House residents stated openly that most pupils of the bilingual schools could not meet the legal requirements of these laws, their sponsorship of these provisions was evidently intended to force immigrant parents to transfer their children to public schools. Characteristically, the compulsory education laws for which the Hull House group lobbied before 1907 failed to include supervision of truancy and nonattendance in parochial schools. Furthermore, in 1911 the Immigrants' Protective League, established by Hull House leaders in 1908, began to act as a clearinghouse for school attendance by obtaining from federal immigration authorities the names of all children of compulsory school age and sending them to school authorities throughout the state of Illinois. Parochial schools were not included among those who received this information.[13]

When Hull House residents realized that the bilingual school system could not be eliminated through this kind of indirect legislation, they supported an alternative demand: that all parochial schools be placed under the supervision of a state education board. The board, it was argued, would ensure that the public school curriculum be introduced into the parochial system; that the language of instruction be English; that foreign languages and ethnic studies be taught as secondary to the American curriculum; and that both the general teachers and the foreign-language teachers had the professional qualifications required of the public school teachers. These changes, the Hull House group believed, were needed "if the principles of our democracy are to endure . . . and the promise of American life is not to be obscured."[14] This act would have transformed the parochial school from an autonomous subcommunity school, whose first priority was to preserve and foster pupils' ethnic identity, into an American public school with an option to teach pupils the language and culture of their parents "for the sake of the family." And above all, since most immigrant teachers lacked the professional qualifications required by boards of education in Illinois, state supervision would eventually have eliminated this school system as such. Given the Hull House group's criticism of the bilingual schools' teaching staff, it may well be that this was in fact their underlying intention. However, due to the strong resistance of the Catholic and the German Lutheran churches, who argued that this supervision violated the freedom of religion, the program was not implemented.[15]

This failure to introduce both indirect legislation and state supervision coincided with an enormous growth in the bilingual school system from the 1890s, especially during the first decade of the twentieth century. Hull House members were obliged to acknowledge that immigrant parents preferred the bilingual school whenever they were in a position to choose between the two educational systems, even though the public school offered free education while the bilingual schools were fee-paying. Hull House members were well aware of the sacrifices an immigrant family made in order to send a child to a parochial school. Furthermore, they observed not only that the bilingual school was much more successful than the public school in preserving the family unit and parental authority, but also that the truancy, nonattendance, and drop-out rates in the bilingual schools were considerably lower than those of immigrant children attending public schools.[16] Although Hull House members did not change their commitment to the public school as the major educational system for both American and immigrant children, they came to realize that, if the public school wished to perform its task in "new immigrant" neighborhoods, it should adopt temporarily some of the features of the bilingual school by introducing "ethnic studies" into the public school curriculum. Hull House came to the conclusion that "the education system should work out methods that will 'educate' the immigrant child along American lines and at the same time will not destroy the traditions round which the family life has been built."[17]

The awareness that such a change in policy was needed was also due to some additional findings of the study on the bilingual schools made by Hull House residents. They realized that immigrant parents were not transmitting their languages and traditions to their children within the family circle but were sending their children to bilingual schools for that purpose. Grace Abbott noted that immigrant parents were anxious to have their children know the language of their country of origin, to close the growing gap between themselves and their more rapidly Americanized offspring. She believed that "the peculiar isolation of the mother keeps her from learning English and often leaves her in almost complete dependence on her native language, and so for the sake of the family life, a knowledge of that language by the children is necessary." She concluded that "if the languages of the neighborhood were taught a few hours a week in public schools, these parents would not prefer the parochial school."[18]

Furthermore, the Hull House group became convinced that the emotional considerations that impelled immigrant parents to make financial sacrifices to send their children to bilingual schools could not be ignored. Grace Abbott stated that "the devotion to their own languages is strongest among the Bohemians, Poles, Slovaks, Lithuanians, and others who came from countries in which because they have struggled for years to resist the efforts of the government to stamp out their language and to substitute German, Russian, or Magyar, freedom of language has come to be regarded by them as an evidence of liberty." From this perspective, Hull House residents began to interpret this insistence on the teaching of immigrant languages as an expression of the commitment to freedom of speech and liberty in the spirit of American democratic traditions.[19] They also began to think that efforts to deny the legitimacy of the foreign language would achieve the opposite of the desired result. As Grace Abbott noted, "this method of assimilation is not a new one . . . the evidence . . . proves overwhelmingly that this method . . . is not only cruel but unsuccessful."[20]

Indeed, the two sociologists, Professor Herbert A. Miller of Olivet College and Professor William I. Thomas of the University of Chicago, based their support of the immigrant leaders' demand to teach their languages in public schools on these grounds. The Bohemian newspaper, *Denni Hlasatel,* reported on 11 March 1912 that "Professor Miller agreed to write in favor of the Bohemian cause from a sociological point of view to the chairman of the Committee of Education Mr. W. Summer." Analyzing the emotional climate within immigrant communities, Professor Miller explained the growth of nationalist feelings among new immigrants from eastern and southern Europe as "a revolt against . . . coercive control . . . against control by power trying to annihilate this consciousness." He believed that any attempt to crush the nationalist feelings among immigrant groups would result in its intensification. Conversely, "when the group no longer feels any restraint on itself as a group, then the free development of the idea of brotherhood stands a good chance." He therefore suggested sympathy with ethnic consciousness and culture rather than an attempt to eradicate them by compulsory means. This attitude was indispensable "before we can hope to assimilate our aliens into Americans . . . In America . . . nationalism persists among our immigrants until they discover that we make no effort to curb it, and dies in the third generation."[21]

Finally, the Hull House group became convinced that immigrants' self-respect as human beings was undermined by the American public's contempt of their cultures. The foreign-language press, which had been involved since the 1880s in a campaign for respect and tolerance, voiced the response of many immigrants to the inferior status accorded to ethnic groups and their traditions when it demanded that immigrant languages and cultures be introduced into the public school curriculum as "a new proof of our cultural maturity" and to show that "from the cultural point of view all languages are of equal value, our literature is as beautiful as that of other nations."[22]

The public school, on the other hand, in its eagerness to Americanize immigrant children ignored the immigrant family. Analyzing the factors that contributed to the success of the bilingual schools and the failure of the public school to protect the family unit, the Hull House group became convinced that the fault of the public school lay in the teachers', lack of knowledge and respect for the immigrant parent. "The contempt for the experiences and languages of their parents which foreign children sometimes exhibit, and which is most damaging to their moral as intellectual life, is doubtless due at least in part to the public school cutting into the family loyalty." Addams suggested that the contrast between the school and the home was one of the major causes for the maladjustment of immigrant children and for juvenile delinquency. The public school "in some way loosens them from the authority and control of their parents, and tends to send them, without a sufficient rudder and power of self-direction, into the perilous business of living."[23] The Hull House group therefore concluded that the main reason for the bilingual school's success in attracting immigrant children, as compared to the public school's, lay in the attitudes towards immigrant cultures. If the public school was interested in succeeding in its task as socializer of the immigrant child and the immigrant family, Addams argued, it ought to respect immigrant cultures. Removing the antagonism between what America stood for and the heritage of the immigrant family would help immigrants and their children to "begin to have a sense of ease in America, a first consciousness of being at home." Instead of "cutting them loose of their parents," Addams suggested "to tie them up in sympathy and understanding."[24]

During the year 1906–7 Addams tested this concept of education for immigrant children at Hull House. Classes in the history of Italy and Ireland were held in the Boys' Clubs for Italian and Irish boys, and two plays dealing with events in Jewish history were performed by a dramatic club consisting mostly of east European Jewish children. Her conclusion was firmly in favor of introducing some ethnic elements into the school curriculum.

> The schools ought to do more to connect these children with the best things of the past, to make them realize something of the beauty and

charm of the language, the history, and the traditions which their parents represent . . . it is the business of the school to give each child the beginning of a culture so wide and deep and universal that he can interpret his own parents and countrymen by a standard which is world-wide and not provincial.[25]

She suggested various ways to do this. "The body of teachers in our great cities could take hold of the immigrant colonies, could bring out of them their handicrafts and occupations, their traditions, their folk songs and folklore, the beautiful stories which every immigrant colony is ready to tell and translate." Public school teachers, she insisted, should teach immigrant children to respect their parents by themselves showing appreciation of some cultural assets such as new immigrants' "primitive art" and "folklore" and by incorporating into the curriculum "beautiful stories on immigrant backgrounds, translated into English."[26] Her suggestion to "bring together the past and the present" went against the current practice of public school teachers, which was to reject immigrants' past experiences and national traditions. Instead of a "feeble attempt to boast of Anglo-Saxon achievement," she suggested that teachers stress the common values shared by the Americans and Poles, Greeks and Jews, such as the longing for liberty and equality. She mentioned stories about Garibaldi and from the history of ancient and modern Greece as examples of how the connection between the American and European traditions could be made.[27]

In an address before the annual conference of the National Education Association in 1908 Addams proposed that ethnic-cultural elements be introduced into the public schools' curriculum. This program aimed both to eliminate the bilingual school system and to adapt the public school to immigrants' needs. Thus several important objectives—the control of immigrant children's socialization and education, the harmonizing of American society, the preservation of the children's respect for their immigrant parents' authority, and the self-respect of immigrants in general—could be accomplished simultaneously.[28]

Jane Addams was not the first to make this proposal. Chicago had been engaged in a long-running battle on this issue since German language and culture had been introduced into the public school curriculum in 1865, on the initiative of the German community.[29] Indeed, as early as 1899 the report of the Educational Commission of the City of Chicago appointed by the mayor on 19 January 1898 and headed by Professor William R. Harper, president of the University of Chicago, justified the teaching of German in Chicago's public schools. It argued that "the demand for German instruction from German born citizens is both natural and to be welcomed. The resident of foreign birth who, making this country the home of his adoption, is willing that his children should grow up without recognition of the natural ties binding them to relatives in the old home lacks one of the elements which go to make good citizenship." For this reason the teaching of German should not be based upon "any theoretical view on the part of experts as to its value in the course." The commission was influenced by the favorable policy on this question adopted in St. Louis and Cincinnati that stressed "the urgency of drawing most German speaking children into the public schools to subvert observable tendencies among Germans to perpetuate exclusive ethnic communities."[30]

Nonetheless, during the years 1900 to 1909, Edwin G. Colley, the superindenpendent of the Chicago school system, made continuous efforts, supported by members of the Chicago Board of Education, to eliminate German language and literature from the grammar school curriculum. He also employed administrative measures to reduce the number of pupils studying, and the number of teachers teaching, German. The teaching of German became enmeshed in a wider controversy over what the content of schooling should be. The *Chicago Tribune,* which represented the views of certain upper-middle-class civic organizations, considered German along with music, physical culture, drawing, and some other subjects to be "fads and frills," a waste of public money. The opposition to the teaching of German was based upon another argument, namely, that the unification of the many races and nationalities that make up this nation is a common speech, used by all peoples in all parts of the country. Others questioned whether it was advisable, upon educational grounds, to teach a modern language other than English in elementary schools. Many educators considered that the elementary school child, especially the immigrant child, was unable to master English unless he concentrated his efforts on one language.[31] Professor Star Willard Cutting of the University of Chicago even objected to teaching some foreign literature in English translation, as suggested by Jane Addams in 1908, since "translation into the mother-tongue must be true to the meaning, rhythm, and melody of the original, if it is to be serviceable in the study of a foreign literature . . . good translations are extremely rare in the whole range of the world's literature. Moreover, even such are no adequate substitute for direct study and appreciation of the original."[32]

Basing their demands on the German precedent, immigrant leaders in Chicago had been campaigning to introduce immigrant languages and literature into the public school curriculum since the 1880s. Their efforts were rewarded in May 1912, when the Board of Education adopted "Report no. 17917, in reference to the addition of modern languages to the list of high school subjects." The decision did not include elementary school pupils, because it was assumed that during these school years the emphasis should be laid upon the teaching of English. The teaching of foreign languages in high schools, however, was considered valuable for educational as well as commercial considerations. As a result immigrant languages could be taught in Chicago high schools on two conditions, namely, that at least twenty pupils were registered for such classes in each school and that teachers teaching immigrant languages met the standards fixed by the Civil Service Commission for high school teachers in general, as well as having the qualifications required for the teaching of a foreign language."[33]

This decision of the Board of Education owed its acceptance in great part to the support given to the cause by Ella Flagg Young, the new Chicago school superintendent, who was a student of John Dewey and a member of the Chicago Liberal Progressive group in which Jane Addams and Hull House were a leading force. Convinced by Professor Cutting's arguments that foreign literature could not be studied properly unless students read it in the original language, and that foreign languages should preferably be taught in high schools, the Hull House group threw its support behind the demand for the teaching of foreign languages in the public high schools. Thus methodological considerations were added to the educational and psychological ones. The teaching of foreign languages and literatures was recommended, also, because it served "to enlarge the students' horizon and to insure the individual against . . . provincialism."[34]

Young referred to all these reasons when explaining her support for the teaching of immigrant languages in public schools. First, "there is no reason why the children should not be proud of their parents' native country and tongue. Making them familiar with the history and literature of the country of their origin would keep the children closer to their mothers and fathers." Second, "up to the present the chasm between the school and the home was almost too great." And finally, "from children brought up in that way there will grow up a generation of enlightened citizens." These arguments were repeated in Young's annual report. They were couched in educational and psychological terms and reflected the views expressed by Jane Addams in 1908.[35]

This measure was, however, considered a temporary expedient rather than the expression of a concept of culture. As William I. Thomas explained, "Language is a tool which its possessor cannot afford to throw away until he has another." He noted, however that "the grandchildren of . . . immigrants have become practically indistinguishable from other Americans. . . . All immigrant groups are losing, even too completely and rapidly, their languages." Liberal Progressives were reconciled to the fact that the measure "came as the inevitable result of public demand, and it will remain just as long as such demand continues." Young herself expressed the Liberal Progressive belief "that in a few years the parents in that particular locality (which is largely composed of descendents from the same race) will be American born, and the desire for the study of the language of the fathers will disappear." In anticipation of this process, she added that "the teachers who taught the language in the earlier years will under the rules governing their certification be competent to teach other subjects, hence the disappearance of the subject from the program will not cause the removal of a good teacher."[36]

The limited role accorded to immigrant languages and literature in the school curriculum was revealed in the new high school course of study adopted by the Board of Education during Young's administration. It did not become part of the general curriculum for American children. Young did not suggest any changes in the teaching of United States history, civics, and literature to reflect the pluralist nature of its society and culture. The idea that the teaching of American history should include the cultural contributions made by immigrant groups and the historical background of these contributions was first brought up at the 1915 conference of the National Education Association. A year later John Dewey, in his address before the association, criticized the public school for failing to teach its pupils "to think and feel in ideas broad enough to be inclusive of the purposes and happiness of all sections and classes." He suggested to do it through the teaching of history.

> This means at least that our public schools shall teach each factor to respect every other, and shall take pains to enlighten all as to the great past contributions of every strain in our composite make-up. I wish our teaching of American history in the schools would take more account of the great waves of migration by which our land for over three centuries has been continuously built-up, and made every pupil conscious of the rich breadth of our national make-up.[37]

Grace Abbott shared John Dewey's criticism, arguing that "the immigrants have been numerically an important factor in the life of the country. The Irish, the German, the Scandinavian, the Italian, the Bohemian, the Pole, the Russian Jew, and all the others who have come have contributed . . . with the Anglo-Saxon American. Together they have builded this country.[38] Yet it was only at the end of 1927 that a "new syllabus for guidance of teaching of history" was introduced into the Chicago public schools, during the administration of Mayor Thompson. It was adopted following a communication from the mayor "Re American Histories" sent to the Board of Education on 22 November 1927.[39]

The secondary role of immigrant studies was reflected also in their optional status and in the limited number of years pupils could study an immigrant language as an optional course. The new course of study represented another compromise—the first being the restriction of ethnic studies to high schools—between ethnic policies and general pedagogical considerations to the disadvantage of the former. Only a few of the thirteen high school courses of study included immigrant languages as an optional study in their curriculum.[40] High school pupils in the office preparatory course were required to study a modern, as opposed to a foreign language, namely, German or French, which was considered more useful for secretaries and clerks. The technical, general trades, arts, and architectural courses had only English in their curriculum. The technical high schools allowed pupils to study any optional course during the third and the fourth year, except for a foreign language in the fourth year. Finally, all the high school two-year courses (the Chicago school system offered twelve such courses) did not allow the optional study of a foreign language. Unfortunately, most of the immigrant children in secondary schools at that time attended technical high schools, vocational courses within general high schools, or the two-year courses. Educational considerations limited their chances to learn a foreign language.[41]

There were yet other obstacles in the way of those immigrant children who wished to study their parents' language and literature. The Chicago new high school course of study gave pupils who took the general science, commercial, household, and teachers' preparatory college courses in high schools the option to study other foreign languages besides German or French. Yet pupils who wished to continue their studies after high school were unable to take advantage of this option, since the admission requirements of the colleges and universities included Latin, Greek, German, or French and did not recognize Polish, Bohmeian, or Hebrew as substitutes for German or French despite Young's efforts in this direction. Her correspondence with President Harry Pratt Judson of the University of Chicago, who was a Liberal Progressive, shows that the university authorities were reluctant to change their policy, even when the Jewish students petitioned the president to introduce their ethnic history and language into the curriculum.[42]

The practical consequences of this decision by the Board of Education were in fact negligible because only an insignificant minority of immigrant children attended public high schools in Chicago before the 1920s (indeed less than 10 percent of all American children attended high schools in the early twentieth century). The average immigrant child left school after the fifth or sixth grade and went to work. There were only several dozen immigrant children from eastern and southern Europe in their neighborhood high school districts. Given this situation, immigrant leaders vowed that "once having established Polish in public high schools," they "will not only keep it there, but will continue to try to secure the establishment of the Polish language in . . . the elementary schools."[43]

The lack of qualified teachers also limited this decision's practicality. Very few immigrant language teachers could meet the professional qualifications required by the Civil Service Commission or pass its examinations. Hull House residents, like other Progressives, were the sponsors and stout supporters of this commission in general, and of professionalism in education in particular. The campaign to establish professional qualifications for public service was an integral part of the Progressive education reform program. As a result, the efforts of immigrant leaders to implement the decision were checked by the very group that supported it. Whenever Liberal Progressives were forced to choose between the demand for professionalism and the so-called immigrant needs, professionalism won.[44] Thus the number of teachers and classes in immigrants' languages was insignificant. Among the new immigrant groups, the east European Jewish community in Chicago had the highest average of high school pupils, but it failed to take advantage of the board's decision in 1912, because no Hebrew teacher in Chicago was qualified to meet the standards set for high school teachers. It was not until 1917 that the *Courier,* the Yiddish-language newspaper, could inform the Jewish community that the first Hebrew teacher had passed the examinations. Other groups faced similar difficulties.[45]

Under these circumstances the opportunity to inculcate respect in the great masses of immigrant children in elementary and high schools towards their parents and their heritages was wasted. The chasm between the home and the public school, and the crisis of the immigrant parent's authority, remained unsolved problems that teachers and parents continued to face. On the other hand, the public school continued its mission "to minimize, obliterate and homogenize" the cultural differences of immigrant children in its efforts "in the process of unification" to create "like-mindedness."[46]

The immediate value of the Board of Education's decision may have been minimal, but its importance for the immigrants' self-respect and the status of their cultures in American society should not be underestimated. Immigrants saw in this decision a recognition by native-born Americans that ethnic languages and literatures were worthy of being included in the American educational system. Immigrant leaders interpreted the board's decision as a departure from the American genteel tradition in which only the study of German, French, classical Greek, and Latin were considered indispensable elements of a good education. It was precisely this sympathetic atmosphere that Hull House's ethnic policies intended to create. The "ethnic program" suggested by Jane Addams in 1908 and the support given by the Chicago Liberal Progressive group to the introduction of immigrant languages into the public high schools expressed the settlement workers' and educators' growing awareness of the alienation between immigrant children and their parents, the parents and the public school, and the immigrant communities and the American public.[47] The favorable attitude towards immigrant languages and culture also represented a more humanitarian method of assimilating new immigrants into American society. Liberal Progressives believed that cultural and social assimilation could be successful insofar as it created the least antagonism between immigrant traditions and ethnic identity and American ones. Unlike nativists and most other Americanizers, Hull House residents were well aware of the economic, cultural, and psychological difficulties faced by newcomers, and identified with their plight. They thought that acculturation was bad insofar as it was undemocratically imposed, had bad effects on both newcomers and the host society, and was greatly injurious to the delicate fabric of human relations indispensable to a democracy. The Hull House group suggested what it believed to be democratic and humanitarian methods for the cultural transformation of newcomers. These included gradual assimilation and recognition of the need to create a sense of continuity between the old and the new, in an atmosphere of mutual respect, tolerance, and understanding. Compulsory means were considered pedagogically useless, as well as inhuman and undemocratic, and much more could be achieved through sympathy, respect, and understanding.[48] In addition to this psychological consideration, Liberal Progressives believed that a democratic society should take great pains to preserve the self-respect and personal integrity of newcomers during the process of acculturation. The dangers of personal and family disorganization and juvenile delinquency were a social price that neither American society nor the newcomers could afford and that would endanger the stability of all American society. Thus for the sakes of the immigrant and the rest of American society, assimilation should be gradual. They believed that the whole process should be organic rather than mechanical, because rapid assimilation would be superficial, that is, it was the adoption of the merely external features of American life and a failure to comprehend the essential meaning of the American idea of democracy and American civilization. Therefore, the future of American democracy depended on the use of suitable methods for the assimilation of newcomers.[49]

Liberal Progressives developed short- and long-range policies to meet the requirements of democratic and humanitarian assimilation. They accepted the fact that ethnic differences could not and should not be eliminated within one generation as most native-born Americans demanded, and that American society would have to live with ethnicity up to the third generation. Given this perspective Liberal Progressives were willing to tolerate and respect ethnic differences even though they conceived of them as transitory phenomena. For the time being they were ready to do their utmost to raise the status of immigrant groups and their cultures in American society in the face of contemptuous, discriminatory, and prejudicial attitudes. Their intention was not to raise the status of the immigrant group as such, but to raise the status of its members as individuals. They therefore viewed ethnic studies in high schools as a temporary expedient, because the transition from one culture to the other was a slow process of adjustment, and totally rejected ethnic persistence as the pattern of immigrant adjustment to American society.[50]

# FIVE

# LEADERSHIP, CULTURAL BROKERAGE, AND "CONTROL THROUGH ALLIANCE"

The gradual emergence of a leadership among the ethnic communities contradicted one of the basic assumptions behind the settlement idea, namely, the leading role of the American middle-class "better element" in the reorganization of the slums and the reunification of the segmented American society. The Hull House group's attitude towards this new ethnic leadership was complex and ambivalent. While disregarding religious leaders and rejecting or manipulating the lower-middle-class ethnic leaders, Hull House displayed a willingness to cooperate with the emerging Americanized middle-class leadership. What determined this attitude was the attempt to gain control of the immigrant masses in order to advance the original objectives of the settlement movement and progressivism. Thus settlement workers and immigrant leaders actually became engaged in a competition for leadership in the slums, a competition that reflected the wider struggle over the nature of American society in the future.

Attacks on immigrant leaders were first voiced by immigrant intellectuals who sought to assimilate culturally and structurally into American society and by immigrant radicals who were opposed to their own group ethnic establishments. These two groups openly accused immigrant businessmen, the foreign press, and the religious as well as lay leaders for being opposed to Americanization and for cultivating a distinct ethnic identity "in order he [the immigrant] may be held as a source of income to those whom he trusts." Immigrant leaders, they argued, used their power "mostly to promote ends of personal vanity and ambition. . . . They have resigned all hope of playing a political role in this country . . . and consider their organization as a training school and a center of future influence." Immigrants' organizations were formed to meet the needs of their leaders, not the real needs of the masses.[1]

Although Hull House residents were much better informed about the situation in immigrant colonies than the average American, their "inside" sources of information were those intellectuals and radicals who represented the antiestablishment marginal elements of immigrant groups (see chapter 6). This situation undoubtedly influenced their attitude towards immigrant leaders. Indeed, it became a consensus in the Hull House circle that the

religious and lower-middle-class immigrant leaders were interested in perpetuating ethnicity and were supported in their efforts by ward bosses and party
machines. Thus, in his study on the Polish community and in other articles,
John Dewey dismissed the notion prevailing among native-born Americans of
"aliens wilfully herding together for fear of becoming transformed into
genuine Americans." He accused American politicians of being interested "in
keeping a group as isolated and fixated that it could easily be handled." While
recognizing the "difficulties of language, economic limitations and exclu-
siveness on the part of native Americans," he also accused immigrant leaders
of a "conspiracy of economic, denominational and political forces with
personal ambition and love of prestige to keep newcomers isolated and out of
real share in American life." He pointed to immigrant leaders as "the forces
which work unceasingly to maintain segregated masses in a block amendable
to ready exploitation by autocratic managers" and called for the "self-
determination" of the immigrant masses in America, for them to free
themselves from their autocratic leaders with the help of the "better element"
in American society. At the same time, Dewey was much more sympathetic
towards the more progressive and enlightened leadership of the Polish
community.[2] Although William I. Thomas also shared the Hull House circle's
view of the lower-middle-class leaders, he pointed out that "the more
important point, however, is not the abuses, but the fact that the immigrant
must have this aid . . . The great American Banks and steamship agencies are
not adapted to his needs."[3]

Liberal Progressives sought to gain control of the immigrant masses
through depriving bosses and lower-middle-class leaders of the sources of
their power. The first objective was to eliminate the network of private
business services that immigrant small businessmen established for newcomers, the employment agencies of the padrones, the commissary system for
room and board in the construction and railroad camps run by bosses, and the
immigrant banks whose major function was to transfer money to the families
of immigrants in Europe. Another objective was to create welfare services as
an alternative to those that ward bosses established in immigrant neighborhoods to provide jobs and relief. In short, Liberal Progressives wished to
transfer all services given to newcomers to governmental and upper-middle-
class agencies and thus to put an end to the economic dependence of "new
immigrants" on the small businessmen of their own groups and on the
political machines. They hoped finally to eliminate the influence and political
control of immigrant small businessmen on the "immigrant vote" and to
terminate their roles as mediators between immigrants and American socioeconomic and political systems, and as interpreters of American institutions.

The Chicago Liberal Progressive group initiated and supported municipal,
state, and federal legislation to achieve these objectives with the cooperation

of civic organizations. These activities were directed by the Immigrants' Protective League, established in 1908 by Hull House leaders. The first two presidents of the league, Judge Julian W. Mack and Alexander A. McCormick, were also highly influential. Two other members of the league's executive, professors Ernst Freund and George H. Mead of the University of Chicago, also made significant contributions to the formulation of policy, Mead having also served as a vice-president. William I. Thomas's wife was a member of the board of trustees.[4]

The bills for the amendment of the employment agency law and for the reorganization of the state free employment offices, which were introduced before the Illinois General Assembly between 1909 and 1915, were intended to transfer the major function of the private employment agencies, namely, the distribution of unskilled labor, especially railroad and construction jobs, to the state free employment offices. Chicago did have private employment agencies, which belonged to native-born Americans and "old immigrants." Since, however, the unskilled immigrants from eastern and southern Europe did not speak English and preferred to be handled by their own countrymen, this kind of labor was either dealt with directly by "new immigrant" agents or indirectly by American agencies using immigrant interpreters (or "bosses") who were paid by the employment agencies to accompany their countrymen to work camps. Thus "new immigrant" agents and "bosses"—mostly Italians and Slavs—played a considerable role in the unskilled labor market. For the same reason the league campaigned to establish a Chicago branch of the federal Bureau of Information, later called the Bureau of Distribution, concerned with interstate distribution of labor. It was also instrumental in the opening of a city employment bureau. From 1912 to 1917 Liberal Progressives were likewise involved in the efforts to enact a law abolishing private banks in Illinois. The law included clauses that prohibited the transfer of immigrants' savings abroad through immigrant banks and altogether abolished small private banks in immigrant neighborhoods. The league supported the establishment of postal banks instead. It also joined other organizations in a campaign for a city civil service law that aimed, in part at transferring the distribution of municipal unskilled and temporary jobs to the Civil Service Commission as a means of depriving ward bosses of their control over them.[5]

The league justified its desire to deprive private employment agencies of their control of the distribution of unskilled labor on the grounds that these agencies were "interested only in the collection of fees, and not in so distributing labor as to serve the large interests of the community." It accused them of charging fees varying from $1 to $14 per man, when the registration fee fixed by an Illinois statute recommended $2; of charging employees for full train fare, when transportation was in fact free or available at reduced rates; of extorting fees for jobs that did not exist; and many other kinds of fraud as well. As early as 1897, investigations held in Chicago by Liberal

Progressives and by federal authorities resulted in charges that immigrant-owned employment agencies, especially Italian padrones dealing with railroad laborers, exploited their own countrymen. In a statement to the Chicago *Evening Post* on November 1897, Jane Addams and Graham Taylor, head residents of the two most famous settlement houses in Chicago, claimed that 90 percent of Italian laborers (constituting the major unskilled labor force in Chicago) were under the "absolute control of padrones," in a state of "slavery," and "under terror of being blacklisted by the padrone."[6] They insisted that "the greatest evil of the system, and the one most to be feared by Americans, is the political influence of the padrones. In this direction they are a tremendous power." They also accused padrones and bosses of supplying their gang workers at construction camps with room and board of inferior quality at high prices.[7]

Other instances of the strategy used to fight the immigrants' private and ward agencies are revealing. Liberal Progressives, through the Immigrants' Protective League, attempted to persuade railroad corporations to regulate and even take over the commissary system run by immigrant bosses in labor camps. The league's Bureau of Information and Social Service, in its capacity as a clearinghouse, directed clients to upper-middle-class charitable organizations as well as recommending them to use the ones run by the city and state.[8] The league thus sought to create an alternative system of services to those provided by immigrant businessmen and ward bosses. This was to take the form of a network of governmental and upper-middle-class voluntary agencies, with the league serving as a clearinghouse and rendering direct services when these were not provided by other agencies.[9]

During 1913, in the wake of the Chicago banking panic of 1912, the league staff investigated 127 of the 200 immigrant banks located in the Chicago area. They found most of the immigrant bankers to be "irresponsible and unreliable persons," noting that even those who were honest were inexperienced and unacquainted with banking procedures. They used the depositors' money in their own businesses and for lack of proper facilities conducted their banking affairs from grocery stores, drugstores, saloons, barbershops, and real estate offices. Since these banks were unincorporated and not subject to any regulation, their assets and liabilities were part of their owner's personal property, and in case of bankruptcy the depositors had no claims on the banker's property. This enabled unscrupulous persons to take advantage of their depositors. Immigrant bankers were also accused of delaying or even failing to transfer money intended for immigrants' families abroad. During most of the first two decades of the twentieth century, Liberal Progressives claimed that this situation remained basically unchanged.[10]

The league presented little evidence of complaints of fraud or bankruptcy against immigrant banks, and the Chicago English press controlled by Progressives, which gave a great deal of publicity to the corruption in private banking, could point to only a few "new immigrant" bankers in this context. One American financial expert even argued that "compared with the tens of millions of dollars entrusted to them [immigrant bankers] the percentage that fails to reach its destination is infinitesimal." Nevertheless, in its report for the year 1917, the league noted with great satisfaction that a private banking law had just been enacted by the general assembly, and "the private banking situation [had] improved . . . Many of the smaller banks which were such a source of exploitation to the immigrant have gone out of existence, and some of the larger private ones in immigrant neighborhoods have become state banks."[11]

The efforts to deprive immigrant lower-class leaders of their influence included campaigns against them in city politics. The Chicago Municipal Voters' League, established in 1896 by the city's civic organizations and supported by Liberal Progressives, published annually its findings on the unscrupulous deeds of aldermen, focusing on those representing immigrant wards. A sampling of the candidates for aldermen recommended by the Chicago Municipal Voters' League reveals that it was involved in campaigns to replace corrupt aldermen of lower-class affiliation with middle-class candidates. This attitude was evident in the support given to John F. Smulski, a Polish-American middle-class leader, graduate of Northwestern University Law School. The political boss of "Polonia's capital," Stanley H. Kunz, a lower-middle-class leader, was continually accused by the Municipal Voters' League of being unfit for office. Yet most Polish-Americans did not read the American papers and were not influenced by Progressive ideas in supporting their ward aldermen. Kunz was elected alderman of the Sixteenth Ward time and again for thirty years. The same trend was evident in the attitude of the Municipal Voters' League toward Italian leaders. Lower-class candidates were rarely supported and even then only for tactical considerations. Thus in 1896, after failing to advance a middle-class candidate, Hull House supported in cooperation with the league a working-class candidate for alderman in the Nineteenth Ward to defeat John Powers, the ward boss. His failure to defeat Powers was another example of the Progressive misconception of the motivations behind the immigrant vote. Jane Addams gradually realized that "in the popular mind a man who laid bricks and wore overalls—the working-class candidate was a builder—was not desirable for an alderman. . . . The district wished its representative to stand up to the best of them."[12]

The preoccupation of native-born Americans in general, and Liberal Progressives in particular, with the "exploitation and fraud" of immigrants by their countrymen can hardly be explained by the actual circumstances. This interpretation of the relationship between the "new immigrant" masses and the small-business group out of which the lower-middle-class leadership was recruited reflected rather the struggle of Liberal Progressives for leadership and control over the immigrant masses. In this struggle for power against the

66

indigenous immigrant brokers, they aimed to destroy these immigrant competitors.

Generally speaking, settlement workers rejected the immigrant lower-middle-class leaders on the basis of the workers' wider concept of leadership, which I had described earlier. Lower-middle-class leaders, in their view, lacking the middle-class value system and refinement and therefore unable to perform a disinterested role, inevitably became advocates of narrow personal and group interests. Hull House leaders were convinced that the immigrant clergy, small businessmen, foreign-language editors, parochial school teachers, and other Old World intellectuals, whose sources of income and leadership careers were dependent upon ethnic segregation and ethnic persistence, were instrumental in keeping the immigrant masses under their influence and control. These leaders sought to establish themselves as indispensable mediators between their groups and American society. Still, the Hull House group made a distinction between those immigrant leaders who were personally unscrupulous—employment agents, bankers, and so forth, who exploited their countrymen economically and politically—and Old World intellectuals who promoted ethnic culture as a means of preserving ethnic identity. Hull House totally rejected the former but made efforts to manipulate the latter into bringing their countrymen under Hull House auspices.[13]

The settlement workers' claim for leadership depended on the argument that in maintaining ethnic identity the lower-middle-class leaders did not represent the real wishes of their constituency. Considering themselves faithful to the idea of democracy, settlement workers claimed that the immigrant leaders did not represent the "consent of the governed."[14] Another argument used against these leaders was that they forfeited their right for leadership by exploiting their positions for personal gain and by neglecting the interests and needs of their constituency. It became the humanitarian, moral, and civic duty of the "better element" to rescue helpless immigrants from their exploiters, to release them from their dependence on unworthy leaders, and to give them and America a chance for a better future. "He [the immigrant] arrives here bewildered, unacquainted with our language, habits and customs, and a ready prey for the scoundrel . . . not merely as a matter of humanity towards the brother and sister in need, but as a matter of duty to ourselves and our children is it important that the newcomer receive the best possible impression of those who are going to be their fellow citizens."[15] Settlement workers explained the immigrant businessmen's control of the immigrant masses in terms of economic dependence. The padrones, immigrant bankers, and grocery and saloon owners in the immigrant neighborhood exploited the helplessness and alienation of newcomers, as well as the neglect of immigrants' needs by the American authorities, and gained their political dependence through economic dependence. In addition to their economic functions, they supplied newcomers with social welfare services and city jobs through their alliance with ward bosses and the two party machines. According to this interpretation these businessmen actually "terrorized" newcomers into voting for machine candidates in payment for services.[16] Another interpretation favored by Hull House was that "simple-minded" newcomers were duped by what they believed to be the disinterested personal kindness of bosses and immigrant politicians, and voted for them as an act of gratitude.[17]

Old World intellectuals were also charged with exploiting for their own personal interests the inarticulate masses, overwhelmed by the new environment. Instead of promoting the learning of English and helping newcomers to become acquainted with American life, they preferred to promote foreign languages and old ways through the foreign-language press and other sociocultural agencies, such as the bilingual school system. The issue was one of priority and orientation, for, as we have seen, the Hull House circle was in no way hostile to immigrants' traditions. Yet settlement workers believed that adjustment to the new environment should have the highest priority, particularly for the younger generation, and this was their aim in manipulating these leaders to bring their countrymen to Hull House.[18]

Hull House leaders were willing to cooperate upon what they considered to be equal terms with the Americanized middle-class leadership. They believed that, unlike the lower middle class, these more Americanized leaders shared their own value system, virtue, and merit and their idea of community and were, therefore, natural allies in the struggle against the immigrant lower-middle-class leadership and its corrupt political allies. This impression was reinforced by a series of meetings between leaders of civic organizations and immigrant middle-class leaders which were sponsored by Hull House in 1916. One Hull House leader noted after one such meeting at the City Club of Chicago "the sense of isolation, of involuntary segregation, of helplessness, revealed in the speeches. Here were men from the alien 'colonies' that did not wish their people to remain alien, but that did not know how to establish close contact with Americans."[19] The middle class, as opposed to the lower class, would therefore serve as cultural brokers between the members of the community and American society. They would assist in gradually eliminating ethnic and cultural barriers, first as representatives of the group, leading to communication on an individual basis, and finally bringing about the dissolution of the immigrant subcommunity. Grace Abbott emphasized the importance of cooperation with these immigrant middle-class leaders:

> Intelligent and able leaders can be found among the foreign born who would be able to mobilize the honest, undirected enthusiasm which many of these people have for civic progress. . . . It is important . . . that these thousands of Slovaks, Ruthenians, Italians and others should be given a chance to ally themselves with the best element in the community and to assist us in making the United States a real democracy.[20]

On the other hand, Hull House leaders could not ignore the statements made by immigrant middle-class leaders in support of maintaining separate ethnic identity, although they tried to dismiss these statements as "ethnic" and "pluralist" rhetoric, which the immigrant middle-class leaders used to camouflage their real views from other immigrant leaders. Such was the interpretation Liberal Progressives gave to the views stated by immigrant middle-class leaders in the controversies on the bilingual school system (see chapters 4 and 8).

The Polish, Bohemian, and east European Jewish middle-class leaders' criticism of the bilingual school system and the Talmud Torahs resembled the Liberal Progressive criticism on the same issues. These leaders deplored the poor accommodation and lack of elementary facilities in the bilingual schools, the low standards and poor methods of teaching, and the teachers' inadequate training. In particular they criticized the deficiencies of the American curriculum of these schools and their clerical orientation. And above all, they demanded that ethnic languages be taught in the public school curriculum, a demand strongly opposed by religious immigrant leaders. Liberal Progressives interpreted the whole range of criticism as part of the middle-class leaders' efforts to transfer immigrant children to public schools. They misunderstood the antagonism that developed between religious and middle-class leaders as a controversy over assimilation versus ethnic persistence.[21] This interpretation influenced at least partly the "ethnic curriculum" proposed by Jane Addams in 1908 in her address before the National Education Association and also motivated Young's support in 1911–12 for the immigrant middle-class leaders' demand to introduce immigrant languages into the public school curriculum.[22]

The primary aim of the settlement workers in the slums was to serve not only as social organizers and political leaders but also as cultural brokers to the immigrant communities, in other words, to establish themselves as representatives both of American society to newcomers, and interpreters of immigrants to the American public. Thus the settlement house became involved in efforts to eliminate ethnic barriers in addition to its role as mediator between the upper and lower classes. The task of creating a unified and harmonized social organism was elaborated to include brotherhood and cooperation between immigrants and native-born Americans. Hull House leaders believed that Liberal Progressive Americans were in a better position than immigrant leaders to make known "to the community the special needs of the newly arrived immigrants." They could mobilize funds and support because "it is through a public organization created [by Americans] to meet these needs that civic, social, and educational resources of the community will be made available for those who are most in need of them." The development of such services required a familiarity with the governmental organizations and a capacity for utilizing official agencies not to be found among the groups most needing help. Above all, the more professional and efficient services that they offered and their disinterested position in society made them better cultural brokers than immigrant leaders and machine politicians and other native-born Americans in general. Since settlement workers were well acquainted with the immigrant colonies and their needs, they had better chances of mobilizing the cooperation of the immigrant masses. "It is only in this spirit of helpful understanding that a public program of Americanization will have the cooperation of the foreign born." Moreover, settlement workers also believed that they were the proper medium through which American institutions, standards, and ideals whould be transmitted to the immigrants, since they represented in their behavior all that was good in American life.[23]

Settlement workers gradually became convinced that cultural brokers should be equally conversant with both the immigrant and American cultures, since they played a crucial role in defining and interpreting the immigrant and American societies to each other and especially in promoting or discouraging a sense of ethnic solidarity and identity. Unlike typical brokers from the dominant group, settlement workers therefore acknowledged that since immigrant leaders were better acquainted with their countrymen, their languages, and their general backgrounds, they were more acceptable as cultural brokers. Under these circumstances it became evident that the objectives of the Hull House circle could not be achieved without the cooperation of the immigrant middle-class leaders. This cooperation, however, took the form of "control through alliance," as the leading role was still reserved for the settlement workers as representatives both of the "better element" in American society and of American culture. Just as the leading role of the American middle class was inherent in the entire nature and ideology of the settlement movement, so the settlement workers' leadership in the field of cultural brokerage was determined by the very fact that they were enlightened middle-class native-born Americans.[24]

The key to the policy of "control through alliance" therefore lay in securing the cooperation of the enlightened members of the immigrant colonies. This included transferring the control of immigrant adjustment to American society from the immigrant lower-middle-class leaders and their allies and immigrant welfare and ethnic institutions, to American governmental and upper-middle-class voluntary agencies, under the auspices of Liberal Progressives. One such agency, the Chicago Municipal Voters' League, was willing to support immigrant middle-class leaders as candidates for the city council. This policy was based upon the underlying Progressive assumption that middle-class leaders were better qualified for a disinterested leading role and was part of a comprehensive plan to end the hold of the political machines on city politics, a hold made possible by the mainly immigrant lower-class vote. The league backed immigrant middle-class candidates financially as well as politically against immigrant lower-class ward bosses in the immigrant wards. Candidates supported by the league were obliged to proclaim their commitment to the league's political reform program and sign a formal commitment. Nonetheless, despite this cooperation at the ward level, no immigrant middle-class leaders were invited to join the inner circle of the league or its executive committee, which formulated policy and directed the league's activities. The league supervised and controlled the work of the aldermen supported by its money. Every year, before the election of candidates, the league published its opinion on how these aldermen had fulfilled their responsibilities, and those who did not meet the league's expectations were not supported again. The league used these publications to influence the city's constituents. Settlement workers supported the league's cause, and some of them were directly involved in its activities. Hull House, for example, cooperated with the league in its efforts to replace John Powers, the boss and alderman of the Nineteenth Ward, where Hull House was situated.[25]

The Immigrants Protective League, unlike the Municipal Voters' League, was willing to give immigrant middle-class leaders recognition and status by inviting them to join its board of trustees, a unique gesture among Progressive agencies. In return these leaders were expected to encourage "new immigrants" to prefer the league's services that directed newcomers to municipal, federal, and American voluntary agencies, instead of those furnished through the economic and political mediation of immigrant lower-middle-class businessmen and politicians. Of course, they believed that these voluntary agencies provided newcomers with better services, given by honest, disinterested, and professional social workers. Even though the influence of these middle-class leaders was crucial in this matter, given the suspicion with which newcomers generally viewed American institutions and agencies, "new immigrants" constituted less than 40 percent of the board members (see table 3), and until the 1920s none of them was elected to the executive committee, which was entrusted with policy decisions. The daily direction of the league's activities and the supervision of its staff of social workers was entrusted to Grace Abbott as director and Sophonisba P. Breckinridge as secretary. Both were Hull House residents and members of the Liberal Progressive circle in Chicago.[26]

Even though Hull House's female residents played an important role in the Immigrants' Protective League and women's immigrant organizations were heavily represented in the league's membership and paid membership fees (see table 4), no immigrant women representing immigrant women's organizations were nominated to the board of trustees. The leaders of these organizations cooperated with the league in its work and occasionally recommended foreign social workers to the league's director; it was, however, a one-sided relationship, since the league wished to become the sole clearinghouse for immigrants' adjustment to the American environment.[27]

71

Table 3 Immigrant Middle-Class Leaders on the Immigrants' Protective League Board of
Trustees

| Years | Profession | Nationality | Other associations |
|---|---|---|---|
| 1909–11 | Physician | Bulgarian | Cook County Hospital |
| | Physician | Italian | Columbus Hospital, president of the White Hand Society of Chicago |
| | Businessman | Bohemian | In 1913 was appointed envoy extraordinary and minister plenipotentiary of the U.S.A. to Romania, Serbia, and Bulgaria |
| | Consul | Italian | |
| | Vice-president of the PNA[a] | Polish | |
| | Director of the Chicago Hebrew Institute | Jewish | |
| 1912–14 | Vice-president of the PNA | Polish | |
| | Social worker, journalist | Jewish | Member of Board of Education of Chicago, 1911–17; the Courier, a Yiddish newspaper |
| | Educator in public schools | Bohemian | Principal of public schools, district superintendent of public schools |
| | Lawyer | Russian | |
| 1915–17 | President of the PNA | Polish | |
| | Social worker, journalist | Jewish | See 1912–14 |
| | Educator in public schools | Bohemian | See 1912–14 |
| | Lawyer | Russian | |
| | Engineer's wife | Jewish | |

Source: Immigrants' Protective League, Board of Trustees Lists, 1909–17, and Annual
Reports, 1909–17, Immigrants' Protective League Papers, University of Illinois Archives,
Chicago.

Note: For biographies of the "new immigrant" membership see A. N. Marquis,*The Book of
Chicagoans* (1911), 2d edition (1915), 3d edition (1917); *The Chicago City Directory* for
the years 1908–20; Francis Boleck, ed., *Who's Who in Polish America* (New York, 1943);
David Droba, ed., *Czech and Slovak Leaders in Metropolitan Area* (Chicago, 1931).

[a]Polish National Alliance.

Table 4  Members of the Immigrants' Protective League in Chicago

| Years | Immigrant organizations | Women's immigrant organizations |
|---|---|---|
| 1909/10 | Bohemian Slavonic Benevolent Society (2 branches)<br>Bohemian Slavonic Society | Auxiliary, Chicago Hebrew Institute<br><br>Women's Auxiliary Polish National Alliance<br>Bohemian Women's Union (14 branches)<br>Bohemian Sisters' Benevolent Union (6 branches) |
| 1912/13 | United Lithuanian Societies<br><br>Polish National Alliance<br><br>Polish Roman Catholic Union of America<br>Austro-Hungarian Benevolent Association<br>Bohemian National Council | Bohemian Women's Union (23 branches)<br>Bohemian Sisters' Benevolent Union (24 branches) |
| 1914/15 | Polish Roman Catholic Union of America<br><br>Polish National Alliance<br><br>United Lithuanian Societies | Bohemian Women's Union S.P.J. (31 branches)<br>Bohemian Women's Union J.C.D. (32 branches)<br>Polish Women's Alliance<br>Bohemian Women's Club (Univ. of Chicago Settlement) |
| 1915/16 | Polish National Alliance<br><br>Bohemian Union of Patriots J.C.V. no. 7 | Bohemian Women's Union (main branch)<br>Bohemian Sisters' Benevolent Union (main branch) |
| 1916/17 | Polish National Alliance | Polish Women's Alliance<br>Bohemian Women's Club<br>Bohemian Women's Union (main branch)<br>Bohemian Sisters' Benevolent Union (main branch) |

Source: Immigrants' Protective League, Lists of Organizations Membership, 1909–17, and Annual Reports, 1909–17, Immigrants' Protective League Papers, University of Illinois Archives, Chicago.

The difference in the roles that the Immigrants' Protective League on the one hand and Hull House on the other assigned to immigrant leaders was a result of the different functions that these two institutions performed in helping immigrants adjust to the American environment. The league was a clearinghouse for information, advice, and welfare services, whereas Hull House sought to socialize and acculturate newcomers and thus unify the segmented society into a harmonized organism. Consequently, even though these immigrant leaders were Americanized, the very nature of Hull House's objectives prevented their playing a leading role within the settlement. William I. Thomas disagreed with Hull House and insisted that the acculturation of newcomers should be entrusted to cultural brokers of the same nationality who were familiar with both ethnic and American cultures, with settlement workers playing a secondary role.[28] "It is a mistake to suppose that a "community center" established by American social agencies can in its present form even approximately fulfill the social function of a Polish parish. It is an institution imposed from the outside . . . these purposes can be attained only by organizing and encouraging social self-help on the cooperative basis.[29] His opinion, however, was not accepted at Hull House.

In accordance with this perception of the primary role of American-born workers, foreign leaders were never invited to represent their groups on the Hull House board of trustees or given any role in the policy making and direction of Hull House. On the other hand, Hull House residents made great efforts to bring their countrymen to Hull House. They established close relations with some leaders by appealing to their national pride and yearning for recognition and respect, by sponsoring "American-ethnic meetings" and "ethnic receptions." It was through these leaders that Hull House extended invitations to philanthropic, literary, dramatic, and other immigrant societies to use Hull House facilities. All these efforts were part of the overall objective of establishing Hull House as the leading neighborhood center in order to implement its ethnic policy of "segregation within integration."[30]

Hull House's method of "control through alliance" in relation to immigrant middle-class leaders can be seen in the role it played in the establishment, in the early 1890s, of the Maxwell Street Settlement. Hull House served as the meeting place when upper-middle-class German Jews tried to get the cooperation of young Americanized east European Jewish leaders (second generation) in establishing a settlement staffed by German Jews. Similarly, Hull House sponsored in the 1890s a meeting of religious, lower- and middle-class Italian leaders seeking to establish an Italian institute. The plan essentially intended to gain the cooperation of middle-class leaders in the institute under the auspices of Hull House. The most comprehensive plan was the attempt in 1910 to establish a neighborhood council, composed of representatives of all the neighborhood societies and organizations, under the direction of Grace Abbott. At its first meeting the council, which was attended by representatives of various American civic and welfare agencies, decided that "delegates from societies in the vicinity are to be gradually added." This ambition, however, was not fulfilled.[31]

The differences between the Immigrants' Protective League and Hull House were reflected also in the compositions of their staff, that is, the cultural brokers in the field. The league employed a staff wholly composed of foreign-born social workers representing every immigrant group in the foreign population of Chicago. Most daily contacts with newcomers were through social workers of the same ethnic group because, as Grace Abbott stated, "the immigrant cannot be adequately guided by an American who does not understand the sources of the difficulties which arise during the period of his adjustment." The newcomer needed cultural brokers able "to speak to him in a language he understands."[32] Hull House on the other hand had a staff mostly composed of upper-middle-class native-born Americans. During the years 1889 to 1929, only about 3 percent of the residents were foreign born. They were employed in the few programs pertaining to immigrant folklore and crafts and in household services. Immigrants were rarely allowed to perform other functions at Hull House.[33]

Hull House leaders believed that foreign-born cultural brokers could not meet the requirements for settlement work. The issue, as we have seen, was the concept of the brokerage role of the upper-middle-class American in American society, which led to the distinction between the function of the social worker and the settlement worker. The latter—the socializer and acculturator—was responsible for molding the patterns of thought and behavior of his or her clientele. Settlement workers were convinced that "real settlement work depends on personality, not on knowledge of language." Moreover, "the persistence of the language of thought or processes of thought, . . . seems almost to be born in us." Thus, foreign-born workers might adopt new ideas, "but thought process is something different." Different thought processes were the outcome of different socialization processes, which shaped the personality of Americanized foreign-born in different ways. Hence, while the foreign-born were preferable as social workers during the early years of adjustment, since a common language and background was indispensable, upper-middle-class Americans were preferable as settlement workers. Nevertheless, settlement workers were aware that familiarity with the immigrant background was vital for their acculturation work. This requirement was met by teaching American settlement workers the history and background of immigrant groups. Such courses were included in the curriculum of the School of Civics and Philanthropy—the Chicago social work training school established by the Chicago settlement leaders—later renamed the School of Social Service Administration. These courses were taught first by Grace Abbott and later by her sister Edith.[34]

In their quest to assert their leadership among the immigrants, the settlement workers assumed that, unlike the religious and lower-class immigrant leadership, the Americanized middle class disapproved of ethnic-cultural persistence as the desirable pattern of immigrant adjustment to American society. The differences between the two groups were, however, more of methods and style than of substance. The middle-class leaders had a wider vision of the role of immigrant groups in American society, but these differences could be attributed to the fact that the two groups represented two generations of leaders (see chapter 8).

Indeed, the differences between immigrant leaders and Liberal Progressives on the idea of community and the nature of American nationalism were far more radical. Despite some similar views and common interests, they in effect represented two different concepts of American society. Immigrant leaders actually stood in the way of the Liberal Progressives' claim to leadership in the slums and in American society as a whole. The crux of the issue was control over the immigrant masses. In their disguised and perhaps only half-conscious struggle for power, Liberal Progressives aimed to force their leadership, as well as their solution to the crisis of American society, upon both "new immigrants" and their leaders.

# PART TWO

## HULL HOUSE AND THE "IMMIGRANT COLONIES"

# SIX:

# HULL HOUSE AND THE IMMIGRANT
# SUBCOMMUNITIES

Hull House's intention to play a major role in immigrant assimilation by becoming the center of communal life in the neighborhood through cooperation with immigrant subcommunities was not fulfilled. Although Hull House performed certain functions in the immigrant subcommunities, it maintained a close relationship mainly with their marginal elements. As we have seen, the desire of both the first and second generations of immigrants to preserve their ethnic entity and identity turned out to be stronger than the assimilating influences of the American environment. Thomas Holland, a Hull House Catholic resident in the early 1920s, was among the few to recognize this situation: "I do not think that Hull House had much impact on the community life", he observed. "It was evident in 1923 that the place was becoming an empty shell."[1]

Nonetheless, as Jane Addams and Hull House sought to adapt their policies to the reality of persistent ethnic identity, differing patterns of relationship emerged between Hull House and the neighboring "new immigrant" communities on Chicago's West Side, the Jews, Italians, and Greeks. These relations were also determined by the different nature of the three communities, which I shall consider in detail below. Although Hull House members failed to understand Jewish ethnicity, they maintained cordial relations with the east European Jewish middle-class leaders. The relations with the Italian community on the other hand were at times strained, as Hull House failed altogether to understand Italians in general and the Italian lower-middle-class leadership in particular. It was most successful with the Greek community, where it created a relationship of cooperation and mutual respect with both the religious and lay leadership. The Greek community, however, was the smallest and the last to settle in the neighborhood. The relationship with it reflected the lessons that Hull House had learned from its contacts with the Jews and Italians, specifically that in Addams's words, the best way to reach new immigrants was "by appealing to their national instincts." It was expressed as early as 1904 and was first applied to Italians. Since Italians were at that time in the prenational stage of consciousness, and they identified themselves along village, town, or regional rather than national lines, Hull

House succeeded in attracting only the Italian intelligentsia. Significantly, Hull House never tried to reach Jews "by appealing to their national instincts."

## The Jewish Community

Jane Addams's conception of the Jews as a religious group and her failure to recognize the importance of the Yiddish language and culture as a unifying factor and an expression of Jewish ethnic identity made it impossible for her to understand the mentality of the east European Jewish community. She failed to understand the strong desire of Jews to remain a community; she was sympathetic towards Jewish suffering, but she never expressed any appreciation of Jewish Yiddish culture or Jewish nationalism (Zionism), as she did for Italian and Greek culture and nationalism.[2]

The attitude of the east European Jewish community towards Hull House was determined by the long history of Jewish segregation, self-esteem, and independence and the community's desire and ability to reconstruct a communal life to which it was accustomed in eastern Europe and which possessed a long tradition of minority self-rule.[3] Contrary to Addams's initial view of immigrants in general as being helpless and in need of guidance and leadership from Hull House, the east European Jewish community on the West Side had able leaders. These leaders created a vital Jewish communal life, established welfare and cultural institutions, and proved their leadership qualities by dealing effectively with the problems of civic rights, anti-Semitism, and immigration restriction. They neither requested nor received guidance or patronage from Hull House or any other source. Indeed, Hull House played only a limited role in the daily life of the Jewish community. While Hull House gained sympathy in Jewish circles because of its support of the Jewish community in the struggle for equal rights and against anti-Semitism and immigration restriction, the Jewish leadership as a whole was reluctant to give Hull House any foothold in the education of its youth or in meeting their social, cultural, and welfare needs.

Hull House had a closer relationship with the marginal Jewish elements, the assimilationists and the radicals. The former participated in Hull House activities and left the Jewish ghetto as soon as they could afford to. The radicals were independently organized and cooperated with Hull House only occasionally. Hull House did have closer connections with some east European Jewish trade union leaders and was intimately involved in industrial disputes and strikes in which east European Jewish workers played a considerable part. Yet this relationship should be seen more in the context of Hull House's industrial relations policies than as an expression of its relations with the Jewish community as such.

Jewish immigrants from eastern Europe began to flow into Chicago starting in the 1860s. A Jewish ghetto was established gradually on the West Side of

Chicago, its population growing from thirty thousand at the beginning of the century to more than seventy thousand in the 1920s. At the beginning of the century the Jewish ghetto comprised parts of the Nineteenth, Seventh, and Eighth wards and was bounded by Polk Street on the north, Blue Island on the west, Fifteenth Street on the south, and Stewart Avenue on the east.[4] The first wave of east European Jews who arrived between the 1860s and the 1870s organized their religious and communal life according to their place of origin. Every such Jewish Orthodox congregation included, in addition to the synagogue, the traditional charitable societies, a Talmud Torah for the younger generation, and a house of learning for the adults. All the social activities were held in the synagogue. This first generation of the east European Jewish community in the ghetto remained faithful to the traditions of their ancestors and made an effort to reconstruct Jewish life in America. This desire was expressed by the establishment of twenty-five Orthodox congregations whose property amounted to $90,000 in 1905. Their registered membership was about two thousand. However, the number amounted to more than ten thousand when one considers the members' families and the many others who visited the synagogue on a less regular basis. During Jewish holidays many *minyanim* (prayer groups) were established. One Hull House resident emphasized the Jewish atmosphere and the strict observation of religious festivals and Jewish tradition in the Jewish ghetto.[5] The Orthodox congregations were directed by Orthodox rabbis and run by a group of lay leaders who were recruited from the more economically successful members of the congregation. While most of the members belonged to the working class, these lay leaders belonged to the lower middle class. They were small businessmen whose business controlled the ghetto's ethnic economy.[6]

The emerging lower-middle-class lay leadership in the ghetto gradually became aware of the need to establish a Jewish *qehilah,* namely, communal organizations to meet the needs of all the Jews in the ghetto. During the 1880s this group of leaders established the Zedoko Kololoth, a relief organization, the Gomelei Chesed Shel Emeth, a burial society, the Chebrah G'miluth Chassodim, a free loan society, and the Women's Free Loan Association. At the beginning of the twentieth century the Beth Moshav Z'keinim, an Orthodox Jewish home for the aged, and the Marks Nathan Jewish Orphan Home were opened.[7] Significantly, these philanthropic organizations were established with the aid of contributions of money not only from the emerging lower middle class but also, and with great sacrifice, from the poor lower-class immigrants. They were set up despite the fact that the German Jewish community had established a number of charitable agencies, first called the United Hebrew Charities and later the Associated Jewish Charities, to help the ghetto population.[8] These lower-middle-class lay leaders together with the religious leaders established, in addition to the Talmud Torahs affiliated with the congregations, communal educational institutions for the Jewish younger generation. The first of these was the Moses Montefiore Talmud Torah opened in 1883, which served as both a day school and an afternoon Hebrew school. Gradually four branches were added to the Montefiore School. In 1900 a Jewish high school was opened, Yeshivath Etz Chaim.[9]

The second wave of east European Jews arrived between the 1880s and the 1910s. This wave included a considerable percentage of nonobservant Jews, those who were not affiliated with an Orthodox congregation but who nevertheless attended the prayers on the Jewish holidays. These Jewish immigrants organized their social and cultural life around *landsmanshaften*, fraternal orders, literary, national (Zionist), and radical societies. The *landsmanshaften* also served as loan associations and sick-benefit and burial agencies, helping newcomers during their early days in the country. Unlike the traditional Orthodox Jews, they were dedicated to their ethnic heritage through commitment to its Yiddish and/or Hebrew culture. They wished to reconstruct the Jewish community along national and ethnic-cultural lines. Concerned about the growing alienation of the younger generation from Judaism in its national and ethnic-cultural aspect, they looked for ways to transmit the Jewish tradition and heritage to their children.[10]

The ghetto soon developed a bustling cultural life. In addition to the amateur theater groups which performed plays in Yiddish and Hebrew, ten Yiddish *Volkstheaters* performed in the years 1905 to 1917, along with professional theaters such as the People's Theater launched in 1887 and the Metropolitan Theater opened in the early 1890s. The Palace Theater was opened in 1919.[11]

The east European Jewish Old World intelligentsia, the Maskilim, mostly arrived during the second wave of Jewish immigration to Chicago. These Jews were nonobservers who, having already challenged the traditional leadership in eastern Europe, considered it incapable of dealing with the problems and challenges of life in modern times. They therefore created their own organizations to meet their social and cultural needs. In 1893 some of them established the Hebrew Literary Society, a unification of two literary societies, which by the turn of the century had become the spiritual and intellectual center of West Side Jewry. By 1912 it housed a library, a reading room, a lecture hall, and club rooms where courses were given on the Hebrew language and Jewish literature and history. The society also offered lectures, cultural evenings, and political debates.[12] The Maskilim were also involved in the establishment of the Hebrew- and Yiddish-language Jewish press. Between 1877 and 1914 at least twelve Yiddish newspapers and periodicals were published in Chicago.[13]

Another group of young east European Jews who belonged to the emerging Americanized middle class were attracted neither to the traditional Orthodox way of life nor to the Maskilim type of societies. Although they themselves were thoroughly Americanized, they rejected American institutions, accusing them of having a patronizing attitude towards newcomers. In 1894 they established the Self-educational Club, which was Jewish in its ethnic composition but was modelled after Hull House and concentrated on teaching young immigrants the English language and American history, besides offering social and cultural programs.[14]

In 1895 a group of young people, some of them members of the Hebrew Literary Society, established the Chicago Zionist Society, which became the Order of Knights of Zion in 1897. The order increased within a short time to several thousands organized in "gates," spreading out of Chicago to the Middle West. The Chicago West Side gates were most influential in the order. By the time of its twentieth annual convention in January 1917, before the Balfour Declaration, it included about fifteen hundred members in thirty gates. The order also established a children's section on the West Side. The order, at least during its early period, represented a mixture of American and east European influences.[15]

The rise of anti-Semitism in Chicago and all over Europe, the yearning for a sense of belonging in the American society from which they were alienated, together with the news of Herzl's new gospel and modern Zionism, all fostered Jewish awareness even in the younger generation. This intensified sense of Jewish identity was expressed during the Dreyfus affair and the Russian pogroms. In response to these events the Jews of the ghetto held mass protest meetings and established a committee to send help to the victims of the pogroms. The Refugees Aid Society was responsible for organizing help for those refugees coming to Chicago. The Jews on the West Side were the victims of many anti-Semitic incidents closer to home: attacks on synagogues, on Jewish families in their homes, and on Jewish peddlers on the streets, as well as discrimination in educational institutions and in jobs. The younger generation responded by establishing defense societies such as the Self-Defense League. Students at the University of Chicago and graduates of the Jewish Training School (established on the West Side by German Jews to Americanize east European Jewish children) formed societies to study Judaism, and two groups of Jewish youngsters formed Zionist societies, Kaddimah and the Clara de Hirsch Gate (the latter formed by young east European Jewish women), which joined the Order of Knights of Zion. About a third of the active members of the order were born and/or educated in the United States. Also, many young people who had drifted away from Judaism began to take an interest in Jewish subjects.[16]

The growing ethnic identity among Americanized young men and women, both the Zionists and the ethnically oriented, brought them into contact with the Maskilim and the Zionist order in Chicago. The alliance between these elements became possible because they all doubted the ability of the religious leadership alone to meet the challenges of life in America. These people were deeply committed to Jewish ethnicity and culture and had no reservations about the need to create a Jewish community and religious life. Nevertheless, they were convinced that the Orthodox congregation could satisfy neither the needs of the second generation growing up in Chicago nor the needs of the Jews as a distinct ethnic group in American society. Their search for a suitable sociocultural framework brought about a reform of the Jewish community and its adjustment to the American environment through a reorganization of the Jewish educational system, establishment of a Jewish American community center, and the creation of a Jewish welfare system along American lines.

Many of these new leaders were Zionists, but they represented a new kind of American Jewish ethnicity rather than the European type of Zionism: the Knights of Zion did not consider immigration to Palestine a solution to the problems of American Jews. While they regarded Europe as an exile, they thought of America as a diaspora and Zionism as a solution to the problems of the Jews in Europe; they defined their own Zionism in terms of material and political aid. This was a combination of Jewish philanthropy and political Zionism and was not essentially different from usual Jewish feelings of solidarity with Jews all over the world, including Palestine.[17]

The growing power and prestige of the second generation of east European Jews in the community's affairs were due to several factors. First, they succeeded—not without a struggle—in gaining the confidence of the Orthodox rabbis of the east European Jewish community. This was possible after some rabbis became convinced that the younger leaders were as committed to the preservation and cultivation of Judaism as themselves and that the only way to win over the second generation was by adapting the community's institutions to the needs of the Americanized younger generation. Second, the Yiddish press, especially the *Courier,* became the major organ for mobilizing the sympathies of West Side Jewry in favor of reorganizing the community's institutions along American Jewish lines. Third, the young second-generation east European Jews joined fraternal organizations and soon became their recognized leaders.

The growing ethnic sentiment among this emerging new leadership combined with the desire of Jewish parents to give their children some knowledge of Judaism. About two-thirds of the nine thousand Jewish children between the ages of six and fourteen in the ghetto received some Jewish education at the beginning of the century. However, Jewish education on the West Side suffered from being concentrated in Orthodox institutions where the traditional type of teachers used methods unsuitable for teaching children who were growing up in America. Parents, Maskilim, Zionists, and ethnically oriented Jews were concerned that the gap between Jewish parents and their children, and between the Jewish young generation and its heritage, would widen unless a fundamental change took place in the mechanisms of Jewish education.[18] Thus began a struggle between Orthodox leaders, whose congregations dominated the Jewish schools, and the new leadership who demanded reform of Jewish education. Harris Horwich, a member of the Knights of Zion and a "scholar in law," started the campaign against the traditional teachers and their old-fashioned methods that was supported by the *Courier,* the Yiddish newspaper with the highest circulation in the ghetto and whose staff included many ardent Zionists. The order also opened in 1900 a Sabbath school whose purpose was "to provide an institution for our children where they can acquire a knowledge of Judaism, of the Hebrew language and Jewish history by methods most adaptable to their surroundings in this country." The educational committee established in 1905 by the conference of the Order of the Knights of Zion encouraged the opening of such modern Sabbath schools, and its influence on the curriculum of the Sabbath and Hebrew schools on the West Side during the first decade of the twentieth century should not be underestimated. Harris Horwich won the support of Ben-Zion Lazar, an Orthodox Jew and president of the Montefiore Talmud Torah, the largest educational institute in the ghetto. Although it was obvious to Lazar that Horwich's motivation was national rather than religious, he supported him because he agreed with Horwich's criticism. They cooperated in establishing for all the branches of the Montefiore Talmud Torah an educational committee, which prepared a new curriculum and started to replace the traditional teachers with more qualified ones. Orthodox and new leaders cooperated also in an effort to unite all the Hebrew schools in the city into one organization. These efforts began in 1907 and culminated in 1912 in the establishment of the Jewish Board of Education for all Talmud Torahs and Sabbath schools. The board included some prominent Zionists: Harris Horwich, Rabbi E. Epstein, Rabbi Budzinsky, and Rabbi Saul Silber. The administrative committee of the board included Benjamin Schiff and Samuel Philipson, also Zionists.[19]

The new leadership also came to the conclusion that a Jewish communal center was needed for American Jewish youth as an alternative to American institutions of the Hull House type and American Jewish institutions of the Self-educational Club type. Such a social center was to combine the American heritage and Judaism; using modern methods it would acquaint Jewish children with both Jewish and American traditions, fostering Jewish ethnic/national consciousness while integrating them into the American environment. The idea of establishing such a Jewish community center was formulated at the end of 1902 by the Kaddimah Gate of the Order of the Knights of Zion, and in November 1903 an association called the Chicago Hebrew Institute was established. About 50 percent of the members of the association—thirteen out of twenty-five—were Zionists.[20] The purpose of the institute, as it was defined in its charter, was "the promotion of education, civic training, moral and physical culture, the amelioration of the condition and social advancement of the Jewish residents of Chicago in the Cook County . . . and maintaining and conducting for that purpose schools, libraries, laboratories, reading class and club rooms, gymnasium, music and lecture halls . . . all to be conducted under Jewish auspices."[21] David Blaustein, one of the first directors of the institute, emphasized another aim when he noted that the "process of Americanization takes care of itself. But it is their Judaism that the people lose so rapidly."[22] Dr. A. Fischkin, the fourth president of the institute, explained in a letter to Julius Rosenwald, asking him for a contribution, that the purpose of the institute was "to be a nucleus for the development of a Russian Jewish society which does not exist yet, to be a forum where their opinion shall find expression and their voice shall be heard."[23] Yet such an institute required the mobilization of the financial, educational, and cultural resources of the whole Jewish community in Chicago. Its initiators' success in mobilizing these resources by enlisting the cooperation of Orthodox, Reform, and nonobservant Jews is evidence of the extent of their influence on the West Side at the beginning of this century. Indeed, their influence was growing as a result of their ability to offer solutions to current problems.

These new leaders, whose ideas and plans had at first encountered great opposition from Orthodox religious leaders, now found the latter in sympathy with the idea of a community center. Orthodox rabbis were gradually realizing that the only means of arresting the alienation of the younger generation from Judaism and of maintaining the unity of the Jewish community was to cooperate with the new leaders. They consented to the establishment of a Jewish community center which would supply the younger generation, especially the nonobservant element, with an alternative to the synagogue. From the moment the enterprise was launched, the Orthodox rabbis helped in their official capacity to publicize the Chicago Hebrew Institute in many ways. It was their support that made possible the mobilization of West Side Jewry's financial resources.[24]

Since these funds were not sufficient to enable the new institution to fulfil the intentions of its founders, the German Jewish Reform community was approached. Its response was enthusiastic: the Reform rabbis gave their support; Dr. Tobias Schanfarber, Dr. Joseph Stolz, Dr. A. R. Levy, and Dr. Emil Hirsch were among the organizers of and speakers at a series of lectures in the West Side Auditorium that raised money to secure a home for the institute; and two Reform rabbis, Schanfarber and Levy, became members of the institute's board of directors. The elder Dr. B. Felsenthal, the only Reform rabbi in Chicago to become a Zionist, was represented in the institute by his son-in-law Dr. A. Fischkin. This support was instrumental in mobilizing the financial support of the German Jewish community, and the entire enterprise made a large contribution to bridging the gap between the German and the Russian Jews.[25]

Until 1907 the institute's program was limited because of a lack of space, but from that year on, after moving to a large building purchased with German Jewish money, it soon became the community center of West Side Jewry. Its buildings and sports facilities occupied three blocks, and the number of weekly participants in its programs grew from 11,368 in 1910 to 16,363 in 1912. (The average attendance at Hull House was 9,000.)[26] The institute offered the Jewish youth sports; social, dramatic, and literary clubs; art and crafts classes; a playground; and courses in the humanities and social, political, and natural sciences. It sponsored concerts, lectures, art exhibitions, and other cultural programs and operated some social welfare services.[27] The Jewish "new immigrants" received courses in English and civics, and the institute also opened a naturalization advisory bureau, an elementary and secondary evening school, and a trade school in order to help newcomers adjust to the American environment. The institute laid stress on educating "new immigrants" in good citizenship by teaching American ideas and traditions and celebrating American national holidays.[28]

However, the uniqueness of the institute lay in its emphasis on teaching Jewish values, culture, and traditions and developing a Jewish ethnic and even national identity. This was achieved by establishing a modern synagogue where services were conducted in Hebrew and English, by celebrating all Jewish religious and national holidays, by lecturing on Jewish topics, by sponsoring concerts of Jewish music, by organizing exhibitions of Jewish art and artists, and by fostering dramatic clubs to perform Jewish plays in Hebrew, Yiddish, and English. In October 1917 the institute established the Hebrew Oratorio Society, whose purpose was "to cultivate, develop and produce Jewish music in all its branches, extending from ancient to modern times." The institute was determined to revive Jewish education by opening a Sabboth and a Hebrew school in which progressive teaching methods were used. The Sabboth school taught religion, and the Hebrew school taught the Hebrew language, Jewish history, and Judaism. In the report of the institute for the year 1913/14, the typical pupil of the Hebrew school was described as "a most desirable type of the Jewish-American boy. Conscious of the great past of his nation, of the glorious contribution of his people to civilization, he makes a proud Jew and a good American Citizen."[29]

The rooms and halls of the institute became the meeting place of various societies and organizations, conferences, mass meetings, and other events. Many of the West Side literary, dramatic, and social clubs, relief societies, landsmanshaften, and socialist and Zionist groups met regularly at the institute, and it became a true community center for the east European Jews of the West Side.[30]

The Zionists made their imprint on the institute during the early years by controlling many of its activities: they comprised more than 50 percent of the board of directors in the years 1904 to 1910, about 30 percent in 1915, and more than 37 percent in 1918. In 1915, when their influence had begun to decline, they still had a majority in the House and Clubs committees, 50 percent in the Religion, Law, and Social committees, and 33 percent in the Education and Building committees, and they were represented in twelve out of fourteen committees. Until the 1920s many of the institute's presidents were Zionists, as were many of the administrative staff and the directors of the different departments and clubs. Many of the members of the Women's Department and their directors were Zionists, too.[31]

Zionism was an integral part of the institute's daily life: the gates of the Order of the Knights of Zion met there regularly, as did the Poale Zion, Hadassah, and Hoachooso societies (the last a Zionist organization for settlement in Palestine). In 1913, fourteen out of fifty-nine of the institute's social clubs declared themselves Zionists. Moreover, the institute was the headquarters of the Young Maccabees, the youth movement of Poale Zion, and of Young Judea, the youth movement of the Zionist Federation of America. The Young Judea youth movement was established in Chicago in 1916 by forty of the institute's clubs. From 29 to 50 percent of the topics discussed at the institute's evening lectures during the first two decades of the twentieth century were concerned with nationalism and Zionism, and a considerable number of the plays performed by dramatic clubs were nationalistic and even Zionist in content. The Zionist organizations conducted all their conferences, mass meetings, and other events, such as Herzl Memorial Meetings, the Balfour Declaration Celebration, and meetings in honor of Zionist leaders from Palestine and America, at the institute.[32]

The institute's periodical, *The Observer,* gave expression to the special relationship between the Zionist movement and the institute in the report of the annual convention of the Order of the Knights of Zion that took place from December 1915 to January 1916.

> It is eminently fit that the Chicago Hebrew Institute—a great Jewish center of intellectual activities—whose fundamental idea and cornerstone was supplied by Zionists, should now again make room in its halls for the Zionist Convention. . . . Many of the present and past prominent figures of the Order of the Knights of Zion have been intimately concerned with the origin and growth of the Institute, if not wholly responsible for its very existence . . . its—the Institute's—attitude towards Zionism has been from the very first of encouragement and good will.[33]

The new leadership sought also to increase Jewish awareness and national identity among the Jewish masses and to lobby and campaign for the interests of the Jewish community. In their efforts to achieve these objectives the new leadership became involved in many public activities. The mass protest meeting against the pogrom of Kishinev in 1903 was organized by Leon Zolotkoff and Bernard Horwich, both leaders of the Knights of Zion and members of the new leadership. Horwich was also the initiator of a mass meeting to mobilize financial aid for the victims of the 1905 pogroms in Russia, and three out of the five members of the committee established to handle the problem were Zionists. Zionist leaders were also active in the Refugees Aid Society, whose task was to help the refugees coming to Chicago. Bernard Horwich and the *Courier* played an important role in the Averbuch affair. The new leaders were also involved in other public issues such as the Beilis trial and the public campaigns against restriction of immigration.[34] (These issues and the Averbuch affair are described below.)

In order to penetrate every phase of Jewish life, the second-generation leaders enrolled as members of the large synagogues to exert influence upon the membership and to mold Jewish public opinion. The Yiddish press, especially the *Courier,* became the major platform for awakening the sympathies of West Side Jewry in support of Jewish nationalism and culture. Abraham S. Braude, the rabbi of Ohave Sholom, one of the biggest congregations on the West Side, pioneered cooperation with the new leaders. He was known as an exceptional type of rabbi, broad-minded and well informed on matters outside the religious world. Rabbi Braude's example was soon followed by his colleagues.

One expression of the increasing Jewish ethnic consciousness among the Jews on the West Side was identification with Jewish ethnicity in general and Zionism in particular. It was, however, A. J. Gershon Lesser, the rabbi of the Beth Hamedrosh congregation during the years 1880 to 1904, who gave the earliest expression to a Jewish national commitment by signing the Blackstone memorial in March 1891. This document was presented to the president of the United States by non-Jews requesting that Palestine be given back to the Jews. Around the turn of the century the other rabbis were following Rabbi Braude's example. In the spring of 1899 Zionists were allowed to hold mass meetings in synagogues whose rabbis only three years earlier had been opposed to Zionism. In 1902, a year before the Union of Orthodox Rabbis in the United States recognized Zionism as the Jewish national movement, six Orthodox congregations on the West Side joined the Knights of Zion. The eulogy for Herzl, in July 1904, was held in a most influential synagogue on the West Side, Anshe Kenesseth Israel. In 1913 the Hamizrachi movement was established in Chicago, and in the same year several Orthodox rabbis in Chicago established the Gauloth Ha'oretz Society for buying land in Palestine. All the Chicago rabbis sat on the dais at the opening of the Knights of Zion annual convention in 1914, and some of the convention's events were held in Orthodox synagogues.[35]

The new leaders also joined fraternal organizations in order to reach the organized Jewish groups. Consequently, the same trend that began developing among Orthodox Jews now appeared among the fraternal orders in Chicago. As a result of the growing influence of these leaders all the Jewish fraternal organizations in Chicago adopted the Zionist program and began to participate in Zionist activities.[36]

This group of new, ethnically aware leaders joined middle-class leaders of other immigrant groups in their efforts to introduce the teaching of immigrant languages and literature into public schools. Harry A. Lipsky, the representative of West Side Jewry on the city's Board of Education, was instrumental in the success of this initiative. As we saw in chapter 4, in May 1912 the board voted (twelve to four) for this proposal. In 1917 Hebrew began to be taught in one public high school in the new Jewish neighborhood on the Northwest Side, Lawndale.. It was also due to these leaders' efforts that the Chicago Public Library stocked Yiddish and Hebrew books. Another achievement was the naming of the public school in Lawndale after Herzl. An attempt to name a street after Herzl failed, however. One of the strongest expressions of the Jewish national feeling was the mobilization of funds by West Side Jewry for the "Bread for Palestine" project sponsored by Zionists after the outbreak of World War I.[37]

The new leadership sought to Americanize the community's social welfare agencies and to add some modern ones. They joined the board of directors of the Jewish orphanage and the home for the aged. Under their influence these agencies were given new and professional management. In 1910 they also established the Josephine Club, a home for homeless girls, and were instrumental in opening the Maimonides Hospital, later renamed Mount Sinai Hospital, in which Orthodox religious supervision for the Orthodox population of Chicago was secured. The most important communal organization on the West Side was the Federated Orthodox Charities, established in 1912 by these second-generation leaders to serve as an umbrella organization for all communal welfare institutions of the east European Jewish community. The establishment of this organization marked the end of West Side Jewry's dependence upon the patronage of the United Hebrew Charities—the leading charitable organization of the German Jewish community.[38]

The emergence of an able second-generation Americanized leadership in the east European Jewish community on Chicago's West Side greatly limited the role played by Hull House in the Jewish community. These leaders proved capable not only of handling the internal affairs of the Jewish community, but also of dealing effectively with the problems confronted by the east European Jews as part of the larger community. These leaders' resentment of the very notion that the east European Jewish community was helpless and in need of outside guidance from German Jews, the already Americanized "old immigrants," or from Hull House was first expressed in 1893. Aware that Jewish youngsters were not joining Hull House clubs in any significant numbers, Jane Addams became involved in German Jews' efforts to establish the Maxwell Street Settlement and in the foundation of the Henry Booth Settlement by the Ethical Culture Society, some of whose prominent leaders were German Jews.

Both settlements were opened in the Jewish ghetto on Chicago's West Side. The second-generation east European Jewish leaders, who were invited to Hull House to discuss the forming of the Maxwell Street Settlement, made it clear that they rejected this initiative as an expression of a patronizing attitude.[39]

As has been indicated above, the Chicago Hebrew Institute was not established as a social center alongside Hull House but as a substitute for Hull House for American Jewish youth. Moreover, east European Jewish organizations rented Hull House facilities very rarely—the Marks Nathan Jewish Orphan Home and some Jewish dramatic clubs rented the Hull House theater hall. No Jewish organization met at Hull House regularly, and no Jewish national event was ever celebrated at Hull House.[40] On the other hand, Hull House never sponsored the celebration of a Jewish national or religious holiday, while celebrating annually the Mardi Gras for Italians, St. Patrick's Cotillion for the Irish, and of course, Christmas.[41]

The east European second-generation leaders played a leading role not only in Jewish community affairs but also in the Zionist movement. Yet Hull House relations with these leaders had nothing to do with their role in the Zionist movement. Unlike Italian and Greek nationalists, Zionists did not turn Hull House into their meeting place and never celebrated Jewish and Zionist events at Hull House or invited any of the Hull House residents to their celebrations. The only mention of Zionism in a Hull House publication was in its 1906/7 *Year Book,* which recorded that Zionists had rented Hull House Hall for several lectures. (This was before the Chicago Hebrew Institute's hall had been built.)[42]

Nonetheless, east European Jewish middle-class leaders cooperated with Hull House on several occasions: the Averbuch affair and the Rudowitz affair in 1908, and the Beilis trial in 1913.[43]

Averbuch, a Russian Jew, was shot to death by the Chicago chief of police in 1908. The police's statement on the case justified the killing, accusing Averbuch of being an anarchist who had come to the home of the chief of police to assassinate him as part of an anarchist conspiracy. The affair was widely discussed in the American press and resulted in public hysteria against immigrants in general and east European Jews in particular. Jane Addams described Hull House's role in the Averbuch affair in terms of "coming to the rescue" of helpless foreigners who had turned to Hull House "in the moment of their perplexity and distress." However, examination of data gives quite a different version of the role played by Hull House and the second-generation Jewish leaders during this affair. The Yiddish *Courier* was the first to discover the discrepancy between the police version and the facts. Immediately, second-generation Jewish leaders formed a committee to investigate the case and hired a lawyer. They were neither helpless nor perplexed but, having assessed the attitude of the American public and officials towards immigrants, preferred to play their role off stage, asking Addams only to do the lobbying for them. One of these leaders, Bernard Horwich, related in his autobiography that the committee "with the aid of many persons interested in social justice [Liberal Progressives and German Jews] made further investigation and found that . . . the poor innocent boy had been killed through a terrible error." Thus Addams and the lawyer Harold L. Ickes represented the Averbuch case in the inquiry on March 24. Most of the money for the case was contributed by a German Jew, Julius Rosenwald—$2,000. Addams gave $600, Bernard Horwich gave $100, and other people gave small sums. The cooperation between Hull House and second-generation Jewish leaders was not limited to the investigation of the case. The reburial of Averbuch in a Jewish cemetery became possible through this cooperation. When asked whether he represented Jews in "this movement for an investigation," Ickes answered, "I cannot answer yes or no to a question of that sort. . . . But I will say, from the question you put to me I know you are on the right track in the matter." The Averbach case had little chance of being treated fairly in the atmosphere of hysteria in those days. The Jewish community greatly appreciated the support given by Addams and some other liberals in this case. Although she did not demand an investigation commission, she saved the case from perhaps becoming a long lasting and vicious anti-Semitic affair by establishing in an article dealing with the case, published on 2 May 1908, that Averbuch had no connection with anarchism. The article was widely discussed in the American press throughout the country. The fact that even Jane Addams was greatly criticized for her role in the case justified the decision of the Jewish leaders to remain in the background.[44]

These Jewish leaders followed the same tactics in the Beilis trial. Beilis was a Russian Jew put on trial by the imperial Russian government in 1913 as a result of a blood libel. The east European Jewish community of Chicago cooperated with the German Jewish community and Chicago liberals on this issue. Formally the great mass protest meeting against the Beilis trial was called by Jane Addams and other liberals, including a group of Christian ministers. Yet the correspondence of Harry Lipsky provides evidence that Jewish leaders were behind the organization of the meeting. Jewish leaders also lobbied among the Illinois congressmen for the United States to lodge a protest with the Russian government.

Second-generation Jewish leaders played a secondary role in the Rudowitz affair, since Rudowitz was not Jewish and the affair had wider implications for American society as a whole. In 1908 the Russian government demanded from the United States the arrest and extradition of Rudowitz, a Lithuanian carpenter, on a trumped-up murder charge, on the basis of an extradition agreement between the two countries. The extradition of Rudowitz, who was a revolutionary and a political refugee, would have been a dangerous precedent that could be used not only against Jewish revolutionists but also against Jews who had deserted the army or avoided conscription in their home countries. Judge Julian W. Mack, one of the leaders of the German Jewish community in Chicago, called a conference that was joined by the second-generation Jewish leaders to mobilize public opinion and lobby against the extradition of Rudowitz. They cooperated with the Political Refugee Defense League—an organization of Russian exiles and American liberals, Jewish socialists, and the American socialist party—which played the leading role in this case. The Chicago Jewish community succeeded in mobilizing public opinion in the Beilis affair thanks to the support of Chicago Liberal Progressives.[45]

The new Jewish leadership also cooperated with the Immigrants' Protective League, in which Hull House residents played a major role. Harry A. Lipsky represented the east European Jewish community on the league's board of trustees. The league sponsored mass meetings against immigration restriction, in cooperation with immigrant leaders. As part of this cooperation, the league's leaders participated in hearings before the House and Senate committees on immigration, in petitions to Congress, and in lobbying at the White House.[46]

Jewish radical and trade union leaders maintained closer relations with Hull House. The east European Jewish radicals were divided into national and cosmopolitan radicals, namely, those with strong Jewish national awareness and those who, despite their pride in their Jewishness, believed in classless, nationless, cosmopolitan socialism. In 1892 the Jewish socialists, led by Abraham Bisno and Peter Sissman, left the Jewish Workingmen's Educational Club, a joint club for socialists and anarchists, and opened their own club, the LaSalle Political Club, whose objective was to educate the Jewish masses in socialism. In 1903 this club became the first Chicago branch of the fraternal order Arbeiter Ring, a socialist Yiddish-speaking organization with headquarters in New York. The Chicago West Side branch multiplied within one year into thirty-one branches with about five thousand members and provided medical care, sick and disability benefits, a burial allowance, and a cemetery and was also involved in educational, social, and cultural work and established Sunday schools for the children of its members.[47]

The Arbeiter Ring gradually gave up its anntinational orientation and became much more involved in the life of the Jewish community. This trend culminated in 1919 when the first Arbeiter Ring schools opened in Chicago. These schools taught Yiddish and its culture, Jewish history, and contemporary Jewish life.[48]

The Labor Zionist Poale Zion movement was organized on Chicago's West Side in 1905. Since it advocated Zionism along with its socialist ideology, it was dedicated to Jewish nationalism and culture. Its youth were educated in Sabbath schools, called the Maccabee schools, in which Yiddish, Hebrew, Jewish history, and Palestinography were taught. The Young Maccabees, its youth movement, grew from five hundred members in 1915 to twenty-one hundred in 1918.[49]

The two Jewish socialist movements on Chicago's West Side established no relations with Hull House as such, and only some of the leaders involved in the Jewish labor movement of Chicago cooperated with Hull House occasionally. Abraham Bisno, the president of the Chicago Cloak Makers' Union, cooperated with Hull House during its investigation of the sweatshop system and was nominated factory inspector by Hull House member Florence Kelley under the Illinois Factory Act of 1893. The fact that both Bisno and Kelley were socialists facilitated the communication between them. Jane Addams lobbied energetically for the factory bill and addressed some Jewish trade union meetings. Yet no special relationship developed between her and Bisno. Sidney Hillman, the leader of the Men's Clothing Workers' Union of Chicago in 1910 and of the Amalgamated Clothing Workers' Union of America from 1914, cooperated with Hull House residents during the strikes of 1910–11 and 1914. Addams helped the strikers in many ways. Yet it was Ellen G. Starr, who became a socialist, with whom Sidney Hillman established close relations. Addams developed cordial relations with Peter Sissman and cooperated with Jewish socialists on public issues such as the Kishinev pogroms and the Rudowitz case.[50]

The only Jewish radical and union leader who had really close connections with Hull House was Philip Davis. He became friendly with Addams, and under her influence he was awarded a scholarship to the University of Chicago and later to Harvard, eventually becoming a settlement worker in Boston. As a result he left the Jewish trade union movement and severed his ties with the Jewish community.[51]

## The Italian Community

The Italian group on Chicago's West Side was not consolidated into one cohesive ethnic community. Unlike east European Jews and Greeks they were subdivided along class, geographical, and cultural lines. The unifying factor of an Italian ethnic consciousness and identity was missing. Jane Addams and Hull House residents succeeded in creating and maintaining a good understanding and cordial relationship with the small southern Italian intelligentsia. They also formed some relations with the Italian socialist party, though not without friction from time to time. Yet these groups had no real influence in the Italian colony. The relationship with the largest segment of the Italian group, the peasants of southern Italy and Sicily, and its leadership, both religious and lay, remained distant and at times hostile for many years. The emergence of the second generation released the tension but did not draw the two groups into cooperation.

Italian immigrants from southern Italy began to flow into Chicago in the 1870s, during which time the "Italian colony" in the Nineteenth Ward was established. The colony in the immediate neighborhood of Hull House included more than five thousand people at the beginning of the century and increased to twenty-seven thousand by 1914. During the years 1870 to 1915, groups of southern Italians settled on Chicago's West Side. As a result, most of the older Italian settlers of the neighborhood, the Italians from the northern regions of Tuscany and Genoa, gradually left for the North Side. The West Side Italian colony became inhabited by southerners from Basilicata, Campania, Apulia (Bari), Calabria, and Sicily and included Italians from Abruzzi in central Italy.[52]

Italian adults in the neighborhood were mostly peasants. Preserving their Old World ways, they limited their social contacts to their village or district of origin. Unlike east European Jews and Greeks they did not develop a great variety of communal institutions apart from churches and mutual benefit societies. The typical southern Italian organization in this neighborhood, as among Italians throughout the country, was the mutual benefit society for insurance and sociocultural purposes, organized according to the villages of origin. Most of the Italian adults in the neighborhood who were deeply attached to their local mores and traditions and extremely family oriented were devoted to their village societies and showed no inclination to come into contact or cooperate with people outside their village, let alone non-Italians. A survey made by the Chicago Department of Public Welfare in 1919 listed 110 Italian mutual benefit societies in Chicago, while Italian sources gave a far higher estimate of between 160 and 400.[53]

As the personal perspectives, or rather the needs, of the Italians in Chicago gradually broadened, there was a concomitant extension of the geographical boundaries of their institutional relations. In 1906 several societies from northern, central, and southern Italy merged into the United Italian Societies. In 1908 the federation launched a campaign to raise funds to acquire a building for the use of its affiliated societies. Many of the central and southern societies on Chicago's West Side belonged to this federation, which by the late 1920s had reached a membership of several thousand. At about the same time the Sicilian societies, including those on Chicago's West Side, merged into the Unione Siciliana, which became a powerful organization under the presidency of Anthony D'Andrea. It grew from eight hundred members in 1910 to several thousand in the early 1920s.[54]

The third stage in the consolidation of the Italian societies and the broadening of the Italian peasant's group identity started in the early 1920s, when a few national fraternal organizations emerged in Chicago, such as the Italo-American National Union and the Chicago branch of the Sons of Italy.[55]

In spite of the ambivalent attitude of southern Italians towards the Catholic church establishment in general and the Irish establishment in America in particular, in 1910 75 percent were church members in the four Italian Catholic churches of the Italian colony on Chicago's West Side. The Guardian

Angel Church in the immediate vicinity of Hull House had one thousand families registered and was obliged to hold five masses every Sunday morning because the church had only four hundred seats. The church Sunday school was attended by 1,433 children who were taught by 125 voluntary teachers. Unlike the impetus in other ethnic groups, the initiative to establish an Italian parish near Hull House came from the Catholic church authorities in Chicago and was financed by German Catholics.[56]

Hull House failed to create close relations and cooperation with the indigenous leadership of the Italian colony except, as in the case of the Jews, with a small group of liberals and radicals. The members of this group came from the southern Italian middle class and included lawyers, physicians, pharmacists, musicians, and small businessmen. They were Italian nationalists and well versed in Italian civilization, and their political orientation was republican. The radicals among them were anticlericalist and opponents of the Catholic establishment. These groups of educated middle-class southern Italians made Hull House the center of their sociocultural activities at the turn of the century. Like other Italians, they were members of mutual benefit societies, some of them affiliated with the United Italian Societies, and it was through them that Hull House became connected with some of the federation's leaders.[57]

Hull House was successful with southern musicians in the neighborhood who were attracted to Hull House by a musical contest organized by the settlement in May 1895. They organized an Italian orchestra which held its rehearsals and concerts at Hull House for two years. Its conductor was Signor Capone, and it numbered forty musicians. Another orchestra, under Maestro Vacchione, was organized in April 1901 following a concert dedicated to the memory of Verdi, which was held at Hull House and organized by a group of young Italian musicians. The orchestra had thirty musicians and held its rehearsals and concerts at Hull House during the first years of its existence. It was Jane Addams who "bought and paid for much needed instruments that cost one hundred dollars."[58]

One of these middle-class leaders was Dr. C. Volini from Naples, the most prominent southern leader in Chicago, whose office was located on 913 South Halsted Street. He was a surgeon in the Catholic hospital for Italians, the Columbus Hospital, and was also on the consulting staff of the Cook County Hospital. His professional success enabled him to transcend ethnic boundaries and become established in American medical circles. He was a member of the American Medical Association and the Chicago Medical Society. At the same time he retained his ethnic connections as a member of the Bellina Lodge, one of the Italian branches of the Knights of Pythias in Chicago. It was through this mutual benefit society that he became one of the leaders of the United Italian Societies. His interest in Italian civilization and nationalism brought him to the Dante Alighieri Society and the Giovane Society, the branch of "Young Italy" in Chicago.[59]

Dr. C. Volini was instrumental in creating the connection between Hull House and a group of southern liberals interested in Italian nationalism and culture. As early as 1899, he addressed an Italian audience at Hull House on the anniversary of the Italian constitution. The relations between this group and Hull House reached their peak during the years 1904 to 1907, when the Dante Alighieri Society held its monthly meetings at Hull House and sponsored a series of Italian plays performed by the society's dramatic club. The close relationship with this group was reflected in the nomination of Volini as representative of the Italian community on the Immigrants' Protective League Board of Trustees for the years 1909 to 1911. The Giovane Society, which was also a member of the United Italian Societies, held its annual commemoration of Mazzini during the years 1903 to 1906 at Hull House. The liberal group apparently transferred most of its activities to the Italian Hall, the building of the United Italian Societies, after its erection was completed, in 1914.[60]

The small left-wing intelligentsia of the neighborhood became affiliated with Hull House through one of its leaders, Alessandro Mastro-Valerio, another southern leader. Mastro-Valerio and his family played a major role in the efforts made by Hull House to attract Italians through Italian receptions, lectures on Italian topics, concerts of Italian operas, and so forth. These efforts continued from 1892 to 1900, yet their main success was to attract radicals, namely, the personal friends of the Mastro-Valerio family, as the *Hull House Bulletin* admitted in 1900. The Mastro-Valerio family became Hull House residents in the early 1890s, and its members became directors of Italian clubs sponsored by Hull House. These were the Mazzini and Maraquete Youth Club and the Italian Circolo for young men and women. In 1906/7 the Italian radical group in the neighborhood made Hull House the meeting place of the radical and anticlerical Giordano Bruno Club.[61]

In its efforts to gain influence among the neighborhood Italians, the Mastro-Valerio group started in 1898 a local newspaper for the Italian West Side community, *La Tribuna*. This newspaper, under the leadership of its owner and editor, Mastro-Valerio himself, conducted the annual campaigns against John Powers, the ward boss, and the campaigns against the Catholic church and its pastors in the neighborhood. The continuous conflicts with the pastor of the Italian church over the naming of the public school in the Italian neighborhood after Garibaldi, the enemy of the church, and the anticlericalism of *La Tribuna* and the Bruno Club during the years 1904 to 1909 identified Hull House with radicalism and anti-Catholicism. This greatly discredited Hull House in the eyes of the Italians in the neighborhood and led Jane Addams to dissociate herself from this group in 1908.[62] The damage, however, was already done. Dunne, the former pastor of the Guardian Angel, who had been nominated to a higher position in the city's Catholic hierarchy, took advantage of the antianarchist hysteria following the murder of a priest in Denver, Colorado, on 23 February 1908 by an Italian anarchist, to conduct an antianarchist campaign in Chicago against the Bruno Club and Jane Addams. The *New World*, the church newspaper, dubbed Hull House a meeting place for anarchists and socialists, referring to Addams as "the professional humanitarian and patron saint of anti-Catholic bigotry in this city." In an interview with the reporter of the Chicago *Record Herald* on 1 March 1908, Addams tried to dissociate Hull House from the controversy by denying any connection between Hull House, the Bruno Club, and anarchism and claiming that Hull House was not responsible for the content of the activities held by the club. She told the reporter that the Bruno Club had been told to leave Hull House in September 1907 because Hull House policy was opposed to using Hull House facilities for political meetings. Nevertheless, the accusations against Hull House and Addams in the Catholic press continued.[63]

Italian socialists and some of the Italian unions used Hull House facilities from time to time, although not on a regular basis. Jane Addams was bitterly attacked several times by the Italian socialist newspaper, *La Parola dei Socialisti*. She was criticized on 21 January 1911 for her refusal to permit the Italian garment workers to continue using the Hull House hall for their meetings because she did not approve of the policy of the union, which was on strike. On 10 January 1914 the newspaper blamed Addams for pretending to be Liberal and Progressive: "Where has your liberal spirit gone?" This accusation was made because of Hull House's refusal to permit the Bruno Club, after its expulsion from Hull House, to hold a meeting there in memory of their anticlerical hero Giordano Bruno.[64]

The relations between Hull House and the pastors of Guardian Angel were marred by fundamental differences in ideology, reflected in their rivalry on various educational and political issues. The pastors considered the public school a threat to the Catholicism of Italian children. Father Dunne became involved in the effort to open a new parochial school for Italian children in the Nineteenth Ward during the late 1890s. Jane Addams and Hull House residents, on the other hand, campaigned for an additional public school for the Italian children. They went from house to house to persuade people to sign a petition for a public school, and Mastro-Valerio's editorials urged Italian parents to send their childrenn to public schools and teach religion at home. Father Dunne, with the cooperation of John Powers, the ward boss, defeated the proposal before the Chicago Board of Education. At this time Missionary Sisters of the Sacred Heart came from Italy to teach Italian children in the Chicago Italian parochial schools, although on Chicago's West Side the first

Italian parochial school was not opened until the second decade of the twentieth century.[65]

The neighboring church's response to the dangers created by Hull House was to extend its activities to include not only religious services and a Catholic settlement but also welfare services through Catholic charitable organizations, to compete with Hull House and other non-Catholic welfare agencies.[66] Father Dunne also played a key role in the opening of a Catholic community center, designed to keep Italian children away from the influence of Hull House, in which efforts he was assisted by the Amberg family—mother and daughter—and the German Catholic community in Chicago. Mary A. Amberg, the head of the Madonna Center Settlement, explained the major argument for the establishment of the Catholic settlement. She stated that institutes of the Hull House type were "dangerous to our Catholic Italian American who confused these 'providing grounds of social spirit,' with the American way of life."[67] It was the formal policy of the Catholic church in Chicago to expose the settlements as proselyting agencies, and the *New World* was the mouthpiece of this policy. Even some Protestant ministers feared that the settlements would become rivals of the parish and a danger to its integrity.[68]

The Catholic community center gradually evolved out of the Guardian Angel Mission, a Sunday school that was opened in the spring of 1898 on Forquer Street with 40 children. By 1903 it had 1,415 children and 115 teachers, and an average of 700 children a year attended the school between 1901 and 1910. The Guardian Angel Mission gradually widened the scope of its activities: an adult evening school opened in 1903 and a children's summer camp in 1904, both of which were held at the neighboring Dante public school because of the shortage of rooms and other facilities. When in 1911 the mission moved to its new quarters, the building of the St. Francis of Assisi School on South Newberry, Mary A. Amberg renamed it the Guardian Angel Social Center. The activities of the social center were modelled on those of Hull House, but it did not became a settlement until 1915. The settlement had fifty-two residents and club directors, mostly Germans, and was renamed the Madonna Center. The major role of Germans—as contributors and volunteers—in the Madonna Center arose from their sense of responsibility to their fellow-Catholics and reflected the similar trend among upper-middle-class native-born Americans who wished to help the underprivileged in American society. In 1913 the social center reached its peak, with three thousand members on its club lists as compared with Hull House's nine thousand members, thus becoming a real challenge to Hull House. The unfortunate need of the Madonna Center to move in 1917 to a new building on West Polk Street and the resulting lengthy interruption in all its activities greatly affected its role in the Italian colony. When it renewed its activities in

November 1917, the settlement had only 1,298 club members, children, young men, and women. This enforced removal, along with financial problems, greatly damaged the chances of the center to compete with Hull House. Unlike the Chicago Hebrew Institute, the Madonna Center never became a major Italian community center.[69]

Nonetheless, while the attacks against Hull House continued in the Catholic press, peaceful co-existence began to develop between Hull House and the new Italian pastor of the Guardian Angel. In December 1906, because of a shortage of rooms and halls, the church started to rent Hull House facilities for some of its activities, such as rehearsals of the church choir and charitable parties. The conversion to Catholicism of Ellen G. Starr, Addams's partner in the establishment of Hull House, further contributed to improving relations between Hull House and the neighboring church. Unlike Father Dunne, the new Italian pastors were sympathetic to Italian nationalism, a fact that also gradually improved the relations between them and Mastro-Valerio and was reflected in the attitude towards Hull House.[70] However, if the neighboring church no longer regarded Hull House as an enemy, it still considered it to be its major competitor for the souls of Italian children. In November 1910 the Italian Teachers' Association of the Guardian Angel Sunday school appealed to the Catholic public for contributions to open a boys' club in order to bring Italian boys from Hull House back to the church, arguing,

> For years the Hull House Boys' Club and other clubs in the neighborhood of the Forquer Street Mission [the Madonna Center] have been robbing the Mission of the boys who, through the efforts of the Association had received religious instruction. These clubs, all conducted by non-Catholics, offer great inducements to the boys. . . . A great many of the Catholic boys, after joining these clubs soon begin to neglect their religion and before very long forget it entirely.[71]

These ambivalent feelings of Italian Catholics towards Hull House were succinctly expressed by Mary Amberg. "All of us had looked upon Hull House as a challenge", she admitted, "yet we never experienced anything but kindness and thoughtfulness and co-operation from Jane Addams."[72]

Although Hull House attempted to create the impression that it attracted the Italian peasants to Hull House, its efforts in this direction were a total failure. A *Chicago Tribune* reporter who was invited to attend an Italian reception in May 1980 described the Italian peasants in peasant dress who attended this meeting. She was told by Jane Addams and Ellen G. Starr that these receptions were attended by southern peasants and the members of the Italian intelligentsia who organized them. Yet in a private letter of May 1890, Starr gave a totally different picture by describing the dresses and jewelry of the well-to-do Italian women at these receptions.[73]

Two major efforts that Hull House made to cooperate with the leaders of the Italian community—well-to-do northern Italians, leaders of benefit societies, and the pastors of the Italian church—were likewise fruitless. In February 1895 Mary Wilmarth and Jane Addams invited Italian leaders to approve the establishment of an Italian welfare institution to be sponsored by Hull House and its friends. The Italian leaders were unwilling to cooperate, and only a few attended the meeting. In 1910 another initiative, to call upon all the societies and organizations to join in a neighborhood council established by Hull House under the direction of Grace Abbott, a Hull House resident and director of the Immigrants' Protective League, also met with no response. Italian leaders were, however, prepared to cooperate on selective issues and on their own terms. Thus in May 1912 they signed the league's petition to the United States Congress against immigration restriction. Modestino Maestro-Giovanni represented the Italian societies on this occasion.[74]

Hull House alienated itself from the lay leadership of the Italian mutual benefit societies, especially the Unione Siciliana, the most powerful Italian organization in Chicago, and some of the Italian unions affiliated with this federation. Hull House residents accused its leaders of exploiting other Italians and wielding power for personal economic and political advantages. The antagonism between the Italian leaders and Hull House was also due to their contradictory interests. The Italian leaders were interested in continued segregation of the Italian community within its own organizations because therein lay the source of their power. Hull House residents were interested in breaking the barriers of ethnicity and integrating Italians into the American environment.[75]

Hull House residents and the Immigrants' Protective League, the agency established on Hull House's initiative to help newcomers, conducted a continuous campaign against the immigrant employment agencies and immigrant banks, especially against those belonging to Italians. However, some Italian padrones and bankers were highly influential, holding positions of leadership in mutual benefit societies and involved in city politics. Luigi Spizzirri was president of the Bergoglieri di Savoia and treasurer of the Società Cristoforo Colombo, both member societies of the United Italian Societies. James Navigato, a resident of the Hull House neighborhood, was president of the Principessa di Napoli Società. Filipi Andrea was president of the Italian Workers' Club and a Republican candidate for county commissioner in 1912. Two other padrones, Vincenzo Rossi and Rocco V. Romano, were candidates for alderman in the First and the Nineteenth wards consecutively in the late 1890s.[76] Other conflicts arose as a result of Hull House's cooperation with the Municipal Voters' League in its efforts to eradicate the ward boss system and the unscrupulous lower-middle-class political leaders in immigrant neighborhoods. As part of these campaigns Italian politicians, mostly saloon owners, padrones, and bankers, were publicly denounced as morally unfit for leadership. Also, Hull House joined enlightened Italians in the neighborhood in challenging the control of the ward by the Democratic party under ward boss John Powers. It cooperated with the alienated small

Italian educated class against the masses, who under the influence of their leaders, as well as the pastor of the Guardian Angel, supported Powers against the Hull House candidates, who were supported by the Italian press and the Italian intelligentsia. The Italians of the neighborhood followed the advice of their leaders and their pastor and voted for John Powers.[77]

The rift between the local Italian leaders and Hull House was not healed even after Addams gave up the fight against Powers. Hull House never supported the Italian Democratic or Republican candidates for ward alderman who campaigned against Powers. However, it seems that the main reason for Hull House's failure to gain the confidence of the Italian community lay elsewhere. Jane Addams failed to understand the Italian peasants' mentality, and although she was sympathetic to their sufferings and difficulties and was sincere in her willingness and efforts to help them, she remained an outsider. During the elections Addams and Hull House not only supported the wrong side as far as Italian peasants were concerned. She also used, with the support of the Italian intelligentsia, Progressive slogans that were totally alien to Italian peasants' background and mentality. They could hardly be attracted by a moral ethos and a demand for social and political reform that they could not understand. Nor did Addams's sympathy for Italian culture and nationalism, which was reflected in Hull House policies, strike a response in Italian peasants who had not yet developed a national consciousness.[78]

Further evidence of the lack of communication among Addams, the Italian intelligentsia, and the southern peasants was revealed in the effort of the Italian Chamber of Commerce, under the influence of Mastro-Valerio, to start an agricultural colony in Alabama in 1892. The inhabitants of the colony were recruited from among the Italian peasants of the Hull House neighborhood, and Hull House gave both moral and financial backing to the program. Despite the failure of this project and the Italian peasants' manifest lack of enthusiasm to join the agricultural colony, Hull House as well as Mastro-Valerio continued to regard agricultural colonies as the best solution to the Italian immigrants' problems. In his testimony before the United States Industrial Commission in 1901, Mastro-Valerio insisted that Italians in America did not become farmers simply because of a lack of means. Until the 1920s *La Tribuna* and *L'Italia* continued to call upon Italians to become farmers. Research has demonstrated that these arguments reflected a lack of understanding of the Italian peasants' wishes in America.[79]

The antagonism between Italian peasants and Hull House was also revealed in matters concerning the Italian family, the education of children, and the role of the child in the adult-centered Italian family. Hull House campaigned against child labor, against the forging of children's ages on work certificates, against premature marriage, and for laws on compulsory education. In their efforts to advance the backward Italian family and instill American norms of behavior they criticized the norms of the Italian family, gave shelter to women who ran away from their husbands, and fought against superstition. Italian peasants regarded this policy as interference in intrafamily relations and assistance to government authorities against the family's interests.[80] A mother whose daughter's work certificate was nullified after Hull House intervention because the child's age had been forged, responded that "Hull House ladies are dreaming to send so old a girl to school."[81]

Father Dunne criticized Hull House's lack of understanding of the problems of Italian peasants, arguing that "Nobody will question the necessity of a child labor law. Those enforcing it, however, should be endowed with discretionary power. The Illinois statute regarding child labor has apparently done more harm than good in its application . . . the requirements of the labor certificate border on the impertinent as well as ridiculous."[82] He accused "the much-advertised social up-lifters" of lobbying for laws that force Italians "into pauperism, 'white slavery,' or other disreputable methods of gaining a livelihood."[83] According to the law, the Board of Education would refuse to issue a certificate to any child unable to read and write the English language, a condition that would deprive Italian widows and families in distress of their only chance of survival if the child was the only wage earner in the family.[84]

The low opinion of Italians that Jane Addams and other Hull House residents expressed on different occasions and their contempt for Italians' personal and moral judgment in choosing their leaders did not improve Hull House's relations with its Italian neighbors and the leaders of the Italian mutual benefit societies. Analyzing the circumstances that enabled "boss rule" in the Nineteenth Ward, Addams identified the major cause as the stage of ethical and moral development of the Italian constituency.

> In certain stages of moral evolution a man is incapable of action unless the result will benefit himself or some of his acquaintances, and it is a long step in moral progress to set the good of the many before the interest of the few, and to be concerned for the welfare of a community without hope of an individual return . . . what headway can the notion of civic purity, of honesty of administration make.[85]

Gradually, Hull House did succeed in attracting more Italian adults, by renting its rooms and facilities at lower prices. Twenty-six different kinds of societies out of about two hundred Italian societies in Chicago held their meetings at Hull House in 1921, and thirty-one in 1929. In this period, Italian societies constituted about 41 percent of the societies that rented rooms at Hull House. Yet most of these societies were dramatic, literary, and charitable clubs of middle-class Italians. Only a few mutual benefit societies met at Hull House regularly.[86]

As the Italian second generation advanced to positions of leadership, the tension between Hull House and the Italian colony was gradually decreased. First, Hull House became reconciled with its neutralized position in the affairs of the Italian colony. The First World War was another factor that eased this tension, since it caused Italians to identify more strongly with the United States; moreover, the cooperation between Hull House and Italian women in the Red Cross and the fact that Hull House served as a recruitment and information center for the American army increased the contact between Italians and Hull House.[87]

## The Greek Community

Hull House relations with the Greek community were entirely different from those with east European Jews or Italians. During the first decade of the twentieth century Hull House succeeded in gaining the confidence and cooperation of the Greek leadership, and as a result, the Greek community's social and cultural activities became concentrated in Hull House and formed, in fact, an independent, self-contained Greek community center within Hull House.

In 1907 the Greek newspaper, *The Star,* called Jane Addams "one of the best friends of Greek people of Chicago," and Dr. Soter, who attended Hull House in the 1910s, described Hull House later in the *Greek Press* as the community center of the Greek community and Addams as the "sweetest physiognomy, the saintliest woman I have ever known."[88] This relationship, however, was achieved by her giving up any effort to interfere in, or even influence, Greek activities at Hull House. Addams, the pacifist, even shut her eyes to the military training and militant nationalism of her Greek friends. In all likelihood, the special relationship with the Greeks was possible because she had learned a lesson from her failures with the Jewish and Italian communities. The sympathy of Hull House residents towards Greek culture and the struggle against the Turkish atrocities also created fertile ground for mutual respect and cooperation. The unique character of the Greek community was another factor in this special relationship. Contrary to the Italians' slow mobility, the Greeks' rapid economic advancement made them less suspicious and more willing to cooperate—on their own terms—with American institutions. Unlike the Jewish community, the smallness of the Greek community made it impossible for it to mobilize the financial resources needed for building a Greek community center, after building a church and a parochial school. Hull House solved their problems, without interfering in their affairs.[89]

Greek immigrants began to settle on Chicago's West Side in the 1890s. The members of the Greek colony in the streets close to Hull House were predominantly from southern Greece, the villages of the province of Arcadia. They were concentrated in what came to be called the Delta, the area surrounded by Halsted, Harrison, Blue Island, and Polk streets. The Greek colony near Hull House grew from 500 in 1904 to 11,500 in 1920 and became the largest Greek community in Chicago.[90]

Unlike the Italian community, the Greek community was characterized by a strong religious, national, and cultural consciousness and identity, and its small middle-class educated leadership, which was closely connected with the religious leader Leon Pegeas, was recognized and respected by the community members. The first community institution established by the Greek community on Chicago's West Side was a Greek Orthodox church, the Holy Trinity, which was opened in 1897 in the building of a former Episcopal church. The predominant role of the Greek church in the Greek community was unquestioned, because of the Greek concept of nationalism in which religion, nationalism, and culture were considered "one in their essential nature." Despite the community's small size and relatively poor resources, its leaders were determined to establish a Greek parochial school to transmit the Greek heritage, language, traditions, and religious faith to its children. In July 1902 a general assembly of the Greek parish decided to open a school, although controversies within the community and financial problems delayed the project for some years. In the meantime an evening school was opened in 1907, managed by the community priest, the Reverend Leon Pegeas. During the first years the curriculum included religion, history of Greece, Greek, English, and commercial business; later some other courses were added. The Greek parochial school, the Socrates School, was opened in 1908 and was controlled by a school committee headed by Pegeas. The number of pupils during its first years ranged between one to two hundred, while the estimated number of the neighborhood children of school age was five hundred. About eight hundred pupils graduated between the years 1908 and 1914. Up to 1917, when the school moved to new quarters, the language of instruction was Greek. English was introduced in that year as a second language, and English-speaking teachers were hired to teach it. The school's structure and curriculum were patterned after schools in Greece, giving the pupils a good background in Greek culture.[91]

The Greeks' social and cultural life focused not only on the church. Along with the establishment of the Holy Trinity, Greek mutual benefit societies were formed according to village of origin. During the first and second decades of the twentieth century the village societies were organized into federations. As the majority of Greeks on Chicago's West Side originated from the province of Arcadia, they were mostly organized in the Pan Arcadian Federation, which was patterned after the Tegea Society, a previous unsuccessful attempt to consolidate Arcadians. The third stage in the development of Greek community organization was characterized by the emergence of national fraternal organizations, the earliest being the Pan-Hellenian Union, whose Chicago branch was started in 1911. In the early 1920s, however, Greek societies became affiliated with one of the two national fraternal organizations, the American Hellenic Educational and Progressive Association (AHEPA) and the Greek American Progressive Association (GAPA).[92]

The more educated members of the community also established literary, dramatic, and national societies in which Greek culture and Greek nationalism were cultivated, such as the Phoenix Greek Society, Greek Amateurs of Chicago, and the Sophocles Dramatic Club.[93]

Hull House housed the Greek community center for almost three decades. The beginning of the ties between Jane Addams and the Greek community can be traced to December 1899, when a group of Greeks was invited to Hull House by Mabel H. Barrow from Boston, for the performance of a Greek play *The Return of Odysseus* before an American audience, a project she initiated all over the country.[94] Addams's aim was to attract Greek members to Hull House, but despite the success of the play and the enthusiastic response of the Greeks, it did not bring Greeks to Hull House. In 1903 another attempt was made to attract Greeks by initiating the performance of another Greek play as a coproduct of Greeks and Hull House. Yet the ice between Greek leaders and Addams melted only after the performance of another Greek play in 1905. The Greek community rented Hull House hall for the first time in March 1905 for the performance of *Athanasius Diakos,* a patriotic play. The income was dedicated to community expenses. In November 1905 the Pan Hellenic Society began to use Hull House for its Greek lectures.

In 1906 a Greek-American meeting, initiated by Greek leaders in order to continue the dialogue on Greek civilization, contributed to the growing mutual respect between Hull House residents and the small Greek community. The Reverend Pegeas played a major role in the organization of the meeting, and during its preparation a special understanding was established between him and Jane Addams. Paul Javaros, a journalist and the only English-speaking Greek in the Greek community at that time, introduced Pegeas to Addams and acted as interpreter at the meetings. Without the approval and cooperation of the priest of the Holy Trinity, the whole idea would not have been realized. Hull House leaders also became friendly with George Kyriakopolos, a Greek lawyer and the president of the Holy Trinity Board of Trustees. This growing cooperation was seen when in October 1907 Addams consented to allow the Holy Trinity to conduct its evening school at Hull House. During the 1910s, the Greeks became the second largest ethnic group at Hull House, after the Italians, although the difference in size was considerable.[95]

Anxious not to make any mistakes in shaping its relations with the Greek colony, Hull House began to study the Greek community in the summer of 1908. Three hundred and fifty Greek households were visited and questionnaires filled for 1,467 persons. From that time Miss Neukom, a Greek-speaking woman, was employed by Hull House to make systematic visits to Greek families. For the Immigrants' Protective League Grace Abbott conducted another piece of research on Greeks, which was published in the fall of 1909.[96]

During this first decade Hull House gradually became the headquarters of an independent, self-contained Greek community center. At this stage Greek leaders began to realize the role Hull House could play both in presenting the glories of Greek culture to American audiences and in providing facilities for

Greek communal, social, cultural, and educational activities. As a result of the cooperation between Hull House and Greek leaders, Greek mutual benefit societies, youth clubs, and adult clubs conducted their meetings at Hull House. Greeks celebrated their national holidays at Hull House and even trained their volunteers for the Balkan War in 1912 at Hull House. In 1914 a Greek community hall, the Athenian Hall, was opened on Polk and Blue Island. Yet even as late as 1929 many Greek societies still held their meetings at Hull House. At that time Greek societies constituted 30 percent of the societies meeting at Hull House (see table 5).[97]

Grace Abbott cooperated with Greek middle-class leaders in her capacity as director of the Immigrants' Protective League. In 1916 George Kyriakopolos and Christ Damaskos, a journalist and one of the leaders of the Greek-American (Republican) Political Club, joined the league in its campaign against the Greek padrone system in Chicago. In May 1912 Peter S. Lambros, a journalist and the leader of the Greek-American (Republican) Political Club, signed a petition against immigration restriction as representative of the Greek community at a mass meeting organized by the league.

The special relations between Hull House leaders and the Greek community were recognized by Dr. Nicholas Salopoulos, the Greek consul in Chicago and one of the owners of the *Saloniki* and, later, of another Greek newspaper, *The Greek Press*. He was also president of the Greek Educational Association organized in 1908, which met regularly at Hull House. In 1909 Jane Addams received an award from Salopoulos, "for meritorious services rendered the immigrants."[98]

Table 5  Greek Societies at Hull House

| Year | Mutual benefit societies | Cultural clubs (adults) | Charitable organizations | Political clubs/unions | Community agencies |
|---|---|---|---|---|---|
| 1910 | 3 | 3[a] | 1[b] | 1[c] | 2[d] |
| 1913 | 3 | 3 | 1 | 1 | 2 |
| 1916 | 3 | 3 | 1 | 1 | 2 |
| 1921 | 10 | 3 | 1 | 1 | 2 |
| 1929 | 11 | 4 | 2 | 3 | 2 |

Source: *Hull House Year Book,* 1910, 23–25; 1913, 24; 1916, 14, 37; 1921, 12–13, 34; 1929, 12–13, 16.

[a]Greek Educational Association, Greek Philharmonic Society, and Greek Pan Hellenic Society/ Union.
[b]Greek Women's Philanthropic Society.
[c]Greek Peddlers' Association.
[d]Holy Trinity Board of Trustees and Greek School Committee.

# SEVEN

# HULL HOUSE AND ITS "NEW IMMIGRANT" CLIENTELE

Although "new immigrants" comprised a considerable portion of Hull House's neighborhood population, ten to fifteen years passed before this was reflected in Hull House membership. This was rooted in the nature of the institute and its staff and the settlement movement, on the one hand, and in the pace of immigrant adjustment to the American environment, on the other hand. Moreover, although Italians were the largest group in the neighborhood (Jews the second, and Greeks the smallest), this situation did not necessarily determine the size and role of each group at Hull House. Hull House was influential among a small segment of those who were fascinated by the American way of life and ethos and sought to leave their ethnic group and integrate into the American mainstream. The majority of the neighborhood people either preferred to preserve their group identity or, lacking the type of personality and qualifications needed for socioeconomic mobility and cultural transformation, were not attracted to Hull House and what it represented. Yet many youngsters took advantage of the facilities offered by Hull House without being influenced by the "Hull House spirit."

When Hull House first opened its doors in September 1889 on Chicago's West Side, the neighborhood was in a state of transformation. Its old residents, native-born Americans, Irish, and Germans, were being replaced by the "new immigrants," mainly Italians, east European Jews, and Greeks.[1] During the first decade of its existence, it was mainly the Americans and "old immigrants," who were English speaking and belonged to the upper level of the working class and the lower middle class, who participated in Hull House activities, even though many of them had already moved out of the neighborhood. "New immigrants" formed a small minority of the Hull House clientele in those days, although they comprised a considerable part of the neighborhood's population. The Italian and the east European Jewish groups were as large as the Irish and native-born American ones, yet the number of Italians who attended Hull House was negligible, and significantly, the ones who did attend belonged to the small Italian intelligentsia, while Greeks did not attend Hull House at all, and only German Jews and a small number of east European Jews participated in its activities.

The ethnic composition of the Hull House clientele began to change around the turn of the century. The number of east European Jews participating in Hull House activities began to rise, and by 1906/7 they had become the largest ethnic group at Hull House. The number of Italians grew slowly but steadily, and Greeks began to attend Hull House at that time, too. These changes coincided with the decrease in the number of native-born Americans and "old immigrants" in the Hull House clientele. The year 1907/8 marked the turning point in the ethnic composition of Hull House: from that year on, "new immigrants" were the majority. Yet the number of east European Jews began to decrease around 1908, and by the second decade of the century the Italians had replaced the Jews as the largest ethnic group at Hull House. In the 1920s Hull House was an "Italian institute" in the sense that the majority of its participants were Italians. As has already been indicated, Hull House gradually modified its cultural policies as a result of the change in the ethnic composition of the neighborhood and the shift in its clientele around 1907 (see chapter 3).

The average number of weekly visitors at Hull House grew, according to its own statistics, from two thousand in 1896 to nine thousand from 1906/7 on. These numbers, however, included not only the Hull House members and students of the Hull House college extension courses who participated in lectures, concerts, sports, and other sociocultural and recreational activities, but also members of societies and organizations that rented rooms and halls for their meetings and were not on the Hull House membership lists. The actual size of the Hull House membership must therefore have been much smaller than that suggested by the weekly number of visitors.[2]

## Patterns of Participation

An analysis of the curve of the graph of "new immigrant" participation in Hull House activities and its composition reveals an interesting difference in the patterns of participation of east European Jews, Italians, and Greeks. The maximum percentages of these groups in the Hull House membership, based on a comparison between immigrant and Hull House sources, are given in Table 6.

Although Hull House programs were formulated to meet the so-called social, cultural, and educational needs of the whole population of the neighborhood—adults, young people, and children—"new immigrant" adults never participated in its activities in any significant way. The membership lists of the Men's Club and the Family Club have not survived, but if one can judge from the membership lists of the Women's Club for the years 1896 to 1926, the lists of the committee members of the adults' clubs, and the high correlation between the ethnic composition of the Women's Club and its committee (see table 7), then the Hull House adult clubs were composed of native-born Americans, Irish, and Germans long after the whole neighborhood had became predominantly a "new immigrant" neighborhood. Indeed, Jane Addams admitted in 1893 that "perhaps of more value than to the newly arrived peasant is the service of the settlement to these foreigners who speak English fairly well."[3]

The Women's Club was patterned after the values of American middle-class women's clubs and was involved in social, civic, and political reform along with its sociocultural programs. Italian and Greek women never participated

Table 6 Composition of Hull House Membership

| Years | Weekly visitors | Approximate membership | Maximum percentages | | | |
|---|---|---|---|---|---|---|
| | | | Native-born Americans and "old immigrants" | East European Jews | Italians | Greeks |
| 1890–1900 | 2,000 | 1,000 | 60 | 25 | 15 | — |
| 1900–1910 | 9,000 | 5,000 | 30 | 35 | 25 | 10 |
| 1910–1920 | 9,000 | 5,000 | 25 | 15 | 40 | 20 |

Sources: *Hull House Bulletin*, Club Lists, 1896–1905/6; *Hull House Year Book*, Club Lists, 1906/7–21, Hull House Papers, University of Illinois Archives, Chicago.

Note: The estimates of Hull House membership according to ethnic groups are based on a comparison between views expressed by contemporaries directly connected with Hull House and the neighborhood, and an analysis of the numbers accumulated from the Hull House *Bulletin* and *Year Book*. The analysis is based on the assumption of the existence of a certain correlation between the ethnic composition of club membership and club committees.

Table 7 Ethnic Composition of the Hull House Women's Club

| Year | Native-born Americans | | Irish | | German (and German Jews) | | East European Jews | |
|---|---|---|---|---|---|---|---|---|
| | Members | Committee members | Members | Committee members | Members | Committee members | Members | Committee members |
| 1896 | — | 60% | — | 40% | — | — | — | — |
| 1902/3 | 64% | — | 20% | — | 13% | — | — | — |
| 1906/7 | 68 | 71 | 13 | 14 | 14 | 14% | 1% | — |
| 1909/10 | 55 | 67 | 14 | 10 | 14 | 19 | 3 | — |
| 1925/26 | 46 | — | 19 | — | 16 | — | — | — |

Source: Hull House Women's Club 1902/3, 1903/4, 1905/6, 1906/7, 1909/10, 1925/26, Louise DeKoven Bowen Papers, Chicago Historical Society; *Hull House Bulletin*, Club Lists, 1896–1905/6; *Hull House Year Book*, Club Lists, 1906/7–1921, Hull House Papers, University of Illinois Archives, Chicago.

Note: There were no Italian or Greek members.

in its activities. While some German Jewish women did belong to the Women's Club, very few east European Jewish women ever participated. Nevertheless, this club was popular among lower-middle-class native-born American and "old immigrant" women, as can be judged by its large membership—250 to 500 women—and its long years of existence.[4]

The continuous efforts made by Hull House to attract Italian women through a separate Italian women's club were not very successful. In 1904 a sewing club for Italian women had sixteen members and lasted a few months. In 1908 not more than 10 percent of the neighborhood mothers who accepted a Hull House invitation to spend a few days at the Hull House summer camp were Italian. During the First World War, Italian women joined the Italian Red Cross group at Hull House, and it was this group of women who formed the Italian Women's Club which met at Hull House in the 1920s under the leadership of Victoria Di Giovanni. The club had only forty-five members and was very small in comparison with the Hull House Women's Club. Lower-class Italian women were not accustomed to leaving their homes except for their church and household duties. This pattern of behavior did not alter after their emigration to America. The very idea that a married woman could leave the house without one of the family's males and lead a social life of her own was alien to the Italian way of life. Those women who were forced by economic necessity to work usually preferred to work at home. Addams became aware of this situation following the invitation of Italian women to the Women's Club. "One evening they [the Women's Club] invited only Italian women, thereby crossing a distinct social gulf . . . The Italian women, who were almost eastern in their habits, all stayed at home, and sent their husbands." That the situation had not changed as late as 1919 is revealed in a letter written by Mrs. Britton, who was in charge of Hull House clubs, in which she complained with reference to Italian women that "the Italians, as usual, are more difficult to reach." This was the pattern of behavior of Italian women of peasant origin in all settlement houses throughout the country.[5]

The Greek Women's Club, which was started in 1910, included twenty-five Greek women who met for social purposes and to study the English language. The club existed until the 1920s although its meetings were irregular and by 1916 its membership had dwindled to twenty. During the First World War some Greek women joined the Greek Red Cross at Hull House and continued to attend for a while after the war. Nonetheless, in spite of the confidence in Greek women that Mrs. Britton expressed in 1919, Hull House failed to maintain a Greek women's club, for the same reasons it failed with Italian women. The pattern of behavior of Greek women did not differ from that of Italian women, both being socialized in peasant conservative societies. Significantly, in accordance with the Hull House attitude to Jewish ethnicity, Hull House records contain no information on efforts to form an east European Jewish women's club.[6]

The Family Club was active from 1900 to 1910, but its supposedly Protestant-oriented programs did not attract "new immigrant" families. Even the number of Irish families was low in comparison with the Women's Club: 38 percent of its members were native-born Americans, 39 percent Germans, and only 16 percent Irish.[7]

The Men's Club established at Hull House found it difficult to attract the neighborhood male population, as was the case in other female-oriented settlement houses throughout the country. Therefore, the Hull House Men's Club facilities were put at the disposal of young men, and it became a young men's club.[8]

The Working People's Social Science Club, another adult club, became a meeting place for native-born American Progressives and the immigrant radical elite. Many of the latter were English and German radicals, yet east European Jewish socialists, anarchists, and "new immigrant" union members participated occasionally. The lack of membership lists makes it impossible to determine the ethnic composition of the club more accurately. The fact that it lasted only seven years, during the first decade of Hull House's existence, may account for its "old immigrant" composition.[9]

While Hull House failed to attract "new immigrant" adults to its clubs, its information office, kindergarten, day nursery, and dispensary did have "new immigrant" clients. Jane Addams admitted that "perhaps the chief value of a settlement to its neighborhood, certainly to the newly arrived foreigner, is its office as an information and interpretation bureau." However, since these welfare agencies were in fact experimental reform projects, they served a very limited number of people. Hull House residents sponsored these projects in order to show municipal and state authorities ways of dealing with the problems of the working class. The Hull House initiative therefore was not designed specifically to meet its neighbors' immediate needs but was part of its general effort to urge the American establishment to create welfare services as part of a comprehensive social and political reform program.[10]

Until the late 1890s, the young people's clubs and the college extension courses were composed of native-born Americans and English-speaking "old immigrants," mostly clerks, typists, salesmen and saleswomen, teachers, and skilled workers. Some of them were men and women of education and refinement who had been forced by circumstances to live in a cheaper neighborhood. Many others were former residents of the vicinity whose economic position had improved and who had already moved to more desirable neighborhoods, but still continued to participate in Hull House activities. Hull House cultural policy was perfectly adapted to the needs of these lower-class native-born Americans and "old immigrants."[11]

The "new immigrant" younger generation did not attend Hull House during its first years. Being unable to distinguish between a mission, a conversion agency, and a nonsectarian social center or settlement house, they were suspicious and kept aloof of all American institutions. East European Jewish youngsters were the first to become aware of the difference and overcome their sense of alienation. Italian and Greek youngsters were much slower in becoming familiar with their new environment.[12]

The younger generation of east European Jews started participating in Hull House activities around the mid-1890s. Their number had grown to a few hundred at the turn of the century, when they comprised about a third of the Hull House club membership. By 1906/7 they were the largest ethnic group at Hull House, although their number never exceeded about one thousand. Subsequently, their proportion in the Hull House clientele decreased to one-fourth, and it continued to dwindle until they became a small minority during the second decade of the twentieth century.

The proportion of Italian youngsters in the Hull House clubs grew very slowly. In 1906/7 it still did not exceed 25 percent of the club membership. Yet the number of Italian children participating in Hull House activities soon began to rise, and by the second decade of the twentieth century they formed a majority.

Greek children began to participate in Hull House activities around 1906, but their number remained negligible until 1913, when it began to rise. They participated in Hull House activities very selectively, and when they reached the age of fourteen they usually joined independent Greek clubs, which rented rooms at Hull House.[13]

The ethnic composition of Hull House youngsters' clubs during the first decade of the twentieth century can be only approximately estimated because of the lack of membership lists, but some notion is provided by the membership lists of the Boys' Club for 1907 and 1908: east European Jewish boys made up the largest group, accounting for 41 percent of the 1,618 members; Italians amounted to 24 percent, Irish 12 percent, Anglo-Saxons 9 percent, Germans 5 percent, Polish 2 percent, and Greeks 1 percent. The ethnic composition of the committee membership lists of Hull House youth clubs also gives an indication of the ethnic composition of Hull House clientele (see Table 8).

Data on the Boys' Club, whose members were between the ages of seven and seventeen, also reveals the kind of boy who was attracted to Hull House. Most of the club's members who attended school went to public schools, rather than parochial schools. Of the club population above the age of compulsory education 52 percent attended high schools, a figure that was far above the average among immigrant children in Chicago and throughout the country. Only a small minority between the ages of fourteen and sixteen were neither in school nor employed, and most of those who had quit school at the age of sixteen worked as salesmen, office boys, manual workers, apprentices, and

Table 8 Ethnic Composition of Committees of Hull House Youth Clubs

| Year | Anglo-Saxons | Irish | German | East European Jews | Italians | Others[a] |
|------|------|------|------|------|------|------|
| 1896 | 44% | 13.5% | 17% | 13.5% | 2% | 10% |
| 1902 | 30 | 13 | 18 | 32 | 5[b] | 7 |
| 1905/6 | 36 | 9 | 7 | 29 | 17 | 2 |
| 1906/7 | 11 | 31 | 8 | 28 | 22 | — |
| 1910 | 20 | 23 | 6 | 20 | 31 | — |

Sources: *Hull House Bulletin*, Club Lists, 1896–1905/6; *Hull House Year Book*, Club Lists, 1906/7–10, Hull House Papers, University of Illinois Archives, Chicago.

Note: No lists are available after 1910.

[a]No Greeks were found in these lists.

[b]Figure from 1903.

semiskilled workers. In Hull House terms it was therefore the "better element" of the immigrant population that attended Boys' Club activities.[14]

Contemporary east European Jews and German Jewish philanthropists disagreed on the extent of east European Jewish participation in Hull House activities during the first decade of its existence. Those who tended to minimize the number of Jewish youngsters attending Hull House activities argued that "the only social center in the early 1890s was Hull House from which the Russian Jewish population kept aloof also because then the distinction between a conversion center and a social center was not recognized, although Hull House was never conducted on a sectarian basis." Another reason for the reluctance of young Jews to attend Hull House was the confrontations between Jewish and non-Jewish children in the neighborhood. This is borne out by the efforts of German Jews, in cooperation with Jane Addams, to establish the Maxwell Street Settlement, the Henry Booth Settlement on Chicago's West Side, and three other settlements in other east European Jewish neighborhoods. If Hull House, which was heavily financed by German Jews and whose clientele in the early 1890s was small, had been successful in attracting Jewish children, there would have been no need for two alternative settlements for the Jewish population. German Jews initiated these settlements in the hope that Jewish settlements would be more successful in overcoming the segregation of the Jewish ghetto. Gradually, however, "numbers of Jews were attracted to Hull House because of the concerts given on Sunday afternoons and because of the educational opportunities [it provided]." This increased participation became possible after Jewish youngsters became better acquainted with the American environment and learned to distinguish between a mission and a nonsectarian settlement house. They joined literary, dramatic, and debating clubs and packed the college extension classes. Hull

House cultural programs were well suited to the educational ambitions of certain types of young east European Jews.[15]

During its early years, Hull House did not seem to encourage the forming of Jewish ethnic clubs, and before 1913 there was no mention in Hull House publications of a Jewish ethnic club as such. It seems that Hull House treated German and east European Jews alike upon the assumption that Jews constituted a religious rather than an ethnic or national group. Since German Jews who attended Hull House during the 1890s joined ethnically mixed clubs, Hull House residents saw no reason to change their policy for east European Jews. Although east European Jewish youngsters did not exhibit any reluctance to join mixed clubs, it is interesting that the club committees' membership for 1896 to 1910 show that they tended to congregate in certain clubs and formed a majority in a third of them. Since new members were admitted by vote of the existing club members and east European Jews were attracted to certain types of clubs—those concerned with drama, literature, social and political topics, and intellectual interests—it makes sense that Jews became concentrated in certain clubs, where they became the majority. Another factor contributing to the formation of de facto Jewish clubs was the tension existing between east European Jewish youngsters and the other youngsters of the neighborhood, Jewish boys being constantly attacked by gangs of Irish and Italian boys.[16]

Unlike east European Jewish boys and girls, Italian youngsters were reluctant to join the Hull House ethnically mixed clubs. The Hull House residents recognized this situation and made efforts to attract Italian youngsters by forming Italian ethnic clubs. Three Italian sports clubs were formed consecutively during the 1890s, but none of them lasted. Hull House was more successful with the four Italian social clubs established by Mastro-Valerio, an Italian resident at Hull House, and Berta Hazard, an Italian-speaking American resident. These clubs were patterned upon the Italian literary and cultural clubs that rented rooms at Hull House. The members of these clubs were newcomers of middle-class background. The rank and file of the Italian youth in the neighborhood, namely, those of peasant background, did not join these clubs but came to Hull House only occasionally to use the playroom and sports facilities. During the first two decades of the twentieth century the number of Italian youngsters participating in Hull House activities grew steadily, the percentage in girls' clubs exceeding that in boys'. Italian girls joined sewing and dancing clubs in their efforts to overcome the Italian tradition of keeping girls at home. Italian boys, on the other hand, preferred to form their own gangs outside of Hull House patronage, making use only of those facilities that they found attractive. Nevertheless, the few Italian clubs that existed at the turn of the century had grown to thirteen in 1907, comprising about one-fourth of the Hull House club membership.[17]

Greek youngsters were the last to start attending Hull House. Their number before the second decade of this century was negligible. Significantly their pattern of participation was entirely different. While the number of Greek children under fourteen in the neighborhood before the 1920s was small, as was reported in the Greek newspapers, the number of boys over fourteen years of age was considerably larger, because of their immigration unaccompanied by parents. Nevertheless, Greek youngsters did not join Hull House clubs. They formed their own ethnic clubs, more Greek than American in nature, using Hull House rooms and other facilities under an agreement between Hull House and the Greek community leaders.[18]

The first ethnic club for Greek youngsters, a sports club, was opened in 1907. It had two directors, an Italian and a Greek, and in December 1908 it was renamed the Greek Educational Association. It was an independent club that rented Hull House facilities and was dedicated to sports and military training, although it also conducted a class to teach English to its members. It elected Jane Addams as honorary president and two other Hull House residents, one of whom spoke Greek, as honorary members. The association at Hull House, which had begun with 90 members, numbered 625 by 1910 when it had established ten branches throughout Chicago. Its first conference was held at Hull House in December 1909. In 1913 the association changed its name to the Greek-American Athletic Club, after many of its members went back to Greece to fight against the Turks, and merged with the Hercules Greek Club in 1914 to form the Greek Olympic Athletic Club, which achieved many victories and medals for Hull House in athletic and boxing contests.[19]

In October 1914 a Greek social club called Peychogoikos Sindemos was formed. It was a Hull House coproject with the Athletic Club to cope with the unemployment caused by the economic recession of 1914. Many young unemployed Greek boys were congregating on the streets, and they needed a meeting place to protect them from police harassment. The club was conducted along Greek cultural lines and held social events with Greek dancing and music. During the period of unemployment it was attended by about eight hundred young people, but by the 1920s its membership had declined to between twenty-five and seventy-five members.[20]

"New immigrant" children followed their older brothers and sisters and started to join Hull House children's clubs at about the same time. Jewish and Italian children found it more natural to belong to ethnically mixed clubs, since most of them were sent to public schools by their parents. Unlike the Germans and Irish, east European Jews and Italians preferred—though for different reasons—public rather than parochial schools. Nevertheless, children of both groups went to Hebrew or Sunday schools for their religious studies. Unlike Jewish and Italian children, most Greek children were segregated in the Greek parochial school in the neighborhood. Naturally,

116

when they began to participate in Hull House activities, they did not join Hull House social clubs, preferring the music, crafts, and sports clubs. A lack of membership lists makes it difficult to ascertain their number. It could not, however, be high since, as we have seen, the Greek colony on Chicago's West Side was considerably smaller than either the Italian or the east European Jewish one.[21]

After 1908 the process of change in the ethnic composition of Hull House's youth clientele was completed. "New immigrants," east European Jews, and Italian became the majority, while the number of native-born Americans, Irish, and Germans decreased significantly. At the same time another trend could be discerned: the rise in the number of Italians and the arrival of the Greeks during the second decade of the twentieth century coincided with a steady decrease in the number of east European Jews attending Hull House activities. Hull House residents responded to this situation by revising their policy towards Jews. Although some earlier experiments could be traced to 1906/7, 1913 marked a turning point when a class in Hebrew literature and Jewish ethnic clubs were launched. This policy was part of Hull House's overall attempt to deal with what was acknowledged in native-born American circles as the revival of ethnicity and immigrant cultures among newcomers. The results, however, were disappointing, as only a small Jewish group participated in Hull House activities from the second decade of the century on.[22]

## The Circumstances That Determined Ethnic Patterns of Participation

The patterns of participation of the younger generation of "new immigrants" in Hull House activities were determined by the nature of Hull House, their ethnic backgrounds, and the pace of their group adjustment to the American environment.

The east European Jewish youngsters who participated in Hull House activities formed a small proportion of their Jewish age group. As we have seen, the majority of Jewish youngsters preferred to establish independent political and cultural clubs and societies, either of the east European Jewish or the American type. Those who attended Hull House constituted a third type of group: some of them, who were more strongly influenced by the Americanization process, preferred American institutions of the Hull House type because of their mixed ethnic composition and American ethos. Others were attracted to Hull House because of its cultural and educational opportunities and attended it in considerable numbers as long as there was no Jewish social center that could meet their needs as Americans and compete with the Hull House facilities and opportunities. When the Jewish community center, the Chicago Hebrew Institute, moved in 1907 to its new quarters and was able to offer the same kind of facilities and activities as Hull House, east European Jewish youngsters preferred it to Hull House. As a result, the number of east European Jews at Hull House gradually dwindled, while those who continued to participate in Hull House activities were mainly the more Americanized and/or alienated from Judaism.[23] Alex Elson, who grew up in the Jewish ghetto, can serve as an example of the type of ethnic youngster who preferred Hull House. He grew up in an immigrant neighborhood and attended Hull House clubs and activities. After graduating from high school he attended law school and worked as a club director at Hull House for a while. He became a widely known lawyer in Chicago but was never deeply involved in the life of the Jewish community. On the other hand, the two sons of Bernard Horwich, a prominent leader of the ghetto community and an ardent Zionist, attended Hull House only as long as there was no Jewish community center in the neighborhood.[24]

The gradual increase in the number of young Italians who participated in Hull House activities was the outcome of their growing familiarity with the American environment, which enabled them, unlike their parents, to distinguish between a social center, a settlement house, and a Protestant mission. As already indicated in chapter 6, the Italian Guardian Angel Mission, which became a Catholic settlement—the Madonna Center—in 1915, attracted some thousands of Italian children over a period of several years. The Catholic settlement developed very slowly due to financial difficulties, and its facilities could never compete with those of Hull House. Significantly, its residents and volunteers were Catholic German Americans of upper-middle-class background, a fact that hardly contributed to its popularity among Italians. In 1917 the settlement was forced to move to new quarters. The poorer facilities in its new building ruined the chances of the Madonna Center to serve as an alternative to Hull House for Italian children. Nonetheless, those children who were especially devoted to the Catholic church never attended Hull House, while the more Americanized children, or those attracted by its better facilities, preferred Hull House in growing numbers.[25] This did not mean that the majority of Italian youth attended Hull House, but rather that Hull House became a social center mainly for the "better element" of Italian youth. The Hull House Boys' Club had a much higher percentage of school attendance for Italians than their city average; 62 percent of the Italian children who joined the Hull House club in 1907/8 were elementary and high school pupils. According to a sample prepared by the United States Immigration Commission in 1908, the percentage of Italian children in the Chicago public schools was lower by about 20 percent, while only 22 percent of Italian youngsters studied in high schools in Chicago in comparison with 31 percent of the boys' club Italian membership. Moreover, the occupational distribution of the Italians at the Hull House Boys' Club was not typical for Chicago or other parts of the United States: 12 percent of young Italians in Chicago were unemployed as compared with only 6 percent in the Hull House Boys' Club; 11 percent of young Americans of Italian origin and 41 percent of Italians in

Table 9 Occupations of Italian Boys in Hull House Boys' Club

| | Italian boys | | Club boys | |
|---|---|---|---|---|
| | Number | Percent | Number | Percent |
| Newsboys | 9 | 6 | 9 | 1 |
| Errand boys | 23 | 16 | 98 | 17 |
| Cabmen, drivers | 4 | 3 | 29 | 5 |
| Industrial workers | 12 | 8 | 85 | 15 |
| Commercial house | 29 | 20 | 108 | 19 |
| Clerks | 3 | 2 | 63 | 11 |
| Workshop apprentices | 46 | 31 | 108 | 19 |
| Other | 11 | 8 | 47 | 8 |
| Not in school and unemployed | 9 | 6 | 21 | 3 |

Source: Hull House Boys' Club, 1907/8, Juvenile Protection Association Papers, University of Illinois.

Chicago were unskilled railroad workers. Peddling was also a typical occupation among young Italians in Chicago. These occupations were not found at all in the Italian sample of the Hull House Boys' Club (see Table 9). Even the percentage of newsboys, another typical occupation among Italian youngsters, was lower in the Hull House sample. The Italian working boys who participated in Hull House activities tended to be the more stable ones who were employed in more prestigious jobs.[26]

The rate of juvenile delinquency among the Italians of the neighborhood was particularly high. Research done by members of the Hull House group, Edith Abbott and Sophonisba P. Breckenridge, demonstrated that a high correlation existed between lack of elementary education, "blind alley occupations"—newsboys, errand boys, peddlers—and delinquency. Thirty-six percent of the children brought before the juvenile court were engaged in these "blind alley occupations." Indeed, Hull House was situated in the Nineteenth Ward, which was one of the worst centers of juvenile delinquency at the beginning of the twentieth century. Needless to say, the delinquent element did not join Hull House clubs but formed their own street corner gangs and became intimately connected with the Italian underworld.[27]

This situation was largely the result of the kind of club directors who worked with the club members and the educational aims of Hull House, which were not adapted to the needs and mentality of the average Italian boy.[28] The male-oriented Italian boys found it most disagreeable to be directed by women. When Hull House residents recognized this problem, they nominated only male directors for Italian boys' clubs. The main problem, however, remained unsolved: an average Italian boy who suffered from cultural and environmental deprivation, who had only six years of education, who had worked since he was twelve or fourteen years of age and had entirely different socialization patterns could not identify with the upper-middle-class white Anglo-Saxon Protestants or even middle-class Germans or Irish intellectuals who volunteered at Hull House. The Italian boy found it difficult to communicate with his club director because of the unbridgeable gap between the model for imitation and his own mentality and personal chances.[29]

The type of director, however, was determined by the very principles of the settlement movement, which aimed to create close contact between upper- and middle-class Americans and the lower classes and to bridge the gap between the classes and unite American society into one integral organism. The educational aims of Hull House were to elevate the children of the working class, to teach them middle-class American values and standards, break down ethnic barriers, and create an integrated society without religious, ethnic, or sexual inequalities. This concept did not encourage the use of Italian directors who would be able to communicate with the Italian children. Of the 382 men and women on Hull House's staff between 1889 and 1929, only 3 percent were Italians, and most of these were engaged in workshops or sports.[30]

The educational goals and pattern of socilization of Hull House contradicted those of the Italian group. In contrast to the individualistic ethos of American society, with its middle-class "child-centered" family, which the Jews always had and Greeks adopted, the Italian peasant family still preserved the old social structure of a "peer group society" and was "adult oriented." The Italians emphasized conformity and loyalty to the "peer group" rather than the development of the individual personality and the ambition to excel which Hull House directors encouraged.[31]

Hull House gradually adapted its cultural policy to the interests of the Italians, shifting the emphasis from educational and cultural programs to sports, dancing, playing, and crafts. These changes took place during the first decade of the twentieth century (see Table 10). Another compromise with reality was the introduction of billiards, bowling, and other games available in the West Side public halls, and a brass band was formed for popular music.[32]

Nevertheless, no changes were introduced in the middle-class norms of behavior and concept of socialization at Hull House. The new cultural policy of Hull House, which was designed to satisfy the needs of the Italian children of peasant background, remained unsuited to the average Italian boy. Hull House daily rules were influenced by its middle-class norms: children under sixteen years were allowed to use its facilities only up to five o'clock in the evening, making it impossible for working boys under this age to attend Hull House, and they were not permitted to take part in games such as billiards and bowling. After seven hours of work, Italian children showed little interest in craft shops, separate dancing groups for boys and girls, educational games, or clubs designed to teach them the principles of parliamentary law. They wanted

Table 10 Change in Hull House Club Policy

| Year | Educational courses | Art, workshop, and craft courses | Debating clubs | Social clubs |
|---|---|---|---|---|
| 1892 | 26 | 7 | | |
| 1896 | | | 13 | 1 |
| 1902 | 32 | 9 | 6 | 6 |
| 1905/6 | 9 | 23 | 5 | 10 |
| 1906/7 | 9 | 21 | 5 | 7 |
| 1910 | 11 | 18 | 2 | 8 |
| 1913 | 8 | 19[a] | | |
| 1916 | 6 | 15[a] | | |

Source: *Hull House Bulletin,* no. 1 (1896): n.p.; no. 1 (1902): 10–11; no. 1 (1905/6): 11–14; *Hull House Year Book,* 1906/7, 8–9, 11–12, 21–26, 35, 37; 1910, 8–13, 21–22, 25–26; 1913, 6–14, 42; 1916, 6–20, 42; Hull House Trade School, 1913, Jane Addams Papers, Peace Collection, Swarthmore College, Swarthmore, Pa.

[a]Hull House trade school included.

to enjoy themselves. Italian girls fit better into Hull House. Paradoxically, Hull House female residents upheld the traditional concept of the female role of Italian girls, teaching them cooking, sewing, and other household arts.[33]

From 1910 more Italian working youngsters began spending their time at Hull House, using its sports facilities and playroom, while others rented rooms for their independent clubs, taking advantage of Hull House's sports facilities. However, Hull House had no influence over these youngsters, and they participated in its programs only occasionally. Thus, for example, the West Side Sportsmen's Club, which began to rent rooms and use Hull House's sports facilities in 1920, hardly exemplified the type of club advocated by Hull House. Its president, William Gargano, a former poolroom owner, could not be considered a favorable type of club president, while many Hull House residents did not trust Robert A. Cairo, the club's director, even though he was for many years a member of the boys' club and a Hull House resident. The club conducted its activities independently, and Hull House residents had no idea of its real nature. They were shocked when in 1931 the police informed them that the club was connected with some of the worst Italian gangsters in Chicago, and that forty-six of the ninety-two of its members had police records.[34]

The participation and gradual increase in the number of Greek children at Hull House was, as we have seen, due to the special relationship that developed between Jane Addams and the leadership of the Greek community on Chicago's West Side. The priest and the lay leaders removed their objection to the participation of their children—up to the age of fourteen—in some of Hull House's activities, after they had made sure that it would not endanger the national religious and cultural goals of the Greek community.[35] Thus Greek children were allowed to participate in activities that did not affect their socialization along ethnic lines. After the age of fourteen they joined Greek clubs that were part of the Greek community center at Hull House and were controlled by the Greek leaders.

The situation described in this chapter indicates that Hull House failed not only to carry out its objective of becoming the community center of the neighborhood, but even to become an important source of influence to the younger generation of immigrants. Hull House was situated in the midst of the ethnic neighborhood but remained a marginal institution.

# EIGHT

# IMMIGRANT LEADERSHIP AND PATTERNS OF ADJUSTMENT TO THE AMERICAN ENVIRONMENT

While Liberal Progressives were marginal in the immigrant communities, they played a major role in interpreting newcomers and their cultures to Americans and vice versa. Their notions of immigrant nationalism and culture are, therefore, central to our understanding of the controversy over the place immigrants and their cultures should occupy in American society. The Liberal Progressives exaggerated and misinterpreted the differences between lower- and middle-class leaders and the relationship between the lower-class leaders and the immigrant masses. Despite their differences, immigrant leaders as a whole were united in their commitment to the survival of ethnic identity, based on the underlying principles of pluralism developed by Horace M. Kallen (see chapter 9). In this they expressed the wishes of most "new immigrants" of the first and second generations. Only a minority had the desire and the capacity to become culturally and structurally totally assimilated into the American mainstream. Most "new immigrants" needed the supporting framework of the ethnic community. The pattern of adjustment to the American environment approved by the rank and file was partial acculturation without assimilation. Residential segregation, along with the existence of immigrant societies and institutions, as voluntary and represented the "consent of the governed."

In shaping the pattern of immigrant adjustment to American society, immigrant leaders went through three stages. The first-generation leadership labored for the survival of group entity and identity. The second generation, represented by the middle-class leadership, struggled against discrimination in American society, for recognition of the status of their group, and for better opportunities for its members. The third generation, which started to participate in community life from the 1920s on, campaigned for their group's ultimate equality of status. The first-generation leaders rarely dared openly challenge Anglo-American supremacy. Second-generation leaders paid lip service to the concept of cosmopolitanism, which challenged the Anglo-American model. The third generation was already in a position to question the cosmopolitan, melting-pot concept of American nationalism, and demanded ultimate equality through cultural pluralism. Nevertheless, the cosmopolitanism of the second generation already implied elements of a pluralist view of American society.

The lower-middle-class leadership whose mentality was molded by the Old World and whose acquaintance with the general society was limited, as in the case of the first generation of immigrants, felt more ethnic than American. They identified themselves as ethnic Americans or Polish Americans, Italian Americans, and so forth and in fact developed a minority consciousness. Their ethnicity was the outgrowth of their European socialization and American conditions. Except for a small group of Old World intellectuals, most of them were in the prenational stage of consciousness. Their quest for a higher degree of self-sufficiency of the immigrant community reflected their feelings of inferiority and yearning for a sense of community, as well as an ethnic consciousness of kind. As first-generation leaders they were preoccupied with laying the foundations of the immigrant community and were mainly involved in the internal affairs of their local communities. As a result, their contacts with the general society were limited to issues directly connected with the elementary needs of their countrymen. Since the American system was not adapted to the needs of newcomers, these leaders built the local immigrant community upon the assumption that it should depend as far as possible upon its own resources for survival. Their minority consciousness was instrumental in their efforts to ensure the survival of their group as an ethnic entity in an Anglo-American environment.[1]

The lower-middle-class leadership, namely, immigrant small businessmen and politicians, was naturally selected by the immigrant communities in their early days. The businessmen, padrones, bankers, and grocery and saloon owners had arrived a few years earlier. They had started at the bottom of the socioeconomic ladder and had succeeded in establishing themselves economically. Being better acquainted with the American environment, they were in a position to take advantage of the new opportunities created by the mass immigration from eastern and southern Europe. They performed an important and useful function for both American employers and the mass of unskilled workers. Being the owners of the few meeting places where the newcomers could gather, these businessmen, of the same ethnic and social background as the newcomers they served, provided in addition information, advice, and personal help. They manipulated the resources of both parties' political machines to take care of their countrymen's needs. For the same purpose they initiated local self-help societies, the mutual benefit societies, to care for the health and other insurance needs of "new immigrants." It was only natural that they became presidents, secretaries, and treasurers of these societies and acted as brokers between the ward boss and the members of ethnic groups who were unable to speak English. These businessmen often acquired party and city jobs because they were the naturally selected and recognized leaders of their communities. Although it is true that some took advantage of their positions for personal gain, their moral standards and motivation did not detract from the fact that they helped their countrymen with jobs, relief, and other kinds of assistance and served as the representatives of their groups' interests. They performed an important role in the adjustment of their countrymen to the realities of the American working-class environment. Newcomers voted for these leaders and for other party machine candidates neither because they were "terrorized" nor because they were naively enchanted by the "personal kindness" of ward bosses. They voted for those who, they believed, represented at least some of what they considered to be their interests.[2]

The rejection of this leadership by Liberal Progressives, who argued that the leaders exploited their countrymen's economic dependence for their personal advantage and "terrorized" them to vote for party machine candidates, was based upon a misinterpretation and exaggeration of the facts.

The major source of misunderstanding between unskilled immigrants and their padrones seems to have been that there were no fixed rules about agency fees, railroad fares, and so forth. The workers did not understand that these were determined by the law of supply and demand and by varying policies of the agents and railroads. As a result, immigrant laborers were often confused and held the agents and bosses responsible for these continuous changes. Evidence gathered from public investigations in New York, Chicago, and other cities proved that the average agency fee for jobs that lasted a few months was $3 to $5. When the fee was $10 to $14, it usually included railroad fares, which were $4 east and $6 west of the Missouri River. Moreover, Progressive critics of the system usually ignored the expenditures involved in this kind of business, such as interpreters, advertisements, and office rent. According to the testimony of Mr. Clapp of Clapp, Norstrom, and Riley, one of the largest agencies in Chicago, the expenditure for placing fifteen thousand laborers amounted to $7,200 a year. The expenditures of the state free employment offices in Chicago, which handled ten to fifteen thousand people a year, ranged between $8,000 to $10,000 during the years 1908 to 1912. A $2 fee scarcely met the agent's expenses. The failure of some voluntary societies to run free employment agencies indicated that both laborers and American employers preferred the services provided by private employment agencies, when given the choice. In spite of their deficiencies, private agencies were more efficient. But above all, the free employment agencies found it impossible to meet the expenses involved in the labor distribution business.[3]

The situation was complicated, as recent studies of the relationship between the Italian padrones and Italian unskilled laborers have shown. The pattern of relationship and norms of behavior of one society cannot be interpreted in terms of those of another. If complaints are an indication of exploitation, the average of 1,000 complaints a year per 200,000 to 300,000 jobs comes to less than half a percent. Padrones and bosses were not as diabolical, nor Italian laborers as helpless and naive, as they were portrayed by Liberal Progressives. Some, no doubt, were unscrupulous, and many took advantage of the dependence of their countrymen in different ways. In that, they were no different from native-born American and "old immigrant" employers, contractors, and employment agents. Unlike the swindlers of diverse origins who appeared in immigrant colonies during periods of depression, collected fees for promised jobs, and disappeared, most padrones and bosses in Chicago were permanent residents of their immigrant communities. They lived there with their families, relatives, and friends who had come from the same villages in Italy, in relatively small, closely knit colonies. They would not have been engaged in continuous, large-scale exploitation of their neighbors. The few who did run away after abusing their countrymen's confidence in them prove that exploitation and fraud were not accepted or tolerated norms in Italian enclaves.[4]

State and federal commissions investigated the exploitation aspects of the padrone and commissary systems. But no commission ever investigated the rates charged by American railroad corporations and contractors for room and board, which amounted to $18 to $20 a month (out of a monthly salary of $35) and included three full meals a day. The monthly expenses for room and board, under the so-called exploitative commissary system, was only $7, enabling Italian laborers to save at least an extra $11 for their families. Besides preferring their own Italian kitchen, Italian workers hoped to save more money by cooking for themselves. An Italian government study of camp conditions, comparing camp food with food available in local villages in Italy, stated that the food eaten by Italian laborers in America was more abundant, varied, and rich. These facts put the accusations against the commissary system in a different light. Investigators were preoccupied with the rates and the unnutritious food sold to immigrant workers by commissary bosses. They never raised the question of how families could have been expected to survive on $15 to $17 a month had they used the alternative offered by American corporations and contractors.[5]

Although the English press in Chicago, controlled by the Progressives, gave a great deal of publicity to the issue of bank fraud, as we saw in chapter 5, it seems that the involvement of the so-called immigrant banks in Chicago in the "bank crisis" in Illinois was negligible.[6] In the absence of a branch system under the Illinois banking law, the immigrant banks were the only banks in the immigrant neighborhoods. These banks not only furnished the only banking facilities available but were also adapted to the needs of their clientele. Immigrant banks were not banks according to American standards, but immigrants could go there at any hour wearing their working clothes and facing no language or mentality barrier. Immigrant bankers handled the immigrants' small money transactions and received their small deposits, which no American national or state bank would handle. Immigrants received banking services without formalities: they could receive their deposits at short notice, as well as credit during seasons of unemployment without having to submit to formal procedures. Moreover, the bankers provided such additional services as forwarding mail, writing letters for the illiterate, cashing paychecks, and acting as legal advisers and interpreters. They even furnished lodging and board at moderate cost and assisted in the management of their clients' property.[7]

Emilio De Stefans, Luigi Spizzirri, and Giuseppe Cugno were considered good padrones. De Stefans and Spizzirri had boardinghouses, groceries, saloons, banks, and steamship agencies on South Clark Street. Giuseppe Cugno had a boardinghouse, saloon, and grocery on Pacific Avenue. In addition to these enterprises they ran employment agencies.[8] As *L'Italia* wrote with reference to the Chicago padrones, "If there is this dishonest race who exploits these men, there is also he who succors these poor ones, who feeds them when they are hungry, defends them in trouble, who tears from their veins the vampires, who saves them from misery and from jail."[9]

The immigrant middle-class leaders, whose personality was shaped partly or wholly by the New World and who had a broader acquaintance with the different aspects of the general society, felt much more at ease in America. They rejected the inferior minority consciousness of the first generation and sought to raise the status of their groups, thus giving legitimacy to group identity as a pattern of immigrant adjustment to, and integration into, American society. They identified themselves as American ethnics, namely, American Poles, or American Italians. They sought to unify the members of their groups on city, state, and national levels and establish national fraternal organizations. These organizations, however, aimed not only at consolidating group solidarity and identity but also at increasing group involvement in American daily life, through group mobility, and at advancing their interests as American ethnics through group pressure. These leaders' methods were more political and Americanized, in comparison with the Old World nationalists who had laid the foundations of organizations. Their success in influencing American attitudes towards their homelands became a barometer of the status of their group in American society. Their Americanization was apparent in their ways of doing things and in their involvement in the daily life of the general community. Yet, paradoxically, their Americanization contributed to intensifying ethnic identity because they were more successful than the first generation in reorganizing and consolidating ethnic communities and in raising the status of their groups in the eyes of their members. In these efforts they rejected the Anglo-American concept of society and adhered to the more liberal concept of America as a cosmopolitan nation. Their interpretation of this term, however, was different from that prevailing among Liberal Progressives. They actually contributed to intensifying the ambiguity of the image of the melting pot. Their cosmopolitanism implied a pluralist rather than a "harmonized-holist" concept of American society. They praised the idea of "diversity within unity" and preferred their own hyphenated Americanism to both the Anglo-American model and the model of Americanism based on the idea of creating a new race out of a cosmopolitan mixture. What Liberal Progressives considered to be a transitional stage was conceived by the second-generation leadership as the desired final pattern for American society.[10]

Cooperation between middle-class immigrant leaders and Liberal Progressives was a common interest. The former needed the help of Liberal Progressives to defend the interests of their groups before the American authorities and public opinion. The latter needed the help of immigrant middle-class leaders to penetrate the immigrant communities. Immigrant middle-class leaders were well aware of the secondary role assigned to them in this cooperation. They also realized that, while the immediate objectives pursued by themselves and the Liberal Progressives were overlapping in the sense that both wished to attract the immigrant masses to their social centers, their final goals were essentially contradictory. Although no unanimity existed on long-range objectives and on the issue of cultural brokerage, immigrant leaders did not underestimate the importance of the sympathy and support they received from Liberal Progressives on short-term issues.

Immigrant middle-class leaders cooperated with Liberal Progressives on issues pertaining to the advancement of their group interests in American society. These included two kinds of issues: those concerned with applying democratic principles to the treatment of newcomers, and those connected with policies of assimilation.

Applying democratic principles included the demand for toleration and respect towards newcomers and their traditions, the campaign against prejudice and discrimination and against restriction of immigration insofar as it reflected racial prejudices, and improvement of the socioeconomic conditions of newcomers. The cooperation was evident in joint protest meetings, memorandums, petitions, and testimonies before city, state, and federal committees, and statements to the American press, as well as intervention on behalf of individual newcomers before police, city, state, and federal authorities. Liberal Progressives became advocates of immigrant rights in American society. Both immigrant leaders and Liberal Progressives sought to establish newcomers' equal rights as human beings and citizens. The immigrant leaders, however, also sought to establish their status and rights as groups, while the Liberal Progressives wished to advance the integration of individual newcomers upon equal terms into the general society. The issue was individual mobility and integration into the mainstream versus group mobility and cultural pluralism.[11]

The second kind of issues pertained to assimilation policies. Immigrant middle-class leaders agreed with the Liberal Progressive interpretation of Americanization in terms of the need to acquire the basic skills to function successfully within the political and economic systems. This meant studying the English language and American history and political institutions, and becoming acquainted with the economic system. Both immigrant leaders and Liberal Progressives recommended partial acculturation as the first stage in adjustment to the new environment. Such an idea of Americanization did not involve the demand to give up segregation, immigrant languages, and traditions immediately upon arrival. The common underlying assumption for assimilation was the understanding that the whole process should be organic rather than mechanical, and therefore, gradual.[12] Although immigrant leaders and Liberal Progressives had different goals, both sought to ease the pressure of compulsory Americanization and rapid assimilation. Immigrant leaders preferred this policy because they needed favorable conditions to establish their groups' distinct identities. Being acquainted with the general society and the different approaches to assimilation, they supported the Liberal line of argumentation and manipulated these arguments in order to reinforce the Liberal Progressives' point of view in the public controversy and to gain their support for the interests of their groups. Thus their support of the Liberal Progressive assimilation policies was based not on a fundamental agreement on principles, but rather on a coincidence of short-range interests. Liberal views were simply more acceptable to the interests of immigrant groups than those of most native-born Americans.

Immigrant middle-class leaders adopted the Liberal Progressive tactics in dealing with the idea of assimilation. This meant leaving the definition of the final goals of assimilation unarticulated and stressing the short-range objectives of assimilation, shifting the emphasis to the destructive effects of artificially accelerated assimilation on both the immigrant and American society, and to means rather than goals. Immigrant leaders warned that

> we must [be] . . . ever alive to the dangers of a rapid and artificial Americanization which may destroy the old values without building up new values in their stead. . . . The immigrant . . . can only see the superficialities of American life and . . . he seizes upon them as the true manifestations of the new environment. While he does not, and indeed, cannot perceive the great ideas underlying the American commonwealth, he quickly enough notices those negative, though accidental features which lie on the surface of American life.[13]

They also pointed to the social and personal disorganization caused by rapid assimilation, especially the gap that arose between parents and children, and juvenile delinquency. Thus the emphasis on gradual and slow assimilation not only left obscured the nature of the assimilation favored by both immigrant middle-class leaders and Liberal Progressives, but also enabled the latter to justify segregation as a humanitarian expedient, at least temporarily.[14]

Immigrant middle-class leaders and Liberal Progressives mutually avoided confrontation on the real nature of their concepts of assimilation. Nevertheless, immigrant leaders dealt with the issue indirectly through the questions of ethnic policies and cultural brokerage. They argued that cultural brokerage and the implementation of ethnic policies or assimilation should be entrusted to social workers and educators of each nationality under the auspices of its middle-class leadership. They based their arguments on the logic of the Liberal Progressives' own assimilation policies, but they manipulated for their own purposes the Liberal Progressives' arguments on the importance of preserving the self-respect of newcomers through self-help and of employing foreign-born social workers able to communicate with their own people. Settlement workers, when pointing out the differences between themselves and native-born American charity organizations, stated that the immigrants' adjustment should be based on work "with the people rather than for the people," if the self-respect of newcomers was to be preserved. Immigrant middle-class leaders used this argument to justify their opposition to the cultural brokerage of native-born Americans. Harry A. Lipsky, for example, a second-generation Jewish leader of east European origin and the representative of the ghetto community on the Immigrants' Protective League Board of Trustees from 1912 to 1914 and on the Chicago Board of Education from 1911 to 1917, argued that "organized or individual initiative and activity, coming from and maintained by sources outside the district involved, encountered the indifference, if not the open hostility of many even of the well informed and better educated residents of the neighborhoods concerned."[15] This was because the educated and more enlightened members of the immigrant communities considered the very efforts of native-born Americans to serve as cultural brokers as representing a patronizing attitude and therefore an insult.[16] Dr. David Blaustein, a social worker, director of the Chicago Hebrew Institute in the first decade of the twentieth century in the Hull House neighborhood, and the representative of the ghetto community on the Immigrants' Protective League Board of Trustees from 1909 to 1911, explained in his address to the Chicago City Club on 17 March, 1909 the role immigrant leaders should play in the "constructive Americanization of newcomers":

> Only an intimate acquaintance with the life of the . . . immigrant in his old and his new environment, only a full understanding of his mentality and psychology, and an adequate appreciation of his traditions and associations may succeed in bridging the terrible chasm between his past and present, . . . and thereby transforming him into a happy and valuable citizen of our great republic.[17]

Following this logic, he suggested that newcomers be Americanized in social settlements staffed with foreign-born workers under the immigrants' own auspices. Yet he agreed that the social workers, educators as well as leaders of the immigrant settlement, should be equally conversant with both the immigrant and American societies and cultures. Czech leaders shared Blaustein's view. During a discussion on the issue in the Czech newspaper *Czechoslovak Review,* one of them noted that "Czech can gain a Czech's confidence much easier than a stranger. Similarly with the Slovaks. Therefore the work must be done by persons of Czech and Slovak origin, among their own people."[18]

The differences between the policies of Hull House and immigrant community centers demonstrated the different goals pursued by them, in both their ethnic composition and cultural orientation. The ultimate objective of the Hull House club policy was the dissolution of the ethnic group through the integration of individuals into the cosmopolitan or ethnically mixed general community; while the ultimate objective of the club policy of immigrant community centers and immigrant settlements was the preservation of ethnicity through the social, ethnic segregation of newcomers. As Dr. Blaustein quite bluntly stated, "Let us assimilate or become Americanized in speech, in dress, in politics, in fact, in every respect, but when it comes to the question of social life, we should, I think, remain our own-selves."[19] Both American settlements and immigrant community centers favored intergroup activities and cooperated in organizing such events. Yet Hull House participated in these activities in order to promote free communication between immigrants and native-born Americans, eliminate ethnic barriers, and create opportunities that would lead to the emergence of a unified, harmonious society composed of individuals of different origins mixed together. Leaders of immigrant community centers, on the other hand, were interested in cooperation and communication between groups. They thought that "immigrants should learn to know each other better" and "learn not to keep aloof from one another," yet their favored pattern of ethnic life was cultural pluralism.[20]

Unlike Hull House, which never made any meaningful efforts to preserve and foster immigrant cultures, immigrant community centers encouraged an ethnic renaissance by promoting ethnic art, music, and drama and by teaching immigrant children the languages, history, and literature of their parents. Thus the role of the east European Jewish community center, the Chicago Hebrew Institute, in the Hull House neighborhood was presented as follows: "It will develop our literature, create or preserve Jewish art in all its functions, stimulate and further Jewish scholarship, so as to make it a powerful factor in the strengthening of the Jewish consciousness. It will reorganize and put on a firm basis the Jewish education of our children . . . and will make Judaism a living, flourishing, impregnable organism."[21] Accordingly, it sponsored lectures on Jewish topics, concerts of Jewish music, Hebrew and Yiddish literary clubs, exhibitions of Jewish art and of Jewish artists in America and Palestine. The dramatic clubs performed plays in Hebrew, Yiddish, and English, written by Jewish writers on topics pertaining to Jewish history, the Bible, and Jewish daily life in Europe and America. Many of these plays dealt with the longing of Jews for Palestine and the dream of national independence. In its efforts to preserve and foster Jewish music, the Hebrew Oratorio Society was established in October 1917, "to cultivate, develop and produce Jewish music in all its branches, extending from ancient to modern times." The institute was permeated by a Jewish atmosphere.[22]

The differences between immigrant middle-class leaders and Liberal Progressives concerning the final goals of assimilation were also revealed in the controversy over the public school versus the parochial school and the introduction of immigrant studies into the public school curriculum (see chapter 4). Unlike Liberal Progressives most immigrant middle-class leaders did not reject parochial schools as such, nor did they desire to transfer immigrant children to public schools as such. Aware that about 50 percent of the immigrant children attended public schools, these leaders wished to introduce the teaching of immigrant languages and literature into the public school curriculum in order to strengthen the attachment of those children to their group and its culture. Nor was there a clear dividing line on this issue between religious and lower-class immigrant leaders on the one hand and middle-class leaders on the other hand. The middle-class leadership itself was divided on this issue. Nevertheless, the controversy should not be seen as a dispute between those who favored ethnic education and those who favored Americanization and assimilation. Middle-class leaders were united in their insistence on the preservation of ethnic identity and disagreed on the means, whether immigrant identity and culture should be transmitted from one generation to another through parochial schools or Sunday and Hebrew schools. The demand that immigrant languages be taught in public schools was aimed at securing the same objectives for those children whose parents were either indifferent or unable to pay the tuition in parochial and supplementary schools.

The cooperation of immigrant middle-class leaders with Hull House on certain issues should not, therefore, be seen as identification with its concept of assimilation. Even the group that rejected the parochial school altogether and insisted that immigrant children should attend public schools still sought to transmit the ethnic heritage, and not only religion, through Sunday or Sabbath schools and the teaching of immigrant languages and cultures in public schools.[23] Liberal Progressives, on the other hand, preferred to think of Sunday schools as religious rather than ethnic schools. Another group of immigrant leaders, probably the majority, demanded that the parochial school curriculum as well as that of the public schools should be reorganized. They wished to adapt the former to the needs of progressive education and to transfer its emphasis from religious to ethnic studies. At the same time they campaigned to introduce ethnic studies into public schools. This demand reflected their belief that it was their right as citizens and taxpayers to transmit their heritage to their children within the public school system. In a situation where 50 percent of immigrant children attended public schools, this policy was understandable.[24]

Christ Damaskos, editor of the *Saloniki*, was a Greek leader closely associated with Hull House. At the same time he opposed the idea of sending Greek children to public schools because "the innocent Greek children are being raised and educated—not in the Greek customs and language, not in the underlying history of our country, not in our sacred Orthodox religion—but in a strange language, strange customs, strange backgrounds and strange mores. . . . It means murder of our nationality."[25] He actually supported the anti–public school policy expressed by the newspaper of the Polish clergy, *Dziennik Chicagoski*, though for different reasons. While the *Dziennik Chicagoski* primarily fought the cause of the Catholic creed, the *Saloniki* was interested in Greek nationalism and culture, as well as religion, and stated that "the parents must be persuaded to send their children to Greek schools instead of American schools."[26]

John Agriostathis, a leader of the Greek Youth Club at Hull House, became in his adulthood the secretary of the board of directors of the Greek parochial school, the Socrates School. In his capacity as secretary he appealed to the members of the Greek community to contribute money for the school, considering it "a noble cause."[27] Its principal, Mrs. C. Kantzou, shared the commitment to America of those who preferred the public school. Yet she sought to achieve it through the parochial rather than the public school. "My sacred duty is to help make good and progressive American citizens out of the pupils entrusted to me," she asserted. "At the same time I am required to mold them into the fine characters worthy of being called Greeks."[28]

The *Greek Star,* edited by Peter S. Lambros, another friend of Hull House, acknowledged the importance of the public school but also stressed that the Greek Sunday school had a vital role to play as a supplement to American education. "The Greek language has always been considered and is still considered by all civilized people the rich and inexhaustible source. . . . The Greek-American youth with his racial and religious traditions and with the American education crowned with his knowledge of the Greek language will be a model citizen of this great republic." [29]

The contradictory attitude of the Zionist group among the east European Jewish middle-class leaders toward parochial schools was typical of many immigrant middle-class leaders. The Yiddish *Courier* declared that only the Ultra-Orthodox group is in favor of establishing parochial schools. The Zionists are, however, opposed to parochial schools or to any type of religious school. They believed that religion and nationalism are two separate matters that the further apart they are, the better is. The Zionists are satisfied with the theory put into practice by Mrs. Ella F. Young of developing and encouraging the national spirit [of the children] of the various nationalities that attend the Chicago public schools. Classes have been organized in the schools in which the language, history, ethics and legends of the various nationalities are taught.[30]

Yet these same leaders cooperated with Orthodox educators in establishing a common board of education for all Jewish schools in Chicago, while the Federated Orthodox Charities, which was controlled by second-generation leaders, many of them Zionists, gave financial support to the Orthodox school system. Furthermore, they were instrumental in establishing Sabbath or Hebrew schools.[31] Other immigrant groups were also divided over the means of achieving ethnic consciousness. An editorial of the Bohemian newspaper *Denni Hlasatel* expressed the attitude of the Bohemian liberal leaders on education for immigrant children: "Our public English-language schools are most important for the children's future. But it would be not only wrong, but also unjust to attribute a minor importance to our Bohemian schools. . . . Send our children not only to public schools but also to our Bohemian schools."[32] It was Professor Jaroslav Zmrhal, a former principal of a Chicago public school and subsequently a district supperintendent of public schools, the Bohemian representative on the Immigrants' Protective League Board of Trustees, who lead the campaign to introduce the teaching of immigrant languages into public schools, in his capacity as secretary of the Bohemian American National Council. He was supported by a group of middle-class leaders such as the architect James B. Dibelka, the Bohemian representative on the Chicago Board of Education at that time. In his appeal to Czech parents, Professor Zmrhal stated that

> the Bohemian American National Council has a whole mass of concurring and sympathetic communications from the ranks of Czech parents who welcomed the idea, not only as a new recognition of the Czech rights and a new proof of our cultural maturity, but primarily as a really practical step, which aside from the educational question will mean chiefly the strengthening of our Bohemianism where it is fundamentally needed—among our student youth.[33]

The *Svornost*, another Bohemian newspaper, supported the demand to teach the Bohemian language in public schools. Nevertheless, it considered that if other immigrant groups did not wish "to see their children denationalized they should maintain private schools for the teaching of their mother tongue just as the Bohemians are doing."[34]

The president and vice-president of the Polish National Alliance were also on the board of trustees of the Immigrants' Protective League. This Polish organization was primarily interested in the advancement of the Polish population within American society and urged Polish parents to send their children to any school of their choice, parochial or public, the emphasis being on education as such.[35] However, its board of directors led the campaign to introduce the teaching of the Polish language and culture into public schools. On 22 September, 1911 the alliance newspaper, *Dziennik Zwiazkowy,* informed its readers that "at last they are to teach the Polish language in Chicago high schools, thanks to the efforts of the Board of Directors of the Polish National Alliance."[36] The newspaper argued that unlike the parochial school the public school denationalized Polish children.

> Such systematic inculcation (of feeling of pride and admiration to the United States) causes the children to loose interest in their own language, the history of their nation, and their customs.
> It is our duty to counteract this influence and demand of the municipal authorities . . . that the Polish language be taught as a separate subject . . . [and] be a shield against loss of national identity and submergence in the boundless sea of Americanism.[37]

The leaders of the Polish National Alliance used other arguments as well in their demand to teach Polish in public schools, the major "being respect for our own [language] because there are considerable numbers of our people in Chicago."[38] On this issue, the Polish intelligentisia and middle-class leadership opposed the wishes of the Polish clergy and the Polish Roman Catholic Union, as revealed by the controversy between the two parties on the pages of the *Dziennik Zwiazkowy* and the *Dziennik Chicagoski,* the publication of the Polish clergy in Chicago. The former newspaper asserted that, "having established Polish in the public high schools, [we] will continue to try to secure the establishment of the Polish language in the American universities, and even in the elementary schools." It insisted, however, that

> this does not mean that we [the Polish National Alliance] are disparaging our Polish parochial schools, and are trying to draw children away from them—not in the least . . . Let him who wants to, send his children there, because there the children will learn Polish and the history of their motherland. But because many Polish children attend the public schools, where Polish is not taught, and their parents either do not want to, or are unable to send them to the parochial schools, therefore, we should try to have the Polish language taught in the public schools, which thousands of Polish children attend, and for which we are taxed.[39]

The leaders of the Polish National Alliance therefore did not reject Polish parochial schools as such, but criticized only their standards of teaching and the curriculum. Addressing the Polish clergy, they pointed out that their constructive criticism had led to the improvement of parochial school standards.[40]

That immigrant middle-class leaders did not agree with the final objectives of the Liberal Progressives' idea of assimilation becomes obvious if we compare the statements that these leaders addressed to their constituency and those addressed to the American public and Liberal Progressives. Robert E. Park, in *The Immigrant Press and Its Control,* has quoted a typical example of the two sets of arguments employed by immigrant middle-class leaders. An editorial on 21 February 1920 in the *Zgoda,* a newspaper of the Polish National Alliance in Chicago, explained in two versions the decision to "devote some of its columns to news items and editorials in the English language." In English, the editor defined his objectives "as explaining Polish-Americans to the American-Polish youth born and brought up in America, who could not read Polish." Moreover, the English version stated that the Polish columns aimed to Americanize Polish-speaking people. "Our policy is to keep the Polish speaking people in continuous contact with America and American institutions . . . interpreting all the desires and aims of America." The Polish version of the same editorial, however, claimed that the English columns were designed "to Polonize" the younger generation, rather than Americanize the older generation, and to ensure that the "protest" of Polish Americans against "American chauvinism" and "in defence of the Polish spirit in the United States . . . reach the highest places."[41]

To be an American was interpreted by immigrants and their leaders in terms of being committed to the idea of democracy and having the freedom and right of self-expression—a right they had been denied in the Old World.[42] Thus, in his address before the members of the Chicago City Club, Dr. David Blaustein, a Jewish leader, asked rhetorically,

> Do we understand by the Americanization of the foreigner that we are to assimilate him with our body politic without any regard for his racial and national characteristics, or do we understand by it that we are to educate him to a proper knowledge of America while letting him develop and work out his salvation on ethnological lines in accordance with his early training and natural instincts?[43]

In other words, he believed that the American Idea meant the development of the love of liberty and patriotism in newcomers, not obliging them to relinquish their ethnicity. On the contrary, America would only be enriched by the variety of cultures and traditions in its midst: "Now that they [the Jewish people] are in the land of liberty, let them have an opportunity for self-expression. This, however, they will not have if . . . they are led entirely to forget their past and give up the ideas and ideals for which they have from time immemorial, been martyrs."[44] Immigrant middle-class leaders employed the "contribution idea" to support their arguments in favor of fostering immigrant cultures. In the name of their right to contribute their share to the shaping of future America, they demanded the right of self-expression not only for first-generation immigrants but for the succeeding generations as well. Jaroslav V. Nirgin, a Bohemian leader, demanded

> the same rights as citizens and workers, and one of these rights is the right to contribute whatever treasure they possess towards the upbuilding of the American ideals . . . the formation of national character. . . . The timber from which is fashioned national character is furnished only by the second and later generations. . . . Now these succeeding generations will be unable to contribute anything of their own . . . if they are not allowed to acquaint themselves with the rich heritage of their ancestors. That can be done only by thorough study of their mother tongue.[45]

The difference between Liberal Progressives and immigrant leaders on the nature of America was succinctly, if somewhat extremely, articulated by a Polish American priest during a discussion with Emily G. Balch, a member of the Liberal Progressive caucus. America, he asserted, was a political federation of ethnic groups.

> America was empty, open to all comers alike . . . There is no such thing as an American nation. . . . The United States is a country, under one government, inhabited by representatives of different nations. . . . I do not think that there will be amalgamation, one race composed of many. The Poles, Bohemians, and so forth, remain such, generation after generation. . . . I do favor one language for the United States, either English or some other, to be used by every one, but there is no reason why people should not have also another language.[46]

Balch's response was typical of the Liberal Progressive view. She was convinced that the priest's concept of America was not shared by all immigrant leaders, expressing at the same time "a sense of shock to a realization of points of view strange to one's own view."[47] She protested that "in spite of my Polish interlocutor's belief that America is not a nation, it has in truth the deepest right to consider itself such."[48]

The main source of the Liberal Progressives' misinterpretation of the views of immigrant middle-class leaders was the former's commitment to their concept of "middle-class ideology." It also sprang from the illusion that agreement on short-range policies reflected a common concept of society, an illusion that was reinforced by the ambivalent language in which both Liberal Progressives and immigrant middle-class leaders couched their views. Liberal Progressives became victims of their own devices. The intentionally ambiguous expression of their views on assimilation and blending was designed to make it easier for immigrants to identify with their views and cooperate with their policies. Immigrant middle-class leaders made full use of this ambiguity. Finally, the Liberal Progressives' optimistic attitude also seems to have been reinforced by a tendency to wishful thinking, regarding the views of immigrants as well as other underpriviledged groups.

# PART THREE

## LIBERAL PROGRESSIVES AND AMERICAN NATIONALISM AND CULTURE

# NINE

# INTERNATIONALISM AND UNIVERSAL BROTHERHOOD

The underlying assumptions upon which the Hull House circle based its idea of American nationalism were environmentalism and the concept of the evolutionary progress of human societies. According to these assumptions the uniqueness of America lay in its being "a democracy founded on internationalism," or universal brotherhood—the highest form of human society. By the same token America's "manifest destiny" was to produce a new kind of civilization, an international or cosmopolitan civilization, and thus accomplish the universal mission that Hellenism and the Roman and British empires had failed to realize.

The history of national struggles in Europe during the nineteenth and early twentieth centuries reflected the principle that both racial and cultural homogeneity were necessary for the emergence of a nationality and for the survival of the national state. This principle was also accepted by democratic societies, and thus the close relationship between nationality, or an ethnic group, and national or ethnic culture became established.[1]

Liberal Progressives considered themselves to be faithful to the American tradition when they questioned the relevance of this principle to American nationalism. Although they agreed that American nationality had in fact been Anglo-American on the eve of independence, because of its predominantly English-speaking population at that time, they also accepted that the United States was a nation of immigrants. Recognizing that the rights of free immigration and asylum, as expressions of the American democratic ideals of equality, freedom, and diversity, determined the nature of American nationality as cosmopolitan in its ethnic origins, they believed that a new American nationality would emerge from the diversity. Nevertheless, as we have seen, they were reconciled with the fact that racial blending and the emergence of a new composite American national type was a long process.[2]

Thus, whereas European nationalism was founded on unity of race, what was peculiarly American was its internationalism. Grace Abbott expressed the Liberal Progressive concept of American nationalism, arguing that "we are many nationalities scattered across a continent . . . we are of many races and are related by the closest of human ties to all the world . . . here in the United

States we have the opportunity of working out a democracy founded on internationalism."[3] The same idea was expressed by John Dewey.[4] Both Addams and Dewey pointed out that humanity, according to the laws of evolutionary progress, was moving from small isolated social units characterized by tribalism, sectionalism, segregation, and xenophobia to larger ones based on the principle of "international nationalism." The national state represented a higher stage in human relations than the family, the parish, the sect, and the province. "It has forced men out of narrow sectionalisms into membership in a larger social unit, and created loyalty to a state which subordinates petty and selfish interests."[5] The Hull House circle anticipated that the next stage in the evolutionary progress of human societies would be the widening of the ethnic scope of national-political units to include people of different nationalities and races.

Jane Addams stated that the trend of humanity towards larger social and political units represented the idea that "the solidarity of the human race" was higher in the scale of human progress than national or ethnic solidarity.[6] Indeed, the idea of universal brotherhood was rooted in the belief that the common interests of human beings predominated over the differences in nationality, language, and culture. Humanity was advancing towards the elimination of the walls of nationality that divided the human race, towards understanding, openness, and communication between people of different backgrounds. Human relations were evolving from war and alienation to peace and friendship, from hatred and isolation to cooperation and sharing. Progress made the disintegration and dissolution of small and segregated units inevitable, and the blending of their members and the emergence of "the great open society" were the imperatives of progress. The new stage in the evolutionary progress of human societies was the international state in which the barriers of nationality or ethnicity and culture would be eliminated to achieve the goal of human existence—universal brotherhood (see chapter 1).[7] In Addams's view, this was already taking place in the United States: "In seeking companionship in the new world the immigrants are reduced to the fundamental qualities and universal necessities of life itself. They develop power of association which comes from daily contact with those who are unlike each other in all save the universal characteristics of man."[8]

This new international nationality was possible because ethnicity and nationality were the products of environment and historical circumstances. Hull House leaders were confident that every human being had the capacity for change and adjustment, and a common racial origin or nationality, therefore, was not indispensable for the creation of national harmony and for the survival of democracy. They believed that the common features of humanity were more fundamental and immutable than the superficial and temporary differences between nationalities based upon language, culture, and national traits.[9] Addams quoted the words of Canon Barnett when she wrote that "the things which make men alike are finer and better than the things that keep them apart, and that these basic likenesses, if they are properly accentuated, easily transcend the less essential differences of race, language, creed and tradition."[10]

Jane Addams discovered the first stage of the inevitable process of the "new internationalism" already at work in America.[11] The immigrant neighborhoods in the slums were the places where people of different origins were forced by circumstances into cooperation and fellowship. "Those who have come to us with all the racial and religious hatreds . . . of a selfish nationalism at home, have lived together in the the United States on the same street, in the same tenement, finding the appeal of a common interest greater than the appeal of a century of bitterness."[12] These common human traits were far more important and should be praised and cultivated in order to elevate the human race and to create universal brotherhood. This meant that the elimination of superficial differences and the unification of individuals of different backgrounds into one harmonious society was the culmination of the evolutionary progress of the human race and the realization of the idea of democracy. The settlement houses served as "cathedrals of humanity" for the fulfillment of this mission, and Addams wished that they "be capacious enough to house a fellowship of common purpose, and . . . beautiful enough to persuade men to hold fast to the vision of human solidarity."[13]

Out of the diversity of races and nationalities a new nationality would emerge in due time, through a process of social and racial blending, although Addams anticipated that "a commingling of racial habits and national characteristics in the end must rest upon the voluntary balance and concord of many forces."[14]

John Dewey believed that the new race or the new nationality would be exalted and superb, because it would bring together the best qualities and traits of all the races and nationalities out of which it was created: "It must be a unity created by drawing out and composing into a harmonious whole the best, the most characteristic, which each contributing race and people has to offer. Our national motto "One from Many," cuts deep and extends far."[15]

Considering the differences between the American and the European solutions to the right of self-expression of nationalities, Dewey argued that political nationalism was not indispensable to cultural nationalism and that the demand for the first was the result of the denial of the second. He believed that the solution in Europe should be ethnic autonomy for its nationalities within a federated political organization. Thus ethnic units would be able to preserve their uniqueness and enjoy, at the same time, the advantages of a political unit large enough to defend their commercial, industrial, and financial interests. At the same time, this federation of nationalities would keep the lines of communication and mutual influence open for cross-fertilization.

Unlike Europe, which for generations had been engaged in national rivalry which could not be easily erased, America had a new message to the world, the creation of an international nationality. This international nationality could become possible because "the principle of nationality receives no recognition in the constitution of a state like ours, where citizenship and nationality are independent." Every human being was equally entitled to American citizenship, and "language, literature, creed, group way, national culture, are social rather than political, human rather than national interests." A nation where all races and nationalities could meet upon equal terms as human beings represented not only the highest stage in the evolution of human societies, but also the realization of the idea that all people were born equal notwithstanding their racial, ethnic, and cultural differences.[16]

The United States was the first international nation and the laboratory and model for universal brotherhood. This human experiment would succeed if American democracy entered upon its second stage, widening its scope from political to social democracy in human relations as well, thus creating the conditions for the elimination of national and cultural differences and the unification of human beings of different origins into one harmonious society.[17]

Two great national leaders, Abraham Lincoln and Giuseppe Mazzini, symbolized for Jane Addams the quest for universal brotherhood. In their thinking the synthesis of political freedom, humanism, and the desire to widen the scope of national-political units by emphasizing the common characteristics of the human race, rather than its national-cultural differences, was most evident. Lincoln represented for Addams the highest ideals of humanism and democracy. He defended these ideals against racial prejudice, discrimination, and exploitation in the name of universal brotherhood. He showed that American nationalism should not be interpreted in racial terms, to separate people of different origin or color from each other, but rather in terms of devotion to the ideal that all men were born equal.[18] Addams stated that Mazzini, "with all his devotion to his country, was still more devoted to humanity" and that his appeal in *The Duties of Man* "transcended all national boundaries and became a bugle call for the duties of man." Both Mazzini and Lincoln represented for her "the sense of the genuine relationship which may exist between men who share large hopes and like desires, even though they differ in nationality, language, and creed." She believed that "those things count for absolutely nothing" and that "unity of spirit might claim right of way over all differences." She hoped that the Italian youth in America, educated upon the ideals of Mazzini, would "indeed become the Apostles of fraternity of nations." She "seemed to detect among . . . those groups of homesick immigrants . . . the beginnings of a secular religion or at least of a wide humanitarianism evolved out of the various exigencies of the situation."[19]

144

Jane Addams's and John Dewey's idea of American nationalism as an expression of universal brotherhood was also influenced by the universalism of Felix Adler and the Ethical Culture Society. Dewey and Addams were closely connected with Felix Adler personally and active in the Ethical Culture Society movement. Both lectured regularly before its local branches, and at its conventions and served on its committees, while Adler was involved in the settlement movement, and his ideas greatly influenced its programs.

Felix Adler, an American Jewish intellectual, applied the cosmopolitan idea in the religious sphere. He envisioned a universal, nondenominational (religious) fellowship, based on a novel, eclectic religio-ethnical ideology; a religiously motivated ideology of universalism for contemporary times. Adler's universal ethical religion developed out of his initial disaffection from Judaism. Cutting his ties with the Jewish socioreligious community in the late 1870s, Adler called upon Jews to end their self-segregation and to dedicate themselves to the moral goal of contributing, upon an individual basis, from their ethnic and religious heritage to humanity. Thus only the best in the Hebrew tradition would be preserved. He urged the replacement of the Jewish and Christian religions with a universal ethical religion. In his cosmopolitan concept of America, the best religious ideas of Judaism and Christianity and the blending of races would create a new religious and racial identity, namely, an American cosmopolitan race, sharing a common universal religion. Although Adler did not concern himself with other ethnic-religious groups, his ideal of creating a new cosmopolitan religious-racial identity implied the dissolution and total cross-assimilation of all immigrant groups.[20]

In the controversy on immigration restriction in the first decades of the twentieth century, the real issue was the terms of admission into the American nationality. Hull House's ideas of environmentalism and universal brotherhood were the response to the nativist theories of heredity, which stated that people of different nationalities were not born equal; that not only their traits but also their capacities were predetermined by group heredity; and that democracy represented the unique racial genius of Anglo-Saxons. Hull House was therefore opposed to the nativist argument that "new immigrants" from eastern and southern Europe should not be admitted to America because they were inferior by heredity and could not change and become true Americans.[21]

John Dewey, who formulated the Liberal Progressive stand in the heredity-versus-environment controversy, argued that the nature of biological heredity was misconceived. Human beings had two distinctive characteristics—language and the capacity to make and use tools, or the capacity to learn. These enabled human beings to assume control of their destinies. Unlike other biological organisms, they were not the victims of evolutionary accident but rather directors of their own evolutionary process. Life was a continuous process of change and readjustment, a process "in which the organism falls out of equilibrium with its environment and restores it."[22]

145

William I. Thomas, who also articulated the Liberal Progressive view, likewise questioned the use of the term "race" with reference to "new immigrants." He argued that the so-called races of Europe were all mongrel and could be classified on the basis of language and custom. Even the Jews were greatly intermixed with both Asiatics and Europeans. He explained the existence of nationality or ethnic traits by "circumstances— . . . a given racial history"—rather than "inborn aptitudes" and insisted that the peculiarities of these groups should be ascribed "to a long train of common experience, not to inborn and ineradicable traits." The changing circumstances would doubtless bring about, in due time, change of traits.[23]

Jane Addams and the Hull House circle also shared some components of Israel Zangwill's idea of American nationalism. Zangwill divided the types of nationality into four categories: simple, complex, compound, and hybrid. The simple type represented a nationality whose "language, race, religion, culture and territory are common to all the group." In the complex type, "all races and religions mingle toward political unity," while in the compound type "they are isolated spatially and united federally." In the hybrid type "they are neither isolated nor united." The United States, like England, belonged to the complex type. It was a melting pot. Yet Israel Zangwill was convinced that history was engaged in a process of creating simple nationalities and so "all nationalities not simple are combinations of simple nationality fused from all the primary they all tend to pass." But "even the nationalities we now call Simple are but the debris of races, and their psychology a palimpsest of cultures and religions." This is due, Zangwill argued, to "the law of change." Harmonious nationalities were invaded throughout history by immigrants or by missionaries and became mixed and blended, the chief factor of change being force. "Either it is weak and is swallowed up by a stronger, or it is strong and swallows up a weaker." As a result, "if a Simple Nationality, the moment it is born, starts changing into a Complex Nationality, so the Complex or Compound Nationality, the moment it is born, starts changing into Simple Nationality." Of all the types, in compound nationalities the process of fusing was the fastest. America was the fastest melting pot, because "love is a swifter factor than force. . . . When a country is loved before it is seen, the fusion begins even before the foot has trod the sacred soil." Zangwill based his melting pot thesis on the assumption that environment was at least as important as heredity, and education was "more than half the creature." He was convinced that "the traits of their [human beings'] common humanity exceeded their differences," and any race "vanished in three generations" if the groups feel content and "are not dominated by each other." He furthermore believed "that it is not any racial obstacle that impedes the Nationality of Man" and "in a century the new American Nationality will be shaped to a European rigidity."[24]

The future lay in a combination of internationalism and nationalism. "Internationalism so far, then, from being the anti-thesis of Nationalism, actually requires nations to inter-relate." Zangwill rejected cosmopolitan universalism, which he believed to be "a more romantic Nationality." The bulk of humanity was fixed to place, and even if it was uniformly civilized, "the world is too big to be conscious or to be governed as a whole." The solution for Europe was federations instead of individual sovereign states, because of its long history of divisiveness. America as a melting pot represented the ideal, "how to maintain the virtues of tribalism without losing the wider vision," or how to preserve the brotherhood of a nation without losing the fellowship of man. This could be achieved because the American melting pot represented the fusion of people of different nationalities into one nationality; similarly all different religions would fuse into a new American religion, one that would represent the universal values common to all religions. The American religion was embodied in the American Constitution, which combined the ideas of the Puritans inspired by the ideal state of Moses.[25]

In his play *The Melting Pot* Zangwill dealt also with the cultural aspect of the melting pot, encouraging the Jews in America to give up their customs and heritages, no matter how painful it might be, because these prevented them from becoming Americans. In becoming Americans they did not sacrifice their "set of moral and ethical precepts," since those were actually part of the American religion. Being a Jew, Zangwill dealt in the play with Jews. Yet his concept of immigrant assimilation was applicable to any immigrant group.[26]

Jane Addams and Liberal Progressives agreed with Zangwill's contentions that a "nationality not simple" was a combination of simple nationalities fused into a new mold, and a complex nationality was a mingling of all races into political unity. Liberal Progressives shared his beliefs that the common traits of humanity exceeded the differences, that environment is at least as important as heredity, and that the future lay in a combination of internationalism and nationalism. The question remains, however, whether they shared Zangwill's concept of cultural assimilation.

Cultural pluralism was formulated in 1915 by Horace M. Kallen. Though no public controversy arose between Chicago Liberal Progressives and Kallen at that time, it is important to analyze the points of agreement and disagreement in order to clarify the Hull House concept of American nationalism, especially because some historians have considered Hull House the forerunner of pluralism.

Indeed, cultural pluralism was inconsistent with the underlying assumption upon which Liberal Progressives based their views in their controversy with Anglo-Saxonism. Kallen rejected the idea of an international nationality and contended that assimilation was an undemocratic and inhuman option. He envisioned America as a "democracy of nations" or a "commonwealth of nationalities." America was "an orchestration of mankind."

> As in an orchestra every type of instrument has its specific timbre and tonality, founded in its substance and form: as every type has its appropriate theme and melody in the whole symphony, so in society, each ethnic group may be the natural instrument, its temper and culture may be its theme and melody and the harmony and dissonances and discords of them all may make the symphony of civilization.

Kallen based his concept of American nationalism and culture on three underlying assumptions: first, that selfhood was inalienable and ancestrally determined; second, that the promise of democracy was individual self-realization, which he conceived as both personal and ethnic; and third, that the true interpretation of *E Pluribus Unum* was diversity within unity, or that permanent group diversity was desirable. These contradicted the three underlying assumptions upon which the nineteenth-century American consensus was based. Kallen's first assumption embodied the idea of "ethnic-cultural determinism." Kallen was paradoxically influenced by the same heredity studies that shaped the thinking of Anglo-American racists, although he interpreted them differently. Rejecting the idea that "the qualities of man are ancestral constants like property in entail," or the notion of hierarchy of inferior and superior races, he believed that "men may change their clothes, their politics, their wives, their religion, their philosophies, to a greater or lesser extent: they cannot change their grandfathers."[27]

Thus, in the controversy between heredity and environment, Kallen took a middle stand. He rejected what he considered to be the common element of both hereditists and environmentalists. "The idea, that one's heredity or one's environment are cause external to the personality of which the personality is the effect, leaves no room for . . . every man's experiences." Kallen believed that "the environment in its broad sense of the world with all its persons, customs, arts, religions, and sciences, undoubtedly determines most of what occurs in man. . . . Most, but not all." On the other hand, "heredity is not a force outside us, compelling us; in fact heredity is our past alive and present within us—in the ways and works of our organs, in the posture and patterns of our minds transformed by experience and transforming it, as new skills and new knowledge are learned, and being learned, suffuse the old and give them new characters and new meaning." As a rule, one has a "personal option," to choose his way out of the alternatives which continually present themselves before him. Yet "our choices must offer fulfillment of our natures, not violations, liberations, not inhibitions." In other words, "whatever may be done to us or by us in the making of our personality, it . . . must be assimilative to the singularity of our organic becoming whose wholeness is our self. If this does not confirm the making, it remains alien." Kallen stated that the whole concept of "natural rights" should be conceived upon the assumption that the "intrinsic positive quality" of mankind, "its psycho-physical inheritance," is "inalterable," "inalienable." Furthermore, "the impress of centuries is indelibly stamped upon it, and no mechanical process can undo the organic development of many generations."[28]

If, Kallen argued, the attributes that make people different—national origin, creed, tradition, and culture—predominate over those that make them alike, then these differences should be respected, preserved, and cultivated. "Democracy involves, not the elimination of differences but the perfection and conservation of differences." If the promise of democracy is to give the individual the best opportunity to exercise his talents for his own sake and for the common good of the whole society, then society should "provide conditions under which he might attain the cultural perfection that was proper to his kind."[29]

Since individuals are "the intersection of a line of ancestry and a line of social and cultural patterns and institutions," people of different ethnic origins are destined to remain in their ethnic-cultural group, and out of different ethnic groups no new ethnic entities can emerge. The inevitable conclusion of pluralists was that any attempt to put the newcomer into an environment that is radically different from the ethnic-cultural environment that shaped his personality, would destroy his social and spiritual equilibrium. The spiritual equilibrium of the individual "is the product of the social forces of his environment." His sense of equilibrium or his "habits, tradition or association—which gives him the feeling of security" is ensured as long as he remains within his familiar surroundings. Ethnicity is a sociocultural way of life, and "the greater the divergence between the old and new environment of the immigrant, the greater must be the disturbance of his equilibrium." Since the impact of the lost equilibrium on both the personality of the immigrant and the whole society is mostly unfavorable, "the only solution left to us is to reconstruct, or rather help the immigrant to reconstruct his old environment, to re-awaken and reinforce the social influences of his former surroundings, so that . . . he may once more possess the sense of equilibrium." In short, ethnic segregation is inevitable, and only some moderate, superficial modifications are possible. "Jews or Poles or Anglo-Saxons, in order to cease being Jews or Poles or Anglo-Saxons, would have to cease to be."[30]

If the individual can liberate and develop his personal capacities, his unique talents and skills, within his ethnic cultural milieu, then individual diversity can be liberated and protected only through the principle of group diversity. The preservation of ethnic diversity is therefore a democratic principle, and in the United States "the whole spirit of those institutions which constitute American nationhood makes for the liberation and harmonious cooperation of nationalities."[31] Furthermore, every national or ethnic group has a destiny to fulfill, which can be realized and perfected within its ethnic environment. Accordingly, the idea of American democracy should be perceived as giving legitimacy to equality, freedom, and diversity for groups as well as to individuals. Kallen considered permanent group diversity as a condition desirable in itself and as a prerequisite so "that every man and every group may have the freest possible opportunity to realize and perfect their natures." "Race reacts selectively to culture . . . the expressions of group life that varying sensibilities and impermeabilities become manifest, and these it is that are creatively significant . . . in no other field (as in culture) has the obscure selective action of temperament appeared more definitively."[32]

Viewing the nature of human society in comparison with the biological world, cultural pluralists interpreted the theory of social evolution as a trend towards greater diversity. Kallen did not hold that the human race was "advancing" in the direction of elimination of races through a process of blending and cross-fertilization and the creation of an international type of society. He did not share the belief that social evolution would produce a new homogeneous type that would blend the best qualities of every one of the races involved. Kallen apprehended that "the likelihood of a new "American" race is remote . . . equally remote also is the possibility of a universalization of the inward bases . . . there comes no assurance that the old types will disappear in favor of a new. Rather will there be an addition of a new type . . . to the already existing older ones. Biologically, life does not unify; biologically life diversifies."[33]

Assuming that ethnic determinism and the direction of evolutionary progress of human societies were leading to the preservation of ethnic diversity and even to greater diversity, Kallen anticipated the emerging of the United States as a "federation of nationalities," or a multicultural society sharing a common political organization. He disagreed with the assumption that a political entity should be based upon ethnic and cultural homogeneity. He believed that a political unit could survive and function successfully in a multiethnic society if a basic elementary consensus existed among a federation of ethnic-cultural subunits cooperating upon equal terms. This elementary consensus should be based on a common economic, political, and educational system, leaving to each group the right to preserve and cultivate its unique ethnic-cultural identity in voluntarily segregated subcommunities and educational, cultural, and ethnic agencies. This was the realization of the American Idea and the ideal of *e pluribus unum,* namely, diversity within unity.[34]

Nevertheless, Kallen wished to keep the lines of communication between groups open in order to ensure the functioning of a "federation of nationalities." "It involves give and take between radically different types, and a mutual respect and mutual cooperation based on mutual understanding." The underlying assumption was that intergroup rather than individual relations were the best social framework to bring together people of different ethnic-cultural backgrounds. Through intergroup activities in all spheres of life—sports, culture, and so forth—people of different groups could learn to know each other better and cooperate for the common welfare of their common homeland.[35]

Unlike Kallen and the pluralists, Liberal Progressives believed that assimilation was both inevitable and desirable and represented a democratic and human solution, if implemented by the appropriate methods. Assimilation did not involve the self-denial or alienation of the individual from his selfhood, because he could express both his personal and ethnic uniqueness through the principle of individual diversity.

John Dewey rejected Kallen's "ethnic determinism" as well as his conclusion that ethnicity was unalterable. He disagreed with Kallen's premise as to the importance and primacy of the early sociocultural environment on the future association of individuals. For Dewey environment and not heredity was the major factor in determining individual association, and therefore in case of change—such as immigration—the new environment and the current interests of the individual would predominate. Since the interests of the individual changed in direct relation to the changing nature of his sociocultural environment, the future association of individuals was "heavily laden with utilitarian purposes." The individual was therefore capable of changing his ethnic identity in a different environment. Dewey based this conviction on his own experience as well. He referred to his own lack of ethnic sentimental interest in a letter to Kallen in 1915, in which he commented on Kallen's article in *The Nation* on the nature of American nationalism. Some scholars have held that Dewey seemed "to have a weak conception of the binding force and strength ethnicity plays in the co-joining of people over long periods of time."[36]

Liberal Progressives also disagreed with the cultural pluralists on the issue of ethnic diversity. Kallen maintained that the richness of a culture depended on the preservation of ethnic diversity: "The deep-lying cultural diversities of the ethnic groups are the strongest shield, the chief defense. They are the reservoirs of individuality, the springs of differences on which freedom and creative imagination depends."[37] Thomas agreed that progress in the arts and the sciences demanded the greatest possible diversity of human speciality and creativity. The more diversified human beings were, the greater the likelihood of progress of civilization towards efficiency and the general welfare of humanity. Unlike the pluralists, however, Thomas rejected the idea that human diversity and creativity were dependent on the preservation of ethnic groups.

> Immigrant groups claim a similar social value—that, on account of their social peculiarities and the fact that they have developed by their past experiences different apperception masses, they are predisposed to individualized functions as groups, and that by perma-

nently organizing along lines of their aptitudes they will not only express their peculiar genius, but contribute unique values to America. . . . It is not apparent that even the most distinct races, the black, white and yellow, are characterized in this way.

Creativity and genius, he argued, were determined by individual capacities rather than by ethnic-cultural affiliation, and the essence of the idea of diversity was individual diversity.[38]

Liberal Progressives therefore denied that ethnic segregation was a prerequisite for individual self-expression and cultural contributions to civilization. Ethnic segregation was disadvantageous to both the individual and the community because only the removal of barriers, and close communication among people of different characters and backgrounds, enriched the individual and society and released forces that otherwise remained limited to small segregated units. An open society in which all individuals mingled freely created the conditions indispensable for the utmost self-realization of the individual for his own benefit and for the common welfare.[39] Jane Addams argued that "if we . . . consciously limit our intercourse to certain kinds of people . . . we not only circumscribe our range of life, but limit the scope of our ethics . . . narrowness of interest . . . deliberately selects its experience with a limited sphere."[40] On the other hand, John Dewey stated that "by breaking down the barriers of class, race and national territory each individual gets an opportunity to escape from the limitation of the social group in which he was born, and come into living contact with a broader environment."[41]

Liberal Progressives likewise rejected the pluralist idea of America as a "federation of nationalities" based upon the concept that political units, democracy included, did not need like-mindedness for their successful functioning, and that a minimal consensus was sufficient. The idea of American nationalism as international, and the belief in a future emergence of a new coherent nationality, were closely connected with the Liberal Progressive concept of American society as a harmonized-holist entity sharing an "apperception mass," a like-mindedness, that is, common values, knowledge, and norms of behavior. Liberal Progressives believed, therefore, that a wide consensus was indispensable for the survival and functioning of American society as well as its democracy. Liberal Progressives and pluralists consequently disagreed on the relationship between democracy and unity. While pluralists considered permanent diversity the natural state of society and the imperative of democracy, Hull House leaders were preoccupied with the phenomena of social and ethnic antagonism and the resulting segmentation of American society. Their idea of society and democracy did not allow for a situation of permanent class conflict and ethnic diversity as a pattern of social or national existence. They believed that the alternatives were either segmentation, which was self-destructive and would bring inevitable chaos, or unity and harmony.[42]

To the Hull House circle a democracy meant the elimination of differences for the sake of equality. Since the things that made people alike predominated over those that made them different and the influences of environment worked towards similarity, the American socioeconomic system and the influence of American institutions and values would result in both acculturation and social assimilation. This idea was the essence of the Hull House concept of sociohumanitarian democracy. According to this idea democracy demanded that newcomers assimilate structurally into American society through free communication, elimination of national and cultural barriers, and social and racial blending (see chapters 1 and 2).

Kallen on the other hand held that since the things that made people different—nationality and culture—predominated, Americanization and upward social mobility into the American middle class (namely, environmental influences) would not result in structural assimilation and the elimination of ethnic groups. He stated that "similarity of class rests upon no inevitable external condition; while similarity of nationality has usually a considerable intrinsic base. Hence the poor of two different peoples tend to be less like-minded than the poor and the rich of the same peoples."[43] Kallen disagreed that a similar environment produced similarity and that like-mindedness was inevitable under common influences.

> Men are men merely, as like as marbles, and destined under uniformity of conditions to uniformity of spirit . . . that likemindedness in virtue of which men are as nearly as possible in fact "free and equal" is not primarily the result of a constant set of external conditions. . . . Its prepotent cause is a prevailing intrinsic similarity which . . . has its roots in that ethnic and cultural unity.[44]

He interpreted the quest for a unified society of universal brotherhood as a tendency to conceive "equal" as "similar" or "identical." He rejected the idea that "so that you may become completely my brother, you must offer up your own different being. Unless you do this you refuse brotherhood." He therefore made a distinction between universal "brotherhood" and universal "friendship" or "fellowship." Brotherhood required elimination of differences as a prerequisite for unity, while friendship accepted differences on a permanent basis as a prerequisite for a free society. Instead of holding that equality means sameness, Kallen suggested adopting the principle of different but equal. Thus the traditional idea of the right of the individual to be different was interpreted by Kallen in terms of the right of the ethnic group to be different and preserve its ethnic-cultural uniqueness.[45]

The Hull House circle reconciled the demand for unity and likemindedness with the "largest possible amount of individual freedom" by recognizing the right of the individual to be different. Adhering to individual pluralism, they left ethnicity as a temporary feature, to be expressed through individuals rather than through ethnic groups.[46]

Since the Hull House circle and Horace M. Kallen disagreed on the direction of the evolutionary progress of human society, they also disagreed on the world mission of America. Kallen's vision of America as a "federation of nationalities" was rejected in favor of the vision of America as the first "international nationality." America's mission was to teach the world that the common features of humanity exceeded its differences and that this shared humanity was enlarging the scope of social units.

So, paradoxical as it may seem, the Hull House circle did accept the underlying assumption shared by all national ideologies, that every nation has a *cultural destiny* to fulfil. Being an international nationality, America had its unique *cultural mission* to human civilization—to create a successful and enduring international or cosmopolitan civilization.[47] Thus the justification and the moral meaning of the creation of a new nation in the New World (composed of people of different ethnic origins and cultures) was the accomplishment of the mission that the Old World had failed to fulfil, namely, the creation of a cosmopolitan civilization. Previous attempts—Hellenist, Roman, English—had failed because they had been forced upon other nations by conquerers and lacked the two indispensable conditions of freedom and equality. The American experiment had better chances of success because it ensured freedom and equality to all the ethnic strains in American society. America was in the process of producing something greater and finer than any of the cosmopolitan civilizations may have produced. The uniqueness of America was its cosmopolitan composition, both ethnic and cultural. The success of this self-imposed mission depended upon the blending of its ethnic groups. Italians, Poles, Germans, and all other types should retain their group distinctiveness ethnically and culturally in their homelands. Those who emigrated to America must become Americans and contribute their share to the racial and cultural melting pot and disappear as Italians, Poles, and so forth. A true cosmopolitan civilization, however, required the contributions of all the ethnic units.[48]

Jane E. Robine, another member of the Liberal Progressive group, envisaged the final result in America of ethnic contributions.

> When the blood of the people which produced Raphael and Michelangelo . . . shall flow in the veins of the American people of the future generations, this people, with the purity of life and religious ideals of the Pilgrims, with the tenacity of the Germans, with the commercial ability of the Jews, with the artistic sense of Italians, will be ready to realize the . . . ideals for which God has prepared it through centuries of work, hope and struggle.[49]

As John Dewey stressed, "Our unity . . . must be a unity created by drawing out and composing into a harmonious whole the best, the most characteristic, which each contributing race and people has to offer."[50]

While both Kallen and the Liberal Progressives shared the belief that every nationality had a cultural "manifest destiny," a unique contribution to add to the common fund of civilization, Kallen rejected any attempt to dissociate national cultures from their ethnic backgrounds. In other words, the contributions of individuals to human civilization were possible through the medium of a national culture only, because the ethnically determined individual was only capable of developing his unique talents and skills within his ethnic environment. This justified the preservation and cultivation of the unique type of culture of every ethnic group in an ethnic environment. Kallen justified his commitment to national cultures also from a historical perspective, considering "the heroic failure of the pan-hellenists, of the Romans, the disintegration and diversification of the Christian church."[51] Similarly, the pluralistic alternative suggested to America by Israel Friedlaender, a Jewish scholar, was a pluralistic civilization consisting of a system of concentric circles. "In the great palace of American civilization we shall occupy our own corner, which we shall decorate and beautify to the best of our taste and ability."[52] Kallen's metaphor of America as an orchestra put a premium on "the different instruments, each with its own characteristic and theme," that would "contribute distinct and recognizable parts to the composition." Accordingly, "each ethnic and cultural community serves as a reservoir of some specific tradition and excellence which one or another of its sons may lift into the powers . . . of the larger national life." Thus the preservation of ethnic cultures in America would be a blessing: "the result in America is a strength and richness . . . which nations of a more homogeneous strain and an imposed culture . . . do not attain."[53]

The difference between the Liberal Progressive and the pluralist view of American civilization was succinctly summarized in Dewey's letter to Kallen in 1915. Expressing his reservations about Kallen's ideas, Dewey stated that he would be willing to adopt the metaphor of America as an orchestra "upon the condition we really get a symphony and not a lot of different instruments playing simultaneously."[54] Dewey stressed the one harmonious melody, while Kallen emphasized the variety of instruments and their distinct tones and themes.

> An orchestra is the free and well-ordered cooperation of unique individualities toward the making of the common tune. . . . Race is . . . to the common culture . . . what an instrument . . . [is] to the music of a symphony. . . . There is a true division of labor in the making of this tune, for although instruments are broadly interchangeable, there are limits set by the timbre to the adequacy and beauty of their utterance.[55]

Significantly, both Dewey and Judge William Mack, president of the Immigrants' Protective League, used Kallen's metaphor in addresses made in

1916. Yet both used it to emphasize unity and harmony, rejecting both Anglo-Saxonism and the "federation of nationalities." Dewey pointed out that "neither Englandism nor New-Englandism, neither Puritan nor Cavalier, any more than Teuton or Slav, can do anything but furnish one note in a vast symphony."[56] Judge Mack added that "the American nation is the harmonious orchestra in which each of the nationalities of the old world is contributing its share in unison to the complete symphony—the spirit of America."[57]

Group culture was therefore not valued for its own sake but as a reservoir of cultural contributions. Eventually, the ethnic groups must disappear, but their immortal heritage would live forever in an American cosmopolitan civilization. Felix Adler expressed this consensus among Liberal Progressives, stating that in the long prospect "the Jewish race, like others must die . . . as Greece is dead and still lives in its poetry, philosophy and art, so the genius of the Hebrew people will live on in the immortal heritage of moral truth which they left to mankind."[58] Dewey expected each cultural section to "maintain its distinctive literary and artistic traditions" for one purpose, "that it might have the more to contribute to others." The essence of his idea of cultural cross-fertilization was "to see to it that all get from one another the best that each strain has to offer from its own tradition and culture . . . so that it shall surrender into a common fund of wisdom and experience what it especially has to contribute."[59] He therefore set the limits to the existence of ethnic-cultural groups, warning that "the dangerous thing is for one factor to isolate itself, to try to live off its past and then to impose itself upon other elements, or at least to keep itself intact and thus refuse to accept what other cultures have to offer, so as thereby to be transmuted into authentic Americanism."[60]

Unlike Kallen, Liberal Progressives believed that a richer cosmopolitan, homogeneous civilization could emerge out of a free mingling of individuals of different cultural backgrounds and personalities, within a unified, open society. They argued that the great civilizations such as the Hellenic, Roman, and English were the result of racial as well as cultural blending and that "the outcome of the process, as shown by a comparison between the contributing elements and the synthesis into which they at last blended, justified the conviction that America's repetition of the experiment will indubitably lead to something finer than any single one of the factors which co-operate to produce it."[61] According to this vision, they insisted that a distinct harmonious civilization created by the cross-fertilization of the best cultural contributions of all groups was the highest achievement of which a society could dream.[62]

# TEN

# THE CONTRIBUTION IDEA AND THE HULL HOUSE CONCEPT OF AMERICAN CIVILIZATION

Despite the Hull House group's rhetoric about the cosmopolitan nature of American civilization, it seems that their eager embracing of the "contribution idea" was more an expression of tactics than a concept of culture. Liberal Progressives did not envisage American civilization in the future to be the sum total of all cultural contributions imparted by the different immigrant groups. To their mind it was not a chemical or even merely mechanical transformation, which would result in the emergence of a new and cosmopolitan American culture. Instead, in accordance with the democratic principle that all newcomers had an equal right to participate in shaping American civilization, the Hull House group conceived this right in terms of equal opportunities in which, through the process of free competition, the best elements would prevail. Moreover, since they were convinced of the inherent superiority of the Anglo-American civilization, which would ensure its triumph in this process, they predicted that American civilization would continue to be essentially Western, that it, Anglo-American, with some selected immigrant contributions, whose impact would be negligible. In this light the contribution idea merely created the illusion of assimilation upon equal terms, whereas newcomers were actually going through a unilateral process of transition from one culture to another.

The contribution idea was intimately connected with the idea of social democracy to which the Hull House group was committed. This concept was elaborated from individual relations to include intergroup relations, which meant recognizing the moral duty of treating every ethnic group—as representing an aggregation of individuals—with respect, as well as according them the right to develop their singularity (see chapter 1). At the same time, the Hull House group adhered to the idea of the moral superiority of the more sophisticated societies over more primitive ones and the responsibilities that the former had towards the evolutionary process of perfection of human societies and civilization articulated by William James and Felix Adler. It was this view, which was in conflict with the Hull House democratic principles, that prevailed, and Hull Houses's concern became the cultural "elevation" of newcomers, rather than the selection and cultivation of immigrant cultural contributions in their own right. Nevertheless, Hull House encouraged the contributions to American civilization of Americanized newcomers, who would enrich its content through their individual talents and artistic skills, upon the assumption that human capacities were individually determined.

The writings of Hull House residents and the Hull House cultural orientation prove that they conceived of American culture, or what was called the genteel tradition, to be already universal or cosmopolitan in nature. This tradition (being an integral part of Western civilization) was seen to be the sum total of the contributions of the Egyptian, Hebrew, Greek, and Roman civilizations. It also included the cultural legacy of the Middle Ages, the Renaissance, and the Enlightenment, as well as the progressive nineteenth-century culture of both Europe and America. Western civilization was a cultural combination of all these into one universal unity, and the genteel tradition was its American manifestation, in which the different threads of all the worthy contributions of the world's civilizations were woven into one organic web.[1]

When, around the turn of the century, the Hull House group was confronted with the increasing cultural diversity within America's large cities and the clash between the American and immigrant cultures, they were confident that their concept of American civilization could cope with the new situation. The contribution idea was the embodiment of this approach, that newcomers' contributions should be added, thus enriching the already cosmopolitan culture of America.[2] A group of intellectuals represented by Randolph Bourne, the Hapgood brothers, and others disagreed with the view of American civilization as being already cosmopolitan. Bourne stated that in contrast to New England and the South, which represented regional cultures highly influenced by English culture, the only American culture was the pioneer culture that appears in Whitman and Emerson and James. Yet this American culture had little influence on the country's traditions and literary expressions. This group deplored American civilization's provincialism, or rather philistinism, and wished to created a truly American cosmopolitan civilization. By cosmopolitanism these intellectuals did not mean the culti-vation of distinct immigrant cultures, which they considered expressions of immigrant parochialism. Rather they envisioned a process of cultural cross-fertilization between Anglo-American and immigrant intellectuals, and the gradual emergence of a cosmopolitan civilization.[3] Their cosmopolitan ideal was based upon the belief that not only did America desperately need immigrants' cultural contributions but also that all newcomers have a right to a voice in the construction of the American ideal. The group conceived of the contribution idea in terms of the culturally distinct individual contributions of newcomers. They believed that the meetings between individuals of different cultural backgrounds would enrich all involved culturally and would lead to expression of their individual contributions to American literature, art, music, and so forth. Thus by creating opportunities for mutual cultural inspiration a cultural cross-fertilization would emerge. Significantly, this cultural meeting was to take place between

> the eager Anglo-Saxon and the acclimatized German or Austrian, the acclimatized Jew, the acclimatized Scandinavian or Italian. . . . Meeting now with this common American background, all of them may yet retain that distinctiveness of their cultures and their national spiritual talents. They are more valuable and interesting to each other for being different, yet that difference could not be creative were it not for this new cosmopolitan outlook which America has given them.[4]

Morris R. Cohen more than any other Jew became "a symbol of cosmopolitanism" for Anglo-Saxons such as Bourne, Oliver Wendell Holmes, Jr., and others.[5] Cohen articulated the consensus of these intellectuals on the future of ethnic cultures in his address "The Future of Jewish Heritage in America." He was strongly opposed to "the idea that all immigrants should wipe out their past," believing that "the cause of liberal civilization in twentieth century America will not be served by wiping out the cultural values of any minority." Yet he was convinced that the gradual disappearance of ethnic cultures "cannot be denied as a fact, at least a long-range fact."[6] Consequently he asserted that "the dynamic principle of American Jewish life is to be found in neither wiping out of special gifts nor withdrawal to the desert (Palestine), but rather in the fruitful bringing together of Jewish and non-Jewish cultural values." This was because the basic principle of American democracy was that "here in these United States men and women of many different backgrounds may cooperate, bringing each his contribution to a greater civilization than has yet existed."[7]

Although Horace M. Kallen, the advocate of cultural pluralism, believed that America had a geniune American culture, the pioneer-puritan culture whose center was New England, he shared the view of the intellectual group on its insignificant cultural value and its parochialism. The trouble with American spiritual life and its "fine arts" lay in their conformity, which "stifles genius and prostitutes talent." Nevertheless, American culture was now in a process of transition from its pioneer-puritan culture to an industrial-immigrant culture, whose center was the Middle West. The value of the new culture lay in its being the result of "the clash of classes, the confrontation of communities" on the one hand and "free association and collaboration of thereby uprooted individuals coming out of all kinds of corporate unities" on the other. Imagination and creativity "come from the impact of diversities . . . and consequent disintegration and readjustment . . . with the emergence of new harmonies." Kallen believed that the quality of the future culture of the United States was dependent on "the variety, pitch and timbre of the forces involved."[8]

Kallen's view was that ethnic cultures in America should serve as permanent reservoirs of individual creativity for the common fund of American civilization. Immigrants who grew up within their ethnic milieu would be able to contribute to a civilization whose uniqueness lay in its being a "federation of cultures." The Jewish community in America served, he believed, as the best example of both cohesiveness and adaptation, in its contributions to the general cultural fund and its "new forms of life and growth." For him this was the desired pattern for cultural enrichment, for the creation of "national fellowship of cultural diversities" and the emergence of "a new and happy form of associative harmony." Kallen disagreed with Morris R. Cohen's views on the future of Jews, ethnic, and other groups in American civilization. Commenting in a letter to Felix Adler in 1915, he expressed his disapproval of "his tendency to minimize the significance and value of Jewish Nationality."[9]

John Dewey was of the opinion that "the only test and justification of any form of political and economic society, it its contribution to art and science—to what may roundly be called culture." He shared the view expressed by the group of intellectuals and Kallen on the need for a new American culture. He also agreed with them that American civilization was in the midst of a cultural transformation. Yet he perceived this transformation as the replacement of an upper-class culture of the old type with the culture of industrial democracy. This new democratic culture was "something to achieve, to create." In this sense "we have as yet no culture. . . . Since we can neither beg nor borrow a culture without betraying both it and ourselves, nothing remains save to produce one."[10] His ideal of a democratic culture led him to reject the old American culture, which he claimed was not an expression of America's distinctiveness. "The old culture is doomed for us because it was built upon a alliance of political and spiritual powers, an equilibrium of governing and leisure classes." It was a class culture that borrowed its ideal of culture from Europe. "The annual pilgrimage . . . to European cathedral and art gallery is the authentic indication of the conscious estimate of the older idea of culture."[11] Similarly Dewey concluded "that America has not yet justified itself." He predicted the emergence of a new civilization: "Our culture must be consonant with realistic science and with machine industry, instead of a refuge from them . . . in a spiritually democratic society every individual would realize distinction. Culture would then be for the first time in human history an individual achievement and not a class possession."[12] Dewey anticipated that immigrants would contribute their share to the creation of a new and harmonious culture as individuals.[13]

Jane Addams and the Hull House group did not join in this criticism and contempt for the genteel tradition nor in its identification by Dewey as a narrow class culture. They did not share the intellectuals' sense of suffocation and claustrophobia from growing within an American particularlistic culture, nor their spiritual need to break through the limiting framework of what they considered an Anglo-Saxon culture and to turn it into a more cosmopolitan and universal one. On the other hand, the Hull House group agreed with Dewey that American culture should become democratic, but for them its democratization meant only that the lower classes would have easier access to its cultural resources and an equal opportunity to contribute.[14]

An analysis of the writings and occasional statements of Addams and the Hull House group, as well as the cultural policy carried out at Hull House, reveals no real effort to absorb "new immigrant" cultural contributions that were not already part of the Western-American civilization. The contribution idea served therefore as a psychological device designed to make newcomers feel that their cultures were respected and found worthy of inclusion in the American common fund, when they were actually engaged in a process of transition from their particularistic cultures to the American so-called universal, cosmopolitan civilization. Hull House was involved neither in cultural blending nor in the preservation and cultivation of immigrant cultures.

Culture at Hull House was essentially the same as that cherished by Americanizers. The major difference lay in how these two groups interpreted the nature of American civilization. While Americanizers emphasized its Anglo-American nature, Liberal Progressives preferred to point to its universal background and to its European, and not only English, cultural influences. The second difference between the two groups lay in the role assigned to immigrant contributions in American civilization. Liberal Progressives proclaimed that American civilization was still in a process of continuous molding according to the flow of immigrant groups into the country, while Americanizers considered it to be a finished product, an organic entity that could absorb only those cultural elements that had something in common with the general American trend. Since they did not consider "new immigrant" cultures to belong to this category, they rejected immigrant contributions. Liberal Progressives on the other hand acknowledged the existence of a common "primitive source" to American and eastern and southern European cultures. Though Liberal Progressives argued that immigrant contributions would enrich American culture, this proved to be mere rhetoric, and behind these statements we can detect a wishful thinking that American civilization would emerge from the process of cross-fertilization essentially unchanged. This hope was rationalized in their interpretation of the views of William James and Felix Adler on culture and society.

Jane Addams, who wrote quite extensively on the role immigrant cultures should occupy in American civilization, developed three major theses: that the past and present should be brought together; that whatever was of value in the immigrants' past should be preserved; and that immigrant cultures should be treated with respect and appreciation.

"The bringing together of the past with the present" was interpreted by Addams in terms of bridging the European and American heritages, blending both civilizations into one organic whole. European civilization was acknowledged as the cultural gift immigrants brought with them and contributed to American civilization. By accepting these contributions American culture added some more cosmopolitan or universal assets to its already universal character.[15] In fact, however, there was no real blending of American and immigrant cultures in the Hull House cultural programs. The European culture at Hull House was not that which the "new immigrant" groups brought with them mainly from southern and eastern Europe. It was mainly English and west European, in accordance with the genteel tradition. While English culture had been the dominant influence since the colonial period, some French influence could be ascertained during the early period of independence and a strong German influence in the late nineteenth century. These foreign influences that contributed their share to the American genteel tradition were not brought by immigrant groups but were the result of cultural relations with these countries. France and Germany, rather than French and German immigrants, were sources of cultural inspiration for Americans. Upper- and upper-middle-class Americans visited western Europe and studied in west European universities, while American intellectuals and men of culture made it a habit to spend several years in the centers of west European civilization.[16]

Jane Addams and other Hull House residents also visited Europe quite frequently, as did their upper-middle-class colleagues. They were the products of the Western-American civilization cultivated in American colleges and universities and which they sought to propagate at Hull House. Furthermore, the Greek and Italian cultures, or rather the heritage of the ancient Greek and Roman world and the Italian culture of the Middle Ages and the Renaissance, so admired and cultivated at Hull House, were certainly not the cultures that the Greek and Italian newcomers brought with them. The former represented the so-called high culture of the Greek and Italian upper and middle classes, while most newcomers from these countries were peasants who had never heard of Michelangelo, Sophocles, or Dante before they came to America. Americans did not need immigrants' cultural brokerage to become acquainted with the Greek and Italian cultures that had been brought to America by its first settlers, through the English cultural tradition. These cultural assets had long ago become an inseparable part of the American genteel tradition.[17]

The willingness of the Hull House group to accept the cultural contributions of newcomers should therefore not be assessed by their acceptance of Greek, Roman-Italian, or German contributions to the already cosmopolitan American civilization. The real nature of the contribution idea should be examined by the Hull House approach towards immigrant cultures entirely alien to the

American civilization, such as the Yiddish or the various Slavic cultures. Indeed, while Hull House devoted many of its cultural programs to Greek, Italian, and German literature, philosophy, and art and also sponsored some special cultural meetings with Greek, Italian, and German neighbors in appreciation of their civilizations, no such programs were ever sponsored—either as part of the general or special ethnic events—for Yiddish culture. This was despite the fact that around the turn of the century, east European Jewish children and youngsters constituted about a third of the Hull House clientele, while the number of Italians and Greeks visiting Hull House at that time was negligible.

Hull House leaders not only ignored Yiddish culture as a source of immigrant contribution, but one of the early Hull House publications even treated it as the expression of the popular or mass culture of uncultured east European Jewish immigrants and called their language a "demoralizing jargon." Hebrew culture, which the Hull House group considered classical, was also given an insignificant role at Hull House in comparison with the place occupied by the Greek and Roman-Italian cultures. While the role of learning and of the spiritual in Hebrew culture was appreciated, "rabbinical casuistry" was considered to be "distorting the minds" of Jewish children. Anyway, the Hebrew heritage was already represented in the Western-American civilization.[18]

The absence of Russian, Polish, and other east European "high cultures" from the Hull House programs also serves as a striking example of the Liberal Progressives' attitude towards alien "high cultures." A considerable portion of the Russian-Jewish intellectuals on Chicago's West Side, not to mention Russians, Poles, and Bohemians, were brought up on these cultures and were well acquainted with their literary resources. Yet except for Tolstoy, who was admired for his social thinking rather than his contributions to literature, no east European writers or poets were represented in Hull House's club and general cultural programs.[19]

The Hull House idea of culture was also expressed graphically in the decoration of the walls of the Hull House theater. The idea was to portray the heroes of many lands, "those cosmopolitan heroes who have become great through identification with the common lot." The heroes selected, however, belonged to the Western and American civilization—Lincoln, Phidias, young David, St. Francis, young Patrick of Ireland, Hans Sachs, Jeanne d'Arc, William Morris, Walt Whitman, Louis Pasteur, and Florence Nightingale—Tolstoy being the only representative of the Slavic cultures. These figures did not represent the composition of Chicago cosmopolitan society and the heroes admired by its ethnic groups.[20]

The role assigned to east European cultures in American civilization by Hull House was also revealed in the ethnic studies program incorporated into the public high school curriculum in 1912 by superintendent Ella Flagg Young (see chapter 4). Her suggestion to add immigrant languages and their literature to those already recognized by the University of Chicago (a suggestion universally rejected) should not be considered as a fundamental change in her cultural orientation but rather as a temporary expedient, as she herself stated. She was confident "that in a few years the parents in the particular locality will be American born and the desire for the study of the language of the father will disappear."[21]

If the culture in the sense of sentiments, attitudes, and ideas is transmitted through acquaintance with the literature, philosophy, and arts of a given civilization, it becomes evident that Hull House was engaged in the acculturation of newcomers, rather than in blending cultures and absorbing immigrant contributions. When Jane Addams spoke of the need "to preserve and keep whatever of value their past life contained," she was referring to the culture of lower-class peasant "new immigrants" from eastern and southern Europe, culture she alluded to as "folklore" and "primitive art." Indeed, the idea to preserve what was of value in these folk cultures became a central theme in the writings of settlement workers from the beginning of the twentieth century, and it was usually in relation to "primitive art" and "ethnic folklore" that the idea of "new immigrant" contributions was mentioned. As early as 1904, Addams pointed out that the American "scholar has furnished us with no method by which to discover men, to spiritualize, to understand, to hold intercourse with aliens and receive what they bring."[22] Settlement workers did, however, identify those contributions worth preserving. Settlement houses and neighborhood community centers sponsored craftsmanship and popular art exhibitions. They organized interethnic pageants, in which the immigrant groups were given opportunities to exhibit their artistic products, their songs and dances, wearing their national dresses, before their own children and the American public.[23]

The terms "immigrant contributions" or "immigrant gifts" as applied to peasant folklore seemed to express a positive or rather sympathetic attitude towards immigrant cultures in comparison with the dismissive approach current among most native-born Americans. Semantically these terms meant donating parts of one's cultural assets as a gift, or offering the most valuable part of a certain entity. The meaning of these terms included the notion that a certain selection took place, by which the best, or the most valuable part, of different peasant cultures was chosen for transplantation into the American culture.

The willingness to receive these immigrant contributions seems to have been influenced by three motivations. One was the desire to give America a "popular culture," a "national folklore," which was nonexistent. A longing for more color, variegation, and exoticism had long been felt by Americans who abhorred the monotony and dullness of American urban life.[24] Americans' romantic longing for a national folklore of their own, similar to what they found on their visits to Europe, such as the magnificent carnivals and the popular folklore and artistry revealed in the country markets, was expressed by Jane Addams: "Surely our life is unromantic and prosaic enough, and the glamour of foreign romance and artistic fancy might well transfigure an age and country so commercialized and destitute of art. America is without a native art, a native music." She suggested a solution to this, asking the American scholar to "go man-hunting into these curious human groups called newly arrived immigrants. Could we take these primitive habits (or domestic custom) . . . and give them their significance and place, they would be a wonderful factor for poesy in cities frankly given over to industrialism."[25] Emily G. Balch, a Liberal Progressive from Boston, likewise envisaged that newcomers would "add valuable varieties . . . to a rather puritanical, one-sided culture . . . poor in the power of creating beauty except in the one great field of literature."[26]

This eagerness to absorb peasant primitive art and folklore was based on the assumption that "folk customs are similar in all nations" and that the immigrants' folklore was therefore not an alien element. Liberal Progressives assumed that "our literature and language, our laws and religion, have received their ideals, forms and their very spirit from the same primitive sources from which these newer immigrants derive their own lives." Nevertheless, Addams stipulated that immigrant contributions were desirable "so far as these are consistent with adopting the ideals of the foster land." Liberal Progressives agreed that "it is not asked that those who come shall disown everything they have brought with them, but . . . shall surrender whatever of the old is not in accord, but within that limitation that representatives of every different race and nation must have recognition in this country." In other words, only those foreign artistic and cultural assets that by their very nature could reinforce already existing American tendencies or were appealing for special reasons were welcomed. This attitude revealed an organic concept of culture.[27]

The second reason for the sympathetic attitude of the Hull House group towards immigrant "folklore" and "primitive art" was the desire to give newcomers a good feeling. By showing respect and appreciation for their cultural assets, Addams wished to counterbalance the contemptuous attitude expressed by native-born Americans towards newcomers and their traditions. Above all, she hoped thus to create a more sympathetic atmosphere, to remove their feelings of estrangement or alienation, and to create a sense of attachment and belonging to America. Jill Conway in a study on upper-middle-class women in the settlement movement has even defined immigrants' engagement in popular art at Hull House as a "therapeutic release."[28]

The third motivation was the desire to transfer immigrant sociocultural activities to American institutions. The Hull House group hoped that interethnic festivals and popular art exhibitions sponsored by American volunteer, municipal, and national institutes would gradually replace segregated immigrant cultural activities. As we have seen, this goal was expressed in the Hull House policy of "segregation within integration."[29]

The settlement's desire to preserve immigrant "folklore" and "primitive art" as a unique contribution to American culture raises the serious question of how these immigrant contributions, selected by Americans, could become inalienable assets of American civilization. Immigrants' "folklore" and "primitive art" had been molded by their rural way of life, as well as European cultural traditions. Those newcomers who had grown up in European villages and had been reared on these customs and traditions were able and willing to preserve their peasant culture. Their children, however, would be able to continue at least some of their parents' traditions only if their particular social and cultural milieu were preserved in America. In the absence of ethnic sociocultural segregation, immigrants' "folklore" and "primitive art" would become museum exhibits within one or two generations. Indeed, since this peasant culture could not be preserved without the ethnic milieu and separate cultural and educational institutes, and since the Hull House group was doing its best precisely to eliminate institutional segregation and absorb newcomers into a harmonious society, the whole contribution idea was reduced to a device to make newcomers feel better, while they were gradually relinquishing their traditional way of life and becoming Americans. The upper-middle-class ladies of Hull House had an almost magical belief in the efficacy of personal expressions of good will in changing the nature of the relationship between native-born Americans and newcomers.

The contribution idea was greatly influenced by the writings of William James and Felix Adler. The Hull House group applied their ideas to ethnic groups upon the underlying assumption that every group was merely an aggregation of individuals. Although James elaborated his idea in relation to primitive and sophisticated societies in general rather than in the context of ethnic groups and American society, his pluralistic world view had some implications for the issue of ethnicity.[30]

The condition of variety is an absolute moral good, because it secures varied individual expressions through groups. The most moral universe is that which satisfies as many individual demands as possible through the most inclusive equilibrium of groups. Every group, even the least worthy, should be permitted to express its pecularities. Thus pluralism requires the right of each group to express its distinctiveness. Nevertheless, the right of the group is derived from the freedom of the individual. Thus liberty means the freedom of individuals, and equality means the moral equivalence of groups composed of different individuals. From this James concluded that primitive societies should be treated with respect and noninterference. Yet he did not advocate isolationism but an international equilibrium based on mutual respect and voluntary interaction among groups of different societies or nationalities.

The moral value of variety was intimately connected with William Jame's concept of the evolutionary progress of human societies. Sophisticated societies have a moral responsibility towards the perfection of the human race and its civilization. This moral duty seems to outweigh the moral value of variety. Sophisticated societies as well as primitive ones are the outcome of historical accident. The character and culture of a race or nationality are mainly the result of the kinds of individuals and geniuses born along the centuries, and the sequence of individual geniuses determines the evolution of group differences. Furthermore, the differences between nationalities are also influenced by different inherited temperaments. But it has nothing to do with differences in intelligence between races or nationalities. Individuals of both primitive and sophisticated societies have the same potential mental capacities and intelligence. Sophisticated societies are simply at a culturally higher stage on the ladder of evolutionary progress, and therefore morally superior.

Being committed to the idea of progress, James sought to reconcile the moral value of variety and the supremacy of the best. Although he advocated noninterference and respect towards the peculiarities of every group, he also held that when a cultural clash between primitive and sophisticated societies was inevitable, the claims of civilization outweighed those of savage tribes.

John Dewey and William I. Thomas contributed the psychological and sociological confirmation to James's thesis. Dewey argued that the differences between the savage and the advanced mind lay in occupational differentiation, and "simple" behavior was the response to a simple mode of production. "So fundamental and pervasive is the group of occupational activities that it affords the scheme or pattern of the structural organization of mental traits. Occupations integrate special elements into a functioning whole." Dewey suggested applying this psychological method to sociology, that is, to the interpretation of social institutes and cultural resources. Viewing the problem in sociological terms Thomas argued that "the human race is one, that human mind is everywhere much the same . . . the savage is very close to us indeed, both in his physical and mental makeup." He agreed with Franz Boaz on the principle that "mental activity follows the same laws everywhere." Thus the differences between ethnic groups and Americans do not lie in mental capacity. "The organization of the mind is on the whole alike in different races."[31]

Consequently, the place a certain society occupies on the cultural ladder is not determined by any special virtue and ability of its race. It "has a certain relation to the nature of the disturbances encountered, and . . . the most progressive have had a more vicissitudinous life." This was the major cause of "the different rate and direction of progress in different peoples." Moreover, "the same crisis will not produce the same effect uniformly . . . different groups take steps in culture in a different order." These differences are the result of the general environmental situation, the nature of the arising crisis, and the character of the ideas already possessed by the group. The latter consists of the operation of "attention," namely, "the mental attitude which takes note of the outside world and manipulates it. It's the organ of accommodation." In short, "notwithstanding the similarity in the form of individual mental processes, the expression of mental activity of a community tends to show a characteristic historical development."[32]

Yet as the contemporary anthropologist Franz Boas stated, "culture is an expression of the achievements of the mind, and shows the cumulative effects of the activities of many minds." If, as Thomas argued, "individual variation is of more importance than racial differences," then "the social rather than the biological aspects of the problem" are of utmost importance, and the presence of extraordinary individuals in a group is of major importance.[33]

The cultural qualities of a society are therefore shaped by environment, historical development, and the incidental rate of individual genius. Yet this does not change the fact that different groups occupy different places on the cultural ladder. Jane Addams described this cultural gap as expressed in the different stage of moral evolution of newcomers: "In certain stages of moral evolution a man is incapable of action unless the result will benefit himself or some of his acquaintances, and it is a long step in moral progress to set the good of the many before the interest of the few, and to be concerned for the welfare of a community without hope of any individual return." Recognizing the equal potential of different individuals and groups does not therefore imply the recognition that they have equal cultural value. Primitive and undeveloped groups are rated lower on the scale of social evolutionary progress; the claims of civilization and democracy outweigh those of savage tribes, as well as newcomers.[34]

Felix Adler's philosophy reinforced these ideas. He developed a universal moral code of human beings' behavior. He stated that "we are to revere that which is potential in all these individuals and groups." He considered this kind of reverence towards backward people to be moral conduct of the highest rank. This attitude "of ideally appreciating others, of seeing them in the light of their possible best, and the feeling of love consequent on this vision is the mightiest lever for tranforming evil into good, and for sweetening the embittered lives of men. No greater boon can anyone receive from another than to be helped to think well of himself."[35]

This reverence towards the potential existing in every human being and the idealization of his "spiritual numen" represented only one aspect of Adler's philosophy. Alder did not think that the less advanced peoples should be allowed to remain in their present stage of evolution. He considered it the duty of the more advanced peoples to uplift and to develop the personalities of the undeveloped peoples and elevate them. This responsibility derived from both the "law of levitation" defined by Adler and the goal of achieving the highest stage in the development of the human race towards perfection. Adler considered the law of levitation in the ethical sphere to be contrary to the law of gravitation. "We actually tend to rise from lower to a higher level in proportion as we bend downward to lift those still lower than ourselves."[36]

On the other hand, "the relation of the less developed to the more advanced peoples should be analogous to that of the child toward the parents. . . . The more advanced peoples are to bring to light the spiritual life latent in the backward." The educational task of the former is "divination of what, under right educational influence, they, the undeveloped, may come to mean for humanity." In short, the task of the civilized nations is "to extend the spiritual realm so as to cover backward, undeveloped peoples, so as to embody them in the corpus spiritual of mankind." This correlation between spiritual perfection and the type of personality developed by Western civilization, and the responsibility of the more civilized peoples to civilize the less civilized or uncivilized peoples, therefore makes it unlikely that the expression of respect towards immigrant cultures would entail efforts to preserve and cultivate primitive cultures.[37]

Jane Addams incorporated these ideas into her concept of social democracy, which was an ethical standard of conduct, "to judge all men by one democratic standard." This was a belief "in the essential dignity and equality of all men . . . and resultant sympathy which are the foundation and guarantee of democracy." Applying this concept to intergroup relations, Liberal Progressives advocated respect and toleration towards people of backward societies and their cultures. They held that every member of society, even the least worthy, should be treated with sympathy and upon equal terms. Addams stated the need to recognize "the good in every man even the meanest."[38]

The Hull House group, therefore, saw the major issue to be not the preservation of immigrant cultures but rather the preservation of the dignity of newcomers and their self-respect as human beings. Addams believed, as Alice Hamilton, also a Hull House resident, put it, that "political equality meant little in comparison with social equality." Nevertheless social equality was interpreted in terms of respect for "new immigrants." The Hull House group believed that "the social ostracism of the "Dago," "Polack," "Hunky," . . . was harder to bear than political corruption and rotten city government. Bad government led to wretched conditions, but it did not degrade the poor man in his own eyes." Addams was quoted as saying that "contempt is the greatest crime against one's fellow man."[39]

At the same time, the Hull House group accepted the idea that the more sophisticated societies had moral responsibilities towards human perfection, and the moral duty of the "better element," namely, the more educated element in every society, was to elevate the underdeveloped. This approach said in effect that "no race should predominate except in so far as it has virtue and ability." Interpreting race as synonymous with society meant that the more sophisticated culture would predominate, not because of its inherent superiority, but because American civilization was more advanced as a result of historical and environmental circumstances. Since the laws of evolutionary progress would weigh the scale towards progress, the predominance of the higher culture on the ladder of sociocultural progress would be secured.[40]

Jane Addams applied this concept of cultural progress and human perfectibility to immigrants, when she formulated the mission of Hull House: to educate these people who came from less sophisticated societies and elevate them on the ladder of civilization. From this perspective she viewed segregation and preservation of ethnic cultures as denying newcomers the advantages and resources of civilization, "the impulse beating at the very source of our lives urging us to aid in the race progress." Hull House residents therefore made great efforts to raise and elevate individual newcomers by developing their artistic and musical talents and their intellectual capacities. In return, they expected these Americanized individuals to contribute their cultural gifts to the common fund.[41]

The Hull House group rejected the idea, prevalent in the dominant Anglo-American group, that the American civilization needed to be protected from the threat of inferior immigrants. Irrespective of his cultural background, every member of society had an equal right to contribute according to his personal capacities to the creation of American civilization. This implied a process by which American culture would be shaped as a result of the free interaction between human types of different cultural backgrounds. Nevertheless, these individuals were to be Americanized.[42]

The Bourne-Hapgood group and Liberal Progressives also shared the view that immigrant contributions should be incorporated into American civilization on an individual basis. Both groups agreed that the ideal model of such an individual was a person "passing out of the socio-religious group on intellectual grounds." This pointed to the type of "cosmopolitanism" advocated by both intellectuals and Liberal Progressives in the long run. The Bourne-Hapgood and the Liberal Progressive groups differed, however, in the importance they attached to the role played by the cultural background of newcomers' individual contributions. The former stressed the contributional enrichment from the viewpoint of cultural cross-fertilization, while the latter envisaged the enrichment of America by individual talents and skills.[43]

Like Liberal Progressives, Randolph Bourne considered it the responsibility of every Anglo-American intellectual to work for the "enterprise of integration into which we can all pour ourselves, of a spiritual welding."[44]

The contribution idea as an expression of respect towards newcomers as human beings and as a means of preserving the dignity of the individual newcomer was first articulated by Felix Adler and later adopted by Jane Addams, the Hull House circle, and Liberal Progressives in general. Adler developed the idea, that the immigrant's past should be respected as a means of preserving his or her self-respect, in the program he submitted to the New York Board of Trustees of the Society for Ethical Culture in November 1906.

This idea was implemented in the Neighborhood Guild and the East Side Ethical Club, later called the Madison Street Settlement, headed by Henry Moscowitz, a Romanian Jewish new immigrant.[45]

Liberal Progressives argued that pride in one's ethnic-cultural background was not inconsistent with cultural and social assimilation. As Dewey envisaged, "Our public schools shall teach each factor to respect every other, . . . When every pupil recognized all the factors which have gone into our being, he will continue to prize and reverence that coming from his own past, but will think of it as honored in being simply one factor in forming a whole, nobler and finer than itself."[46] Adler himself served as an example of such an American, who proudly identified himself as a man of Jewish ethnic-racial origin who had left his socioreligious brotherhood. Adler's concept of assimilation included identification with his new nationality and its culture without rejecting the past. He stated that everyone should

> keep in touch with one's racial past, to keep in touch with the roots out of which one sprang, because always the sap of life comes of those roots; it is a part of self-respect not to cut off one's memory, not to wish to bury the past out of sight—a part of self-respect, and it is part of the best kind of spiritual development to know the fountain out of which one has been drawn, to know the past.[47]

Other Americanized Jewish intellectuals echoed the same feelings. They were anxious to preserve their self-respect by emphasizing the cultural background of their contributions to American civilization.[48]

Even though the contribution idea regarding immigrant group cultures was intended to serve as no more than a psychological device, its importance should not be underestimated. Its impact on the self-respect of "new immigrants" was enormous and created a dynamic of its own. It established the principle of "equal value" or the "equal opportunity" of each cultural group to contribute its share to the common American fund. This in turn encouraged "new immigrant" leaders to demand the realization of this principle. Liberal Progressives were (perhaps unintentionally) paving the way for more liberal cultural policies in the future.

The contribution idea also had a profound impact on the Liberal Progressives' self-image. They satisfied their democratic conscience by appearing to legitimize the free interaction of influences on American civilization, upon the principle of what they believed to be fair competition. Their confidence, however, that the law of evolutionary progress would ensure the predominance of the best enabled them to believe that American civilization would successfully maintain its basic characteristics, just as the Anglo-Saxon civilization had succeeded in the British Isles.[49]

# ELEVEN

# THE HULL HOUSE CONCEPT OF AMERICAN NATIONALISM AND CULTURE IN THE SPECTRUM OF CONTEMPORARY VIEWS

The ambivalence found in the writings of Liberal Progressives on the nature of American nationalism and culture makes it difficult to determine to which of the three concepts prevailing around the turn of the twentieth century—pluralism, cosmopolitanism, or Anglo-Americanism—the Liberal Progressive concept of nationalism and culture best belongs. For example, Liberal Progressives could be interpreted as pluralists on the basis of some of their statements. John Dewey wrote that "each national group should be given an opportunity to cultivate its own distinctive individuality and maintain its distinctive literary and artistic traditions."[1] In the same vein Jane Addams called for a realistic definition of American nationalism based not "upon a common national history and land occupation . . . not upon a consciousness of homogeneity but upon a respect for variation . . . the future patriotism of America must not depend so much upon conformity as upon respect for variety."[2] Grace Abbott argued further that, "if encouraged to express his own characteristics, the Slav and the Italian would give to American life [his] . . . self expression . . . given opportunity, English, Irish, Polish, German, Scandinavian, Russian, Magyar, Lithuanian, and all other races of the earth can live together, each making his own contribution to our common life."[3]

Other statements seem to associate these writers more with the cosmopolitan concept. Dewey argued that "our unity . . . must be a unity created by drawing out and composing into a harmonious whole the best, the most characteristic, which each contributing race and people has to offer."[4] Addams and Abbott praised American new cosmopolitanism and internationalism: "it is to be hoped that we shall have the courage to be unlike Europe in both our nationalism and our internationalism."[5]

These writers criticized Anglo-Saxonism on numerous occasions. Abbott and Addams disapproved the efforts to mold newcomers along the Anglo-Saxon model.[6] Addams felt uneasy observing "the somewhat feeble attempt to boast of Anglo-Saxon achievement . . . [and] This lack of a more cosmopolitan standard."[7] Dewey likewise believed that "any one who assumes that one racial strain, any one component culture, no matter how early settled it was in our territory, or how effective it has been in its own land, is to furnish a pattern to which all other strains and cultures are to conform, he is a traitor to an American Nationalism.''[8]

However, when we examine the various ideas expounded both implicitly and explicitly by the Hull House group—their views on community as a harmonized-holist entity; their views on cultural and social assimilation and ethnic policies; the notions of environmentalism, evolutionary progress, and the international nature of American nationalism; the contribution idea; and America's ''manifest destiny''—all these add up to a coherent concept of the role newcomers and their cultures should occupy in America, and therefore also of the nature of American nationalism and culture.

Although Liberal Progressive rhetoric seemed cosmopolitan and pluralist at times, its seeming pluralism was due to some confusion over the very definition of the term ''cultural pluralism.'' Contemporary and later scholars often overlooked the general context within which these apparently pluralist ideas were expressed and the consequent policies executed. As we have seen, Liberal Progressives considered pluralism merely a sociocultural fact, a description of the present situation, not a norm or their future vision of America.[9] The Hull House group also differed with pluralism on such fundamental issues as the role and pace of environmentalism, the laws of evolutionary progress of human societies, and the interpretation of the idea of democracy. These differences were reflected both in their views on assimilation and their concept of American nationalism and culture, as shown in previous chapters, and draw a clear line between Hull House and pluralist thinkers.

During the years 1890 to 1919, which are within the scope of this study, Liberal Progressives shared, with reservations, a monist rather than a pluralist world view. John Dewey himself, who can be seen as the philosopher of the Chicago Liberal Progressive group, did not consider himself a pluralist.[10] In a letter to William James in 1903 he admitted ''that it may be the contrived working of the Hegelian bacillus of reconciliation of contradictions in me, that makes me feel as if the conception of process gives a basis for uniting the truths of pluralism and monism.''[11] Indeed, it seems that Dewey considered himself a monist rather than a pluralist, pointing out that ''if this harmony exists, we seem to have not a sheer plurality but already an organized system; if it does not we have only chaos, no universe.''[12] Dewey's objections were also formal: pluralism as a matter of definition and of applying the definition to reality.

Dewey's philosophy has indeed been described in terms of the uniting of opposites, as reflected in George E. Axtelle's definition: ''Dewey's philosophy falls into none of these categories [monist or pluralist], and if it were not a barbarism and a contradiction in terms, the label might be ''pluralist monism . . .'' He saw the world both organized and continuous, and as varied, creative, individualized.''[13] Other scholars agreed with Axtelle that ''Dewey's relationship to pluralism was at best problematic." Seymour W. Itzkoff and Jay Wissot wrote that "Dewey implied that the pluralist society does not exist as an end in itself." Of course the definition of cultural pluralism is problematic and may be interpreted differently in different historical contexts. But the judgment of Dewey's contemporary and the philosopher of pluralism Horace M. Kallen should be considered seriously. Kallen saw William James and not John Dewey as the pluralist of pragmatism. Kallen realized that Dewey's "sense of the solidarity and continuity of the ethnic groups was much weaker than Bourne's." Yet he misinterpreted the meaning of Dewey's idea of hyphenism, assuming it was close to his.[14]

The Chicago Liberal Progressive group viewed pluralism as a temporary situation to be replaced by harmony, unity, and coherence. As Lucia and Morton White show, Dewey's idea of community before the 1920s, which was determined by his "Hegelian view of history," was heavily loaded with a preindustrial vision of a unified community. As long as he remained committed to the idea that close interpersonal communication and a thoroughly unified social organism were indispensable to the survival of American society and democracy, he was not a pluralist.[15]

Jane Addams and the Hull House circle shared Dewey's idea of community. Addams insisted that residents of Hull House were "bound to regard the entire life of their city as organic, to make an effort to unify it, and to protest against its over-differentiation."[16]

William I. Thomas challenged cultural pluralism openly. Disputing the ideas of Louis Brandeis, Alexander M. Duskin, and Isaac B. Berkson, he rejected the underlying assumption upon which they built their theories.[17]

It is possible that during the 1920s and the 1930s Liberal Progressives lost their belief in the chances to realize their idea of community and became reconciled with the idea of diversity within unity, developed by Robert E. Park. But even Park interpreted diversity in terms of occupational-cultural differences within a system of organic solidarity, not ethnic-cultural diversity.[18]

However, although they were divided on essentials, the Hull House circle shared some of the views expressed by pluralists. Both groups insisted that newcomers and their cultures should be respected and appreciated and were opposed to the policy of accelerated assimilation carried out by the Americanization movement. They objected to pressures for the immediate repudiation of immigrant languages, traditions, and customs as well as to the demand for immediate desegregation of immigrants and dissolution of their communities. It was these views, which were shared by pluralists, that obscured the real Hull House vision of America and made it seem ambivalent and inconsistent, especially since the Hull House circle and pluralists also adopted similar policies in their institutions. Hull House formed ethnic clubs and developed ethnic cultural programs similar in some respects to those of immigrant community centers. Yet the ethnic policies in the centers represented a certain idea of the immigrant's way of life and adjustment to the American environment, whereas Hull House's policies were designed as temporary measures to ensure the eventual unification of American society along lines totally unacceptable to pluralists: their aim was to establish favorable conditions for cultural transformation, the dissolution of ethnic segregation, and the political, social, and cultural incorporation of newcomers into the general community.

Finally, cultural pluralism as an alternative to contemporary ideas on American nationalism and culture did not become a public issue before the 1920s, and the term did not enter the American vocabulary before that time. Except for a few intellectuals such as Randolph Bourne and the Hapgood brothers, Kallen's articles published in 1915, in which this alternative idea was first expounded, did not attract public attention. Nor did the Chicago Liberal Progressive group respond publicly to these articles. (John Dewey merely comments in an unpublished letter to Kallen.)[19]

Since Liberal Progressive thinking before the 1920s evidently does not fit the label pluralism, we should consider the Hull House circle's concept of nationalism and culture in relation to the other two prevailing concepts—a more moderate version of the idea of Anglo-American conformity.

The members of the Hull House circle did not ignore the idea of cosmopolitanism and its symbol, the melting pot, as they ignored Kallen's idea of a "federation of nationalities." The Liberal Progressives' rhetoric as well as their idea of community and premises on environmentalism, the evolutionary progress of human societies, American internationalism and the idea of universal brotherhood, sociohumanitarian democracy, and the "manifest destiny" of American nationalism—all point to the conclusion that Liberal Progressives were cosmopolitanists. Nonetheless, it seems that they were cosmopolitanists only as far as the fusing of races and ethnic groups was concerned. Their cultural cosmopolitanism was a matter of tactics and rhetoric. John Dewey even acknowledged that "the theory of the Melting Pot always gave me rather a pang. To maintain that all the constituent elements, geographical, racial and cultural in the United States should be put in the same pot and turned into a uniform and unchanging product is distasteful. . . . The concept of uniformity and unanimity in culture is rather repellent."[20] However, the context of this statement indicated that he was rejecting the notion that all newcomers should be molded into Anglo-Saxons. Indeed, the melting pot idea was used by contemporaries to express two different conceptions of American nationalism, the cosmopolitan and Anglo-Saxon, and Dewey pointed out that although he himself "never did care for the melting pot metaphor," nonetheless "genuine assimilation to one another not to Anglo-Saxondom—seems to be essential to an American."[21]

Both he and Adams also proclaimed their dislike of conformity, of "a uniform and unchanging product" or a "drilled homogeneity," which "promoted a standardization favorable of mediocrity." At the same time, they did not condemn conformity in itself. Everything depended on what was conformed to and why. Narrow-minded conformity based upon one strain in American society was bad. But the harmony created out of a cross-fertilization of individuals of different cultures was a step up in the scale of social evolution of human cultures, because individual pluralism secured a more abundant and rich culture than one created by individuals of the same racial strain: "Things act and react upon one another, and in so doing are reciprocally transformed. This interactive relationship between things creates unity, and harmony on a higher scale."[22]

While Liberal Progressives clearly stated their concept of the international nature of American nationalism, their statements on the nature of American civilization were more equivocal. They seem to have defined American civilization to be cosmopolitan or international by virtue of its being a branch of Western civilization. Furthermore, the principles of democracy made it necessary to accept "new immigrants" as equals, recognizing their right to participate in the shaping of American civilization. As William I. Thomas argued, "We must make the immigrants a working part of our system of life, ideal and political, as well as economic, or lose the character of our culture. Self-preservation makes this necessary; the fact that they bring valuable additions to our culture makes it desirable."[23] At the same time, the need for like-mindedness for the survival and functioning of democracy and the moral duty of the more advanced elements in American society implied that the more sophisticated upper-class culture could and should be dominant. Chapter 10, on the Liberal Progressive view of the role of immigrant contributions in the American culture and its expression in Hull House cultural programs, has confirmed this interpretation. As Emily G. Balch put it, American culture "must be a spiritual fusion . . . [and] assimilation—the growth into similarity in speech, ways and thoughts."[24]

Although Americanizers and Liberal Progressives agreed on the inevitability of a unified, coherent society for the survival and functioning of American society and its democratic form of government, they were divided on the content and policies of assimilation. Liberal Progressives, as we have seen, advocated cultural and structural assimilation. The paradox of the Americanization movement lay in its demand for unity, cultural conformity, and acculturation without racial, social, or structural assimilation. They insisted that newcomers give up their languages, heritages, and customs upon arrival, learn English and civics, dissolve their ethnic colonies and subcommunities, and disperse throughout the country as individuals, without being integrated structurally. Both Americanizers and Liberal Progressives agreed on the need for an underlying cultural consensus, but while Americanizers insisted on strict conformity or a thoroughly uniform consensus, Liberal Progressives preferred a looser or more liberal definition, namely, like-mindedness. Yet both thought of America in terms of an Anglo-American civilization.

Americanizers were not directly involved in the controversy on environmentalism versus heredity. Although they were torn between heredity, enthnocentrism, and environmentalism in practice, they did not reject environmentalism altogether. Indeed, the whole idea of the Americanization movement—the education of newcomers—was based on the belief that newcomers were capable of changing and adjusting to their new environment and that the American institutions and environment could influence newcomers. Thus, despite considerable doubts about the chances and desirability of assimilation in general, the Americanization movement was engaged in a comprehensive semicompulsory acculturation effort, in cooperation with federal authorities.[25]

Hull House and Americanizers also disagreed on the principles of sociohumanitarian democracy in integrating newcomers into American society, that is, on the belief that newcomers should be welcomed as equals as a prerequisite for successful assimilation not only into the political but also into the social system. Americanizers were willing to accept newcomers upon equal terms by recognizing their right to citizenship. They did not wish to accept them as equals socially and approve structural assimilation, namely, intermarriage and the fusing of both Americans and newcomers into a new race. Although Americanizers were resigned to the inevitable blending of all nationalities in America in the far future, they were reluctant to accept newcomers into their primary groups and social organizations. Their idea of the role of the Anglo-American Protestant elite as acculturators rationalized the segregation and preservation of the Anglo-American Protestant group and its control. Liberal Progressives developed instead the idea of virtue and merit and the control of the "better element," namely, the enlightened members of the disinterested (upper) middle class.

The very fact that Liberal Progressives participated in the Americanization movement points to the consensus they shared with the movement. Although they were not the leading force in the movement, they were deeply involved in its activities on local, state, and federal levels. Jane Addams was a member of the National Committee of One Hundred, which was established in 1916 by the federal Bureau of Education upon the recommendation of a national conference of educators, businessmen, newspaper editors, representatives of patriotic societies, social and settlement workers, and labor organizations to coordinate and control the Americanization movement. The Immigrants' Protective League under the direction of Grace Abbott and Sophonisba P. Breckinridge, both members of the Hull House circle, cooperated with the movement as did Hull House and other settlement houses in Chicago and throughout the country. Although the league had little influence in the national and Illinois state committees organized by the Americanization movement, it was influential in the Joint Committee on the Education and Naturalization of the Foreign-Born Adults and in the Joint Committee on Americanization organized in Chicago. The former was established in summer 1916 by the league in cooperation with Chicago City Club, representing Chicago's "better element." This committee was joined by other local clubs and organizations of the Chicago upper middle class. The newcomers were represented by the Association of Foreign Languages Newspapers. The Joint Committee on Americanization was also composed of representatives of upper-middle-class clubs and organizations, and the newcomers were represented by the Foreign-Born Citizens Committee and the Association of Foreign Languages Newspapers.[26]

These two joint committees differed from their counterparts throughout the country in formulating what the league considered "sympathetic and constructive Americanization." This included consulting the immigrant leaders represented by the above-mentioned organizations before formulating the committees' policies, and cooperating with immigrant organizations in implementing the policies upon equal terms. Unlike the Americanization programs in other parts of the country, these committees' programs were based upon the principle of face-to-face relations rather than the mass approach of the "red-blooded policy of Americanization." Hull House served as a model of sympathetic and constructive Americanization. From the outset, Hull House held classes to teach newcomers English, and after the naturalization law of 1906 the house also conducted naturalization and citizenship classes. In 1912 it established its School of Citizenship. The director of the school, Charles Schwartz, a young Jewish lawyer, was chairman of the Americanization Committee of the City Club and later chairman of the Joint Committee on Americanization in Chicago and on the state level. He published in 1916 a pamphlet containing the material taught in the Hull House civics classes. The school was advertised in the foreign-language press and through cards and handbills circulated in the neighborhood. Gradually other settlements and organizations, such as the YMCA, began to hold similar classes. In 1915 the public school authorities started classes in citizenship in two of the public schools. Ten other evening schools had similar classes conducted by teachers, including Hull House residents.[27]

The Hull House circle criticized the Americanization movement from within. They rejected the compulsory methods of Americanizing newcomers through concentrated public pressure—immediate repudiation of ethnic identity and immigrant cultures and dissolution of immigrant subcommunities. They considered these methods cruel, undemocratic, and in any case counterproductive and advocated instead an attitude of toleration and respect and a policy of gradual assimilation. The Americanization movement wished to take a shortcut to acculturation, while the Hull House circle did not think shortcuts were possible or desirable. Unlike Americanizers who believed that acculturation could be completed within one generation, the Hull House circle argued that it was a three-generation process that depended upon a policy of understanding towards immigrants and their cultures.[28]

These differences in acculturation policies can be traced to a different evaluation of immigrant cultures and immigrant motives for immigration. Although both Americanizers and Liberal Progressives shared the view that an apperception mass was a prerequisite for the survival of democracy, Americanizers had little confidence in the willingness of newcomers to become acculturated. By contrast Liberal Progressives assumed that, since immigrant cultures and American civilization had "common primitive sources," it would be easy for immigrants to adopt American values, ideas, sentiments, and ways of doing things and that since they immigrated voluntarily, they would want to become acculturated. These assumptions explain their sympathetic attitude towards newcomers. Americanizers, on the other hand, not only found essential differences between immigrant and American cultures but also suspected that the immigrants came to America because of the economic and political advantages it afforded, and intended to preserve and cultivate their ethnic-cultural identity on American soil. These arguments justified, they believed, a policy of compulsory acculturation and the demand that newcomers give up their foreign languages and cultures as well as their allegiance to their homelands as a prerequisite for citizenship.

Moreover, unlike Americanizers, Liberal Progressives believed that, by recognizing newcomers' cultures as valuable and their right to influence American civilization through their contributions, they would enable newcomers to feel that they were not betraying their ancestors and their selfhood while they were making the transition from one culture to the other. Francis Hackett, an Irish immigrant who was a Hull House resident, expressed this idea.

> America dawned for me in a social settlement. It dawned for me as a civilization and a faith. . . . It was the first place where I found a flame by which the melting pot melts. . . . The place bristled with hyphens. But the Americanism was of a kind that opened to the least pressure from without. . . . To inherit him [Lincoln] becomes for the European not an abandonment of old loyalties, but a summary of them in a new.[29]

The crucial issue, however, when examining the Liberal Progressives' views in relation to the Americanization movement is what role they expected the Anglo-American strain to play in the harmonious orchestra of America. Liberal Progressives clearly rejected Anglo-Saxon racism and chauvinism, prejudice, and ethnic discrimination; they criticized the underlying assumption, typical of Anglo-Americans, that the United States was "an imaginary

179

homogeneous Anglo-Saxon population.'' Nonetheless, they did not reject their Anglo-Saxon heritage and fully recognized America's indebtedness to the influences that had shaped American political and cultural traditions.[30] As Emily G. Balch pointed out,

> at the time of the Revolution fully one-fifth of the population spoke some other language than English, and . . . not over one-half were of Anglo-Saxon blood. . . . But in spite of all temptations to belong to other nations, the background and basis of the population is and always has been essentially English . . . the strain that has predominated, the men that have shaped and led the nation, have been mainly English or English-speaking. . . . America . . . is essentially English in blood and more so in literary and political traditions.[31]

Liberal Progressives believed that they were living up to these traditions in following their concept of assimilation. Balch spoke for all Liberal Progressives in rejecting the view expressed by a Polish American priest that ''there is no such thing as an American nation.''[32] She responded to his idea, arguing that ''in spite of my Polish interlocutor's belief that America is not a nation, it has in truth the deepest right to consider itself such. It is an organic whole, . . . colored by one tradition and bound together . . . by one conception of the country's mission and of the means—liberty, enlightenment and prosperity—by which that mission is to be accomplished.''[33]

This view of American civilization led Liberal Progressives to reject the Americanizers' belief that the right to participate in shaping that civilization should be restricted, that it was ''natural and proper'' that the essential framework of American government and culture, which were shaped by the first settlers, should ''be left in the hands of the descendants of those who originally introduced them and carried them on,'' a demand that Liberal Progressives considered undemocratic.

> There is a fear that the control will slip from the hands of those who have enjoyed it from the beginning of our country. . . . You cannot admit that a proprietary class, once created, can continue by right of inheritance. . . . We cannot go on in this country and simply assume that the descendants of the same people are going to continue as a matter of course in control.[34]

Thus Liberal Progressives rejected compulsory acculturation while believing that the American social, economic, and cultural systems and Americanizing influences made acculturation inevitable. Emily G. Balch noted that ''the different immigrant groups neutralize one another's influence'' and that immigrants were much more influenced by the Anglo-American model than the ''old settled American community'' was modified by immigrant influences.[35] She summed up the Liberal Progressive confidence in the American environment in what she called the ''laws of imitation.''

The choice between customs in which men differ is sometimes selective—a conscious or unconscious acceptance of the better adapted of the different copies. More often, perhaps, the choice is determined, not by intrinsic superiority, but by some general rule of preference. In a state of society where custom reigns, the preference is for the old and established, as such; where fashion and progress are the ruling ideas, what is novel is preferred for that reason. Again, that which has prestige of any sort is regularly preferred . . . the socially inferior copies the socially superior; backward nations, the leading nation of the day; the minority, the majority, and so on . . . under the joint influence of convenience, ambition, and the natural human desire to be like other people, and especially to be like those who occupy the high seats . . . the unifying change goes on.[36]

Supported by the theories of Felix Adler and William James as well as sociologists, Liberal Progressives were confident that the more sophisticated culture would predominate,[37] although they warned that "no race should predominate except in so far as it has virtue and ability. . . . They [have] got to deserve the control if they are going to have it."[38] Nevertheless, Liberal Progressives did not intend to leave the issue to the free interplay of natural forces. The need for like-mindedness for the survival and functioning of democracy, along with the moral duty of the more advanced elements in society to elevate the less advanced or the underprivileged, gave the "better element" both the responsibility and the right to interfere in the process of acculturation. As Jane Addams stated, "Americanism was then regarded as a great cultural task and we eagerly sought to invent new instruments and methods with which to undertake it."[39]

# AFTERWORD

## MYTH AND REALITY

The myth that developed around Hull House's leaders, its relations with the immigrant communities, and its cultural orientation does not accord with the realities that we have examined in detail. The extent of these relations was exaggerated and Hull House's idea of American and ethnic cultures misinterpreted. The myth of Hull House prevailed in Progressive circles, but no traces of such a myth could be found among the mass of immigrants themselves. Indeed, the myth of Jane Addams's saintly mission among the poverty-stricken immigrants seems to have assuaged the sense of guilt experienced by the American "better element" when confronted by the ills of American society.

Hull House, as a Liberal Progressive institution, failed to carry out its goal of becoming an influential factor in the neighborhood by cooperating with middle-class immigrant leaders and "controlling them through alliance." Hull House failed also to turn itself into the major neighborhood community center and to accelerate the assimilation of "new immigrants" into the American mainstream. Only gradually did Hull House and other Liberal Progressive leaders recognize the reality of persistent ethnic identity and become reconciled with this reality.

As we have seen, Liberal Progressives were faithful to the traditional liberal Anglo-American concept of American nationalism and culture. They rejected Anglo-Saxon racism and criticized Americanizers' chauvinism. They considered simple nationalities, or ethnicity, a lower stage in the evolution of human societies and praised the harmony of internationalist America as the highest stage of development. However, in this period when the ideas of nativism and semicompulsory Americanization according to the narrow European concept of nationalism adopted by the proponents of the so-called Anglo-Saxon conformity were dominant, Liberal Progressives may be seen as conservative—or at least traditionalist—in their adherence to the idea of universal or international nationalism in America. For the Liberal Progressives the uniqueness of American nationalism was its being cosmopolitan or international in the tradition of the old idea *e pluribus unum*, interpreted as unity out of diversity. They anticipated that in due time a new American nationality would emerge out of the racial melting pot.[1]

Paradoxically, Liberal Progressives wanted this new unity to preserve American institutions and culture as they had "grown out of American experience and Anglo-Saxon traditions"—the English language and the Anglo-American-oriented cultural patterns. Sooner or later newcomers would come to "share the most valuable products of American civilization." They still considered this American civilization to be cosmopolitan because it was based on a universal Western civilization and influenced by immigrants' individual contributions. According to their vision America was the true heir to the Hellenistic, Roman, and English empires in fulfilling its mission to the world by creating a cosmopolitan civilization, just as the Hellenistic, Roman, and English cosmopolitan civilizations had originally been national cultures adopted—voluntarily or involuntarily—by different national groups. America's cosmopolitan civilization would therefore be essentially Anglo-American, but Liberal Progressives believed that the major difference between it and former cosmopolitan civilizations lay in the condition of freedom and equality that the American civilization offered its cosmopolitan population.[2]

Liberal Progressives used the contribution idea to reconcile their recognition that the United States was already "an area of cultural characterization" that had a legitimate right to preserve the character of its culture, with the right of newcomers to participate in the shaping of American civilization. As we have seen, John Dewey and Jane Addams interpreted the contribution idea to mean that immigrants should be given equal opportunities to influence and shape American civilization by contributing their individual endowments, while William I. Thomas added that these immigrant contributions would be accepted as "valuable additions to our culture," that is, to the already articulated American civilization. Yet Liberal Progressives were confident that the best elements, namely, the more developed Anglo-American civilization, would predominate. In the long run the same civilization, which nativists and Americanizers called Anglo-American, and Liberal Progressives called international or cosmopolitan, would prove its qualities by influencing individuals of different ethnic-cultural backgrounds. The real contribution would not be isolated elements of immigrant cultures, but rather the integration of the talents, skills, and creativity of Americanized newcomers as individuals into the larger entity of American civilization, thus making it cosmopolitan in that sense.[3]

The Liberal Progressive concept of assimilation therefore emerged as an alternative to the current Anglo-American concept of American nationalism and culture, under the influence of the intellectual climate of the Progressive Era, its social thinking, philosophy, and values. Hull House presented it as a humanistic-democratic option to what they considered an inhuman and undemocratic concept of assimilation.

The Liberal Progressive concept of assimilation was considered cosmopolitan by contemporaries and pluralist by some later scholars. The contemporary impression arose because the Liberal Progressive rhetoric was largely cosmopolitan, and contemporaries believed that the controversy on the preferable type of assimilation before the 1920s was between Americanizers and their concept of Anglo-American conformity, and Liberal Progressives and their cosmopolitan (or melting pot) concept of American society and culture. The pluralist impression arose because, as has been stated, before the 1920s the boundaries between the concepts of cosmopolitanism and pluralism were often confused and undefined. Kallen contributed to clarifying the two terms in the early 1920s, by stressing the differences between brotherhood and fellowship, cosmopolitanism, and universalism. Liberal Progressives interpreted these two sets of terms as synonymous, while pluralists distinguished between them. For the former, brotherhood and cosmopolitanism equated equality with sameness, through racial, social, and cultural cross-fertilization; while for the latter, fellowship and universalism meant "equal and different," the inherent value of differences, and the need to perfect and preserve them through cultural pluralism.

What made the effort to define the Liberal Progressives' concept of assimilation even more complicated was that they adopted a cosmopolitan view of American society, while their idea of culture was imbued with the concept of the evolutionary progress of cultural systems and the predominance of the more advanced and sophisticated ones over the less developed. The contribution idea was advanced to reconcile their cosmopolitan view of society with their notion of the Anglo-American (or Anglo-Saxon) civilization. American civilization was by definition cosmopolitan in the sense that it was a part of Western civilization and because the individual contributions of Americanized and acculturated immigrant intellectuals were welcomed.

It can be concluded, therefore, that Hull House leaders did not have a pluralist view of society during the years 1890 to 1919. Yet their concept of humanitarian social democracy and their benign policies of assimilation created a dynamic that unintentionally paved the way for a more pluralist view of society in the 1930s. Their opposition to the compulsory eradication of differences, their insistence that immigrant cultures be tolerated, contributed to the redefinition of liberalism in the 1930s. It was the inner logic of these attitudes that advanced the cause of pluralism.

# NOTES

## Introduction

1. John Higham, *Strangers in the Land: Patterns of American Nativism, 1860–1925* (New Brunswick, N.J., 1955), 9, 19–34; Hans Kohn, *American Nationalism: An Interpretative Essay* (New York, 1957), 139–75; John Higham, *Send These to Me: Jews and Other Immigrants in Urban America* (New York, 1957), 3–4, 20, 29–66, 225–28; Barbara M. Solomon, *Ancestors and Immigrants: A Changing New England Tradition* (Chicago, 1956), 1–22; Milton M. Gordon, "Assimilation in America: Theory and Reality," *Daedalus* 90 (1961): 265–74; Philip Gleason, "The Melting Pot: Symbol of Fusion or Confusion," *American Quarterly* 16 (1964): 20–46; Arthur Mann, *The One and the Many: Reflections on the American Identity* (Chicago, 1979), 46–136; Leo Pfeffer, "American Individualism and Horace Kallen's Idea," in Horace M. Kallen, *Cultural Pluralism and the American Idea* (Philadelphia, 1956), 159–64.

2. David F. Bowers, ed., *Foreign Influences in American Life* (Princeton, N.J., 1944), 45; Nathan Glazer, "Ethnic Groups in America: From National Culture to Ideology," in Morris Berger et al., *Freedom and Control in Modern Society* (New York, 1964), 161–66.

3. Higham, *Strangers in the Land*, 32–34, 86–97; Higham, *Send These to Me*, 37–45; Solomon, *Ancestors and Immigrants*, 23–102; Henry P. Fairchild, "The Melting Pot Mistake," in Benjamin M. Zeigler, ed., *Immigration* (Boston, 1953), 19–25; Gordon, "Assimilation in America," 263–74.

4. Higham, *Strangers in the Land*, 131–93; Solomon, *Ancestors and Immigrants*, 1–22; Milton M. Gordon, *Assimilation in American Life: The Role of Race, Religion, and National Origins* (New York, 1964), 84–114; Emory S. Bogardus, "Cultural Pluralism and Acculturation," *Sociology and Social Research* 34 (November-December 1949): 125–27.

5. Higham, *Strangers in the Land*, 97–218; Higham, *Send These to Me*, 45–53; Solomon, *Ancestors and Immigrants*, 60–171; E. A. Goldenweiser, "Walker's Theory of Immigration," *American Journal of Sociology* 18 (1912): 342–51; Mann, *One and the Many*, 125–35; Joseph Lee, "Assimilation and Nationality," *Survey*, January 1908, 1453–55.

6. Higham, *Strangers in the Land*, 9, 32–33, 195–217; Kohn, *American Nationalism*, 139–75; Edward G. Hartmann, *The Movement to Americanize the Immigrant* (New York, 1948), 13–37, 267–76; Henry P. Fairchild, "The Restriction of Immigration," *American Economic Review* 12, supplement (March 1912): 53–63; "Dis-

cussion on Restriction of Immigration,'' ibid., 63–78; Bogardus, ''Cultural Pluralism and Acculturation,'' 125–27; R. Fred Wacker, ''Assimilation and Cultural Pluralism in American Social Thought,'' *Phylon* 40 (1949): 325–33.

7. Joseph Leftwich, *Israel Zangwill* (London, 1957), 251–59; Maurice Wohlegelern-ter, *Israel Zangwill* (New York, 1964), 175–86; Elsie B. Adams, *Israel Zangwill* (New York, 1971), 107–32; John S. Mizrer, ''Israel Zangwill: Between Orthodoxy and Assimilation,'' Ph.D. dissertation, University of Pennsylvania, 1966, 135–70.

8. David A. Hollinger, ''Ethnic Diversity, Cosmopolitanism, and the Emergence of the American Liberal Intelligentsia,'' *American Quarterly* 28 (May, 1975): 133–51; Wacker, ''Assimilation and Cultural Pluralism,'' 325–33; Higham, *Send These to Me,* 211–12; Horace M. Kallen, ''Democracy versus the Melting Pot,'' in *Culture and Democracy in the United States* (New York, 1970), 67–125; Gordon, *Assimilation in American Life,* 132–59.

9. Robert A. Woods, ed., *Americans in Process: A Study of the North and West Ends* (Boston, 1902); Robert A. Woods, ed., *The City Wilderness: A Study of the South End* (New York, 1893); Robert A. Woods, *The Neighborhood in Nation-Building* (Boston, 1923); Robert A. Woods and Albert J. Kennedy, *The Zone of Emergence* (Cambridge, Mass., 1962); B. M. Solomon, *Ancestors and Immigrants,* 63, 70, 77–78, 136, 141–43; Robert A. Woods and Albert J. Kennedy, *The Settlement Horizon: A National Estimate* (New York, 1922), 331.

10. B. M. Solomon, *Ancestors and Immigrants,* 80, 131, 141–43; George C. White, ''Social Settlements and Immigrant Neighbors, 1886–1914,'' *Social Service Review* 33 (1959): 58–59; Alvin Kogut, ''The Settlements and Ethnicity: 1840–1914,'' *Social Work* 17 (May 1972): 26–27; Woods, *City Wilderness,* 38, 51, 110, 233–35, 307; Robert A. Woods, ''The University Settlement Idea,'' in Jane Addams et al., *Philanthropy and Social Progress* (Boston, 1893), 63–66; Robert A. Woods, ''University Settlements: Their Point and Drift,'' *Quarterly Journal of Economics* 14 (October 1899): 73–78; Robert A. Woods, ''The Clod Stirs,'' *Survey,* March 1902, 1929; Woods, *Americans in Process,* 50–51, 69, 146, 317–21, 358–70, 372–82; Robert A. Woods, ''Social Work: A New Profession,'' *International Journal of Ethics* 16 (October 1905): 25, 30–32, 38; Robert A. Woods, ''The Neighborhood in Social Reconstruction,'' *American Journal of Sociology* 19 (1914): 586–87; Andover House Association, Circular 9, Report for the Year 1892–93, South End House Records, Boston; South End House Association, Reports of the Settlement for the Years 1896–1921, South End House Records, Boston; J. Lee, ''Assimilation and Nationality,'' 1453–55.

11. Allen F. Davis, *American Heroine: The Life and Legend of Jane Addams* (London, 1973), 198–211; *Evening Post* (Chicago), 4 March 1908; *Evening Sun* (New York), 27 September 1912, both in Addams Newspaper Clippings, Jane Addams Papers, Swarthmore College Peace Collection, hereafter SCPC.

12. *Times* (Pittsburgh), 14 May 1895; *Ledger* (Philadelphia), 1 July 1895; *Herald* (Syracuse), 30 March 1896; unknown-newspaper clipping, 17 October 1903; *Herald* (Washington, D.C.), 8 September 1912; *Advance,* 18 September 1913; *American Magazine* 67 (September 1906); and *Current Literature,* April 1916; all in Addams Newspaper Clippings; *Wyoming Press,* 24 February 1906, Taylor Newspaper Clippings, Graham Taylor Papers, Newberry Library, Chicago; *News Tribune* (Duluth, Minn.), 18 April 1906, Taylor Newspaper Clippings; A. F. Davis, *American Heroine,* 198–207.

13. Graham Taylor, "Jane Addams: Interpreter," *Review of Reviews* (December 1909): 688–94; *Record Herald*, 3 December 1909, Addams Newspaper Clippings, SCPC; Graham Taylor, "Jane Addams: Neighbor and Citizen," pamphlet, February 1936, 3–9.

14. Jane Addams, "The Friendship of Settlement Work," *Charities*, 28 March 1903, 315–16; Jane Addams, "The Chicago Settlements and Social Unrest," *Charities and the Commons*, 2 May 1908, 155–67.

15. *Advance*, 18 September 1913; *Sunday Magazine*, 19 April 1908; *Current Literature*, August 1910; Kenneth O. Morgan, "The Legend of Saint Jane," *Historical Biography*, 13 June 1975, 648–49; *Christ Science Monitor*, 22 November 1912; *Public Ledger* (Philadelphia), 16 March 1908, *Herald* (Washington, D.C.), 5 and 26 April 1908; all newspapers in Addams Newspaper Clippings, SCPC.

16. Steven J. Diner, "Department and Discipline: The Department of Sociology at the University of Chicago, 1892–1920, *Minerva* 13 (Winter 1975): 514–53; Martin Bulmer, *The Chicago School of Sociology* (Chicago, 1984); By-laws of University of Chicago Settlement, box 1, folder 3c, Mary E. McDowell Papers, Chicago Historical Society, hereafter CHS; University of Chicago Settlement Committee, 1894–1902, box 1, folder 3b, McDowell Papers.

17. Hull House Board of Trustees, Minutes of the Board for 1895–1915, Hull House Papers, University of Illinois Archives, Chicago.

18. John W. Leonard, ed., *Woman's Who's Who of America: 1914/1915* (New York, 1915), 33–34, 38–39, 124, 912; Erma C. Lee, ed., *The Biographical Cyclopaedia of American Women* (New York, 1925), 1–7; Edward T. James et al., *Notable American Women, 1607–1950* (Cambridge, Mass., 1971), 1:2–4, 16–22, 233–36, 2:462–64, 3:697–99; James T. White, *The National Cyclopaedia of American Biography* (New York, 1956), 54–55, 581; Morris Janowitz, ed., *William I. Thomas on Social Organization and Social Personality* (Chicago, 1966), i–lviii; George Herbert Mead, "The Social Settlement: Its Basis and Function," *University of Chicago Record* 12 (1908): 108–10; John Dewey, "The School as Social Center," in National Education Association, *Proceedings* (1902), 373–83; Jane Addams and William I. Thomas Correspondence, 20 March 1907, 27 December 1909, 12 December 1911, 1, 9, and 18 August, 14 October 1922, Jane Addams Correspondence, Jane Addams Papers, SCPC.

19. Janowitz, *Thomas on Social Organization*, xvi, xxvii; Robert E. Park and Herbert A. Miller, eds., *Old World Traits Transplanted* (Chicago, 1925), 259–308.

20. J. Christopher Eisele, "John Dewey and the Immigrants," *History of Education Quarterly* 15 (Spring 1975): 67–85; Walter Feinberg, "Progressive Education and Social Planning," *Teachers College Record* 73 (May 1972): 485–505; Charles L. Zerby, "John Dewey and the Polish Question: A Response to the Revisionist Historians," *History of Education Quarterly* 15 (Spring 1975): 17–30; Charles A. Tosconi, Jr., and Van Cleve Morris, *The Anti-Man Culture: Bureau-Technocracy and the Schools* (Urbana, Ill., 1972), 139–54; Michael Katz, *Class, Bureaucracy, and Schools* (New York, 1971), 113–25; Clarence J. Karier, "Liberal Ideology and the Quest for Orderly Change," in Karier et al., *Roots of Crisis: American Education in the Twentieth Century* (Chicago, 1973), 84–107; Paul C. Violas, "Jane Addams and the New Liberalism," ibid., 66–83; Mark M. Krug, *The Melting of the Ethnics: Education of the Immigrants, 1880–1914* (Bloomington, Ind., 1976); Robert A.

Carlson, *The Quest for Conformity: Americanization through Education* (New York, 1975); G. C. White, "Social Settlements and Immigrant Neighbors," 55–66; Kogut, "Settlements and Ethnicity," 22–31; Higham, *Strangers in the Land,* 120–23, 251–54; Gordon, *Assimilation in American Life,* 137–40; Frederic Lilge, "The Vain Quest for Unity: John Dewey's Social and Educational Thought in Retrospect," in Reginald D. Archambault, ed., *John Dewey on Education* (New York, 1966), 51–71; Jay Wissot, "John Dewey, Horace Meyer Kallen, and Cultural Pluralism," *Educational Theory* 25 (Spring 1975): 186–96; Seymour W. Itzkoff, *Cultural Pluralism and American Education* (Scranton, Pa., 1969), 34–67; Seymour W. Itzkoff, "The Sources of Cultural Pluralism," *Educational Theory* 26 (Spring 1976): 231–33; J. Christopher Eisele, "Dewey's Concept of Cultural Pluralism," *Educational Theory* 33 (Summer-Fall 1983): 149–56.

21. Higham, *Strangers in the Land,* 120–23, 251–54, quote from page 122.

22. Carlson, *Quest for Conformity,* 79–93, quote from page 93.

23. Krug, *Melting of the Ethnics,* 5–14, 63–77, quote from pages 72, 74.

24. G. C. White, "Social Settlements and Immigrant Neighbors," 55–66; Kogut, "Settlements and Ethnicity," 22–31; Richard N. Juliani, "The Settlement House and the Italian Family," in Tenth Annual Conference of the American Italian Historical Association, *Proceedings* (Toronto, 1977), 107–8.

25. Eisele, "John Dewey and the Immigrants," 67–85; Tosconi and Morris, *Anti-Man Culture,* 139–54; M. Katz, *Class, Bureaucracy, and Schools,* 113–25; Karier, "Liberal Ideology," 84–107; Higham, *Send These to Me,* 199–201; Feinberg, "Progressive Education and Social Planning," 485–505; Zerby, "Dewey and the Polish Question," 17–30; Gordon, *Assimilation in American Life,* 139–40; Lilge, "Vain Quest for Unity," 51–71; Wissot, "Dewey, Kallen, and Cultural Pluralism," 186–96; Itzkoff, *Cultural Pluralism and American Education,* 34–67; Itzkoff, "Sources of Cultural Pluralism," 231–33; Eisele, "Dewey's Concept of Cultural Pluralism," 149–56.

26. Gordon, *Assimilation in American Life,* 137–40.

## Chapter One

1. Clarke E. Chambers, "The Belief in Progress in Twentieth-Century America," *Journal of the History of Ideas* 19 (April 1958): 197–224; Rush Weter, "The Idea of Progress in America," ibid., 16 (June 1955): 401–15; Jane Addams, *Democracy and Social Ethics* (Cambridge, Mass., 1902), 1–177; Jane Addams, "The New Internationalism," in National Arbitration and Peace Congress, *Proceedings* (April 1907), 213–16; Jane Addams, "Nationalism: A Dogma?" *Survey,* February 1920, 524–26; Jane Addams, *Newer Ideals of Peace* (New York, 1907), 1–30, 209–38; *Milwaukee Living Church,* 12 November 1910, Addams Newspaper Clippings, SCPC.

2. Felix Adler, "Some Characteristics of the American Ethical Movement," in Adler, ed., *The Fiftieth Anniversary of the Ethical Movement, 1876–1926* (New York, 1926), 3–29, quotes from pages 21, 28; Addams, *Democracy and Social Ethics,* 1–177.

3. Chambers, "Belief in Progress," 197–224; Weter, "Idea of Progress in America," 401–15; Addams, *Democracy and Social Ethics,* 1–177; Addams,

"Nationalism: A Dogma?" 524–26; Addams, "New Internationalism," 213–16; Addams, *Newer Ideals of Peace,* 1–30, 209–38.

4. John Dewey, *Democracy and Education* (New York, 1916; reprinted 1944), 1–11, 81–99, quote from page 4.

5. Ibid.

6. Ibid., 81–99, quote from page 83; Anthony Flew, "Democracy and Education," in Richard S. Peters, ed., *John Dewey Reconsidered* (London, 1977), 76–101. Bantock is quoted by Flew, page 87.

7. Addams, "The Subjective Necessity for Social Settlements," in Jane Addams et al. *Philanthropy and Social Progress* (Boston, 1893), 1–26; Jane Addams, "The Objective Value of the Social Settlement," ibid., 27–56; Addams, *Democracy and Social Ethics,* 1–12, 137–76: Addams, *Newer Ideals of Peace,* 93–150; Jane Addams, "A New Impulse to an Old Gospel," *Forum* 14 (November 1892): 345–58; Morton and Lucia White, *The Intellectual versus the City* (Cambridge, Mass., 1962), 139–54; Jean B. Quandt, *From the Small Town to the Great Community: The Social Thought of Progressive Intellectuals* (New Brunswick, N.J., 1970), 3–35; Daniel Levine, *Jane Addams and the Liberal Tradition* (Madison, Wis., 1971), 34–41, 160–78; John C. Farrell, *Beloved Lady: A History of Jane Addams' Ideals on Reform and Peace* (Baltimore, 1967), 17–26; Jane Addams, "The Settlement as a Factor in the Labor Movement," in Jane Addams et al., *Hull House Maps and Papers* (Boston, 1895), 183–206.

8. Addams, "Subjective Necessity," 1–11, quotes from pages 2, 4; Addams, "Old Gospel," 345–48.

9. Addams, "Subjective Necessity," 7, 5, 22; Addams, "Settlement Factor in the Labor Movement," 200–201. See also Addams, *Democracy and Social Ethics,* 1–12; 26 May 1909, Addams Newspaper Clippings, SCPC.

10. Addams, "Subjective Necessity," 23, 26, and see 1–11.

11. Addams, "Subjective Necessity," 1–11; Addams, *Democracy and Social Ethics,* 1–12; Addams, "Settlement Factor in the Labor Movement," 200–201; *Record Herald,* 26 May 1909, Addams Newspaper Clippings, SCPC.

12. Addams, *Democracy and Social Ethics,* 1–12.

13. William James, "On a Certain Blindness in Human Beings," in *Talk to Teachers on Psychology: And to Students on Some of Life's Ideals* (1900; reprint, Boston, 1939), 113–29, quotes from pages 113, 115.

14. Addams's concept of social disorganization and reorganization, as well as her ideas of personal disorganization, was greatly influenced by the theories of Emile Durkheim. This concept of social organization and change was later embodied in William I. Thomas's sociological writing, especially *The Polish Peasant in Europe and America* (1918), and in the theories of Robert E. Park. See Janowitz, *Thomas on Social Organization,* xxix–lii; Maurice R. Stein, *The Eclipse of Community: An Interpretation of American Studies* (Princeton, N.J., 1961), 20–33; Addams, "Subjective Necessity," 1–26; Jane Addams, *Twenty Years at Hull-House* (New York, 1910), 1, 3, 5, 13–15, 30–38, 49–50, 366–67, 432; Jane Addams, *The Spirit of Youth and the City Streets* (New York, 1909), 108–9, 120–24, 135–46; Addams, *Democracy and Social Ethics,* 1–11; Addams, *Newer Ideals of Peace,* 121, 216, 236–37; Quandt, *From the Small Town,* 3–35; M. and L. White, *Intellectual versus the City,* 147–50.

15. Addams, "Objective Value," 27–56; Jane Addams, "Hull House, Chicago: An Effort toward Social Democracy," *Forum* 14 (November 1892): 226–41; Douglas Sloan, "Cultural Uplift and Social Reform in Nineteenth-Century Urban America," *History of Education Quarterly* 19 (Fall 1979): 361–72; Helen L. Horowitz, "Varieties of Cultural Experience in Jane Addams' Chicago," *History of Education Quarterly* 14 (Spring 1974): 69–86; Emily K. Abel, "Middle-Class Culture for the Urban Poor: The Educational Thought of Samuel Barnett," *Social Service Review* 82 (December 1978): 596–620; Addams, "Subjective Necessity," 1–27; Levine, *Addams and the Liberal Tradition*, 3–41; Harriet Katz, "Workers' Education or Education for the Worker?" *Social Service Review* 82 (June 1978): 265–74.

16. Charles Nagel, "Address," in Immigrants' Protective League, *Seventh Annual Report* (1916), 26, Immigrants' Protective League Papers, University of Illinois Archives, Chicago, hereafter IPL; Mack's response, ibid.

17. Abel, "Middle-Class Culture," 600–616; Paul C. Violas, "Progressive Social Philosophy: Charles H. Cooley and Edward A. Ross," in Clarence J. Karier et al., *Roots of Crisis: American Education in the Twentieth Century* (Chicago, 1973), 40–65; Violas, "Addams and the New Liberalism," 81–83; Karier, "Liberal Ideology," 84–107; Samuel P. Hays, "The Politics of Reform in Municipal Government in the Progressive Era," *Pacific Northwest Quarterly* 55 (October 1964): 157–69; Addams, "Subjective Necessity," 1–27; Dorothy G. Becker, "Social Welfare Leaders as Spokesmen for the Poor," *Social Case Work* 49 (February 1968): 82–89; Allen F. Davis, *Spearheads for Reform: The Social Settlements and the Progressive Movement, 1890–1914* (New York, 1967), 33–39; James Weinstein, *The Corporate Ideal in the Liberal State, 1900–1918* (Boston, 1968), 16, 21; Edward C. Banfield and James Q. Wilson, *City Politics* (Cambridge, Mass., 1966), 125–45; Michael Johnston, *Political Corruption and Public Policy in America* (Monterey, Calif., 1982), 36–68; Addams, *Democracy and Social Ethics*, 221–77; Felix Adler, *An Ethical Philosophy of Life* (New York, 1920); Samuel F. Bacon, *An Evaluation of the Philosophy and Pedagogy of Ethical Culture* (Washington, D.C., 1933); Clarence M. Case, *Social Process and Human Progress* (New York, 1931); Horace L. Friess, *Felix Adler and Ethical Culture* (New York, 1981), 56–57; Herbert Gintis and Samuel Bowles, "The Contradictions of Liberal Educational Reform," in Walter Feinberg and Henry Rosemont, Jr., eds., *Work, Technology, and Education: Dissenting Essays in the Intellectual Foundations of American Education* (Urbana, Ill., 1975), 97–98.

18. Abel, "Middle-Class Culture," 611, 614–16; Daniel J. Elazar, *American Federalism: A View from the States* (New York, 1972), 40–102; Banfield and Wilson, *City Politics*, 125–45; Johnston, *Political Corruption*, 36–68; Hays, "Politics of Reform," 157–69; Addams, *Democracy and Social Ethics*, 221–77; J. R. Pole, "Historians and the Problem of Early American Democracy," *American Historical Review* 67 (April 1962): 626–46.

19. Addams, *Democracy and Social Ethics*, 1–101, 137–277; Addams et al., *Hull House Maps*, 138–206; Addams, *Newer Ideals of Peace*, 124–50; Abel, "Middle-Class Culture," 596–620; Sloan, "Cultural Uplift," 361–72; Becker, "Social Welfare Leaders," 82–89.

20. Abel, "Middle-Class Culture," 596–620; Sloan, "Cultural Uplift," 361–72; Becker, "Social Welfare Leaders," 82–89; A. F. Davis, *Spearheads for Reform*, 3–39; Addams, "Subjective Necessity," 12–18.

21. Addams, "Subjective Necessity," 4–5.

22. Addams, *Democracy and Social Ethics*, 1–101, 137–277; Addams et al., *Hull House Maps*, 138–206; Addams, *Newer Ideals of Peace*, 124–50; Abel, "Middle-Class Culture," 596–620; Sloan, "Cultural Uplift," 361–72; Becker, "Social Welfare Leaders," 82–89.

23. John P. Rousmaniere, "Cultural Hybrid in the Slums: The College Woman and the Settlement House, 1889–1894," *American Quarterly* 22 (1970): 45–66; Jill Conway, "Jane Addams: An American Heroine," *Daedalus* 93 (1964): 761–80.

24. Residents Lists, 1889–1929, Hull House Papers; *Hull House Bulletin*, no. 1 (1896), no. 4 (1896): 6, no. 1 (1903): 9; *Hull House Year Book*, 1906–7, 16; William E. McLennan, "Settlement Men's Clubs," read before the Conference of the National Federation of Settlements, 5 June 1917, Chicago Federation of Settlements Papers, CHS.

25. *Hull House Year Book*, 1907/8, 12; Chicago School of Civics and Philanthropy, *Bulletin*, July 1914, 9, box I, Taylor Papers. See also Grace Abbott, *From Relief to Social Security* (Chicago, 1940); Sophonisba P. Breckinridge, "Frontiers of Control in Public Welfare Administration," *Social Service Review* 1 (March 1927): 84–99; Grace Abbott, "Developing and Protecting Professional Standards in Public Welfare Work," *Social Service Review* 5 (September 1931): 384–94; Edith Abbott, *Social Welfare and Professional Education* (Chicago, 1931); Earle E. Eubank, "The Schools of Social Work of the United States and Canada: Some Recent Findings," *Social Service Review* 2 (June 1928): 263–73; Chicago School of Civics and Philanthropy, *Bulletin*, 1912–18, box I, Taylor Papers.

26. A. F. Davis, *Spearheads for Reform*, 40–83, 103–47, 170–93, 194–217; Levine, *Addams and the Liberal Tradition*, 59, 111–25, 160–78; Addams et al., *Hull House Maps*, 27–90; Addams, *Twenty Years*, 154–230, 281–341; Jane Addams, "Trade Unions and Public Duty," *American Journal of Sociology* 4 (January 1899): 448–62; Jane Addams, "The Present Crisis in Trade-Union Morals," *North American Review* 179 (August 1904): 178–93; Addams, *Democracy and Social Ethics*, 137–77.

27. Addams, "Subjective Necessity," 1–26; Addams, *Twenty Years*, 89–153, 342–400; Friess, *Felix Adler and Ethical Culture*, 94–100, 121–37; Levine, *Addams and the Liberal Tradition*, 67.

28. See notes 7 and 15.

29. Addams, *Twenty Years*, 177–97; Addams, *Democracy and Social Ethics*, 178–220; Addams, *Newer Ideals of Peace*, 236–37; Sophonisba P. Breckinridge and Edith Abbott, *The Delinquent Child and the Home* (New York, 1912); Edith Abbott and Sophonisba P. Breckinridge, *Truancy and Non-attendance in the Chicago Schools* (Chicago, 1917); Robert E. Park, *Human Communities* (Glencoe, Ill., 1952); Mollie R. Carroll, *Labor and Politics: The Attitude of the American Federation of Labor towards Legislation and Politics* (Boston, 1923); John R. Commons, *History of Labor in the United States, 1896–1932* (New York, 1918–35). See also note 14.

## Chapter Two

1. Jonathan D. Sarna, "From Immigrants to Ethnics: Toward a New Theory of Ethnicization," *Ethnicity* 5 (1978): 370–78; Rudolph J. Vecoli, "Contadini in Chicago: A Critique of the Uprooted," *Journal of American History* 51 (December 1964): 404–17; Oscar Handlin, *The Uprooted* (New York, 1951); Karel D. Bicha,

"The Survival of the Village in Urban America: A Note on Czech Immigrants in Chicago to 1914," *International Migration Review* 5 (1971): 72–74; Stein, *Eclipse of Community*, 1–134; Raymond Breton, "Institutional Completeness of Ethnic Communities and the Personal Relations of Immigrants," *American Journal of Sociology* 70 (1964): 198–201; Ethna O'Flannery, "Social and Cultural Assimilation," *American Catholic Sociological Review* 29 (1961): 195–206; Walter Hirsch, "Assimilation as Concept and Process," *Social Forces* 21 (October 1942): 35–39; Park and H. A. Miller, *Old World Traits Transplanted*, 287–96; Joseph P. Fitzpatrick, "The Importance of 'Community' in the Process of Immigrant Assimilation," *International Migration Review* 1 (Fall 1966): 5–16; Phillip R. Kunz, "Immigrants and Socialization: A New Look," *Sociological Review* (Great Britain) 16 (1968): 363–75. The process through which immigrant communities reached institutional completeness will be elaborated in chapter 3.

2. Park and H. A. Miller, *Old World Traits Transplanted*, 308.

3. Ibid., 259–87, quotes from pages 264, 270–71, 265, 271. The term "apperception mass" was used by William I. Thomas.

4. Ibid., 265, 273, 269, 270.

5. Graham Taylor, "Report of the Committee on Distribution and Assimilation of Immigrants," National Conference of Charities and Correction, *Proceedings* (1913), 26–27.

6. Grace Abbott, *The Immigrant and the Community* (New York, 1917), 247–81; Grace Abbott, "Adjustment—Not Restriction," *Survey*, January 1911, 528; Jane Addams, "Recent Immigration: A Field Neglected by the Scholar," *Education Review* 29 (March 1905): 245–63; Jane Addams, "Pen and Book as Tests of Character," *Survey*, January 1913, 419–20; Grace Abbott, "The Democracy of Internationalism," *Survey*, August 1916, 478–80.

7. Park and H. A. Miller, *Old World Traits Transplanted*, 259–87, quotes from pages 260, 268, 264.

8. Breckinridge and E. Abbott, *Delinquent Child and the Home*, 56–57.

9. Park and H. A. Miller, *Old World Traits Transplanted*, 286.

10. Ibid., 280–308; Addams, *Democracy and Social Ethics*, 9–11; Addams, *Twenty Years*, 77–83; Dewey, *Democracy and Education*, 81–99; Philip H. Phenix, "John Dewey's War on Dualism," in Reginald D. Archambault, ed., *John Dewey on Education* (New York, 1966), 46.

11. Park and H. A. Miller, *Old World Traits Transplanted*, 308.

12. Charles Zublin, "The Chicago Ghetto," in Jane Addams et al., *Hull House Maps and Papers* (Boston, 1895), 110–11; Addams, *Democracy and Social Ethics*, 200. See also Stein, *Eclipse of Community*, 20–33; Park and H. A. Miller, *Old World Traits Transplanted*, 105–6.

13. Addams, "Recent Immigration," 259–62. See also Addams, *Democracy and Social Ethics*, 170; Addams, "Settlement Factor in the Labor Movement," 183–204.

14. Park and H. A. Miller, *Old World Traits Transplanted*, 296–308, quotes from pages 304, 302, 305, 306.

15. Jane Addams, "Americanization," in American Sociological Society, *Publication* 14 (1919): 213–14, quote from page 213. See also Jane Addams, "Foreign-born Children in the Primary Grades," in National Education Association, *Journal of*

*Proceedings and Addresses* (1897), 107–8; Jane Addams, "The Public School and the Immigrant Child," in ibid. (1908), 99–102; Addams, "Recent Immigration," 252–54; Addams, *Twenty Years*, 231–58; Addams, "Nationalism: A Dogma?" 524–26; G. Abbott, *Immigrant and the Community*, 225–98; Edith Abbott, "Grace Abbott and Hull House, 1908–1921," *Social Service Review* 24 (September 1950): 379; Sophonisba P. Breckinridge, *New Homes for Old* (New York, 1921), 238, 247.

16. Addams, "Public School and the Immigrant Child," 99–102; Addams, "Foreign-born Children in the Primary Grades," 107–8; G. Abbott, *Immigrant and the Community*, 67, 221–46; Breckinridge and E. Abbott, *Delinquent Child and the Home*, 55–69; Breckinridge, *New Homes for Old*, 170–86, 231–32, 238, 247; Sophonisba P. Breckinridge, "Education for the Americanization of the Foreign Family," *Journal of Home Economics* 11 (May 1919): 187–92; Mary E. McDowell, "The Struggle in the Family Life," *Charities and the Commons*, 3 December 1904, 196–97; City of Chicago, *Fifty-eighth Annual Report of the Board of Education* (1912), 112–15.

17. Park and H. A. Miller, *Old World Traits Transplanted*, 287–308, quotes from pages 289, 296, 294. See also Robert E. Park, *The Immigrant Press and Its Control* (Chicago, 1922).

18. Grace Abbott, "The Immigrant as a Problem in Community Planning," in American Sociological Society, *Publication* 12 (1917): 166–73; Grace Abbott, "The Education of Foreigners in American Citizenship," in National Conference for Good City Government, *Proceedings* (1910), 375–84; Julian W. Mack, "Address of the President," in IPL, *Seventh Annual Report* (1916), 26–28; Addams, "Americanization," 210; G. Taylor, "Committee on Distribution and Assimilation," 26–36.

19. Addams, "Americanization," 210.

20. Addams, *Twenty Years*, 235–36.

21. Addams, "Americanization," 210. See also Addams, "Recent Immigration," 278.

22. Park and H. A. Miller, *Old World Traits Transplanted*, 272–80.

23. Jane Addams, "Recreation as a Public Function in Urban Communities," *American Journal of Sociology* 17 (1912): 616–17; Addams, "Recent Immigration," 245–63; Addams, "Americanization," 206–14; Addams, *Twenty Years*, 21–42, 77, 111–12, 120–258, 426; Addams, *Newer Ideals of Peace*, 4, 16–17, 39–40, 75–78, 214–16, 253; Jane Addams, "Civic Associations' Night," *City Club Bulletin* (Chicago) 5 (May 1912): 212–13. Francis Hackett, a Hull House resident of Irish origin, felt that Hull House was successful in creating a sense of community among its immigrant members, by developing such a feeling of continuity. Francis Hackett, "As an Alien Feels," *New Republic*, 3 July 1915, 304–5.

24. Park and H. A. Miller, *Old World Traits Transplanted*, 280, 265, 286–87. See also William I. Thomas, "The Prussian-Polish Situation: An Experiment in Assimilation," *American Journal of Sociology* 19 (March 1914): 624–39.

25. *American* (Chicago), 23 March 1912, Addams Newspaper Clippings, SCPC; Park and H. A. Miller, *Old World Traits Transplanted*, 284–86, quote from page 284. See also Mary Reynolds to Jane Addams, 25 March 1912, Speranza Papers, Immigration Research Center, University of Minnesota, St. Paul.

26. G. Abbott, *Immigrant and the Community*, 255–98.

27. Breckinridge, *New Homes for Old,* 189–90.

28. G. Abbott, *Immigrant and the Community,* 267–98; Edith Abbott, "Grace Abbott: A Sister's Memories," *Social Service Review* 13 (September 1939): 379; Grace Abbott to Paul U. Kellogg, 2 November 1916, box 48, *Survey* Papers, Social Welfare History Archives Center, University of Minnesota, Minneapolis; Jane Addams to Paul U. Kellogg, 22 November 1916, box 48, *Survey* Papers; Paul U. Kellogg to Grace Abbott, 2 March 1917, box 48, *Survey* Papers; *Evening Post* (New York), 6 December 1916, Addams Newspaper Clippings, SCPC.

29. Breckinridge, *New Homes for Old,* 50–84, 130–53, 228–39, 243–54, 294.

30. Addams, "Subjective Necessity," 20; *Record Herald,* 26 May 1909, Addams Newspaper Clippings, SCPC.

## Chapter Three

1. On the development of religious and secular agencies, see William Warner and Leo Srole, *The Social Systems of American Ethnic Groups* (New Haven, 1945), 103–282; Breton, "Institutional Completeness," 198–201; James W. Sanders, *The Education of an Urban Minority: Catholics in Chicago, 1833–1965* (New York, 1977), 1–72; Joseph J. Parot, *Polish Catholics in Chicago, 1850–1920* (DeKalb, Ill., 1981); Charles Shanabruch, *Chicago Catholics: The Evolution of an American Identity* (Notre Dame, 1981); M. Andrea, "The Societies of St. Stanislaus Kostka Parish, Chicago," *Polish American Studies* 9 (January-June 1952): 27–37; Zublin, "Chicago Ghetto," 91–114; Victor Greene, *For God and Country: The Rise of Polish and Lithuanian Ethnic Consciousness in America* (Madison, 1975), 83–91; Joseph Miaso, *The History of Polish Education in the United States* (New York, 1977), 97–148; Victor Greene, "Becoming American: The Role of Ethnic Leaders: Swedes, Poles, Italians, Jews," in Melvin G. Holli and Peter d'A. Jones, eds., *The Ethnic Frontier: Essays in the History of Group Survival in Chicago and the Midwest* (Grand Rapids, Mich., 1977), 143–78; Edward Mazur, "Jewish Chicago: From Diversity to Community," in ibid., 270–91; Joseph J. Barton, "Eastern and Southern Europeans," in John Higham, ed., *Ethnic Leadership in America* (Baltimore, 1978), 150–75; Irving Cutler, "The Jews of Chicago: From Shtetl to Suburb," in Peter d'A. Jones and Melvin G. Holli, eds., *Ethnic Chicago* (Grand Rapids, Mich., 1981), 47–60; Andrew T. Kopan, "Greek Survival in Chicago: The Role of Ethnic Education, 1890–1980," in ibid., 80–139; Edward R. Kantowicz, "Polish Survival through Solidarity," in ibid., 179–210. See also chapter 2, note 1.

2. Mark P. Curchack, "The Adaptability of Traditional Institutions as a Factor in the Formation of Immigrant Voluntary Associations: The Example of the Landsmanshaften," *Kroeber Anthropology Social Papers* 42 (1970): 88–98.

3. Mary B. Treudley, "An Ethnic Group's View of the American Middle Class," *American Sociological Review* 2 (1946): 715–22; Miaso, *History of Polish Education,* 60–96; 149–75; Warner and Srole, *Social Systems of American Ethnic Groups,* 271–73; Fitzpatrick, "Importance of Community," 14–15; Andrea, "Societies of St. Stanislaus Kostka Parish," 27–37; Constance Krasowska, "The Polish National Alliance and the Liberation of Poland," *Polish American Studies* 12 (January-June 1955): 11–18; Joseph A. Wytrwal, *America's Polish Heritage* (Detroit, 1961); Edward R. Kantowicz, *Polish-American Politics in Chicago, 1888–1940* (Chicago,

1975), 57–95; Greene, *For God and Country,* 67–68; David Blaustein, "The Problem of Immigration in the United States," *City Club Bulletin* (Chicago), 1909, 363–70; Barton, "Eastern and Southern Europeans," 150–75: D. J. Lawless, "Attitudes of Leaders of Immigrant and Ethnic Societies in Vancouver towards Integration into Canadian Life," *International Migration Quarterly Review* 2 (1964): 201–11; Park and H. A. Miller, *Old World Traits Transplanted,* 119–44.

4. Addams, "Subjective Necessity," 4–5.

5. See chapter 1 and chapter 2, notes 1 and 2.

6. Addams, *Twenty Years,* 129–254, 322–70; Addams, "Objective Value," 27–56; G. Abbott, *Immigrant and the Community,* 105–37, 221–46, 295–96.

7. Hackett, "As an Alien Feels," 303–5; Addams, "Objective Value," 38–45; *Hull House Bulletins,* 1896–1906; Alice Miller, "Hull House," *Charities Review* 1 (February 1890): 167–73; "Hull House: A Social Settlement," 1892, Hull House Papers; Addams, *Twenty Years,* 101–9; Jane Addams, "Hull House and Its Neighbors," *Charities,* 7 May 1904, 450–51; Florence Kelley, "Hull House," *New England Magazine* 18 (July 1898): 550–66; Elzina P. Stevens, "Life in a Social Settlement: Hull House," *Chicago Self Culture* 9 (March 1899): 42–51; Sloan, "Cultural Uplift," 361–72; Horowitz, "Varieties of Cultural Experience," 69–86; Abel, "Middle-Class Culture," 596–620; H. Katz, "Workers' Education," 265–74; Addams, "Subjective Necessity," 2, 7–10. See chapter 1.

8. Zublin, "Chicago Ghetto," 104–5; G. Abbott, *Immigrant and the Community,* 231–32; E. Abbott and Breckinridge, *Truancy,* 68, 81, 264–87; Ella Flagg Young, "The Secular Free Schools," in National Education Association, *Proceedings* (1916), 63–68; Addams, "Foreign-born Children in the Primary Grades," 104–12.

9. Breckinridge and E. Abbott, *Delinquent Child and the Home,* 55–56.

10. Miaso, *History of Polish Education,* 98–200; Ellen Marie Kuznicki, "The Polish American Parochial Schools," in Frank Mocka, ed., *Poles in America* (Stevens Point, Wis., 1978), 435–60; Ellen Marie Kuznicki, "A Historical Perspective on the Polish American Parochial School," *Polish American Studies* 35 (1978): 5–12; E. Abbott and Breckinridge, *Truancy,* 264–87; G. Abbott, *Immigrant and the Community,* 230–34; Breckinridge and E. Abbott, *Delinquent Child and the Home,* 55–56.

11. Addams, "Americanization," 206–14; Park and H. A. Miller, *Old World Traits Transplanted,* 270–308; G. Abbott, *Immigrant and the Community,* 221–98.

12. *Evening Post* (Chicago), 8 November 1897; Elmer E. Cornwell, Jr., "Bosses, Machines, and Ethnic Groups," *Annals of the American Academy of Political and Social Sciences* 353 (May 1964): 27–37, hereafter *Annals;* Sonya Forthal, "Relief and Friendly Service by Political Precinct Leaders," *Social Service Review* 7 (December 1933): 616–18; Harold F. Gonsell, *Machine Politics, Chicago Model* (Chicago, 1937), 69–125; Addams, *Democracy and Social Ethics,* 221–77; G. Abbott, *Immigrant and the Community,* 256, 264; Allen F. Davis, "Jane Addams vs. the Ward Boss," *Journal of the Illinois State Historical Society* 53 (Autumn 1960): 247–65; Barton, "Eastern and Southern Europeans," 150–75; Lawless, "Attitudes towards Integration," 201–11; John Higham, "Leadership," in Michael Walzer et al., *The Politics of Ethnicity* (Cambridge, Mass., 1982), 69–92; Holli and Jones, *Ethnic Frontier;* Jones and Holli, *Ethnic Chicago;* Helen Busyn, "Peter Kiolbassa: Maker of

Polish America," *Polish American Studies* 8 (July-December 1951): 65–84; Helen Busyn, "The Political Career of Peter Kiolbassa," ibid. 7 (January-June 1950): 8–22; Kantowicz, *Polish-American Politics in Chicago,* 45–71. The relationship between Hull House and immigrant leaders is dealt with in two of my articles: Rivka Lissak, "Myth and Reality: The Pattern of Relationship between the Hull House Circle and the 'New Immigrants' on Chicago's West Side, 1890–1919," *Journal of American Ethnic History* 2 (Spring 1983): 21–50; Rivka Lissak, "Liberal Progressives and 'New Immigrants': The Immigrants' Protective League of Chicago, 1908–1910," in *Scripta Hierosolymitana* (Jerusalem, 1987), 32:79–103. It will be further elaborated in chapters 5 and 8.

13. See note 12; G. Abbott, *Immigrant and the Community,* 103–4, 261–66; Colin E. De'Ath and Peter Padbury, "Brokers and the Social Ecology of Minority Groups," in George L. Hicks and Philip E. Leis, eds., *Ethnic Encounters* (Belmont, Calif., 1977), 181–200; Marilyn A. Trueblood, "The Melting Pot and Ethnic Revitalization," ibid., 153–67; Park, *Immigrant Press and Its Control,* 448–68; Park and H. A. Miller, *Old World Traits Transplanted,* 97–115, 145–258, 287–96; Treudley, "An Ethnic Group's View," 715–24.

14. "Hull House's Unique Melting Pot Experiment," *Evening Post* (New York), 2 December 1916, Addams Newspaper Clippings, SCPC.

15. Immigrants' Protective League, Annual Reports' Lists of the Board of Trustee Membership 1909–1917, IPL Papers; G. Abbott, *Immigrant and the Community,* 261–66; Breckinridge, *New Homes for Old,* 192, 223–26, 272–76; Graham R. Taylor, "Chicago Settlements in Ward Politics," *Charities and the Commons* 16 (May 1906): 183–85; Chicago Municipal Voters' League, Annual Reports on Aldermanic Candidates, 1897–1925, Chicago Municipal Voters' League Records, CHS; Joan S. Miller, "The Politics of Municipal Reforms in Chicago during the Progressive Era: The Municipal Voters' League as a Test Case, 1896–1920," master's thesis, Roosevelt University, Chicago, 1966; Allen F. Davis, "Raymond Robins: The Settlement Worker as Municipal Reformer," *Social Service Review* 33 (June 1959): 131–41.

16. Addams, *Twenty Years,* 342–99; Horowitz, "Varieties of Cultural Experience," 69–86; Addams, "Objective Value," 38–44; William S. B. Mathew, "Editorial Bric-a-Brac," *Music* 17 (1899): 179–82; *Hull House Bulletin,* no. 7 (1905/6), 4–6; *Hull House Year Book,* 1906/7, 6–7, 10–12, 32–35; 1910, 6–7, 10–11, 34–39; 1913, 6–14, 34–36; 1916, 6, 9–11, 18–22; National Federation of Settlements, "Report of Second Conference of the National Association of Music Schools," 1912, box 17, National Federation of Settlements Records, Social Welfare History Archives Center, University of Minnesota, Minneapolis; Harry A. Lipsky, "Citizen Making in Chicago," *Survey,* May 1906, 883; Jane Addams, "The Waste of Talent among the Poor; or, Our Waste of Nationalities," 18 May 1907, 1–6, box 9, Addams Papers, SCPC; *Herald* (Washington, D.C.), 26 April 1908, Addams Newspaper Clippings, SCPC.

17. Victor S. Yarros, "Settlements and Community Centers," *Jewish Social Service Quarterly* 2 (June 1926): 258.

18. "The Work of Hull House," *Republican* (Springfield, Mass.), 19 March 1904, Addams Newspaper Clippings, SCPC.

19. Addams, *Twenty Years,* 235–36.

20. Addams, *Twenty Years*, 231–34, 388–89; N. Marks, "Two Women's Work," in Allen F. Davis and Mary L. McCree, eds., *Eighty Years at Hull House* (Chicago, 1969), 29–33; *Hull House Bulletin*, no. 7 (1896): 8, no. 4 (1897): 9, no. 7 (1898): 4, no. 1 (1900): 7.

21. *Hull House Bulletin*, no. 12 (1899), no. 2 (1902), no. 1 (1903/4), no. 1 (1905/6); Edith C. Barrows, "The Greek Play at Hull House," *Commons* 9 (January 1904): 6–10; Clinton Hall, "The Greek Play," *Charities* 12 (February 1904): 125; Addams, *Twenty Years*, 388–89.

22. Addams, *Twenty Years*, 348; *Hull House Year Book*, 1906/7, 28; 1910, 30–31; 1913, 31–32; 1916, 37.

23. First Report of the Labor Museum at Hull House, 1901/2, Hull House Papers; *Hull House Year Book*, 1906/7, 10–11; 1910, 10–11; 1913, 9–11; 1916, 9–11; Addams, "Hull House and Its Neighbors," 450–51.

24. Hull House Women's Club Membership Lists, 1902/3, 1903/4, 1905/6, 1906/7, 1909/10, 1925/26, Bowen Papers, CHS; *Hull House Bulletins*, 1896–1905/6; "Hull House: A Social Settlement," 1 March 1892; E. P. Stevens, "Life in a Social Settlement," 49.

25. *Hull House Bulletin*, nos. 1–8 (1897), no. 1 (1901/2): 9–13, no. 2 (1903/4): 9–17, no. 1 (1905/6): 14.

26. *Hull House Bulletin*, no. 12 (1899): 9–10, no. 1 (1903/4): 15–16, no. 1 (1905/6): 3–4, 23; *Hull House Year Book*, 1906/7, 37; 1910, 25, 32; 1921, 12–13, 34; 1929, 13, 15–16; Addams, *Twenty Years*, 257, 388–89, 424–26; Graham R. Taylor, "Recreation Developments in Chicago Parks," *Annals* 35 (January-June 1910): 304–321; Mary E. McDowell, "The Field Houses of Chicago and Their Possibilities," *Charities and the Commons*, 3 August 1907, 535–38; Guy L. Shipps, "Utilizing Neighborhood Groups," in National Conference of Charities and Correction, *Proceedings* (1914), 401–7; Graham R. Taylor, "City Neighbors at Play," *Survey*, July 1910, 549–59; John Daniels, *America via the Neighborhood* (New York, 1920), 102–46, 182–202; Edward W. Stevens, "Social Centers, Politics, and Social Efficiency in the Progressive Era," *History of Education Quarterly* 12 (Spring 1972): 16–33.

27. *Hull House Year Book*, 1906–7, 23–27; 1910, 25–29; 1913, 26, 28–30, 32; 1916, 14, 33–37.

28. Addams, *Twenty Years*, 342, 346–48; *Hull House Year Book*, 1906/7, 21–23, 41–43; 1910, 20, 44–47; 1913, 17–22, 41–42; 1916, 26–30, 39–41.

29. *Hull House Bulletin*, 1896–1905/6; *Hull House Year Book*, 1906–16; Addams, *Twenty Years*, 387–88, 390–95; Yarros, "Settlements and Community Centers," 246.

30. Addams, *Twenty Years*, 77–79, 83, 91, 115–27.

31. Dewey, "School as a Social Center," 381.

32. Theodore Roosevelt, "Character and Civilization," *Outlook*, 8 November 1913, 527–28.

33. Ferenc M. Szasz, "The Stress on Character and Service in Progressive America," *Mid-America* 63 (October 1981): 145–54; Woods and Kennedy, *Settlement Horizon*, 137; Addams, "Subjective Necessity," 20; *Record Herald*, 26 May 1909, Addams Newspaper Clippings, SCPC.

34. List of Plays Produced by the Hull House Players, 1899–1939, Hull House Papers; Edith de Nancrede, "Dramatic Work at Hull House," *Neighborhood* 1 (January 1928): 23–28; Laura D. Pelham, "The Story of the Hull House Players," *Drama* 6 (May 1916): 249–62; Madge C. Jenison, "A Hull House Play," *Atlantic Monthly*, July 1906), 83–92; Addams, *Twenty Years*, 387–95; "The Three Gifts: A Labor Play," *Charities and the Commons*, 3 March 1906, 844–46; C. A. Benson, "Social Settlement Theatre: Hull House and Karamu House," Ph.D. dissertation, University of Wisconsin, 1965, 35–37; Sheldon Cheney, *The New Movement in the Theatre* (New York, 1924), 183–84; Mary B. Caughey, "A History of the Settlement House Theaters in the United States," master's dissertation, University of Louisiana, 1927, 42–43.

35. Addams, *Twenty Years*, 342–99; Horowitz, "Varieties of Cultural Experience," 69–86; Addams, "Objective Value," 38–44; Mathew, "Editorial Bric-a-Brac," 179–82; *Hull House Bulletin*, no. 7 (1905/6): 4–6; *Hull House Year Book*, 1906/7, 6–7, 10–12, 32–35; 1910, 6–7, 10–11, 34–39; 1913, 6–14, 34–36; 1916, 6, 9–11, 18–22; National Federation of Settlements, "Report of Second Conference of the National Association of Music Schools."

36. Addams, *Twenty Years*, 378–80.

37. Ibid., 377.

38. Ibid., 371–72; Addams, "Objective Value," 42–43, quote from page 42.

39. Addams, *Twenty Years*, 375.

40. Addams, "Waste of Talent," 1–6. See also Lipsky, "Citizen Making in Chicago," 883.

41. *Herald* (Washington, D.C.), 26 April 1908, Addams Newspaper Clippings, SCPC.

42. Addams, *Twenty Years*, 346–47, 391–95, 435.

43. *Hull House Bulletin*, no. 3 (1896): 2, no. 1 (1902): 3, 9, no. 1 (1905/6): 4–5, 10; *Hull House Year Book*, 1906/7, 7–9; 1910, 8–9; 1913, 6–7; 1916, 6–8; Yarros, "Settlements and Community Centers," 246; Francis Hackett, "Hull House: A Souvenir," *Survey*, June 1925, 275–80; Addams, "Objective Value," 38–44.

44. *Hull House Bulletin*, no. 7 (1896): 2, no. 1 (1902): 3, no. 1 (1905/6): 4; *Hull House Year Book*, 1906/7, 8; 1910, 8. No language courses except English were given after 1910.

45. The proportion of educational courses to art, workshop, and craft courses was 26 to 7 in 1892; 32 to 9 in 1902; 9 to 23 in 1905; 9 to 21 in 1906/7; 11 to 18 in 1910; 8 to 19 in 1913; and 6 to 15 in 1916. *Hull House Bulletin*, no. 1 (1896), no. 1 (1902): 10–14, no. 1 (1905/6): 11–14, 18–19; *Hull House Year Book*, 1906/7, 9–10, 11–12, 21–26, 35, 37; 1910, 8–13, 21–22, 25–26, 44–47; 1913, 6–14, 42; 1916, 6–20, 42.

46. "Hull House: A Social Settlement," 1892; *Hull House Bulletin*, no. 1 (1896), no. 1 (1902): 10–14, no. 1 (1905/6): 11–14, 18–19; *Hull House Year Book*, 1906/7, 9–10, 11–12, 21–26, 35, 37; 1910, 8–13, 21–22, 25–26, 44–47; 1913, 6–14, 42; 1916, 6–20, 42; Addams, *Twenty Years*, 349–50; interviews by Rivka Lissak with Antonio Sorrentino, Nicollette Mallone, Florence Scala, Libonnati, August 1977.

## Chapter Four

1. Park and H. A. Miller, *Old World Traits Transplanted*, 270–71. Dewey adds, "What they must have in common in order to form a community on society are aims, beliefs, aspirations, knowledge—a common understanding—like mindedness."

2. Dewey, *Democracy and Education*, 3–9, 81–99. See chapter 1.

3. John Dewey, "Splitting Up the School System," *New Republic* 2 (1915): 283–84. See also Charles P. Megan, "Parochial School Education," ibid. 3 (1915): 72; John Dewey, "Industrial Education: A Wrong Kind," ibid. 2 (1915): 71–73.

4. Addams, "Foreign-born Children in Primary Grades," 104–12, quote from page 105; Ella Flagg Young, *Isolation in the School* (Chicago, 1900), 46–47. See also Addams, "Public School and the Immigrant Child," 99–102; Young, "Secular Free Schools," 63–68.

5. G. Abbott, *Immigrant and the Community*, 230–34; E. Abbott and Breckinridge, *Truancy*, 68, 81, 264–87; Young, *Isolation in the School*, 50–52.

6. Breckinridge and E. Abbott, *Delinquent Child and the Home*, 55–56.

7. Ibid. See also G. Abbott, *Immigrant and the Community*, 230–234; E. Abbott and Breckinridge, *Truancy*, 66–68, 81, 264–87.

8. Breckinridge and E. Abbott, *Delinquent Child and the Home*, 55–56. See also Addams, "Public School and the Immigrant Child," 99–102; Addams, "Foreign-born Children in the Primary Grades," 104–12; G. Abbott, *Immigrant and the Community*, 230–34, 267–98; Addams, "Civic Associations' Night," 212–13.

9. G. Abbott, *Immigrant and the Community*, 232–34.

10. Ibid., 230–34; E. Abbott and Breckinridge, *Truancy*, 68, 81, 264–87; Breckinridge and E. Abbott, *Delinquent Child and the Home*, 56–69.

11. Zublin, "Chicago Ghetto," 104–5.

12. E. Abbott and Breckinridge, *Truancy*, 68.

13. G. Abbott, *Immigrant and the Community*, 230–34; E. Abbott and Breckinridge, *Truancy*, 66–91, 263, 287; Addams, "Objective Value," 49–50; Ray S. Baker, "Hull House and the Ward Boss," *Outlook*, 28 March 1898, 770; Anne F. Scott, "Saint Jane and the Ward Boss," *American Heritage* 12 (December 1960): 96; *La Tribuna*, 9 September 1906, reel 30, Chicago Foreign Language Press Survey, Chicago Public Library, 1942, hereafter FLPS; City of Chicago, Board of Education, *Proceedings*, 18 December 1895, 198; 22 September 1897, 99; 29 January, 1908, 444–45; 11 February 1908, 500–01; 26 February 1908, 550; Charles Shanabruch, "The Repeal of the Edwards Law: A Study of Religion and Ethnicity in Illinois Politics," *Ethnicity* 7 (1980): 310–32; Daniel W. Kucerna, *Church-State Relationship in Education in Illinois* (Washington, D.C., 1955), 108–75; Breckinridge and E. Abbott, *Delinquent Child and the Home*, 55–69; Sanders, *Education of an Urban Minority*, 1–55.

14. E. Abbott and Breckinridge, *Truancy*, 286.

15. G. Abbott, *Immigrant and the Community*, 230–34; E. Abbott and Breckinridge, *Truancy*, 66–91, 263–87; Daniel W. Kucera, *Catholic Elementary and Secondary Schools under Illinois Law* (Chicago, 1950), 1–48; Kucerna, *Church-State Relationship*, 108–75; Breckinridge and E. Abbott, *Delinquent Child and the Home*, 55–69; Sanders, *Education of an Urban Minority*, 1–55.

16. G. Abbott, *Immigrant and the Community*, 230–34; E. Abbott and Breckinridge, *Truancy*, 91, 114–64, 263–87, 450–54; Breckinridge and E. Abbott, *Delinquent Child and the Home*, 55–69; Breckinridge, *New Homes for Old*, 159–62; Miaso, *History of Polish Education*, 105; John Landesco, *Organized Crime in Chicago* (Chicago, 1929), 240; John Landesco, "Crime and the Failure of Institutions in Chicago's Immigrant Areas," *Journal of the American Institute of Criminal Law*

*and Criminology,* 23 (July-August 1932): 240–41; Kuznicki, "Polish American Parochial Schools," 436.

17. G. Abbott, *Immigrant and the Community,* 233–34.

18. Ibid., 230–32; E. Abbott and Breckinridge, *Truancy,* 264–87; Ella Flagg Young, "Modern Languages in High Schools," *Journal of Education,* 5 December 1912, 597.

19. G. Abbott, *Immigrant and the Community,* 230–32.

20. Ibid., 276–77.

21. Herbert A. Miller, "The Rising of National Individualism," *American Journal of Sociology* 19 (March 1914): 592–605, quotes from pages 593, 598, 599. See also Herbert A. Miller, *The School and the Immigrant* (Cleveland, 1916), 37–38; W. I. Thomas, "Prussian-Polish Situation," 624–39. Dean Summer was not president of the Board of Education at that time. He was chairman of the committee on school management within whose jurisdiction was the school curriculum. City of Chicago, Board of Education, *Proceedings,* 26 July 1911, 39.

22. *Denni Hlasatel,* 7 December 1911, 26 January 1922. See also *Chicago Chronicle,* 20 February 1905; *Dziennik Zwaizkowy,* 6 October 1911, 1 and 4 November 1911, reel 48, FLPS; *Courier,* 7 June 1912, reel 31, FLPS; *Denni Hlasatel,* 28 November, 6 and 15 December 1911, 1 April 1912, reel 1, FLPS.

23. Addams, "Foreign-born Children in the Primary Grades," 107; Addams, "Public School and the Immigrant Child," 99–102, quote from page 100. See also McDowell, "Struggle in the Family Life," 196–97.

24. Addams, "Public School and the Immigrant Child," 102, 100.

25. Ibid., 99–102, quote from page 100. See also *Hull House Year Book,* 1906/7, 22, 38–39.

26. Addams, "Public School and the Immigrant Child," 101.

27. Addams, *Twenty Years,* 231–43; Addams, "Recent Immigration," 252–58; G. Abbott, *Immigrant and the Community,* 226–28.

28. Park and H. A. Miller, *Old World Traits Transplanted,* 265.

29. Julia Wringley, *Class Politics and Public Schools, Chicago 1900–1950* (New Brunswick, N.J., 1985), 55.

30. City of Chicago, Report of the Education Commission Appointed by the Mayor 19 January 1898 (Chicago, 1899), 129–38, quotes from page 131; Steven L. Schlossman, "Is There an American Tradition of Bilingual Education? German in the Public Elementary Schools, 1840–1919," *American Journal of Education* 91 (February 1983): 139–86, quote from page 150.

31. Wringley, *Class Politics,* 55; Hannah B. Clark, *The Public Schools of Chicago* (Chicago, 1897), 109–10; Jean E. Fair, "The History of Public Education in the City of Chicago, 1894–1914," master's thesis, University of Chicago, 1939, 42–69; Mary J. Herrick, *The Chicago Schools: A Social and Political History* (Beverly Hills, Calif., 1971), 60–61, 73–74, 81–89; City of Chicago, Board of Education, *Proceedings,* 15 February 1896, 319; 23 February 1893, 329; 20 March 1893, 362, 376; 26 April 1893, 434; 19 August 1896, 69; 7 February 1900, 285; 21 February 1900, 306; 28 February 1900, 471–72; 1 May 1901, 584, 619; 26 June 1901, 739; 22 January 1902, 286; 21 June 1905, 786; Young, "Modern Languages in High Schools," 597; City of Chicago, Report of the Educational Commission, 130–32.

Notes to pages 56–59

32. Star Willard Cutting, "The Teaching of Foreign Modern Literature in Our Schools," *Educational Bi-Monthly* 7 (December 1912): 97–103, quote from page 99.

33. Wringley, *Class Politics*, 55; City of Chicago, Board of Education, *Proceedings*, 14 June 1899, 655; 6 September 1899, 53; 4 October 1899, 102, 105; 29 May 1900, 454; 13 June 1900, 472, 475, 487; 27 June 1900, 496–98; 8 March 1911, 724–25; 1 May 1912, 903, 950; City of Chicago, *Fifty-eighth Annual Report*, 112–15; *Chicago Chronicle*, 20 February 1905, Addams Newspaper Clippings, SCPC; *Dziennik Zwaizkowy*, 6 October 1911, 26 November 1910, 1 and 4 November 1911, reel 48, FLPS; *Courier*, 7 June 1912, reel 31, FLPS; *L'Italia*, 12 January 1913, reel 30, FLPS; *Denni Hlasatel*, 28 November, 6, 7, and 15 December 1911, reel 1, FLPS.

34. G. Abbott, *Immigrant and the Community*, 230. See also City of Chicago, *Fifty-eighth Annual Report*, 112–15; Cutting, "Teaching of Foreign Modern Literature," 97–103; City of Chicago, Board of Education, *Proceedings*, 19 August 1893, 69; 30 June 1897, 635–36; 18 April 1900, 394–95; 1 May 1912, 903, 950; John S. Nollen, "Aims of the Teaching of Modern Languages in the Secondary Schools," *School Review* 19 (January-December 1911): 550–54.

35. Young, "Modern Languages in High Schools," 597. See also *Denni Hlasatel*, 15 December 1911, 1 April 1912, reel 1, FLPS; City of Chicago, *Fifty-eighth Annual Report*, 112–15; *Indianapolis Star*, 9 November 1911, Addams Newspaper Clippings, SCPC.

36. Park and H. A. Miller, *Old World Traits Transplanted*, 284, 305, and see page 282; City of Chicago, Report of the Educational Commission, 130–32, quote from page 131; Young, "Modern Languages in High Schools," 597. See also G. Abbott, *Immigrant and the Community*, 230–32; Breckinridge and E. Abbott, *Delinquent Child and the Home*, 55–56.

37. John Dewey, "Nationalizing Education," in National Education Association, *Proceedings* (1916). See also National Education Association, *Proceedings* (1915), 245; Dewey, *Democracy and Education*, 214; Henry Johnson, *Teaching of History in Elementary and Secondary Schools* (New York, 1940), 53–66; Bruno Lasker, *Race Attitudes in Children* (New York, 1929), 139–59.

38. G. Abbott, *Immigrant and the Community*, 316–17.

39. *New York Evening World*, 22 October 1927; City of Chicago, Board of Education, *Proceedings*, 23 November 1927, 519–20; 11 January 1928, 701; Lasker, *Race Attitudes in Children*, 156–57.

40. City of Chicago, Board of Education, *Proceedings*, 18 February 1914, 867–79, 909–10.

41. Ibid., 18 February 1917, 867–79.

42. Ella Flagg Young to President Harry P. Judson, 4 March 1913, box 71, folder 2, University Presidents' Papers, University of Chicago Special Collections; James R. Angell to Ella Flagg Young, 7 March 1913, University Presidents' Papers; James R. Angell to President Harry P. Judson, 8 March 1913, University Presidents' Papers; A. F. Nightingale, Superintendent of High Schools, to President William R. Harper, 22 September 1892, 16 November 1892, 12 February 1896, 30 March 1896, 16 May 1896, 27 May 1896, 22 September 1896, box 9, folders 3–4, University Presidents' Papers; James R. Angell, "New Requirements for Entrance and Graduation at the University of Chicago," *School Review* (January-December 1911): 489–97; W. Betz, "College Entrance Requirements in Modern Languages," ibid., 406–9; Franklin W.

201

Johnson, "The New Harvard Entrance Requirements," ibid., 412–13; Charles H. Judd, "Reasons for Modifying Entrance Requirements," *Education* 32 (September 1911–June 1912): 266–77.

43. *Dziennik Zwiazkowy,* 4 November 1911, reel 48, FLPS. See also Miaso, *History of Polish Education,* 140–42, 155, 181, 194; Kuznicki, "Polish American Schools," 454; Kuznicki, "Historical Perspective," 8; Milo H. Stuart et al., "Report of the Survey of Schools of Chicago, Illinois: Secondary Education in Chicago," Columbia University, New York, 1932, 5.

44. Joseph B. Kingsbury, "The Merit System in Chicago from 1895 to 1915," *Public Personnel Studies* 3 (November 1925): 306–11, and 4 (February 1926): 154–84; Joseph B. Kingsbury, "The Merit System in Chicago from 1915 to 1923," ibid. 4 (November 1926): 306–19; City of Chicago, Civil Service Commission, Annual Reports, 1896–1916; Fair, "Public Education in Chicago," 43–53; Herrick, *Chicago Schools,* 73–75, 81–86; City of Chicago, *Fiftieth Annual Report of the Board of Education* (1904), 54–58; *Fifty-first Annual Report of the Board of Education* (1905), 160–67.

45. *Courier,* 7 June 1912, 30 July 1917, 12 May 1922, reel 35, FLPS.

46. Dewey, *Democracy and Education,* 3–9, 81–99; Addams, "Foreign-born Children in Primary Grades," 104–12; Addams, "Public School and the Immigrant Child," 99–102; Young, "Secular Free Schools," 63–68; Young, *Isolation in the School,* 46–47; Parker, "Jane Addams of Hull House," 14.

47. Addams, "Public School and the Immigrant Child," 99–102. See chapter 10 on the cultural theories of the Liberal Progressives.

48. G. Abbott, "Adjustment—Not Restriction," 528; Addams, "Pen and Book," 419–20; Victor S. Yarros, "Hull House Unique Melting Pot Experience," *Evening Post* (New York) 2 December 1916, Addams Newspaper Clippings, SCPC; G. Abbott, "Immigrant in Community Planning," 166–73; G. Abbott, *Immigrant and the Community,* 221–98; Addams, "Nationalism: A Dogma?" 524–26; Park and H. A. Miller, *Old World Traits Transplanted,* 259–308; Addams, "Recent Immigration," 245–63; Addams, "Subjective Necessity," 20.

49. Kunz, "Immigrants and Socialization," 363–75; S. N. Eisenstadt, *The Absorption of Immigrants* (Glencoe, Ill., 1955); Addams, "Public School and the Immigrant Child," 99–102; Addams, "Foreign-born Children in the Primary Grades," 107–8; Breckinridge and E. Abbott, *Delinquent Child and the Home,* 55–69; G. Abbott, *Immigrant and the Community,* 67, 221–98; Breckinridge, *New Homes for Old,* 170–86, 231–32, 238, 247; City of Chicago, *Fifty-eighth Annual Report,* 112–15; Park and H. A. Miller, *Old World Traits Transplanted,* 43–118; McDowell, "Struggle in the Family Life," 196–97; G. Abbott, "Immigrant in Community Planning," 166–73; Janowitz, *Thomas on Social Organization,* 195–202; Mack, "Address of the President," 26–28; G. Abbott, "Education of Foreigners in American Citizenship," 375–84; G. Taylor, "Committee on Distribution and Assimilation," 26–36.

50. Addams, "Americanization," 213–14; Addams, *Twenty Years,* 231–58; Addams, "Public School and the Immigrant Child," 99–102; Addams, "Foreign-born Children in the Primary Grades," 107–8; Addams, "Recent Immigration," 252–54; Edith Abbott, "Grace Abbott and Hull House, 1908–1921," *Social Service Review* 24 (1950): 379; G. Abbott, *Immigrant and the Community,* 225–98; Fitzpatrick, "Importance of 'Community,'" 5–16; Park and H. A. Miller, *Old World Traits Trans-*

Notes to pages 61–65

*planted,* 259–308; W. I. Thomas, "Prussian-Polish Situation," 624–39; H. A. Miller, "Rising of National Individualism," 592–605; McDowell, "Struggle in the Family Life," 196–97; Breckinridge, *New Homes for Old,* 238, 247.

## Chapter Five

1. Park and H. A. Miller, *Old World Traits Transplanted,* 105–6, and see 121–44, 227–35; Park, *Immigrant Press and Its Control,* 50–59, 76; Timothy L. Smith, "Lay Initiative in the Religious Life of American Immigrants, 1880–1950," in Tamara K. Hareven, ed., *Anonymous Americans: Exploration in Nineteenth-Century Social History* (Englewood, N.J., 1971), 215; George E. Pozzetta, "Immigrants and Craft Arts: Scuola d'Industrie Italiane," in Tenth Annual Conference of the American Italian Association, *Proceedings* (Toronto, 1977), 141.

2. John Dewey, "Autocracy under Cover," *New Republic,* 24 August 1918, 103–6, quotes from pages 103, 105. See also Zerby, "Dewey and the Polish Question," 17–30; Eisele, "Dewey and the Immigrants," 67–85; Feinberg, "Progressive Education and Social Planning," 485–505.

3. Park and H. A. Miller, *Old World Traits Transplanted,* 121.

4. See Rivka Lissak, "Liberal Progressives," 79–103.

5. IPL, *First Annual Report* (1909/10), 27–28; IPL, *Fourth Annual Report* (1913), 16–20; IPL, *Fifth Annual Report* (1914), 15–16; IPL, *Sixth Annual Report* (1915), 10–30; IPL, *Eighth Annual Report* (1917), 14–16; E. Abbott, "Grace Abbott and Hull House," 384–85; E. Abbott, "Sister's Memories," 359–74; Grace Abbott, "The Chicago Employment Agency and the Immigrant Worker," *American Journal of Sociology* 14 (1908): 289–305; William Dillingham, *Reports of the Immigration Commission* (Washington, D.C., 1911), 37:324; Edward Beckner, *A History of Labor Legislation in Illinois* (Chicago, 1929), 398–418; Kingsbury, "Merit System from 1895 to 1915" (November 1925), 306–11, (February 1926), 154–65, 178–84; see note 1 above; *Chicago Chronicle,* 16 September 1906; *Chicago Tribune,* 16 September 1906, both in Addams Newspaper Clippings, SCPC.

6. G. Abbott, *The Immigrant and the Community,* 26–54, quote from page 44; *Evening Post* (Chicago), 8 November 1897. See also Florence Kelley, "The Italians of Chicago: A Social and Economic Study," in the *Ninth Special Report of the Commissioner of Labor, United States Bureau of Labor* (Washington, D.C., 1897); Florence Kelley, "Italians in Chicago," *Bulletin of the Department of Labor* (United States Bureau of Labor) 2 (1897): 691–727; Dillingham, *Immigration Commission* 18:331–43; Illinois Bureau of Labor Statistics, *Tenth Annual Report of the Free Employment Offices for the Year Ending September 30, 1908* (Springfield, 1909), 76–84; Illinois Bureau of Labor Statistics, *Thirteenth Annual Report of the Free Employment Offices for the Year Ending September 30, 1911* (Springfield, 1912), 91–111; Illinois Bureau of Labor Statistics, *Fourteenth Annual Report of the Free Employment Offices for the Year Ending September 30, 1912* (Springfield, 1913), 100–121; City of Chicago, *Report of the Mayor's Commission on Unemployment* (Chicago, 1914), 48–75.

7. *Evening Post* (Chicago), 8 November 1897. See also G. Abbott, *Immigrant and the Community,* 26–54, 191–92; G. Abbott, "Chicago Employment Agency," 289–305; Humbert S. Nelli, *Italians in Chicago, 1880–1930* (New York, 1970), 55–67; John Koren, "The Padrone System and Padrone Banks," *Bulletin of the*


203

*Department of Labor* 2 (1897): 113–29; Frank J. Sheridan, "Italian, Slavic, and Hungarian Unskilled Immigrant Laborers in the United States," *Bulletin of the Bureau of Labor* (United States Bureau of Labor) 72 (1907): 403–86; IPL, *Fourth Annual Report* (1913), 17; Dillingham, *Immigrant Commission* 18:331–43, 37:179–95; Lillian D. Wald and Frances A. Kellor, "The Construction Camps of the People," *Survey,* January 1910, 449–65; Gino C. Speranza, "Handicaps in America," ibid., 465–72; Frances A. Kellor, "Who Is Responsible for the Immigrant," *Outlook,* 25 April 1914, 912–17; Luciano J. Iorizzo, "The Padrone and Immigrant Distribution," in Silvano M. Tomasi and Madeline H. Engel, eds., *The Italian Experience in the United States* (New York, 1970), 52–58; Humbert S. Nelli, "The Padrone System: An Exchange of Letters," *Labor History* 17 (1976): 406–12.

8. IPL, *Fourth Annual Report* (1913), 17, 21–22; IPL, *Fifth Annual Report* (1914), 16–17; IPL, *Sixth Annual Report* (1915), 20–21; IPL, *Seventh Annual Report* (1916), 18.

9. IPL, *Ninth Annual Report* (1918), 2.

10. City of Chicago, *Journal of the Proceedings of the City Council of Chicago for the Council Year 1911/12* (Chicago, 1912), 408–9, 690, 1477; City of Chicago, *Journal of the Proceedings of the City Council of Chicago for the Council Year 1912/13* (Chicago, 1913), 1811, 2036, 3367–72; City of Chicago, *Journal of the Proceedings of the City Council of Chicago for the Council Year 1914/15* (Chicago, 1915), 182, 466, 486; City of Chicago, *Journal of the Proceedings of the City Council of Chicago for the Council Year 1915/16* (Chicago, 1916), 1609; City of Chicago, *Journal of the Proceedings of the City Council of Chicago for the Council Year 1916/17* (Chicago, 1917), 2202–7, 2810, 4402; City of Chicago, *Journal of the Proceedings of the City Council of Chicago for the Council Year 1917/18* (Chicago, 1918), 272–73, 1164–65; State of Illinois, *Journal of the House of Representatives of the Fiftieth General Assembly for the Year 1917* (Springfield, 1917), 85, 147, 198, 228–29, 247, 302–3, 636, 846, 916, 952, 1148; State of Illinois, *Journal of the Senate of the Fiftieth General Assembly for the Year 1917* (Springfield, 1917), 430, 438, 531–32, 655, 798–99, 828–30, 842–43, 876–83, 897–901, 918, 920–21, 1237, 1295, 1304–7, 1326–29; State of Illinois, *Laws of the State of Illinois Enacted by the Fiftieth General Assembly, 1917* (Springfield, 1917), 206–15; Frederic Cople Jaher, *The Urban Establishment: Upper Strata in Boston, New York, Charleston, Chicago, and Los Angeles* (Chicago, 1982), 472–573; Joel A. Tarr, "J. R. Walsh of Chicago: A Case Study in Banking and Politics, 1881–1905," *Business History Review* 40 (1966): 451–66; R. G. Thomas, "Bank Failures in Chicago before 1925," *Journal of the Illinois State Historical Society* 28 (October 1935): 188–203; Frank C. James, *The Growth of the Chicago Banks* (New York, 1938), 2:824–66, 909–23; Frances Murray Huston, *Financing an Empire: History of Banking in Illinois* (Chicago, 1926), 1:201, 208, 453, 551–87.

11. Charles F. Spear, "What America Pays Europe for Immigrant Labor," *North American Review* 187 (January 1908): 106–16. See also IPL, *Fourth Annual Report* (1913), 17–20; IPL, *Sixth Annual Report* (1915), 10–12; IPL, *Eighth Annual Report* (1917), IPL, *Ninth Annual Report* (1918), 19–20; G. Abbott, *Immigrant and the Community,* 81–94; Luciano J. Iorizzo, "Italian Immigration and the Impact of the Padrone System," Ph.D. dissertation, University of Syracuse, 1966, 100–160.

12. A. F. Davis, *Spearheads for Reform*, 155–58, quote from page 156. See also John B. Miller, "The Politics of Municipal Reform in Chicago during the Progressive Era: The Municipal Voters' League as a Test Case, 1896–1920," master's dissertation, Roosevelt University, Chicago, 1966, 23–30; Chicago Municipal Voters' League, Official Records of Aldermen for the Years 1896–1925, Chicago Municipal Voters' League Records; Chicago Municipal Voters' League, Minutes of the Executive Committee, 20 February 1908, 25 February 1910, Chicago Municipal Voters' League Records; Kantowicz, *Polish-American Politics in Chicago*, 57–71, which includes a sketch of the candidates' curricula vitae.

13. *Evening Post* (Chicago), 9 November 1897; Addams, *Democracy and Social Ethics*, 221–77; G. Abbott, *Immigrant and the Community*, 256, 264; IPL, *First Annual Report* (1909/10), 5; Jane Addams, "Why the Ward Boss Rules," *Outlook*, 2 April 1898, 879–82; A. F. Davis, "Jane Addams vs. the Ward Boss," 247–65; Wald and Kellor, "Construction Camps of the People," 449–65; Kellor, "Who Is Responsible for the Immigrant," 912–17; Smith, "Lay Initiative," 214–49. See chapter 1, notes 15–23.

14. Dewey, "Autocracy under Cover," 103–6.

15. IPL, *First Annual Report* (1909/10), 5.

16. Kantowicz, *Polish-American Politics in Chicago*, 45–98; Busyn, "Political Career of Peter Kiolbassa," 8–22; Busyn, "Peter Kiolbassa: Maker of Polish America," 65–84; Barton, "Eastern and Southern Europeans," 150–75; Greene, "Becoming American," 158–65; Breckinridge, *New Homes for Old*, 108, 118, 124–229; Addams, *Democracy and Social Ethics*, 231–33, 235, 248–50; Peter Roberts, *The New Immigration* (New York, 1912), 63–77, 109–16; Nelli, *Italians in Chicago*, 63; Rudolph J. Vecoli, "Chicago's Italians prior to World War I: A Study of Their Social and Economic Adjustment," Ph.D. dissertation, University of Wisconsin, 1963, 259–61; Sharlene Hesse-Biber, "The Ethnic Ghetto as Private Welfare," *Italian Americana* 3 (1976): 9–14; John S. and Leatrice D. MacDonald, "Chain Migration, Ethnic Neighborhood Formation, and Social Networks," *Milbank Memorial Fund Quarterly* 42 (January 1964): 82–93; Perry Duis, "The Saloon in a Changing Chicago," *Chicago History* 4 (1975/6): 219–20; Addams, *Democracy and Social Ethics*, 221–77; Baker, "Hull House and the Ward Boss," 769–71; Scott, "Saint Jane and the Ward Boss," 12–17, 94–99; A. F. Davis, "Jane Addams vs. the Ward Boss," 247–65; Addams, "Why the Ward Boss Rules," 879–82; Forthal, "Relief and Friendly Service," 616–18; Banfield and Wilson, *City Politics*, 115–21; Johnston, *Political Corruption*, 36–57; Gonsell, *Machine Politics, Chicago Model*, 69–125; Cornwell, "Bosses, Machines, and Ethnic Groups," 27–37.

17. Addams, *Democracy and Social Ethics*, 221–77.

18. Park and H. A. Miller, *Old World Traits Transplanted*, 92–101; Hutchins Hapgood, *The Spirit of the Ghetto* (New York, 1902), 47–52, 79, 97, 114, 196, 261, 270, 283–94.

19. *Evening Post* (Chicago), 2 December 1916, Addams Newspaper Clippings, SCPC.

20. G. Abbott, *Immigrant and the Community*, 261–66, quote from page 265.

21. E. Abbott and Breckinridge, *Truancy*, 282–86; G. Abbott, *Immigrant and the Community*, 228–35; *Dziennik Chicagoski*, 2 June 1891, 11 July 1908, reel 48, FLPS;

Miaso, *History of Polish Education,* 97–171; Kuznicki, "Polish American Parochial Schools," 444–56; *Svornost,* 27 February 1880; *Dziennik Zwaizkowy,* 26 November 1910, 4 November 1911, reel 1, FLPS; *Denni Hlasatel,* 7 December 1911, 14 June 1917, reel 1, FLPS.

22. Addams, "Public School and the Immigrant Child," 99–102; *Denni Hlasatel,* 15 December 1911, 11 March 1912, 1 April 1912, reel 1, FLPS; Herbert A. Miller, "Treatment of Immigrant Heritages," in National Conference of Social Work, *Proceedings* (1919), 730–38; G. Abbott, *Immigrant and the Community,* 228–35.

23. G. Abbott, *Immigrant and the Community,* 103–4, and see 261–65, 282–98; Breckinridge, *New Homes for Old,* 223–24; IPL, Annual Reports, 1909–17.

24. Addams, "Chicago Settlements and Social Unrest," 157–62; Lawless, "Attitudes towards Integration," 201–11; Eisenstadt, *Absorption of Immigrants,* 189–202; De'Ath and Padbury, "Brokers and the Social Ecology of Minority Groups," 181–200; Trueblood, "Melting Pot," 153–67; Addams, "Americanization," 211; G. Abbott, *Immigrant and the Community,* 261–65; Park, *Immigrant Press and Its Control,* 448–68.

25. Addams, *Twenty Years,* 322; A. F. Davis, "Raymond Robins," 131–41; Lincoln Steffens, *The Shame of the Cities* (New York, 1904), 162–94; G. R. Taylor, "Chicago Settlements in Ward Politics," 183–85; Sigmund Zeisler, "The Municipal Voters' League," *World Review,* 25 January 1902, 3–11; Sidney I. Roberts, "Chicago Civic Profiles," *Men and Events* 34 (1958): 22–23, 31–32; Sidney I. Roberts, "The Municipal Voters' League and Chicago Boodlers," *Journal of the Illinois State Historical Society* 53 (Summer 1960): 117–48; J. S. Miller, "Politics of Municipal Reforms," 31–36; Chicago Municipal Voters' League, Annual Reports on Aldermanic Candidates, 1897–1925, Chicago Municipal Voters' League Records; Municipal Voters' League, Executive Committee Minutes, 30 December 1903–2 January 1931, Chicago Municipal Voters' League Records; Addams, *Democracy and Social Ethics,* 221–73; G. Abbott, *Immigrant and the Community,* 252–66.

26. IPL, Board of Trustees Lists, 1909–17, Annual Reports, 1909–17. For biographies of the "new immigrant" membership: A. N. Marquis, *The Book of Chicagoans* (1911), 2d edition (1915), 3d edition (1917); *The Chicago City Directory* for the years 1908–20; Francis Boleck, ed., *Who's Who in Polish America* (New York, 1943); David Droba, ed., *Czech and Slovak Leaders in Metropolitan Area* (Chicago, 1931).

27. IPL, Lists of Organizations Membership, 1909–17, Annual Reports 1909–17.

28. IPL, Annual Reports, 1901–17; Breckinridge, *New Homes for Old,* 192, 223–26, 272–76.

29. Janowitz, *Thomas on Social Organization,* lvi–lvii.

30. Record of Hull House Association, 1895–1920, Hull House Papers; List of Members of the Hull House Board of Trustees, 1903–10, box 2, series 13e, Addams Papers, SCPC.

31. *Hull House Year Book,* 1910, 10; *L'Italia,* 15–16 February, 24–25 August 1895, *La Tribuna,* 11 February 1895, and *Inter-Ocean* (Chicago), 11 February 1895, Addams Newspaper Clippings, SCPC; Rabbi Joseph Stolz to J. Witkowsky, 2 November 1893, Stolz Papers, box 2249, American Jewish Archives, Cincinnati; Philip P. Bregston, *Chicago and Its Jews: A Cultural History* (Chicago, 1933), 48–49; Hyman L. Meites, *History of the Jews of Chicago* (Chicago, 1924), 184–85.

32. G. Abbott, *Immigrant and the Community*, 103, 195. See also Ethel Bird, "Informal Discussion on the Value of the Foreign Born Language Worker," in National Conference of Social Work, *Proceedings* (1919), 746; IPL, Annual Reports, 1909–17; Elizabeth L. Holbrook to Sophonisba P. Breckinridge, 23 December 1918, box 3, S. P. Breckinridge Papers, Library of Congress; Ruth Fitzsimons to Sophonisba P. Breckinridge, 2 August 1919, Breckinridge Papers; Edith T. Bremer, "The Foreign Language Worker in the Fusion Process: An Indispensable Asset to Social Work," in National Conference of Social Work, *Proceedings* (1919), 740–46; Virginia N. Murray, "The Training and Use of Nationality Workers," in ibid. (1922), 484–87; Breckinridge, *New Homes for Old*, 181–82, 228, 244–49, 281–86.

33. Hull House Residents Lists, 1889–1929, Hull House Papers; *Hull House Year Book*, 1906/7, 5–13; 1910, 8–14; 1913, 8–18; 1916, 8–11, 28, 36, 42.

34. Sidney A. Teller, "Informal Discussion on the Value of the Foreign Born Language Worker," in National Conference of Social Work, *Proceedings* (1919), 746. See also Abel, "Middle-Class Culture," 600–616; Sloan, "Cultural Uplift," 361–72; Aimee Sears, "Training of American Workers for Successful Work among Immigrants," in National Conference of Social Work, *Proceedings* (1922), 482–84; Kate H. Claghorn, "The Work of Voluntary Immigrant Protective Agencies," in ibid. (1919), 747–54; G. Abbott, *Immigrant and the Community*, 103–4, 292–95; *Tribune* (Detroit), 19 August 1916, DGI Series, box 1906, Addams Papers, SCPC; Chicago School of Civics and Philanthropy, *Bulletin*, vol. 1 (July 1909), 33; no. 5 (July 1910), 137; no. 12 (July 1911), 16–17; no. 15 (March 1912), 17; no. 24 (July 1914), 19; no. 39 (April 1918), 22, box I, Taylor Papers; Course on Immigration, box 11, folder 2, box 12, folder 9, Edith Abbott Papers, University of Chicago Library.

## Chapter Six

1. Thomas Holland to Rivka Lissak, 5 August 1978.

2. Addams, *Twenty Years*, 232, 256–58, 426, 436–37; Addams, *Newer Ideals of Peace*, 70; Addams, "Recent Immigration," 245–63.

3. Bregston, *Chicago and Its Jews*, 331–58; Mrs. Benjamin Davis, "Religious Activity," in Charles S. Bernheimer, ed., *The Russian Jew in the United States* (Philadelphia, 1905), 250; Zublin, "Chicago Ghetto," 101–11; Rabbi E. Mushkin to Rivka Lissak, interview, August 1977.

4. E. Abbott and Sophonisba P. Breckinridge, *The Tenements of Chicago, 1908–1935* (Chicago, 1936), 85–92; Mrs. Benjamin Davis, "General Aspects of the Population of Chicago," in Charles S. Bernheimer, ed., *The Russian Jew in the United States* (Philadelphia, 1905), 58; Louis Wirth, *The Ghetto: A Study of Isolation* (Chicago, 1928), 278; "Jewish Social and Recreational Needs of the Jewish Community of Chicago," 1922, Jewish People's Institute Papers, CHS; Zublin, "Chicago Ghetto," 93; Meites, *History of the Jews*, 317, 339.

5. Bregston, *Chicago and Its Jews*, 51–54; Mrs. B. Davis, "Religious Activity," 174; Mrs. B. Davis, "General Aspects," 58; Minnie F. Low, "Philanthropy," in Charles S. Bernheimer, ed., *The Russian Jew in the United States* (Philadelphia, 1905), 92; I. K. Friedman, "Amusements and Social Life," in ibid., 252–54; Morris A. Gutstein, *A Priceless Heritage: The Epic Growth of Nineteenth Century*

*Chicago Jewry* (New York, 1953), 43–45; Morris A. Gutstein, *Profiles of Freedom: Essay in American Jewish History* (Chicago, 1967), 105–24; Bernard Horwich, *My First Eighty Years* (Chicago, 1939), 145–52; Meites, *History of the Jews,* 176, 657–76; Seymour J. Pomerenz, "Aspects of Chicago Russian Jewish Life, 1893–1915," in Simon Rawidowicz, ed., *The Chicago Pinkas* (Chicago, 1952), 117, 126–29; Zublin, "Chicago Ghetto," 108; *Courier,* 4 April 1910, reel 35; 24 October 1910, reel 32, FLPS.

6. Beth Moshav Z'keinim, Twentieth Anniversary, Lists of Board of Directors, 1901–2, Jewish Chicago Historical Society; Marks Nathan Jewish Orphan Home History, Jewish Chicago Historical Society; Meites, *History of the Jews,* 151–240; Bregston, *Chicago and Its Jews,* 102–217.

7. See note 5; Menahem B. Sacks, "Orthodox Shul," in *One Hundred Years of Chicago Jewry, Sentinel,* Jubilee Issue (August 1948): 30–31; Beth Moshav Z'keinim, Twentieth Anniversary, Jewish Chicago Historical Society; Federated Orthodox Charities, Board of Directors Minutes, folders 43–46, Marks Nathan Jewish Orphan Home, Jewish Chicago Historical Society; Meites, *History of the Jews,* 151–240.

8. Beth Moshav Z'keinim, Twentieth Anniversary, List of Contributors, 1920, Jewish Chicago Historical Society; Marks Nathan Jewish Orphan Home History 1906–23, 1925, Jewish Chicago Historical Society; Minutes of the United Hebrew Charities 1888–1900 and the Associated Jewish Charities 1900–1923, Jewish Chicago Historical Society.

9. C. L. Mishkin, "Talmud Torahs," in *One Hundred Years of Chicago Jewry, Sentinel,* Jubilee Issue (August 1948): 41, 45, 48–49, 102; Samuel M. Blumenfield, "Education," in ibid., 26, 114, 116; Harold Korey, "The History of Jewish Education in Chicago," master's dissertation, University of Chicago, 1942.

10. A. Margolin, "Landsmanshaften," in *One Hundred Years of Chicago Jewry, Sentinel,* Jubilee Issue (August 1948): 69, 95; Charles E. Kaye, "Fraternal Orders," in ibid., 79, 82; Charles E. Kaye, "Fraternal Orders: Those National Groups Having Local Chapters in Chicago," *Sentinel,* special issue (1960): 188–89; William Jay Robinson, "Helping Each Other: The Story of the Landsmanshaften," ibid., 198–99; Pomerenz, "Chicago Russian Jewish Life," 126–29.

11. M. Margolin, "The Yiddish Stage," in *One Hundred Years of Chicago Jewry, Sentinel,* Jubilee Issue (August 1948): 81, 84–85; Danny Newman, "The Yiddish Theatre," *Sentinel,* special issue (1960), 109–11.

12. Bregston, *Chicago and Its Jews,* 49–79, 115–23; Mrs. B. Davis, "Religious Activity," 181; Gutstein, *Priceless Heritage,* 403–9; Gutstein, *Profiles of Freedom,* 141–44; Horwich, *My First Eighty Years,* 228, 231, 268; Meites, *History of the Jews,* 167–201, 549–766.

13. Ben Aronin, "The Jewish Press," *Sentinel,* special issue (1960): 112–13; Meites, *History of the Jews,* 358–64.

14. Bregston, *Chicago and Its Jews,* 49–79; Mrs. B. Davis, "Religious Activity," 181; Gutstein, *Priceless Heritage,* 403–9; Gutstein, *Profiles of Freedom,* 141–44; Horwich, *My First Eighty Years,* 228, 231, 268; Meites, *History of the Jews,* 167–201, 549–766.

15. Eviatar Friesl, "The 'Knights of Zion' in Chicago and Their Relations with the Zionist Federation in America, 1898–1916," in Daniel Carpi, ed., *Zionism* (Tel Aviv,

1970), 1:122–24; Nathan D. Kaplan, "Zionism," in *One Hundred Years of Chicago Jewry, Sentinel,* Jubilee Issue (August 1948), 39, 50; Meites, *History of the Jews,* 195–96, 202; *Maccabaean* 1 (December 1901): 134; 2 (February 1902): 95–96; 2 (June 1902): 338–39; 30 (January 1917): 136–37, 144.

16. Bregston, *Chicago and Its Jews,* 88, 94–100, 137–38; Marnin Feinstein, *American Zionism, 1884–1904* (New York, 1965), 30; Gutstein, *Priceless Heritage,* 403–9; Horwich, *My First Eighty Years,* 122–25, 130, 135–37, 228–34, 254–58; Jacob R. Marcus, "European Bibliographical Items on Chicago," in Simon Rawidowicz, ed., *The Chicago Pinkas* (Chicago, 1952), 178–79; Meites, *History of the Jews,* 167–68, 195, 197, 203–5, 234, 244–49, 290, 408; Chayim M. Rothblatt, "Chicago Hebrew Press," in Simon Rawidowicz, ed., *The Chicago Pinkas* (Chicago, 1952), NG; M. J. Sable, "Some American Jewish Organizational Efforts to Combat Anti-Semitism," Ph.D. dissertation, New York, 1964, 46; Wirth, *Ghetto,* 44, 101–6, 128–29, 180–81, 189, 192, 268, 271–72; *Hameliz,* 7 March 1886, 502; *Reform Advocate,* 18 February 1899, 20 May 1905, FLPS; *Illinois Staats Zeitung,* 19 April 1901, reel 37, FLPS; *Chicago Chronicle,* 20 November 1905, reel 36, FLPS; *Courier,* 22 January 1905, reel 36, FLPS; *Record Herald* (Chicago), 22 November 1905, Addams Newspaper Clippings, SCPC.

17. Ben Halfern, "The Americanization of Zionism," *American Jewish History* 69 (September 1979): 15–33; *American Jewish Year Book* (New York, 1900/1), 181.

18. Gutstein, *Priceless Heritage,* 249; Korey, "Jewish Education in Chicago," 80–127.

19. Korey, "Jewish Education in Chicago," 80–81, 104, 126–27, quote from page 80. See also Bregston, *Chicago and Its Jews,* 53–54, 63–67, 94–97, 247–48; Feinstein, *American Zionism,* 214, 238; Meites, *History of the Jews,* 563; Rothblatt, "Chicago Hebrew Press," pp. MD, MH, ND; *Maccabaean,* 3 (June 1902): 342, 4 (January 1905): 55.

20. Kaplan, "Zionism," 32; Meites, *History of the Jews,* 216–18, 225; Max Shulman, "The First American Disciples," in *Theodor Herzl Memorial, New Palestine* (New York, 1929), 223.

21. Meites, *History of the Jews,* 218. See also *Observer,* no. 4 (1914/15): 16.

22. Meites, *History of the Jews,* 226. See also Zvi Scharfstein, *History of Jewish Education* (Jerusalem, 1970), 3:55; *Courier,* 13 October 1907, reel 32, FLPS.

23. Dr. A. Fischkin to Julius Rosenwald, 11 March 1908, box 18, Julius Rosenwald Papers, University of Chicago Manuscript Room.

24. Kaplan, "Zionism," 38; Shulman, "First American Disciples," 223.

25. Bregston, *Chicago and Its Jews,* 89–97, 119–20, 331–33; Horwich, *My First Eighty Years,* 223–34, 237, 272–82; Kaplan, "Zionism," 39, 50; Anita L. Leberson, "Zionism Comes to Chicago," in Isidore S. Meyer, ed., *Early History of Zionism in America* (New York, 1958), 177; Meites, *History of the Jews,* 216–26, 243; Scharfstein, *History of Jewish Education* 3:55; Shulman, "First American Disciples," 223; *American Hebrew,* 21 April 1899, 841; *Observer,* no. 6 (1913/14): 47–53, 59.

26. Chicago Hebrew Institute, Minutes of the Meeting of the Board of Directors, 19 January 1910, box I, Jewish Community Centers of Chicago Papers, CHS, hereafter JCC Papers; *Observer,* November 1912, reel 31, FLPS; Lusil Pintozzi to Rivka Lissak, interview, 29 August 1977.

27. *Messenger*, November 1909; *Observer*, no. 12 (1911/12), no. 1 (1913/14), no. 1 (1918/19), no. 2 (1918/19); *Courier*, 10 October 1909, 15 October 1913, 15 April 1918, reel 31; *Reform Advocate*, 13 February 1926, reel 34; all in FLPS.

28. Chicago Hebrew Institute, Minutes of the Meeting of the Board of Directors, 1907/8, box I, JCC Papers; *Messenger*, November 1909; *Observer*, no. 12 (1911/12); *Courier*, 16 July 1915, reel 31, FLPS.

29. *Observer*, no. 6 (1913/14) 15. See also Bregston, *Chicago and Its Jews*, 234, 291; Horwich, *My First Eighty Years*, 274–75; *Messenger*, November 1909; *Observer*, no. 12 (1911/12), no. 1 (1913/14), no. 1 (1914/15), no. 6 (1918/19); *Courier*, 9 December 1907, 16 October 1908, 8 December 1911, 6 March 1916, 10 July 1917, 10 November 1920, reel 35, FLPS; *Forward*, 23 February 1919, reel 33, FLPS; Chicago Hebrew Institute, Hebrew Oratorio Society, October 1917, box 6, Rosenwald Papers.

30. Meites, *History of the Jews*, 226; *Observer*, no. 1 (1914/15); *Courier*, 31 October 1907, reel 39; 2 January 1914, reel 39; 5 February 1915, reel 33; 18 and 21 September 1916, reels 32, 39, FLPS; *Forward*, 6 March 1919, reel 33, FLPS.

31. Bregston, *Chicago and Its Jews*, 119; Kaplan, "Zionism," 50–52; Meites, *History of the Jews*, 217–18; Shulman, "First American Disciples," 223; Chicago Hebrew Institute, Minutes of the Meeting of the Board of Directors, 19 January 1910, 30 June 1915, 22 December 1915, 21 March 1918, JCC Papers; *Observer*, no. 6 (1913/14): 1–58, no. 7 (1913/14): 14, no. 10 (1913/14): 7–8, no. 3 (1914/15): 18, no. 4 (1914/15): 13, no. 3 (1915/16): 8.

32. On the weekly activities of Zionist clubs and youth movements, see Clubs and Societies Lists in the Chicago Hebrew Institute *Observer*, page 2, every month. On Zionist clubs and youth movement special activities, see *Observer*, no. 6 (1913/14): 22, no. 6 (1915/16): 70–71, no. 11 (1915/16): 16, no. 6 (1916/17): 78–79, no. 10 (1916/17): 9–10, no. 11 (1916/17): 23, no. 12 (1916/17): 17, no. 6 (1917/18): 57–59, 61, nos. 10–11 (1917/18): 14; *Courier*, 24 September 1916, reel 39, FLPS. For Zionist special cultural events, see *Observer*, no. 2 (1914/15): 18, no. 6 (1914/15): 61–63, no. 2 (1915/16): 15, no. 6 (1915/16): 88, no. 13 (1915/16): 10–11; *Courier*, 3 March 1916, reel 39, FLPS. For Zionist mass meetings and conventions, see *Messenger*, November 1909; *Observer*, no. 2 (1913/14): 7, 8, no. 8 (1913/14): 17, no. 9 (1913/14): 16, no. 10 (1913/14): 16, no. 2 (1914/15): 15, no. 6 (1914/15): 55, nos. 7–8 (1914/15): 27, no. 2 (1915/16): 15–16, no. 3 (1915/16): 7–10, no. 4 (1915/16): 15–16, no. 8 (1915/16): 10, no. 9 (1915/16): 10, no. 11 (1915/16): 18, no. 6 (1916/17): 71, no. 9 (1916/17): 13, no. 3 (1917/18): 9–10; *Courier*, 31 October 1907, 15 January 1909, 22 April 1910, reel 39, FLPS.

33. *Observer*, no. 2 (1915/16): 15, no. 3 (1915/16): 8.

34. Bregston, *Chicago and Its Jews*, 57, 71, 102–282; Horwich, *My First Eighty Years*, 254–78; Meites, *History of the Jews*, 203–4, 224–50, 549–640; Judah Rosenthal, "Beginnings of the Eastern-European Jewish Settlement in Chicago," in Simon Rawidowicz, ed., *The Chicago Pinkas* (Chicago, 1952), KZ–KH.

35. Bregston, *Chicago and Its Jews*, 6, 224, 232, 246–49; Feinstein, *American Zionism*, 214; Gutstein, *Priceless Heritage*, 129, 405; Horwich, *My First Eighty Years*, 233–34; Kaplan, "Zionism," 39, 50; Meites, *History of the Jews*, 164–67, 202–3, 643–44; Shulman, "First American Disciples," 223–24; *American Hebrew*, April

1899, 841; *Chicago Interior,* 10 September, 1903, 1186; *Maccabaean* 2 (June 1902): 342, 339; 4 (January 1903): 62; *Courier,* 10 July 1913, 2 January 1914, reel 39, FLPS.

36. Bregston, *Chicago and Its Jews,* 277; Gutstein, *Priceless Heritage,* 50–52; Gutstein, *Profiles of Freedom,* 115–22; Meites, *History of the Jews,* 131, 643–44, 661, 664, 666, 670; Shulman, "First American Disciples," 223; *Die Welt,* no. 28 (1900): 16; *Maccabaean* 9 (July 1905): 24; *Courier,* 20 June, 13 October 1910, 12 June 1917, reel 38, FLPS; *Observer,* no. 2 (1915/16): 15, no. 3 (1915/16): 8.

37. Bregston, *Chicago and Its Jews,* 246–49; Meites, *History of the Jews,* 202–3, 228, 234–35, 289–95; Shulman, "First American Disciples," 223–24; *Courier,* 2 May, 7 June 1912, reel 31, FLPS; *Haychudi,* no. 31 (1910): 15; *Sentinel,* 19 March 1915; *American Jewish Year b Book* (1917/18), 239.

38. Bregston, *Chicago and Its Jews,* 102–282; Meites, *History of the Jews,* 203–50; Rosenthal, "Eastern-European Jewish Settlement," KZ-KH; Horwich, *My First Eighty Years,* 254–78.

39. Bregston, *Chicago and Its Jews,* 48–51; Meites, *History of the Jews,* 186, 217; Horwich, *My First Eighty Years,* 158.

40. *Hull House Year Book,* 1906/7, 29, 38–39; 1910, 42; 1913, 38.

41. *Hull House Year Book,* 1906/7, 28, 32, 48; 1910, 30, 31; 1913, 31, 32; 1916, 20, 37.

42. *Hull House Year Book,* 1906/7, 48.

43. Addams, "Chicago Settlements and Social Unrest," 155–66; Addams, *Twenty Years,* 403–16; James Rudin, "From Kishinev to Chicago: The Forgotten Story of Zazar Averbuch," *Midstream* 18 (1972): 63–75; Bregston, *Chicago and Its Jews,* 8, 9, 13, 17–18, 48–51, 55–57, 66, 72–73, 88–90, 97, 102–4, 137–38, 180–85, 213, 222, 230, 232–37, 239–41; A. F. Davis and McCree, *Eighty Years at Hull House,* 107; Mrs. B. Davis, "Religious Activity," 172–75, 48, 65, 82–120; Gutstein, *Profiles of Freedom,* 141; Gutstein, *Priceless Heritage,* 272–73, 351–55; Horwich, *My First Eighty Years,* 131, 135, 144, 151, 158, 257–58, 262–65, 293–307; Frederick C. Giffin, "The Rudowitz Extradition Case," *Journal of the Illinois State Historical Society* 75 (Spring 1982): 61–72; Low, "Philanthropy," 94; Meites, *History of the Jews,* 150–51, 168, 184–86, 190, 194, 196, 204–5, 217, 231, 245–49, 304, 359, 453–69, 554, 580–89, 596–99, 604, 616–21, 630–40; Pomerenz, "Chicago Russian Jewish Life," 127; *American* (Chicago), 6 November 1910, Addams Newspaper Clippings, SCPC; *Chicago Post,* 2 May 1908, Addams Newspaper Clippings, SCPC; *Chicago Tribune,* 19 May 1903, 3 May 1908, 12 and 21 December 1908, 30 October 1910, Addams Newspaper Clippings, SCPC; *Courier,* 20 June 1910, reel 38, 29 October, 1920, reel 33, FLPS; *Evening Post* (Chicago), 4, 5, and 25 November 1910, Addams Newspaper Clippings, SCPC; *Forward,* 3 August 1920, reel 33, FLPS; *L'Italia,* 28 September 1915, reel 30, FLPS; *La Parola dei Socialisti,* 21 January 1911, reel 30, FLPS; *New York Times,* 6 November 1910, Addams Newspaper Clippings, SCPC; *Record Herald,* 19 May 1903, 28 November 1910, Addams Newspaper Clippings, SCPC; Clarence Darrow to Jane Addams, 11 September 1901, Addams Papers, SCPC; John O. Bentall, State Secretary of the Socialist Party of Chicago, to Jane Addams, 17 December 1908, Addams Papers, SCPC; Sidney Hillman to Jane Addams, 22 December 1915, Hull House Papers.

44. Addams, "Chicago Settlements and Social Unrest," 159; Horwich, *My First Eighty Years,* 262–65, quote from page 264; unknown newspaper, n.d. See also

Bregston, *Chicago and Its Jews,* 180–85; Rudin, "From Kishinev to Chicago," 63–75; *Evening Post* (Chicago), 2 May 1908; *Record Herald,* 3 and 5 May 1908; *Chicago Tribune,* 3 May 1908; *Republican* (Denver), 7 May 1908; *Republican* (Springfield, Mass.), 7 May 1908; *Public,* 8 May 1908; all newspapers from series 13a, box 9, Addams Papers, SCPC.

45. Meites, *History of the Jews,* 245–49; Bregston, *Chicago and Its Jews,* 225–28; unknown newspaper, 12 December 1908, Addams Newspaper Clippings, SCPC; Giffin, "Rudowitz Extradition Case," 61–72.

46. U.S. House of Representatives, Petition and Memorials, 62A-H10.2, National Archives, Washington; U.S. House of Representatives, night letter to Congressman Charles E. Fuller, 8 May 1912, 62A-H10.2, National Archives; *Evening Post* (Chicago), 18 May 1912, box 15, folder May 1912, Addams Papers, SCPC; Addams, *Twenty Years,* 400–426; Bregston, *Chicago and Its Jews,* 181–82, 225–28; Meites, *History of the Jews,* 245–49; Addams, "Chicago Settlements and Social Unrest," 155–66.

47. Meites, *History of the Jews,* 673; Abraham Bisno, *Abraham Bisno: Union Pioneer* (Madison, 1964), 1–100; Gutstein, *Priceless Heritage,* 302–7; Kaye, "Fraternal Orders," 82; Gutstein, *Profiles of Freedom,* 25.

48. Meites, *History of the Jews,* 203, 653–54, 667; Milton J. Silberman, "Zionism: The Chicago Movement, 1910–1960," *Sentinel* (1960): 172; *Observer,* 1914/15, 1916, 1918; *Courier,* 3 and 24 September 1916, 19 May 1918, reel 39, FLPS.

49. Mark M. Krug, *History of the Yiddish Schools in Chicago* (Chicago), 1–67; Kaye, "Fraternal Orders," 82; Meites, *History of the Jews,* 654.

50. Addams, *Twenty Years,* 201–2; A. F. Davis, *Spearheads for Reform,* 123–27; Josephine Goldmark, *Impatient Crusader* (Urbana, Ill., 1953), 1–72; Bisno, *Abraham Bisno: Union Pioneer,* 88, 98–99, 115–24, 144–45, 171–72; Joseph M. Jacobs, "The Story of the Jewish Trade Union Movement," *Sentinel* (1960): 79–84; Matthew Josephson, *Sidney Hillman: Statesman of American Labor* (Garden City, N.Y., 1952), 42–57; Ellen G. Starr, "The Chicago Clothing Strike," *New Review* (March 1916): 62–64; Sidney Hillman to Ellen G. Starr, 22 December 1915, Sidney Hillman to Ellen G. Starr, 27 February 1939, Jacob S. Potobsky to Ellen G. Starr, 24 February 1939, series 3, box 11, folder 122, Ellen G. Starr Papers, Sophia Smith Collection, Smith College, Northampton, Mass.; Wildred Carsel, *A History of the Chicago Ladies Garment Workers' Union* (Chicago, 1940), 28–29, 98–99, 124–25, 170–71; *Chicago Tribune,* 19 May 1903; *Record Herald,* 19 May 1903; *Chicago Tribune,* 12 and 21 December 1908; the three newspapers from Addams Newspaper Clippings, SCPC.

51. Philip Davis, *And Crown Thy Good* (New York, 1952), 82–183.

52. Vecoli, "Chicago's Italians prior to World War I", 6–81, 98–120, 138–55; Agnes S. Holbrook, "Maps, Notes, and Comments," in Jane Addams et al., *Hull House Maps and Papers* (Boston, 1895), 3–26; Nelli; *Italians in Chicago,* 34–37.

53. Breckinridge, *New Homes for Old,* 218, 239, 241, 246; Edward M. Dunne, "Memoirs of 'Zi Pre,' " *Ecclesiastical Review* 49 (August 1913): 192–203; "The Italian and the Settlement," *Survey,* 12 April 1913, 58–59; Park and H. A. Miller, *Old World Traits Transplanted,* 151–58; Nelli, *Italians in Chicago,* 73, 77, 103, 153, 170–78, 193–94, 198, 209, 232, 350, 350–59; Kate G. Prindiville, "Italy in Chicago," *Catholic World* 76 (July 1903): 452–61; Giovanni E. Schiavo, *The Italians*

in *Chicago: A Study in Americanization.* (Chicago, 1928), 6, 55–57, 68–70; Vecoli, "Contadini in Chicago," 406–8, 414; William F. Whyte, *Street Corner Society: The Social Structure of an Italian Slum* (Chicago, 1958), 99; Vecoli, "Chicago's Italians prior to World War I," 138–55; Frank Orman Beck, "The Italian in Chicago," *Bulletin of the Chicago Department of Public Welfare* 2 (February 1919): 22–23.

54. Beck, "Italian in Chicago," 23; Schiavo, *Italians in Chicago,* 65; Nelli, *Italians in Chicago,* 105, 134–38, 173–79; *L'Italia,* 5 December 1908, reel 31, FLPS; *La Tribuna,* 28 April 1906, reel 31, FLPS.

55. Nelli, *Italians in Chicago,* 174–76, 239, 242; Park and H. A. Miller, *Old World Traits Transplanted,* 132–33; Schiavo, *Italians in Chicago,* 59.

56. Prindiville, "Italy in Chicago," 452–61; Humbert S. Nelli, "Italians in Urban America: A Study in Ethnic Adjustment," *International Migration Review* 1 (1967): 47–49; Rudolph J. Vecoli, "Prelates and Peasants: Italian Immigrants and the Catholic Church," *Journal of Social History* 2 (Spring 1969): 217–68.

57. Addams, *Twenty Years,* 231–33, 256–58; Addams, "Objective Value," 37; *L'Italia,* 23 March 1889, 25 January 1890, 13 February, 29 October 1892, 8 January, 16 September 1893, 3 June, 25 November 1899, 24 May 1902, 26 September 1903, 10 December 1904, 14 January 1905, 12 January 1913, 28 February 1914, 7 February 1915, reels 30, 31, FLPS; *Hull House Bulletin,* 1904–5; IPL, List of Board of Trustees Members, 1909–11, in *First Annual Report* (1909/10), 3.

58. *La Parola,* 19 July 1913, Hull House Papers; see also *Hull House Bulletin,* no. 7 (1896): 8, no. 2 (1897): 8–9, no. 4 (1901): 15, no. 1 (1902): 2, 15–16, no. 2 (1902): 13–14, no. 2 (1903/4): 14, no. 1 (1905/6): 2.

59. Marquis, *Book of Chicagoans* (1917); *L'Italia,* 3 June 1899, 16 September 1893, 14 January 1905, 12 January 1913, 28 February 1914, 7 February 1915, reels 30, 31, FLPS; IPL, List of Board of Trustees Members, 1909–11, in *First Annual Report* (1909/10), 3.

60. See notes 7 and 58; *Chicago City Directory,* vols. 1901–4; *Hull House Bulletin,* no. 4 (1901): 15, no. 1 (1902): 2, 15, no. 2 (1902): 2, no. 2 (1903/4): 11–14, 17, no. 1 (1905/6): 2, 15, 23; *Hull House Year Book,* 1906/7, 49; Addams, *Twenty Years,* 256, 257–58; *L'Italia,* 14 May, 1892, reel 30, 23 May 1903, reel 31, 19 December 1908, reel 30, 10 June 1911, reel 31, FLPS; *La Tribuna,* 11 and 18 June 1904, 15 July 1906, 13 August 1907, reels 30, 31, FLPS.

61. Mary L. McCree, "The First Year of Hull House, 1889–1890: Letters by Jane Addams and Ellen G. Starr," *Chicago History* (Fall 1970): 101–14; Marks, "Two Women's Work"; Addams, *Twenty Years,* 232, 362; *Hull House Bulletin,* no. 1 (1896), no. 6 (1896): 7, no. 7 (1896): 8, no. 1 (1897): 9, no. 5 (1897): 7, no. 11 (1898): 8, no. 1 (1900): 7, no. 4 (1901): 15, no. 1 (1902): 2, no. 1 (1903/4): 10, no. 1 (1905/6): 11, 14; *Hull House Year Book,* 1906/7, 23, 28; 1919, 31; 1913, 32; 1916, 37; *L'Italia,* 4–5 May 1895, 9 April 1904; *La Parola,* 17 January 1908, 27 September 1913; *Record Herald,* 1 March 1908; all newspapers from reels 30, 31, FLPS.

62. *New World,* 30 April, 11 and 25 June 1904; *L'Italia,* 11 June, 2 July 1904; *La Tribuna,* 11 and 25 June, 2 July 1904, 20 August 1904, 9 September 1906; *Chicago Tribune,* 1 March 1908; *Record Herald,* 1 March 1908; all newspapers from reels 30, 31, FLPS; Addams, "Objective Value," 49–50; Baker, "Hull House and the Ward Boss," 770; A. F. Davis, *Spearheads for Reform,* 153, 161–62; Scott, "Saint Jane and the Ward Boss," 96.

63. *New World,* 29 February 1908. See also *La Parola,* 5 March 1908, reel 31, 10 January 1914, reel 30, FLPS; *Record Herald,* 1 March 1908, reel 30, FLPS; *New World,* 7 March, 25 April 1908, 22 and 27 February, 6 March 1914.

64. *La Parola,* 17 January 1908, reel 30, FLPS; *Record Herald,* 1 March 1908, reel 30, FLPS; *New World,* 29 February, 7 March, 25 April 1908, 6 March 1914.

65. Florence Kelley to Henry Lloyd, 26 September 1898, Henry Lloyd Papers, Wisconsin State Historical Society, Madison; Addams, "Objective Value," 49–50; Baker, "Hull House and the Ward Boss," 770; Scott, "Saint Jane and the Ward Boss," 96; Father Sam De Vito, Our Lady of Pompei Parish, to Rivka Lissak, interview, 16 July 1979; Sister Carmela (Mary Filibert), Order de Notre Dame, to Rivka Lissak, interview, 8 July 1979; *New World,* 17 June 1899, 2 February 1907.

66. Mary A. Amberg, *Madonna Center* (Chicago, 1976), 40–46; *New World,* 10 April 1914, 8 October 1915, 30 November 1917.

67. Amberg, *Madonna Center,* 39.

68. Robert Free, "Settlements or Unsettlements," *Nineteenth Century* 63 (March 1908): 365–80; John P. Walsh, "The Catholic Church in Chicago and the Problems of Urban Society, 1893–1915," Ph.D. dissertation, University of Chicago, 1948, 36–37; *L'Italia,* 24–25 August 1895, reel 30, FLPS; *New World,* 18 March 1899, 20 August 1904, 22 February 1913.

69. Amberg, *Madonna Center,* 40–46, 67–82, 100–110; *New World,* 8 October 1895, 26 November 1910, 22 March 1913, 30 November 1917.

70. Amberg, *Madonna Center,* 83; *Hull House Year Book,* 1906/7, 28–29; Vecoli, "Prelates and Peasants," 258–59; Thomas W. Holland to Rivka Lissak, 5 August 1978.

71. *New World,* 26 November 1910.

72. Amberg, *Madonna Center,* 83.

73. McCree, "First Year of Hull House," 101–14; Marks, "Two Women's Work."

74. *Hull House Year Book,* 1910, 10; *Inter-Ocean* (Chicago), 11 February 1895, Addams Newspaper Clippings, SCPC; *L'Italia,* 15–17 February, 24–25 August 1895, reel 30, FLPS; *La Parola,* 19 July 1913, reel 30, FLPS; *La Tribuna,* 11 February 1895, Newspaper Clippings, Hull House Papers; Italian Institute, circular sent by Alex. Mastro-Valerio to Italian leaders, 15 February 1895, Hull House Papers; Mrs. James A. Britton to Miss Longan, 23 August 1919, Addams Papers, SCPC; U.S. House of Representatives, night letter to Congressman Charles E. Fuller, 8 May 1912; *Evening Post* (Chicago), 18 May 1912, Addams Newspaper Clippings, SCPC.

75. Nelli, *Italians in Chicago,* 79–80, 105–12, 123, 134, 138, 173–74; *Evening Post* (Chicago), 8 November 1897; see also chapter 5.

76. Vecoli, "Chicago's Italians prior to World War I," 53–62, 89–91, 235–337; Schiavo, *Italians in Chicago,* 65; *L'Italia,* 27 May 1899, 16 December 1911, 16 January 1912, reels 30, 31, FLPS; Chicago Municipal Voters' League, Official Records of Aldermen, 1897, Chicago Municipal Voters' League Records; Illinois Bureau of Labor Statistics, *Tenth Annual Report,* (1909), 76–84; Illinois Bureau of Labor Statistics, *Thirteenth Annual Report,* (1912), 91–111; Illinois Bureau of Labor Statistics, *Fourteenth Annual Report,* (1913), 100–121; G. Abbott, "Chicago Employment Agency," 289–305; E. Abbott, "Sister's Memories," 359, 367–69; G. Abbott, *Immigrant and the Community,* 83–95; Nelli, *Italians in Chicago,* 62–63, 79–80, 105; Humbert S. Nelli, "The Italian Padrone System in the United States,"

*Labor History* 5 (Spring 1964): 153–67; Iorizzo, "Padrone and Immigrant Distribution," 55, 58, 74; Vecoli, "Contadini in Chicago," 412–13; IPL, Annual Reports, 1909–17.

77. Chicago Municipal Voters' League, Official Records of Aldermen for the Years 1896–1925, Chicago Municipal Voters' League Records; A. F. Davis, "Jane Addams vs. the Ward Boss," 247–65; Nelli, *Italians in Chicago*, 88–124; Jane Addams, "Ethical Survivals in Municipal Corruption," *International Journal of Ethics* 8 (April 1898): 273–91; Scott, "Saint Jane and the Ward Boss," 12–17, 94–99; *Chicago Record*, 26 January 1898, Addams Newspaper Clippings, SCPC; *Inter-Ocean* (Chicago), 6 March 1898, Addams Newspaper Clippings, SCPC; *Times Herald*, 6 and 29 March 1898, Addams Newspaper Clippings, SCPC; *Evening Post* (Chicago), 7 March 1898, Addams Newspaper Clippings, SCPC; *Chicago Tribune*, 8 March 1898, Addams Newspaper Clippings, SCPC.

78. Nelli, *Italians in Chicago*, 22, 73, 98–100, 170–81, 138; Vecoli, "Contadini in Chicago," 405–13; Vecoli, "Prelates and Peasants," 231.

79. Addams, *Twenty Years*, 232–33; Bertha Hazard, "A Working Colony as a Social Investment," *Charities*, 7 May 1904, 452–53; Florence Kelley, "The Settlements: Their Lost Opportunity," *Charities and the Commons*,7 April 1906, 80–82; Nelli, *Italians in Chicago*, 16–20, 250; *L'Italia*, 16 November 1918, 19 August 1919, reel 31, FLPS; *United States Industrial Commission* (Washington, D.C., 1901), 15:497.

80. Addams, *Twenty Years*, 102–10, 154–76, 199–200; Addams, "Objective Value," 46; "Italian and the Settlement," 58–59; Anthony Sorrentino, *Organizing against Crime: Re-developing the Neighborhood* (New York, 1977), 75; Herbert J. Gans, *The Urban Villagers: Group and Class in the Life of Italian Americans* (Glencoe, N.Y., 1962), 1–260; Francis A. J. Ianni, "The Italo-American Teen-Ager," *Annals* 338 (November 1961): 73–76; Breckinridge, *New Homes for Old*, 50–51; E. Abbott, "Grace Abbott and Hull House," 510; E. Abbott, "Sister's Memories," 369–71; Dunne, "Memoirs of 'Zi Pre,' " 192–203.

81. E. Abbott and Breckinridge, *Truancy*, 277.

82. Dunne, "Memoirs of 'Zi Pre,' " 195.

83. Ibid., 195–96.

84. Ibid., 196.

85. Addams, *Democracy and Social Ethics*, 226–27.

86. Nelli, *Italians in Chicago*, 173; *Hull House Bulletin*, no. 1 (1905/6): 3–4; *Hull House Year Book*, 1906/7, 37; 1910, 25, 32; 1921, 12–13, 34; 1929, 13, 15–16.

87. *Hull House Year Book*, 1929, 25–27; Florence Scala to Rivka Lissak, interview, 2 August 1977.

88. *Star*, 25 October 1907, reel 23, FLPS; *Greek Press*, 25 November 1964, Hull House Papers.

89. *Chicago Tribune*, 9 April 1939, Greek Community Folder, West Side Historical Society Papers, University of Illinois; *Greek Press*, 25 November 1964, Hull House Papers; Grace Abbott, "Study of Greeks in Chicago," *American Journal of Sociology* 15 (November 1909): 386–87; Thomas Burgess, *Greeks in America* (New York, 1970), 123–25; George A. Kourvetaris, *First and Second Generation Greeks in Chicago* (Athens, 1971), 49–95; Edward A. Steiner, *On The Trail of the Immigrant* (New York, 1906), 286–87; Kopan, "Greek Survival in Chicago," 99–109.

90. Kopan, "Greek Survival in Chicago," 84–90; Burgess, *Greeks in America*, 124; *Greek Press*, 25 November 1964, Hull House Papers; Kourvetaris, *First and Second Generation*, 49–50; Steiner, *On the Trail*, 291; City of Chicago, Board of Education, *Proceedings* (1904/5), 97, 101–8; *Hull House Year Book*, 1906/7, 36; 1916, 33, 42; Dr. S. D. Soter to Rivka Lissak, 24 July 1979.

91. Kopan, "Greek Survival in Chicago," 90–99, 121–26, 135–38; *Chicago Tribune*, 9 April 1939, Greek Community Folder, West Side Historical Society Papers; *Greek Press*, 25 November 1964, Hull House Papers; *Star*, 15 and 22 March, 25 October, 29 November 1907; *Saloniki*, 29 November, 20 December 1913; 10 October, 5 December 1914; 31 July, 18 September, 9 October 1915; 22 and 29 July 1916; 18 August 1917; 8 July 1918; 25 June 1921; 10 July 1929, reels 23–26, FLPS.

92. Kopan, "Greek Survival in Chicago," 106–9, 116–21; Burgess, *Greeks in America*, 123, 125; Kourvetaris, *First and Second Generation*, 64–66; Steiner, *On the Trail* 286–87; *Greek Press*, 25 November 1964, Hull House Papers; *Chicago Tribune*, 9 April 1939; George Christakes, *Greek Immigrants in the United States* (Kansas, 1965), 14–16; *Hull House Year Book*, 1910, 23–25; 1913, 24; 1916, 14, 37; 1921, 12–13, 34; 1929, 12–13, 16, 45.

93. Kopan, "Greek Survival in Chicago," 106–7; *Chicago Tribune*, 9 April 1939; *Hull House Year Book*, 1921, 13; 1929, 45.

94. Addams, *Twenty Years*, 388–89; *Hull House Bulletin*, no. 12 (1899): 2–3; Kopan, "Greek Survival in Chicago," 110–11; *Chicago Record*, 13 December 1899.

95. Addams, *Twenty Years*, 256–57, 388–89; Barrows, "Greek Play at Hull House," 6–10; Burgess, *Greeks in America*, 124; Hall, "Greek Play," 125; *Hull House Bulletin*, no. 1 (1905/6): 23; *Hull House Year Book*, 1906/7, 36–37, 48; 1916, 33; *Star*, 17 March, 24 November, 1 December 1905; 30 March, 29 June, 6 July, 19 October 1906; 25 January, 25 October, 22 November 1907, reel 23, FLPS; Kopan, "Greek Survival in Chicago," 109–14; *Greek Press*, 25 November 1964.

96. Burgess, *Greeks in America*, 125–26; *Hull House Year Book*, 1910, 51; G. Abbott, "Study of Greeks in Chicago," 386–87.

97. Kopan, "Greek Survival in Chicago," 109–16; Addams, *Twenty Years*, 256–57, 388–89; Barrows, "Greek Play at Hull House," 6–10; Burgess, *Greeks in America*, 123–26; Kourvetaris, *First and Second Generation*, 64–66; Steiner, *On the Trail*, 286–87, 291; *Chicago Tribune*, 9 April 1939; *Greek Press*, 25 November 1964; *Hull House Bulletin*, no. 1 (1905/6): 23; *Hull House Year Book*, 1906/7, 36, 37, 48; 1910, 23, 24, 29, 51; 1913, 25, 30–31, 39; 1916, 14; 1921, 11–13, 34; 1929, 12–16; *Loxias*, 2 November 1912, 1 and 21 November 1914, reel 23; 14 April 1915, reel 26, FLPS; *Saloniki*, 29 November 1913, reel 23, 17 April 1915, reel 26, 8 April 1916, reel 23, FLPS; *Star*, 24 November, 1 December 1905; 30 March, 29 June, 6 July, 19 October 1906; 25 January, 25 October, 22 November 1907, reel 23; 2 July 1909, reel 26, FLPS.

98. *Greek Press*, 25 November 1964; *Saloniki*, 10 October 1914, 18 September 1915, 25 September 1917, 1 and 8 June 1918, reel 23, FLPS; *Dziennik Chicagoski*, 10 October 1914, 18 September 1915, 11 December 1915, reel 48, FLPS; *Star*, 11 August 1905, reel 23, FLPS.

## Chapter Seven

1. Holbrook, "Maps, Notes, and Comments," 3–26; City of Chicago, Board of Education, *Proceedings* (1898/99), 187–89, (1904/5), 97, 101–8; City of Chicago,

Board of Education, *School Census of the City of Chicago* (1908), 12–19, (1910), 8–14, (1914), 19–23.

2. Addams, *Twenty Years*, 179–83, 342; Addams, "Objective Value," 36–37; "Hull House Outline Sketch," in Jane Addams et al., *Hull House Maps and Papers* (Boston, 1895), 216–18; Kelley, "Hull House," 560–61; A. Miller, "Hull House," 170–71; E. P. Stevens, "Life in a Social Settlement," 49–50; "Hull House: A Social Settlement," 1892; *Hull House Bulletin*, Club Lists, 1896–1905/6; *Hull House Year Book*, Club Lists, 1906/7–21, Hull House Papers; Hull House Women's Club, 1902/3–6/7, 1909/10, 1925/26, Bowen Papers.

3. Addams, "Objective Value," 36–37.

4. Hull House Women's Club, 1902/3–6/7, 1909/10, 1925/26, Bowen Papers; *Hull House Bulletin*, Club Lists, 1896–1905/6; *Hull House Year Book*, Club Lists, 1906/7–21; Addams, *Twenty Years*, 358.

5. Addams, *Twenty Years*, 358–59, and see 209, 350. See also *Springfield Daily*, 15 November 1898, Addams Newspaper Clippings, SCPC; Breckinridge, *New Homes for Old*, 39; Nelli, *Italians in Chicago*, 77; Park and H. A. Miller, *Old World Traits Transplanted*, 152, 158; G. De Filippis to Rivka Lissak, interview, 17 August 1977; Nicollette Mallone to Rivka Lissak, interview, 17 August 1977; Florence Scala to Rivka Lissak, interview, 2 August 1977; Addams, "Objective Value," 37; Breckinridge, *New Homes for Old*, 218, 239, 241, 246; Mrs. James A. Britton to Miss Longan, 23 August 1919, Addams Papers, SCPC; Hull House Women's Club, 1902–10, 1925/26, Bowen Papers; *Hull House Bulletin*, no. 2 (1903/4): 14; *Hull House Year Book*, 1916, 42; 1929, 26–27; Hull House Summer Record, 1907/8, Juvenile Protective Association Papers, University of Illinois, hereafter JPA Papers; "Italian and the Settlement," 58–59; Whyte, *Street Corner Society*, 99.

6. *Star*, 12 August 1907; *Saloniki*, 17 January, 5 September 1914, reel 23, FLPS; *Hull House Year Book*, 1910, 24–25; 1916, 37; 1929, 27; Mrs. James A. Britton to Miss Longan, 23 August 1919, Addams Papers, SCPC.

7. *Hull House Bulletin*, no. 1 (1900): 7, no. 1 (1902): 11, no. 1 (1905/6): 14–15; *Hull House Year Book*, 1906/7, 26; 1910, 28.

8. "Hull House: A Social Settlement," 1892; *Hull House Bulletin*, no. 1 (1896), no. 4 (1896): 6, no. 1 (1903): 9.

9. Addams, *Twenty Years*, 179–83, 342; Addams, "Objective Value," 36–37; "Hull House Outline Sketch," 216–18.

10. Addams, "Objective Value," 44–47; Nelli, *Italians in Chicago*, 73, 74–76; Woods and Kennedy, *Settlement Horizon*, 191; *La Parola*, 19 July 1913, reel 30, FLPS; *L'Italia*, 24 August 1895, reel 30, FLPS; *Hull House Year Book*, 1913, 41; Hull House Relief Account, 1891–94, Hull House Papers; Pasqualino Scala to Rivka Lissak, interview, 4 September 1977; G. De Filippis to Rivka Lissak, interview, 17 August 1977.

11. Kelley, "Hull House," 560–61; A. Miller, "Hull House," 170–71; E. P. Stevens, "Life in a Social Settlement," 49–50; Addams, "Objective Necessity," 38–44; Hackett, "Hull House: A Souvenir," 275–80; Addams, "Subjective Necessity," 1–26; Addams, *Twenty Years*, 89–153, 342–400; Friess, *Adler and Ethical Culture*, 94–100, 121–37; Levine, *Addams and the Liberal Tradition*, 67. See chapter 3 on Hull House cultural policy.

12. Zublin, "Chicago Ghetto," 104, 108; Bregston, *Chicago and Its Jews,* 17–18; Meites, *History of the Jews,* 184–85; Nelli, *Italians in Chicago,* 186; Schiavo, *Italians in Chicago,* 75; Vecoli, "Prelates and Peasants," 228–33; A. F. Davis and McCree, *Eighty Years at Hull House,* 22; Gans, *Urban Villagers,* 110–13, 211; Paul J. Campisi, "Ethnic Family Patterns: The Italian Family in the United States," *American Journal of Sociology* 52 (May 1948): 448; Ianni, "Italo-American Teen-Ager," 73.

13. Figures for membership of these youngsters come from Addams, *Twenty Years,* 179–83, 342; Addams, "Objective Value," 36–37; "Hull House Outline Sketch"; Kelley, "Hull House," 560–61; A. Miller, "Hull House," 170–71; E. P. Stevens, "Life in a Social Settlement," 49–50; "Hull House: A Social Settlement," 1892; *Hull House Bulletin,* Club Lists, 1896–1905/6; *Hull House Year Book,* Club Lists, 1906/7–29; Hull House Women's Club, 1902/3–6/7, 1909/10, 1925/26, Bowen Papers.

14. Hull House Boys' Club, Membership Lists 1907/8, JPA Papers.

15. Meites, *History of the Jews,* 184–85, and see 391–92. See also Bregston, *Chicago and Its Jews,* 17–18; Philip Davis, "Educational Influences," in Charles S. Bernheimer, ed., *The Russian Jew in the United States* (Philadelphia, 1905), 214, 217; Low, "Philanthropy," 87–89; Hackett, "Hull House: A Souvenir," 72; "Hull House Outline Sketch," 224–25; A. Miller, "Hull House," 169; Hannah G. Solomon, *Fabric of My Life* (New York, 1946), 93–96; Wirth, *Ghetto,* 188; Yarros, "Hull House Unique Melting Pot Experiment"; "Hull House: A Social Settlement," 15 January 1895; *Hull House Bulletin,* Club Lists, 1896–1905/6; *Hull House Year Book,* Club Lists, 1906/7–16; Hull House Boys' Club, 1907/8, JPA Papers; Joseph Stolz to J. Witkowsky, 2 November 1893, box 2249, Stolz Papers; *Record Herald,* 19 April 1893, box 2249, Stolz Papers; Zublin, "Chicago Ghetto," 104, 108; *Reform Advocate,* 22 September 1894; Rabbi Morris A. Gutstein to Rivka Lissak, interview, 22 August 1977; Hull House Players Membership List, 1898–1924, Hull House Papers; Alex Elson to Rivka Lissak, interview, 23 August 1977; Moshe Ghitzes to Rivka Lissak, interview, 11 September 1977; Nat M. Kahn to Rivka Lissak, November 1977; Thomas W. Holland to Rivka Lissak, 5 August 1978.

16. P. Davis, "Educational Influences," 217; *Hull House Year Book,* 1906/7, 38; 1913, 8; 1921, 37–39; Alex Elson to Rivka Lissak, interview, 23 August 1977; Benny Goodman's sister to Rivka Lissak, interview, 11 September 1977.

17. Jane Addams, *Second Twenty Years at Hull-House: September 1909 to September 1929* (New York, 1930), 397; Addams, "Objective Values," 36–37; Lilian A. Brandt, "Transplanted Birthright: The Development of the Second Generation of the Italians in an American Environment," *Charities,* 7 May 1904, 496; Gans, *Urban Villagers,* 158; Higham, *Strangers in the Land,* 118; John Landesco, "The Life History of a Member of the '42 Gang,' " *Journal of Criminal Law and Criminology* 24 (March 1933): 969; Nelli, *Italians in Chicago,* 92; Sorrentino, *Organizing against Crime,* 46–49; *Evening Post* (Chicago), 2 December 1916, Addams Newspaper Clippings, SCPC; "Hull House: A Social Settlement," 1 March 1892, 15 January 1895, Hull House Papers; *Hull House Bulletin,* no. 1 (1896): no page numbers, no. 5 (1896): 7, no. 8 (1897): 7, no. 1 (1898): 9, no. 4–5 (1898): 8, no. 6 (1898): 8, no. 7 (1898): 6, no. 8–9 (1899): 7, no. 4 (1901): 15, no. 2 (1903/4): 14–17, no. 1

(1905/6): 11, 14, 15; *Hull House Year Book,* 1906/7, 21–28, 41–43; 1910, 20, 25–29, 31, 44; 1913, 17–22, 28–32, 41–42; 1916, 17, 26–29, 33–37, 39; 1921, 35–39; Hull House Boys' Club, 1907/8, JPA Papers; Hull House Summer Record, 1907/8, JPA Papers; Hull House Players Membership List, 1898–1924, Hull House Papers; M. Ghitzes, interview, 11 September 1977; M. Gamboni, interview, 14 September 1977; G. De Filippis to Rivka Lissak, interview, 17 August 1977; Antonio Sorrentino to Rivka Lissak, interview, 2 August 1977; Thomas W. Holland to Rivka Lissak, 5 August 1978; Ellen G. Starr to M. Blaisdell, 18 May 1890, Starr Papers; *Chicago Tribune,* 19 May 1890, Addams Newspaper Clippings, SCPC; *L'Italia,* 4–5 May 1895, reel 30, 9 April 1904, reel 31, FLPS. From 1890 to 1900 Hull House membership was 60–65 percent native-born American and "old immigrant," 25 percent east European Jew, and 10–15 percent Italian. From 1900 to 1907 membership was 40–45 percent native-born American and "old immigrant," 35 percent east European Jew, and 20–25 percent Italian. The Hull House Summer Record for 1907/8 indicates the predominance of girls in the Italian membership: picnics had an attendance that was 20 percent Italian, 60 percent of them girls; summer camp had an attendance that was 12 percent Italian, 78 percent of them girls.

18. George J. Rakas, "Recollections of Jane Addams," August 1972, box 10, series 4, Addams Papers, SCPC; *Hull House Year Book,* 1910, 51; 1913, 41; 1916, 33, 42; 1921, 24; Hull House Boys' Club, 1907/8, JPA Papers; S. D. Soter, "Jane Addams"; *Saloniki,* 5 December 1914, 9 October 1915, 8 April 1916, reel 23, FLPS; Thomas W. Holland to Rivka Lissak, 5 August 1978; Alex Elson to Rivka Lissak, interview, 23 August 1977.

19. *Star,* 29 November 1907; *Loxias,* 27 January 1909, 7 and 21 November 1914; *Saloniki,* 5 February 1916, 4 March 1916, 31 March 1917, 22 November 1919, reel 23, FLPS; Soter, "Jane Addams"; Dr. S. D. Soter to Rivka Lissak, 24 July 1979; *Hull House Year Book,* 1910, 23; 1913, 23, 26–27; 1916, 12–14, 31–32; 1921, 9–10.

20. *Hull House Year Book,* 1916, 14, 31; 1921, 10, 29; 1929, 11–15.

21. *Hull House Bulletin,* 1896–1905/6; *Hull House Year Book,* 1906/7, 21–23, 41–43; 1910, 20–23, 44–47; 1913, 17–21, 41–43; 1916, 26–30, 39–41; 1921, 23–29.

22. *Hull House Year Book,* 1906/7, 38–39; 1913, 9; 1916, 33–36; 1921, 35–39; Arthur N. Horwich to Rivka Lissak, 17 August 1978; Nat M. Kahn to Rivka Lissak, 2 March 1978.

23. Bregston, *Chicago and Its Jews,* 8–9, 13–15, 115–16; Mrs. B. Davis, "Religious Activity," 177–81; Gutstein, *Priceless Heritage,* 403–9; Gutstein, *Profiles of Freedom,* 140–44; Horwich, *My First Eighty Years,* 228, 231, 233–34, 237, 268, 272–82; Meites, *History of the Jews,* 167–68, 187, 195–98, 201, 216–26, 243, 549–50, 643–48, 653–58, 766; *Reform Advocate,* 11 November 1893, 4 May 1901, reel 35, 13 February 1926, reel 34, FLPS; *Courier,* 13 October 1907, reel 32, 22 November 1907, 2 May 1909, 7 April 1910, 9 October 1912, 31 January 1913, reel 35, FLPS; Ira Berkow, *Maxwell Street* (Garden City, N.Y., 1970), 73–74; Bregston, *Chicago and Its Jews,* 89–90, 96–97, 119, 331–33; Kaplan, "Zionism," 39, 50; Leberson, "Zionism Comes to Chicago," 177; McCree, "First Year of Hull House," 114; Shulman, "First American Disciples," 223; Scharfstein, *History of Jewish Education* 3:55; *American Hebrew,* 21 April 1899, 841; *Chicago Hebrew Institute*

*Messenger,* November 1909, reels 31, 37, FLPS; *Observer,* December 1911, reel 31, FLPS; Chicago Hebrew Institute, Minutes of the Meeting of the Board of Directors, 1907/8, Chicago Hebrew Institute Papers, CHS; Chicago Hebrew Institute, Minutes of the Meeting of the Board of Directors, 19 January 1910, Chicago Hebrew Institute Papers; *Hull House Year Book,* 1910, 6; 1913, 6–7; Dr. Fischkin to Julius Rosenwald, 11 March 1908, Rosenwald Papers; Lusil Pintozzi to Rivka Lissak, interview, 29 August 1977.

24. Alex Elson to Rivka Lissak, interviews, 2 March 1973, 23 August 1977; Arthur N. Horwich to Rivka Lissak, 17 August 1978.

25. E. Abbott and Breckinridge, *Tenements of Chicago,* 94–95; Amberg, *Madonna Center,* 40–46, 52–59, 63–65, 67–82, 100–110; Nelli, *Italians in Chicago,* 189–94; Schiavo, *Italians in Chicago,* 75; *L'Italia,* 2 May 1903, reel 31, FLPS; *La Tribuna,* 14 January 1905, reel 39, FLPS; *New World,* 8 October 1895, 26 November 1910, 22 March 1913, 30 November 1917.

26. Addams, *Twenty Years,* 106–25, 198–207, 250–54, 323–28; E. Abbott and Breckinridge, *Truancy,* 121–29; Breckinridge and E. Abbott, *Delinquent Child and the Home,* 72–75, 81–82, 130–38, 150–53; William L. Bodine, "Compulsory Education in Chicago," in Sophonisba P. Breckinridge, ed., *The Child in the City* (Chicago, 1912), 155, 264; Breckinridge, *New Homes for Old,* 157, 161, 167; Gertrude H. Britton, "An Intensive Study of the Census of Truancy," 1906, Hull House Papers; John J. D'Alesandro, "Occupational Trends of Italians in New York City," in Francesco Lordasco and Eugene Bucchioni, eds., *The Italians* (Clifton, 1974), 425–26; Dillingham, *Immigration Commission* 26:308–11, 313–14, 318, 27:144–46, 149, 30:566; Gans, *Urban Villagers,* 24–25; Edward P. Hutchinson, *Immigrants and Their Children, 1850–1950* (New York, 1956), 174; Landesco, "Crime and the Failure of Institutions," 238–48; Mary F. Matthews, "The Role of the Public School in the Assimilation of the Italian Immigrant Child in New York City, 1900–1914," in Silvano M. Tomasi and Madeline H. Engel, eds., *The Italian Experience in the United States* (New York, 1970), 138–39; Henry Moscowitz, "The Place of the Immigrant Child in the Social Program," in Sophonisba P. Breckinridge, ed., *The Child in the City* (Chicago, 1912), 264; Anne E. Nicholes, "From School to Work in Chicago," *Charities and the Commons,* 12 May 1906, 231, 233–34; Frederick M. Thrasher, *The Gang: A Study of 1,313 Gangs in Chicago* (Chicago, 1927), 8–37, 67; Steiner, *On the Trail,* 271, 276; Carroll D. Wright, *Seventh Special Report of the Commissioner of Labor: The Slums of Baltimore, Chicago, New York, and Philadelphia* (New York, 1894), 76; Woods and Kennedy, *Settlement Horizon,* 213; *Hull House Year Book,* 1929, 31; Hull House Boys' Club, 1907/8, JPA Papers; Nelli, *Italians in Chicago,* 55–72; Dunne, "Memoirs of 'Zi Pre,' " 193–99.

27. E. Abbott and Breckinridge, *Truancy,* 123–25; Breckinridge and E. Abbott, *Delinquent Child and the Home,* 72–75, 130–38, 150–53; Landesco, "Crime and the Failure of Institutions," 241–43; Nicholes, "From School to Work," 231, 233; Woods and Kennedy, *Settlement Horizon,* 213.

28. Sorrentino, *Organizing against Crime,* 46–47; Gans, *Urban Villagers,* 37–38; Landesco, "Crime and the Failure of Institutions," 241–47; Thrasher, *Gang,* 8, 10, 11–15, 18–19, 23, 26–28, 32–37; William F. Whyte, "Social Organization in the Slums," *American Sociological Review* 8 (February 1943): 38; Antonio Sorrentino to Rivka Lissak, interview, 2 August 1977.

29. Addams, "Subjective Necessity," 1–26; Addams, *Twenty Years*, 41–42, 113–28, 452; A. F. Davis, *Spearheads for Reform*, 3–26; A. F. Davis, *American Heroine*, 53–66.

30. Addams, *Twenty Years*, 281–96, 323–41; Breckinridge, *New Homes for Old*, 238; Campisi, "Ethnic Family Patterns," 447; P. Davis, *And Crown Thy Good*, 95, 108; A. F. Davis, *Spearheads for Reform*, 60–83, 170–93; Gans, *Urban Villagers*, 39–40, 45–103, 126–33, 148, 154, 159, 219, 222, 229–42, 252–53, 279; Kelley, "Settlements: Their Lost Opportunity," 79–82; Kelley, "Hull House," 565; Maryal Knox, "Social Settlement and Its Critics," *Survey*, August 1914, 486–87; Whyte, *Street Corner Society*, 98–107; Woods and Kennedy, *Settlement Horizon*, 74, 137–274.

31. Addams, "Subjective Necessity," 1–17; G. Abbott, *Immigrant and the Community*, 195; Bremer, "Foreign Language Worker," 740–46; Gans, *Urban Villagers*, 272–77; Hackett, "Hull House: A Souvenir," 275–80; David G. Loth, *Swope of General Electric: The Story of Gerald Swope and General Electric in American Business* (New York, 1958); Lillian D. Wald, "Qualifications and Training for Service with Children in a Crowded City Neighborhood," in Sophonisba P. Breckinridge, ed., *The Child and the City* (Chicago, 1912), 246–47; Whyte, *Street Corner Society*, 44, 98–107; Edward and Charles Yeomen, eds., *Who's Who in Chicago* (Chicago), various volumes; Residents Lists, 1889–1929, Hull House Papers; *Hull House Bulletin*, no. 1 (1905/6): 15; *Hull House Year Book*, 1906/7, 5–13, 41–42; 1910, 5, 8–14, 21; 1913, 5, 8–14, 18; 1916, 5, 8–11, 28, 36, 41–42.

32. "Hull House: A Social Settlement," 1892; *Hull House Bulletin*, no. 1 (1896): n.p.; no. 1 (1902): 10–11; no. 1 (1905/6): 11–14; *Hull House Year Book*, 1906/7, 8–9, 11–12, 21–26, 35, 37; 1910, 8–13, 21–22, 25–26; 1913, 6–14, 42; 1916, 6–20, 42; Hull House Trade School, 1913, Addams Papers; Gertrude H. Britton, "The Boy Problem in the Nineteenth Ward," November 1920, Hull House Papers; *Weekly Times* (Denver), 24 August 1898, Addams Newspaper Clippings, SCPC; *New York Evening Telegram*, 3 March 1910, Addams Newspaper Clippings, SCPC; "First Report of a Labor Museum at Hull House," 1901/2, Hull House Papers.

33. Addams, *Twenty Years*, 147; Brandt, "Transplanted Birthright," 497; Gans, *Urban Villagers*, 65–70; Landesco, "Member of the '42 Gang,' " 970–98; Sorrentino, *Organizing against Crime*, 130; Thrasher, *Gang*, 83–101; Woods and Kennedy, *Settlement Horizon*, 75; Louise DeKoven Bowen to Mary R. Smith, 9 January 1932, Addams Papers, SCPC; *Hull House Bulletin*, no. 1 (1896): n.p., no. 1 (1902): 13–14, no. 1 (1905/6): 11, 18–19; *Hull House Year Book*, 1906/7, 21; 1910, 20, 44–47; 1929, 31; Nicollette Mallone to Rivka Lissak, interview, 17 August 1977; Florence Scala to Rivka Lissak, interview, 2 August 1977; Libonnati to Rivka Lissak, interview, 23 August 1977; Antonio Sorrentino to Rivka Lissak, interview, 2 August 1977.

34. Gans, *Urban Villagers*, 133, 153, 155–56; Landesco, "Member of the '42 Gang,' " 969; Landesco, *Organized Crime in Chicago*, 126–27, 180, 196, 200–201; *Hull House Year Book*, 1921, 9; 1929, 11–12; Robert A. Cairo to Jane Addams, 21 December 1931, Addams Papers, SCPC; Louise DeKoven Bowen to Jane Addams, 8 January 1932, Addams Papers, SCPC; Louise DeKoven Bowen to Mary R. Smith, 9 January 1932, Addams Papers, SCPC; Louise DeKoven Bowen to Mary R. Smith, 14 January 1932, Addams Papers, SCPC; Libonnati to Rivka

Lissak, interview, 23 August 1977; William J. Granata to Jane Addams, 11 January 1932, Addams Papers, SCPC.

35. Rakas, "Recollections of Jane Addams"; *Hull House Year Book,* 1910, 51; 1913, 41; 1916, 33, 42; 1921, 24; Hull House Boys' Club, 1907/8, JPA Papers; Soter, "Jane Addams"; *Saloniki,* 5 December 1914, 9 October 1915, 8 April 1916, reel 23, FLPS; Thomas W. Holland to Rivka Lissak, 5 August 1978; Alex Elson to Rivka Lissak, interview, 23 August 1977

## Chapter Eight

1. Edith G. Balch, *Our Slavic Fellow Citizens* (New York, 1910), 393; Barton, "Eastern and Southern Europeans," 150–75; Higham, "Leadership," 69–92; Greene, "Becoming American," 144–75; Warner and Srole, *Social System of American Ethnic Groups,* 103–282; Eisenstadt, *Absorption of Immigrants,* 16, 61, 188–202, 231, 236–37, 247, 262–63.

2. Barton, "Eastern and Southern Europeans," 150–75; Greene, "Becoming American," 158–65; Breckinridge, *New Homes for Old,* 108, 118, 124–229; Addams, *Democracy and Social Ethics,* 231–33, 235, 248–50; P. Roberts, *New Immigration,* 63–77, 109–16; Nelli, *Italians in Chicago,* 63; Vecoli, "Chicago's Italians prior to World War I," 259–61; Hesse-Biber, "Ethnic Ghetto as Private Welfare," 9–14; MacDonald and MacDonald, "Chain Migration," 82–93; Duis, "Saloon in a Changing Chicago," 219–20.

3. *Evening Post* (Chicago), 9 November 1897; Addams, *Democracy and Social Ethics,* 221–27; G. Abbott, *Immigrant and the Community,* 256, 264; IPL, *First Annual Report* (1909/10), 5; Addams, "Why the Ward Boss Rules," 879–82; A. F. Davis, "Jane Addams vs. the Ward Boss," 247–65; Wald and Kellor, "Construction Camps of the People," 449–65; Kellor, "Who Is Responsible for the Immigrant," 912–17; Smith, "Lay Initiative," 214–49; Koren, "Padrone System and Padrone Banks," 113–29; Sheridan, "Unskilled Immigrant Laborers," 403–86; Vecoli, "Chicago's Italians prior to World War I," 235–78; Nelli, *Italians in Chicago,* 55–87; Edwin Fenton, *Immigrants and Unions: A Case Study: Italians and American Labor, 1870–1920* (New York, 1975), 71–135; Robert F. Harney, "The Padrone and the Immigrant," *Canadian Review of American Studies* 5 (1974): 101–18; MacDonald and MacDonald, "Chain Migration," 82–97; Hesse-Biber, "Ethnic Ghetto as Private Welfare," 45–54; Greene, "Becoming American," 158–61; Breckinridge, *New Homes for Old,* 118, 193; Charles B. Phipard, "The Philanthropist-Padrone: What Is Being Done to Raise the Standard through Competition and Example," *Survey,* 7 May 1904, 470–72; "Table of Complaint and Services for the Year 1915," folder 53, IPL Papers; Robert F. Harney, "The Padrone System and Sojourners in the Canadian North, 1885–1920," in George E. Pozzetta, ed., *Pane e lavoro: The Italian American Working Class,* Proceedings of the Eleventh Annual Conference of the American Italian Historical Association, 1978 (Toronto, 1980), 119–37; Addams, *Twenty Years,* 207; Bisno, *Abraham Bisno: Union Pioneer,* 144–45; Beckner, *History of Labor Legislation in Illinois,* 153–55.

4. Frances A. Kellor, *Out of Work: A Study of Employment Agencies, Their Treatment of the Unemployed, and Their Influence upon Homes and Business* (New York, 1904); *Report of the Commission of Immigration of the State of New York*

(Albany, 1909); *Reports of the Industrial Commission on Immigration and on Education* (Washington, D.C., 1901), vol. 15; *Final Report of the Industrial Commission* (Washington, D.C., 1902), vol. 19; Wald and Kellor, "Construction Camps of the People," 449–65; Kellor, "Who Is Responsible for the Immigrant," 912–17; Koren, "Padrone System and Padrone Banks," 113–29; Sheridan, "Unskilled Immigrant Laborers," 403–86; Dillingham, *Immigration Commission;* Charlotte Erickson, *American Industry and the European Immigrants, 1860–1885* (Cambridge, Mass., 1957), 70–93, 99–105. See notes 26–42.

5. G. Abbott, *Immigrant and the Community,* 26–54, 191–92; G. Abbott "Chicago Employment Agency," 289–305; Nelli, *Italians in Chicago,* 55–67; Koren, "Padrone System and Padrone Banks," 113–29; Sheridan, "Unskilled Immigrant Laborers," 403–86; IPL, *Fourth Annual Report* (1913), 17; Dillingham, *Immigration Commission* 18:331–43, 37:179–95; Wald and Kellor, "Construction Camps of the People," 449–65; Speranza, "Handicaps in America," 465–72; Kellor, "Who Is Responsible for the Immigrant," 912–17; Iorizzo, "Padrone and Immigrant Distribution," 52–58; Nelli, "Padrone System: An Exchange of Letters," 406–12.

6. IPL, *Fourth Annual Report* (1913), 17–20; IPL, *Sixth Annual Report* (1915), 10–12; IPL, *Eighth Annual Report* (1917), 19–20; G. Abbott, *Immigrant and the Community,* 81–94; Iorizzo, "Italian Immigration," 100–160; Spear, "What America Pays Europe for Immigrant Labor," 106–16; Dillingham, *Immigration Commission* 37:203–350.

7. G. Abbott, *Immigrant and the Community,* 81–94; Dillingham, *Immigration Commission* 37:212–20; IPL, *Fourth Annual Report* (1913), 17–20; IPL, *Sixth Annual Report* (1915), 8; IPL, *Ninth Annual Report* (1918), 19–20.

8. Vecoli, "Chicago's Italians prior to World War I," 235–78.

9. *L'Italia,* 20 July 1889, reel 30, FLPS.

10. Balch, *Our Slavic Fellow Citizens,* 393; Barton, "Eastern and Southern Europeans," 150–75; Zublin, "Chicago Ghetto," 101; Higham, "Leadership," 69–92; Miriam Blaustein, *Memories of David Blaustein* (New York, 1913), 33–59, 163–75, 190–99; Warner and Srole, *Social Systems of American Groups,* 103–282.

11. U.S. House of Representatives, Petition and Memorials, 62A-H10.2, National Archives; U.S. House of Representatives, night letter to Congressman Charles E. Fuller, 8 May 1912; *Evening Post* (Chicago), 18 May 1912, box 15, folder May 1912, Addams Papers, SCPC; Addams, *Twenty Years,* 400–426; Bregston, *Chicago and Its Jews,* 181–82, 225–28; Meites, *History of the Jews,* 245–49; Addams, "Chicago Settlements and Social Unrest," 155–67.

12. D. Blaustein, "Problem of Immigration," 363–70; Israel Friedlaender, "The Americanization of the Jewish Immigrant," *Survey,* May 1917, 103–8; *Evening Post* (New York), 2 December 1916, box 34, Addams Papers, SCPC; B. Simek, "More about Americanization," *Czechoslovak Review* 3 (August 1919): 231–333; Joseph Stybr, "Americanization," ibid. 3 (June 1919): 153–54.

13. Friedlaender, "Americanization of the Jewish Immigrant," 106; Jaroslav V. Nirgin, "Teaching of Bohemian in High Schools and Colleges," *Bohemian Review* 1 (May 1917): 11–12.

14. D. Blaustein, "Problem of Immigration," 363–70; Friedlaender, "Americanization of the Jewish Immigrant," 103–8; *Evening Post* (New York), 2 December

1916, Addams Papers, SCPC; Simek, "More about Americanization," 231–333; Stybr, "Americanization," 153–54; Nirgin, "Teaching of Bohemian," 11–12.

15. Lipsky, "Citizen Making in Chicago," 884; A. N. Marquis, *Who's Who in Chicago* (Chicago, 1917); Bregston, *Chicago and Its Jews*, 181–82, 225–28, 246–49; Meites, *History of the Jews*, 202–3, 228, 234–35, 245–49, 289–95; Shulman, "First American Disciples," 223–24; *Courier*, 2 May, 7 June 1912, reel 31, FLPS; *Haychudi*, no. 31 (1910): 15; *Sentinel*, 19 March 1915; *American Jewish Year Book*, (1917/18), 239; U.S. House of Representatives, Petition and Memorials; U.S. House of Representatives, night letter to Congressman Charles E. Fuller, 8 May 1912; *Evening Post* (Chicago), 18 May 1912, Addams Papers, SCPC; Addams, *Twenty Years*, 400–426; Addams, "Chicago Settlements and Social Unrest," 155–67.

16. Bregston, *Chicago and Its Jews*, 48–53; Meites, *History of the Jews*, 186, 217; Dr. A. Fischkin to Julius Rosenwald, 11 March 1908, Rosenwald Papers; Lipsky, "Citizen Making in Chicago," 884; Breckinridge, *New Homes for Old*, 99, 303–4.

17. D. Blaustein, "Problem of Immigration," 363–70, quote from page 367. See also M. Blaustein, *Memories of David Blaustein*, 107–8, 201–2, 207–8, 216–21, 290–91, 299–300; IPL, *First Annual Report* (1909/10), 2; Meites, *History of the Jews*, 226; *Courier*, 13 October 1907, reel 32, FLPS.

18. E. F. Prantner, "Americanization: Our Problem," *Czechoslovak Review* 3 (March 1919): 98–99; see also D. Blaustein, "Problem of Immigration," 367.

19. M. Blaustein, *Memories of David Blaustein*, 220–21.

20. D. Blaustein, "Problem of Immigration," 367.

21. Israel Friedlaender, "The Problem of Judaism in America," in *Past and Present: A Collection of Jewish Essays* (Cincinnati, 1919), 237–72, quote from page 272.

22. Lissak, "Myth and Reality," 26–27.

23. *Star*, 21 October 1904, reel 23, FLPS.

24. *Dziennik Zwiazkowy*, 26 November 1910, 4 November 1911, 5 September 1914, reel 48, FLPS; Korey, "Jewish Education in Chicago," 80–127; E. Abbott and Breckinridge, *Truancy*, 66–91, 263–87; Nirgin, "Teaching of Bohemian," 11–12.

25. *Saloniki*, 18 September 1915, reel 23, FLPS.

26. *Dziennik Chicagoski*, 10 October 1914, 18 September 1915, 11 December 1915, reel 48, FLPS; *Saloniki*, 10 October 1914, reel 23, FLPS.

27. *Saloniki*, 1 and 8 June 1918, reel 23, FLPS.

28. Ibid., 25 September 1917.

29. *Star*, 11 August 1905, reel 23, FLPS.

30. *Courier*, 19 August 1913, reel 32, FLPS.

31. Korey, "Jewish Education in Chicago," 80–127; Federated Orthodox Charities, Minutes of the Meetings of the Board of Directors, January 1919–October 1922, folder 41, Federation Papers, Jewish Archives, Spertus College, Chicago.

32. *Denni Hlasatel*, 4 September 1915, reel 1, FLPS.

33. Ibid., 7 December 1911, 11 March 1912.

34. *Svornost*, 14 February 1879, reel 1, FLPS.

35. IPL, *Fourth Annual Report* (1913), 4; IPL, *Sixth Annual Report* (1915), 4; Boleck, *Who's Who in Polish America;* Wytrwal, *America's Polish Heritage*, 173–80, 194–212, 227–35; *Dziennik Zwiazkowy*, 4 November 1911, reel 48, FLPS.

36. *Dziennik Zwiazkowy,* 26 November 1910, reel 48, FLPS.

37. Ibid., 5 September 1914.

38. Ibid., 26 November 1910.

39. Ibid., 4 November 1911. See also *Dziennik Chicagoski,* 19 January 1891, reel 48, FLPS.

40. *Dziennik Zwiazkowy,* 4 November 1911, reel 48, FLPS.

41. Park, *Immigrant Press and Its Control,* 210–13.

42. D. Blaustein, "Problem of Immigration," 363–70; Friedlaender, "Americanization of the Jewish Immigrant," 103–8; Nirgin, "Teaching of Bohemian," 1–12; Prantner, "Americanization: Our Problem," 98–99; Stybr, "Americanization," 153–54.

43. D. Blaustein, "Problem of Immigration," 366.

44. Ibid., 366–67.

45. Nirgin, "Teaching of Bohemian," 11–12.

46. Balch, *Our Slavic Fellow Citizens,* 398–99.

47. Ibid., 397–99, quote from page 398.

48. Ibid., 403.

## Chapter Nine

1. Michael Walzer, "Pluralism in Political Perspective," in Walzer et al., *The Politics of Ethnicity* (Cambridge, Mass., 1982), 1–6.

2. Addams, "Civic Associations' Night," 212–13; G. Abbott, *Immigrant and the Community,* 221–98; Breckinridge and E. Abbott, *Delinquent Child and the Home,* 55–56; Emily G. Balch, "What It Means to Be an American," 22 February 1916, in Mercedes Randall, ed., *Beyond Nationalism: The Social Thought of Emily G. Balch,* 33–40; Balch, *Our Slavic Fellow Citizens,* 396–425; Dewey, "Nationalizing Education," 183–89; John Dewey, "The Principle of Nationality," *Menorah Journal* 3 (October 1917): 203–9; Nagel, "Address," 20–26; Addams, "Recreation as a Public Function," 610–15.

3. G. Abbott, *Immigrant and the Community,* 277.

4. Dewey, "Nationalizing Education," 183–84; John Dewey, "Nationalism and Its Fruits," in Joseph Ratner, ed., *Intelligence in the Modern World: John Dewey's Philosophy* (New York, 1939), 467–74; Merle Curti, "John Dewey and Nationalism," *Orbis* 10 (1967): 1103–19.

5. Dewey, "Nationalizing Education," 183. See also Dewey, "Nationalism and Its Fruits," 467–74; Curti, "Dewey and Nationalism," 1103–19. See chapter 1.

6. Addams, "Subjective Necessity," 26.

7. Addams, "Recreation as a Public Function," 615–19; Merle Curti, "Jane Addams on Human Nature," *Journal of the History of Ideas* 22 (April-June 1961): 240–53; Addams, *Twenty Years,* 23–64, 75–88, 111–12; Addams, "Recent Immigration," 253–54, 261–63; Addams, "Subjective Necessity," 20–21, 26; Addams, "New Internationalism," 213–16; Addams, "Nationalism: A Dogma," 524–26; Addams, *Newer Ideals of Peace,* 15–30, 209–38.

8. Addams, *Newer Ideals of Peace,* 14.

9. Addams, *Twenty Years,* 23–88, 111–13; Addams, "Subjective Necessity," 1–7, 19–23, 26; Addams, *Democracy and Social Ethics,* 1–12; Addams, "New

Internationalism," 213–16; Addams, "Recreation as a Public Function," 615–19; Addams, "Nationalism: A Dogma," 524–26.

10. Addams, *Twenty Years*, 112–13.

11. Addams, *Newer Ideals of Peace*, 15–30, 209–38; Addams, "New Internationalism," 213–16; Addams, "Recreation as a Public Function," 615–19; Addams, "Recent Immigration," 261–63; G. Abbott, *Immigrant and the Community*, 267–81.

12. Abbott, *Immigrant and the Community*, 278–79.

13. Addams, *Twenty Years*, 77–88, 111–12, quote from page 83; Curli, "Addams on Human Nature," 240–43; Addams, "Subjective Necessity," 15; Henry Steele Commager, "Foreword," in Jane Addams, *Twenty Years at Hull-House* (New York, 1961), ix.

14. Addams, "Recent Immigration," 263.

15. Dewey, "Nationalizing Education," 185.

16. Dewey, "Principle of Nationality," 203–9, quote from page 205; John Dewey, "America in the World," *Nation*, 14 March 1918, 287. See also Dewey, "Nationalizing Education," 183–98; Eisele, "Dewey and the Immigrants," 67–85; Dewey, "Nationalism and Its Fruits," 467–74; Curti, "Dewey and Nationalism," 1103–19.

17. Addams, "New Internationalism," 213–16; Addams, "Recent Immigration," 261–63; Addams, *Democracy and Social Ethics*, 1–12; Addams, "Subjective Necessity," 1–7.

18. Addams, *Twenty Years*, 23–64, 76–79; A. F. Davis, *American Heroine*, 162–65, 174.

19. Addams, *Twenty Years*, 76–79.

20. Howard B. Radest, *Toward Common Ground: The Story of the Ethical Societies in the United States* (New York, 1969), 65, 106, 122, 155, 254, 265; Benny Kraut, *From Reform Judaism to Ethical Culture: The Religious Evolution of Felix Adler* (Cincinnati, 1979), 119–214; Friess, *Adler and Ethical Culture*, 68, 119, 214; Benny Kraut, "Francis E. Abbot: Perceptions of a Nineteenth Century Religious Radical on Jews and Judaism," in Jacob R. Marcus and Abraham J. Peck, eds., *Studies in the American Jewish Experience* (Cincinnati, 1981), 90–113.

21. Addams, "Americanization," 213; Curti, "Addams on Human Relations," 240–53; Addams, "Recent Immigration," 245–63; G. Abbott, *Immigrant and the Community* 247–98; Addams, "Pen and Book," 419–20; G. Abbott, "Adjustment—Not Restriction," 528; Addams, "Recreation as a Public Function," 615–19.

22. George E. Axtelle, "John Dewey and the Genius of American Civilization," in Douglas E. Lawson and Arthur E. Lean, eds., *John Dewey and the World View* (London, 1964), 35–62, quote from page 46; Dewey, *Democracy and Education*, 1–22.

23. Park and H. A. Miller, *Old World Traits Transplanted*, 301–8, quote from page 302.

24. Israel Zangwill, *The Principle of Nationalities* (London, 1917), 39–40, 43–49, 54–64.

25. Ibid., 81–91. See also Neil L. Shumsky, "Zangwill's *The Melting Pot:* Ethnic Tensions on Stage," *American Quarterly* 27 (March 1975): 29–41.

26. Shumsky, "Zangwill's *The Melting Pot*," 29–41; G. Abbott, *Immigrant and the Community*, 278–79.

27. Kallen, *Culture and Democracy*, 44–233, quotes from pages 124–25, 122. See also Horace M. Kallen, *The Education of Free Men: An Essay toward a Philosophy of Education* (New York, 1949), 149–73; Horace M. Kallen, *Cultural Pluralism and the American Idea* (Philadelphia, 1956), 5–101; Alfred J. Marrow, ed., *What I Believe and Why—Maybe* (New York, 1971); Wissot, "Dewey, Kallen, and Cultural Pluralism," 186–96; Itzkoff, *Cultural Pluralism and American Education*, 34–66; Itzkoff, "Sources of Cultural Pluralism," 231–33; Wacker, "Assimilation and Cultural Pluralism in American Social Thought," 325–33.

28. Kallen, *Education of Free Men*, 149–73, quotes from pages 169–70, 171, 162; Friedlaender, "Americanization of the Jewish Immigrant," 106–7, quote from page 107. See also Kallen, *Culture and Democracy*, 122–23.

29. Kallen, *Culture and Democracy*, 121, and see 122–25, 168–201.

30. Friedlaender, "Americanization of the Jewish Immigrant," 103–8, quotes from pages 104, 107; 103–8; ibid., 122–23.

31. Horace M. Kallen, "Nationality and the Hyphenated American," *Menorah Journal* 1 (April 1915): 79–85, quote from page 81. See also Kallen, *Culture and Democracy*, 120–25, 168–201; Kallen, *Education of Free Men*, 149–73; Marrow, *What I Believe*, 124–27.

32. Kallen, *Culture and Democracy*, 44–232, quote from pages 181–82. See also Glazer, "Ethnic Groups in America," 158–73; Gordon, "Assimilation in America," 274; Higham, *Send These to Me*, 196–230; Kohn, *American Nationalism*, 170–71; Kallen, *Cultural Pluralism*, 5–101, 171–208; Kallen, "Nationality and the Hyphenated American," 79–85.

33. Kallen, *Culture and Democracy*, 97, 119–20.

34. Ibid., 67–125, 191–201.

35. Kallen, *Education of Free Men*, 116–18, 174–84.

36. John Dewey to Horace M. Kallen, 31 March 1915, box 2493–2521, Horace M. Kallen Papers, American Jewish Archives, Cincinnati; Eisele, "Dewey and the Immigrants," 67–85; Axtelle, "Dewey and the Genuis of American Civilization," 35–62; Phenix, "Dewey's War on Dualism," 39–51; Lilge, "Vain Quest for Unity," 51–71; Wissot, "Dewey, Kallen, and Cultural Pluralism," 186–96; Itzkoff, *Cultural Pluralism and American Education*, 34–67; Itzkoff, "Sources of Cultural Pluralism," 231–33; Eisele, "Dewey's Concept of Cultural Pluralism," 149–56; J. Theodore Klein, "Review Article: Human Nature and the Ideal of Cultural Pluralism," *Educational Theory* 22 (Fall 1972): 479–84; Spencer J. Maxcy, "Ethnic Pluralism, Cultural Pluralism, and John Dewey's Program of Cultural Reform: A Response to Eisele," *Educational Theory* 34 (Summer 1984): 301–5.

37. Kallen, *Culture and Democracy*, 202–32, quote from page 229.

38. Park and H. A. Miller, *Old World Traits Transplanted*, 296–302, quoted from pages 299, 230, 301.

39. Dewey, *Democracy and Education*, 81–88; Robert M. Barry, "A Man and a City: George Herbert Mead in Chicago," in Michael Novak, ed., *American Philosophy and the Future* (New York, 1968), 173–92; Addams, *Democracy and Social Ethics*, 9–11; Addams, "Americanization," 213; Curti, "Addams on Human Relations," 240–53; Addams, "Recent Immigration," 245–63; G. Abbott, *Immigrant and the Community*, 247–98; Addams, "Pen and Book," 419–20; G. Abbott,

"Adjustment—Not Restriction," 528; Addams, "Recreation as a Public Function," 615–19; Kallen, *Cultural Pluralism,* 97, 119–20.

40. Addams, *Democracy and Social Ethics,* 9–11.

41. Dewey, *Democracy and Education,* 87.

42. Ibid., 81–99; Flew, "Democracy and Education," 76–101; Balch, *Our Slavic Fellow Citizens,* 403; see chapter 1.

43. Kallen, *Culture and Democracy,* 88–96, quote from page 93. See also Marrow, *What I Believe,* 129–38.

44. Kallen, *Culture and Democracy,* 88–89, 92.

45. Marrow, *What I Believe,* 129–38, quote from page 130. See also Kallen, *Culture and Democracy,* 88–96, 120–25.

46. Park and H. A. Miller, *Old World Traits Transplanted,* 262.

47. Horace J. Bridges, *On Becoming an American* (Boston, 1918), 94–149; Friess, *Adler and Ethical Culture,* 68–69, 124–25, 327; John Dewey, "Universal Service as Education," *New Republic,* 22 April 1916, 309–10, 334–35; Dewey, "Nationalizing Education," 183–89; G. Abbott, *Immigrant and the Community,* 267–81; Addams, *Twenty Years,* 23–88, 231–37. Bridges was a major figure in the Ethical Culture movement.

48. Bridges, *On Becoming an American,* 94–149.

49. Jane E. Robine, "The Foreign Born American," *Outlook* 83 (1906): 893.

50. Dewey, "Nationalizing Education," 184–85.

51. Kallen, *Culture and Democracy,* 118–20, 124–25, 202–32, quote from page 118. See also Kallen, *Education of Free Men,* 117–18.

52. Friedlaender, "Problem of Judaism in America," 253–78, quote from pages 276–77.

53. Kallen, *Culture and Democracy,* 118–20, 124–25; Kallen, *Education of Free Men,* 117–18.

54. John Dewey to Horace M. Kallen, 31 March 1915, Kallen Papers; Eisele, "Dewey and the Immigrants," 71–72.

55. Kallen, *Culture and Democracy,* 180–81.

56. Dewey, "Nationalizing Education," 184–85. See also Dewey, "Autocracy under Cover," 103–6; Dewey, "Universal Service as Education," 309–10, 334–35; John Dewey to Horace M. Kallen, 31 March 1915, Kallen Papers.

57. Mack, "Address of the President," 26–27.

58. Friess, *Adler and Ethical Culture,* 68.

59. Dewey, "Nationalizing Education," 183–85, quote from page 185.

60. Ibid., 183.

61. Bridges, *On Becoming an American,* 94–149, quote from page 138. See also Friess, *Adler and Ethical Culture,* 68–69, 124–25, 327; Addams, "Recent Immigration," 263; Dewey, "Nationalizing Education," 184–85.

62. Phenix, "Dewey's War on Dualism," 39–51.

## Chapter Ten

1. David F. Bowers, "The Problem of Social and Cultural Impact," in Bowers, ed., *Foreign Influences in American Life* (Princeton, N.J., 1944), 3–38; Howard M. Jones, *The Age of Energy: Varieties of American Experience, 1865–1915* (New York, 1971), 200–201, 216, 259–82; Henry F. May, *The End of American Innocence: A*

*Study of the First Years of Our Own Time, 1912–1917* (New York, 1960), 3–120; Addams, *Twenty Years,* 1–87, 347, 371–99.

2. Bridges, *On Becoming an American,* 94–149; Friess, *Adler and Ethical Culture,* 68–69, 124–25, 327; Dewey, "Universal Service as Education," 309–10, 334–35; Dewey, "Nationalizing Education," 183–89; G. Abbott, *Immigrant and the Community,* 267–81; Addams, *Twenty Years,* 23–88, 231–37; Robine, "Foreign Born American," 893.

3. David A. Hollinger, "Ethnic Diversity, Cosmopolitanism, and the Emergence of the American Liberal Intelligentsia," *American Quarterly* 28 (May 1975): 133–50; Randolph S. Bourne, "Trans-National America," in Carl Resek, ed., *War and the Intellectuals: Essays by Randolph S. Bourne, 1915–1919* (New York, 1964), 107–23; Randolph S. Bourne, "The Jew and Trans-National America," ibid., 124–33; Norman Hapgood, "The Jews and American Democracy," *Menorah Journal* 2 (October 1916): 201–5; Max Grossman, "Morris Cohen, Felix Adler, and the Ethical Movement," *Ethical Outlook* 49 (1923); Norman Hapgood, "The Future of the Jews in America," *Harper's Weekly,* November 1915, 511–12.

4. Bourne, "Trans-National America," 118.

5. Morris R. Cohen, *A Dreamer's Journey* (Boston, 1949), 222–24, 227; Bourne, "Jew and Trans-National America," 132; Hollinger, "Ethnic Diversity," 133–36; Kraut, *From Reform Judaism to Ethical Culture,* 124.

6. Cohen, *A Dreamer's Journey,* 219–28, quotes from pages 220, 226, 224. Randolph Bourne seemed to be unable to differentiate the views of Horace M. Kallen from those of Morris R. Cohen. See especially Morris R. Cohen, "Zionism: Tribalism or Liberalism," *New Republic,* 8 March 1919, 182–83; Horace M. Kallen, "Zionism and Liberalism," in *Judaism at Bay: Essays toward the Adjustment of Judaism to Modernity* (New York, 1932), 111–20.

7. Cohen, *A Dreamer's Journey,* 228.

8. Kallen, *Culture and Democracy,* 201–32, quotes from pages 205, 210, 211.

9. Ibid., 231, 232. See also Horace M. Kallen to Felix Adler, 9 April 1915, box 10, folder 5. Kallen Papers.

10. John Dewey, "American Education and Culture," in Joseph Ratner, ed., *Intelligence in the Modern World: John Dewey's Philosophy* (New York, 1939), 725–28, quotes from pages 725, 726.

11. Ibid., 727.

12. Ibid., 725, 727, 728.

13. Dewey, "Nationalizing Education," 183–85; Dewey, *Democracy and Education,* 81–99.

14. Addams, "Public School and the Immigrant Child," 99–102; Addams, "Foreign-born Children in the Primary Grades," 106–7; Addams, "Subjective Necessity," 20; *Record Herald,* 26 May 1909, Addams Newspaper Clippings, SCPC.

15. Addams, *Twenty Years,* 233–34; Addams, *Newer Ideals of Peace,* 16, 75–78, 253; Addams, "Recent Immigration," 252–54.

16. H. M. Jones, *Age of Energy,* 218–82; May, *End of American Innocence,* 3–120; Bowers, "Problem of Social and Cultural Impact," 3–38.

17. Addams, *Twenty Years,* 1–87, 347, 348, 388–95; Farrell, *Beloved Lady,* 37–51; Levine, *Addams and the Liberal Tradition,* 1–35; Glazer, "Ethnic Groups in America," 168; Nathan Glazer, "Immigrant Groups and American Culture," *Yale*

*Review* 48 (1958/59): 385–86; Hollinger, "Ethnic Diversity," 133–51; H. M. Jones, *Age of Energy,* 218, 259–82; May, *End of American Innocence,* 3–120; Bowers, "Problem of Social and Cultural Impact," 3–38.

18. Zublin, "Chicago Ghetto," 101–7.

19. Addams, *Twenty Years,* 259–80, 342–70.

20. Ibid., 395–99, quote from pages 395–96.

21. Young, "Modern Languages in High Schools," 597.

22. Addams, "Recent Immigration," 225.

23. Addams, "Objective Value," 35–38; Addams, *Twenty Years,* 231–32, 242–47; Addams, *Newer Ideals of Peace,* 164, 203; Addams, "Recreation as a Public Function," 617; Jane Addams, "Report of the Committee on Immigrants," in National Conference of Charities and Correction, *Proceedings* (1909), 214; Victor Von Borosini, "Our Recreation Facilities and the Immigrant," *Annals* 35 (January-June 1910): 359–60; Graham Taylor to Jane Addams, 20 May 1916, Chicago Commons Papers, CHS; Graham Taylor to Jane Addams, 10 May 1916, Chicago Commons Papers, CHS; Robert T. Wallach, "The Social Value of the Festival," *Charities and the Commons,* 2 June 1906, 315–19; Adeline Moffet, "The Exhibition of Italian Arts and Crafts in Boston," *Survey,* April 1909, 51–53; Pozzetta, "Immigrants and Craft Arts," 141–42, 146.

24. H. M. Jones, *Age of Energy,* 261–63; Addams, "Recreation as a Public Function," 616–17; Addams, "Recent Immigration," 255; Donald D. Egbert, "Foreign Influences in American Art," in David F. Bowers, ed., *Foreign Influences in American Life* (Princeton, N.J., 1944), 99–125; G. Abbott, *Immigrant and the Community,* 274–77.

25. *Herald* (Washington, D.C.), 26 April 1908, box 15, Addams Newspaper Clippings, SCPC.

26. Balch, *Our Slavic Fellow Citizens,* 404–5.

27. G. Taylor, "Committee on Distribution and Assimilation," 27; *Christ Science Monitor,* 22 November 1912, Addams Newspaper Clippings, SCPC; Nagel, "Address," 22. See also Park and H. A. Miller, *Old World Traits Transplanted,* 264–70; Egbert, "Foreign Influences in American Art," 99–125.

28. Addams, *Twenty Years,* 235–37, 240–46; *Christ Science Monitor,* 22 November 1912, Addams Newspaper Clippings, SCPC; Hackett, "As an Alien Feels," 304; Conway, "Jane Addams: An American Heroine," 761–80.

29. Wallach, "Social Value of the Festival," 315–19; Von Borosini, "Our Recreation Facilities and the Immigrant," 357–67; G. R. Taylor, "Recreation Developments in Chicago Parks," 304–21; G. R. Taylor, "City Neighbors at Play," 549–59; Woods and Kennedy, *Settlement Horizon,* 47, 354, 425–26.

30. Larry C. Miller, "William James and Twentieth-Century Ethnic Thought," *American Quarterly* 31 (Fall 1979): 533–55; William James, *The Will to Believe and Other Essays* (Cambridge, Mass., 1896), 216–62.

31. William I. Thomas, "Standpoint for the Interpretation of Savage Society," *American Journal of Sociology* 15 (September 1909): 145–63, quotes from pages 146, 153; William I. Thomas, "Race Psychology: Standpoint and Questionnaire, with Particular Reference to the Immigrant and the Negro," ibid., 17 (May 1912): 725–775, quote from page 726. See also Franz Boaz, *The Mind of Primitive Man*

(New York, 1911), 180–202; John Dewey, "Interpretation of Savage Mind," *Psychological Review* 9 (May 1902): 217–30.

32. W. I. Thomas, "Savage Society," 157, 163, 156.

33. Boaz as quoted in W. I. Thomas, "Race Psychology," 727, 726.

34. Addams, *Democracy and Social Ethics*, 1–70, 221–77, quote from pages 226–27.

35. Adler, *Ethical Philosophy of Life*, 208–48, 324–40, quotes from pages 245, 232.

36. Ibid., 222.

37. Ibid., 325, 331, 332.

38. Addams, *Democracy and Social Ethics*, 15, 6–7. See also Alice Hamilton, *Exploring the Dangerous Trades* (Boston, 1943), 59.

39. Hamilton, *Exploring the Dangerous Trades*, 59.

40. Nagel, "Americanization," 20–26.

41. Addams, "Subjective Necessity," 10–18.

42. Nagel, "Address," 20–26; G. Abbott, *Immigrant and the Community*, 247–98.

43. Kraut, *From Reform Judaism to Ethical Culture*, 119–25; Max Grossman, "Cohen, Adler."

44. Bourne, "Trans-National America," 123.

45. Kraut, *From Reform Judaism to Ethical Culture*, 119–214; Radest, *Toward Common Ground*, 122–32; Harry P. Kraus, *The Settlement House Movement in New York City, 1886–1914* (New York, 1980), 43, 50–55, 88, 111–12, 199–204.

46. Dewey, "Nationalizing Education," 184–85.

47. Quoted in Kraut, *From Reform Judaism to Ethical Culture*, 175.

48. Cohen, *A Dreamer's Journey*, 222–24, 227; Bourne, "Jew and Trans-National America," 132; Hollinger, "Ethnic Diversity," 133–36; Kraut, *From Reform Judaism to Ethical Culture*, 124.

49. Bowers, "Problem of Social and Cultural Impact," 3–38; Bridges, *On Becoming an American*, 135–49.

## Chapter Eleven

1. Dewey, "Principle of Nationality," 205.

2. Addams, "Recreation as a Public Function," 616–17.

3. G. Abbott, *Immigrant and the Community*, 276.

4. Dewey, "Nationalizing Education," 185.

5. G. Abbott, *Immigrant and the Community*, 277–81, quote from page 281. See also Addams, "New Internationalism," 214–15.

6. G. Abbott, *Immigrant and the Community*, 236; Addams, "Recent Immigration," 246–54.

7. Addams, "Recent Immigration," 253–54.

8. Dewey, "Nationalizing Education," 184–85.

9. Kogut, "Settlements and Ethnicity," 22–31; G. C. White, "Social Settlements and Immigrant Neighbors," 55–66; Juliani, "Settlement House and the Italian Family," 107–8; Krug, *Melting of the Ethnics*, 5–14, 63–77; Eisele, "Dewey's Concept of Cultural Pluralism," 149–56; Wissot, "Dewey, Kallen, and Cultural Pluralism," 186–96; Itzkoff, *Cultural Pluralism and American Education*, 34–66.

10. Lilge, "Vain Quest for Unity," 52–71; John Dewey, "Pluralism," *Dictionary of Philosophy and Psychology* (New York, 1902), 306; Axtelle, "Dewey and American Civilization," 45–46.

11. John Dewey to William James, March 1903, in Ralph Barton Perry, *The Thought and Character of William James* (Cambridge, Mass., 1948), 306.

12. Dewey, "Pluralism," 306.

13. Axtelle, "Dewey and American Civilization," 45–46.

14. Kallen, *Culture and Democracy,* 131–32. See also Itzkoff, *Cultural Pluralism and American Education,* 60; Wissot, "Dewey, Kallen, and Cultural Pluralism," 192.

15. Morton and Lucia White, "The Plea for Community, Robert Park, and John Dewey," in Morton and Lucia White, *The Intellectual versus the City* (Cambridge, Mass., 1962), 139–54.

16. Addams, *Twenty Years,* 127.

17. Park and H. A. Miller, *Old World Traits Transplanted,* 299–302.

18. White, "Plea for Community," 139–54; Stein, *Eclipse of Community,* 20–33.

19. The term "cultural pluralism" was first used by Horace M. Kallen in his book *Cultural Pluralism and the American Idea,* published in 1924. Kallen, "Democracy versus the Melting Pot," 67–125; John Dewey to Horace M. Kallen, 31 March 1915, Kallen Papers; Eisele, "Dewey and the Immigrants," 71–72; Hollinger, "Ethnic Diversity," 133–51.

20. Dewey, "Principle of Nationality," 205–6.

21. John Dewey to Horace M. Kallen, 31 March 1915, Kallen Papers.

22. Phenix, "Dewey's War on Dualism," 42–47, quote from page 42.

23. Park and H. A. Miller, *Old World Traits Transplanted,* 264.

24. Balch, *Our Slavic Fellow Citizens,* 407.

25. Friedlaender, "Americanization of the Jewish Immigrant," 106–7; Kallen, *Education of Free Men,* 149–73; Kallen, *Culture and Democracy,* 122–23; Hartmann, *Movement to Americanize the Immigrant;* John F. McClymer, "The Federal Government and the Americanization Movement, 1915–1924," *Prologue* (Spring 1978): 23–41.

26. IPL, *Seventh Annual Report* (1916), 26–28; IPL, *Ninth Annual Report* (1918), 26; Hartmann, *Movement to Americanize the Immigrant,* 44–56; Gwyneth M. Fulcher, "Americanization of the Immigrant in Chicago," *Social Service Review* (October 1918): 17, (November 1918): 8–10, (December 1918): 9, (January 1919): 9; Grace Abbott, "True Americanization," *Americanization Bulletin* 1 (November 1918): 4; John Daniels, "National Immigration Conference," *Survey,* December 1911, 1358–59; "National Committee of One Hundred," *School and Society* 4 (October 1916): 557; Circular of the Joint Committee on Americanization, Chicago, 1919, supplement 3, box 6, Schwartz Papers, University of Illinois Archives; G. Abbott, "Immigrant in Community Planning," 166–72; President Wilson to Charles P. Schwartz, 14 October 1916, Schwartz Papers.

27. G. Abbott, "True Americanization," 4; G. Abbott, "Immigrant in Community Planning," 166–72; *Hull House Year Book,* 1913, 24; 1916, 15; Charles P. Schwartz, "Lessons in Citizenship for Naturalization," 7th ed. (Chicago, 1929); "Short Biography of Charles P. Schwartz," Schwartz Papers.

28. G. Abbott, "True Americanization," 4; Addams, "Americanization," 206–14.

29. Hackett, "As an Alien Feels," 304.

30. G. Abbott, *Immigrant and the Community,* 222. See also Breckinridge and E. Abbott, *Delinquent Child and the Home,* 55–56; Addams, "Recent Immigration," 252–57.
31. Balch, *Our Slavic Fellow Citizens,* 401–2.
32. Ibid., 398–99.
33. Ibid., 403.
34. Nagel, "Address," 25–26.
35. Balch, *Our Slavic Fellow Citizens,* 410–12.
36. Ibid., 411–12.
37. L. C. Miller, "William James and Twentieth-Century Ethnic Thought," 533–55; Adler, *Ethical Philosophy of Life,* 208–48, 324–40.
38. Nagel, "Address," 25–26.
39. Addams, "Americanization," 210.

## Afterword

1. Higham, *Strangers in the Land,* 9–34.
2. E. Abbott and Breckinridge, *Truancy,* 266–67.
3. Park and H. A. Miller, *Old World Traits Transplanted,* 264.

# SELECT BIBLIOGRAPHY

This bibliography is divided into the following sections: Manuscript Collections, Annual Reports and Proceedings, Printed Government Material, Journals and Newspapers, Works by Jane Addams, Works by Hull House and Other Settlement House Workers, Immigrant Colonies, and General Sources. The section Immigrant Colonies is subdivided further into East European Jews, Italians, and Greeks. In the General Sources writings about Felix Adler, John Dewey, William James, Horace M. Kallen, George Herbert Mead, William I. Thomas, and Ella Flagg Young are listed after writings by those authors.

## Manuscript Collections

Abbott, Grace and Edith. Papers. University of Chicago Library.
Addams, Jane. Papers. Peace Collection, Swarthmore College, Swarthmore, Pa.
Bowen, Louise DeKoven. Papers. Chicago Historical Society.
Breckinridge, Sophonisba P. Papers. Library of Congress, Washington, D.C.
Chicago City Club Papers. Chicago Historical Society.
Chicago Hebrew Institute Records. Chicago Historical Society.
Chicago Municipal Voters' League Records. Chicago Historical Society.
Chicago School of Civics and Philanthropy Papers. University of Chicago.
Dewey, John. Papers. Southern Illinois University Archives, Carbondale.
Prescott F. Hall Scrapbook of Newspaper Clippings. Widener Library, Harvard University, Cambridge.
Hull House Papers. University of Illinois Archives, Chicago.
Immigrants' Protective League Papers. University of Illinois Archives, Chicago.
Immigration Restriction League Papers. Houghton Library, Harvard University, Cambridge.
Jewish Community Papers. Jewish Chicago Historical Society, Spertus College, Chicago.
Kallen, Horace M. Papers. American Jewish Archives, Cincinnati.
Mead, George H. Papers. University of Chicago Library.
National Federation of Settlements Records. Social Welfare History Archives Center, University of Minnesota, Minneapolis.
Starr, Ellen G. Papers. Sophia Smith Collection, Smith College, Northampton, Mass.

Survey Papers. Social Welfare History Archives Center, University of Minnesota, Minneapolis.

Wald, Lillian D. Papers. Columbia University Library, New York City.

_____. Papers. New York Public Library, New York City.

Woods, Robert A. Papers. Houghton Library, Harvard University, Cambridge.

## Annual Reports and Proceedings

American Federation of Labor. Proceedings, 1907–15.

City of Chicago. Board of Education. Annual Reports and Proceedings, 1897–1919.

Hull House. Bulletins and Year Books, 1896–1929.

Immigrants' Protective League. Annual Reports, 1909–17.

National Conference of Charities and Correction. Proceedings, 1897–1917.

National Conference of Social Work. Proceedings, 1917–20.

## Printed Government Material

Dillingham, W. *Reports of the Immigration Commission.* 42 vols. Washington, D.C.: 1911.

## Journals and Newspapers

*American Journal of Sociology.*

*Annals of the American Academy of Political and Social Sciences.*

*Charities.* 1897–1905.

*Charities and the Commons.* 1905–9.

*The Chicago Foreign Language Press Survey.* Chicago Public Library, 1942.

*Commons.* 1896–1905.

*New World.* Chicago Catholic church organ.

*Social Service Review.*

*Survey.* 1909–20.

## Works by Jane Addams

Addams, Jane. "The Subjective Necessity for Social Settlements." In Jane Addams et al., *Philanthropy and Social Progress,* 1–26. Boston: Thomas Y. Crowell Co., 1893.

_____. "Objective Value of a Social Settlement." In Jane Addams et al., *Philanthropy and Social Progress,* 27–56. Boston: Thomas Y. Crowell Co., 1893.

_____. "The Settlement as a Factor in the Labor Movement." In Jane Addams et al., *Hull House Maps and Papers,* 183–206. Boston: Thomas Y. Crowell Co., 1895.

_____. "Foreign-born Children in the Primary Grades." In National Education Association, *Journal of Proceedings and Addresses* (1897), 104–12.

_____. "Ethical Survivals in Municipal Corruption." *International Journal of Ethics* 8 (April 1898): 273–91.

_____. "Why the Ward Boss Rules." *Outlook,* 2 April 1898, 879–82.

_____. "Trade Unions and Public Duty." *American Journal of Sociology* 4 (January 1899): 448–62.

_____. "A Function of the Social Settlement." *Annals of the American Academy of Political and Social Sciences* 13 (May 1899): 323–45.

_____. *Democracy and Social Ethics.* Cambridge: Harvard University Press, 1902.

_____. "First Report of the Labor Museum at Hull House, Chicago, 1901–1902." *Unity,* 13 March 1902, 20–23.

Select Bibliography

_____. "What the Theatre at Hull House Has Done for the Neighborhood People." *Charities,* 29 March 1902, 284–86.

_____. "Hull House and Its Neighbors." *Charities,* 7 May 1904, 450–51.

_____. "Immigrants and American Charities." In Illinois Conference of Charities and Correction, *Proceedings* (1905), 11–18.

_____. "Recent Immigration: a Field Neglected by the Scholar." *Education Review* 29 (March 1905): 245–63.

_____. "Social Settlements in Illinois." Transactions of the Seventh Annual Meeting of the Illinois State Historical Society. In Illinois State Historical Library, *Publications* 11 (1906), 162–71.

_____. *Newer Ideals of Peace.* New York: Macmillan Company, 1907.

_____. "The Public School and the Immigrant Child." In National Education Association, *Journal of Proceedings and Addresses* (1908), 99–102.

_____. "The Chicago Settlements and Social Unrest." *Charities and the Commons,* 2 May 1908, 155–66.

_____. *The Spirit of Youth and the City Streets.* New York: Macmillan Company, 1909.

_____. "Report of the Committee on Immigrants." In National Conference of Charities and Correction, *Proceedings* (1909), 213–15.

_____. "Foreword." In Immigrants' Protective League, Chicago, *Annual Report* (1909/10), 4.

_____. *Twenty Years at Hull-House.* New York: Macmillan Company, 1910.

_____. "Recreation as a Public Function in Urban Communities." *American Journal of Sociology* 17 (March 1912): 615–19.

_____. "Jane Addams' Page." *Ladies Home Journal,* January 1913, 25.

_____. "Pen and Book as Tests of Character." *Survey,* January 1913, 419–20.

_____. "Jane Addams' Page." *Ladies Home Journal,* February 1913, 23.

_____. "Jane Addams' Page." *Ladies Home Journal,* March 1913, 27.

_____. "Jane Addams' Page." *Ladies Home Journal,* April 1913, 27.

_____. "Jane Addams' Page." *Ladies Home Journal,* May 1913, 27.

_____. "Jane Addams' Page." *Ladies Home Journal,* June 1913, 21.

_____. "Patriotism and Pacifists in Wartime." *City Club of Chicago Bulletin,* 18 June 1917, 184–90.

_____. "Americanization." In American Sociological Society, *Publication* 14 (1919): 206–14.

_____. *Second Twenty Years at Hull-House: September 1909 to September 1929.* New York: Macmillan Company, 1930.

## Works by Hull House and Other Settlement House Workers

Abbott, Edith. "Grace Abbott and Hull House, 1908–1921." *Social Service Review* 24 (1950): 374–94, 24 (1950): 493–518.

_____. "Grace Abbott: A Sister's Memories." *Social Service Review* 13 (1939): 351–407.

Abbott, Edith, and Sophonisba P. Breckinridge. *Truancy and Non-attendance in the Chicago Schools.* Chicago: University of Chicago Press, 1917.

Abbott, Grace. "The Chicago Employment Agency and the Immigrant Worker." *American Journal of Sociology* 14 (November 1908): 289–305.

237

———. "The Bulgarians of Chicago." *Survey,* January 1909, 653–60.

———. "The Treatment of Aliens in the Criminal Courts." *Journal of Criminal Law and Criminology* 2 (1911): 554–64.

———. "Immigration and Crime." *Journal of Criminal Law and Criminology* 6 (1915): 522–32.

———. *The Immigrant and the Community.* New York: Century Company, 1917.

———. "The Immigrant as a Problem in Community Planning." In American Sociological Society, *Publication* 12 (1917): 166–73.

———. "Educational Needs of Immigrants in Illinois." In Illinois State Immigrants' Commission, *Bulletin* (Springfield), 1 (1920).

Blumberg, Dorothy R. *Florence Kelley: The Making of a Social Pioneer.* New York: A. M. Kelley, 1966.

Breckinridge, Sophonisba P. *New Homes for Old.* New York: Harper and Brothers, 1921.

———, ed. *The Child in the City.* Chicago: Hollister Press, 1912.

Breckinridge, Sophonisba P., and Edith Abbott. *The Delinquent Child and the Home.* New York: Charities Publication Committee, 1912.

Cheney, Sheldon. *The Art Theater.* New York: A. A. Knopf, 1917.

———. *The New Movement in the Theatre.* New York: M. Kennerley, 1924.

Davis, Philip. *And Crown Thy Good.* New York: Philosophical Library, 1952.

Goldmark, Josephine. *Impatient Crusader: Florence Kelley's Life Story.* Urbana: University of Illinois Press, 1953.

Hackett, Francis. "As an Alien Feels." *New Republic* 3 (July 1915): 303–5.

———. "Hull House: A Souvenir." *Survey,* June 1925, 275–80.

Hamilton, Alice. *Exploring the Dangerous Trades.* Boston: Little, Brown and Company, 1943.

Hawkins, Gaynell. *Educational Experiments in Social Settlements.* New York: American Association for Adult Education, 1973.

Jenison, Madge C. "A Hull House Play." *Atlantic Monthly,* July 1906, 83–92.

Kelley, Florence. "Hull House." *New England Magazine* 18 (July 1898): 550–66.

———. "The Settlements: Their Lost Opportunity." *Charities and the Commons,* 7 April 1906, 79–82.

Knox, Maryal. "Social Settlement and Its Critics." *Survey,* August 1914, 486–87.

McDowell, Mary E. "The Field Houses of Chicago and Their Possibilities." *Charities and the Commons,* 3 August 1907, 535–38.

Miller, Alice. "Hull House." *Charities Review* 1 (February 1890): 167–73.

Moffat, Adeline. "The Exhibition of Italian Arts and Crafts in Boston." *Survey,* April 1909, 51–53.

Moscowitz, Henry. "Music School Settlements." *Survey,* June 1911, 462–63.

———. "The East Side in Oil and Crayon." *Survey,* May 1912, 271–73.

Nancrede, Edith de. "Dramatic Work at Hull House." *Neighborhood* 1 (January 1928): 23–28.

Nicholes, Anna E. "From School to Work in Chicago: A Study of Central Office That Grants Labor Certificates." *Charities and the Commons,* 12 May 1906, 231–35.

Pelham, Laura D. "The Story of the Hull House Players." *Drama* 6 (May 1916): 249–62.

Stevens, Elzina P. "Life in a Social Settlement: Hull House." *Chicago Self Culture* 9 (March 1899): 42–51.

Taylor, Graham R. "City Neighbors at Play." *Survey,* July 1910, 549–59.

Tucker, Irwin J. "Forty Years at Hull House: The Story of Jane Addams." *World Tomorrow,* September 1929, 367–71.

Von Borosini, Victor. "Our Recreation Facilities and the Immigrant." *Annals of the American Academy of Political and Social Sciences* 35 (January-June 1910): 357–67.

Woods, Robert A. "The University Settlement Idea." In Jane Addams et al., *Philanthropy and Social Progress,* 57–97. Boston: Thomas Y. Crowell Company, 1893.

_____. "University Settlements: Their Point and Drift." *Quarterly Journal of Economics* 14 (October 1899).

_____. "The Clod Stirs." *Survey,* March 1902, 1929.

_____. *The Neighborhood in Nation-Building.* Boston: Houghton Mifflin Company, 1923.

_____, ed. *The City Wilderness: A Study of the South End.* New York: Houghton Mifflin Company, 1893.

_____. *Americans in Process: A Study of the North and West Ends.* Boston: Houghton Mifflin Company, 1902.

Woods, Robert A., and Albert J. Kennedy. *The Settlement Horizon: A National Estimate.* New York: Russell Sage Foundation, 1922.

_____. *The Zone of Emergence.* Cambridge: MIT Press, 1962.

## Immigrant Colonies
### East European Jews

Barnard, Harry. *The Forging of an American Jew: The Life and Time of Judge Julian W. Mack.* New York: Herzel Press, 1974.

Berkow, Ira. *Maxwell Street.* Garden City, N.Y.: Doubleday and Company, 1970.

Bernheimer, Charles S., ed. *The Russian Jew in the United States.* Philadelphia: J. C. Winston Company, 1905.

Bisno, Abraham. *Abraham Bisno: Union Pioneer.* Madison: University of Wisconsin Press, 1964.

Blaustein, Miriam. *Memories of David Blaustein.* New York: McBride, 1913.

Bregston, Philip P. *Chicago and Its Jews: A Cultural History.* Chicago: private publication, 1933.

Cutler, Irving. "The Jews of Chicago: From Shtetl to Suburb." In Peter d'A. Jones and Melvin G. Holli, eds., *Ethnic Chicago.* Grand Rapids, Mich.: William B. Erdmans Publishing Company, 1981.

Feinstein, Marnin. *The First Twenty-Five Years of Zionism in the United States.* New York: Columbia University, 1964.

_____. *American Zionism, 1884–1904.* New York: Herzel Press, 1965.

Friedlaender, Israel. *Past and Present: A Collection of Jewish Essays.* Cincinnati: Ark Publishing Company, 1919.

Friesl, Eviatar. "The 'Knights of Zion' in Chicago and Their Relations with the Zionist Federation in America, 1898–1916." In Daniel Carpi, ed., *Zionism,* 1:121–49. Tel Aviv, 1970.

————. *The Zionist Movement in the United States.* Tel Aviv: Tel Aviv University Press, 1970.

Gutstein, Morris A. *A Priceless Heritage: The Epic Growth of Nineteenth Century Chicago Jewry.* New York: Bloch Publishing Company, 1953.

————. *Profiles of Freedom: Essay in American Jewish History.* Chicago: Chicago College of Jewish Studies Press, 1967.

Hart, Sara L. *The Pleasure Is Mine: Autobiography.* Chicago: Valentine-Newman, 1947.

Horwich, Bernard. *My First Eighty Years.* Chicago: Argus Books, 1939.

Josephson, Matthew. *Sidney Hillman: Statesman of American Labor.* Garden City, N.Y.: Doubleday, 1952.

Korey, Harold. "The History of Jewish Education in Chicago." Master's dissertation, University of Chicago, 1942.

Leberson, Anita L. "Zionism Comes to Chicago." In Isidore S. Meyer, ed., *Early History of Zionism in America.* New York: American Jewish Historical Society, 1958.

Meites, Hyman L. *History of the Jews of Chicago.* Chicago: Jewish Historical Society of Illinois, 1924.

*One Hundred Years of Chicago Jewry. Sentinel,* Jubilee Issue (August 1948).

Rawidowicz, Simon, ed. *The Chicago Pinkas.* Chicago: College of Jewish Studies, 1952.

Scharfstein, Zvi. *History of Jewish Education.* 4 vols. Jerusalem: R. Mass, 1970.

Seman, Philip E. "The Jewish Community Center Idea." *Jewish Center* 1 (1922): 13–18.

Shulman, Max. "The First American Disciples." In *Theodor Herzl Memorial, New Palestine,* 223–24. New York, 1929.

Solomon, Hannah G. *Fabric of My Life.* New York: Bloch Publishing Company, 1946.

Werner, Morris R. *Julius Rosenwald: The Life of a Practical Humanitarian.* New York: Harper and Brothers, 1939.

Wessel, Bessie B. "Ethnic Family Patterns: The American Jewish Family." *American Journal of Sociology* 53 (1948): 439–42.

Wirth, Louis. *The Ghetto: A Study in Isolation.* Chicago: University of Chicago Press, 1928.

Zublin, Charles. "The Chicago Ghetto." In Jane Addams, et al., *Hull House Maps and Papers,* 91–114. Boston: Thomas Y. Crowell Company, 1895.

## Italians

Amberg, Mary A. *Madonna Center.* Chicago: Loyola University Press, 1976.

Beck, Frank Orman. "The Italian in Chicago." *Bulletin of the Chicago Department of Public Welfare* 2 (February 1919): 5–32.

Brandt, Lilian A. "Transplanted Birthright: The Development of the Second Generation of the Italians in an American Environment." *Charities,* 7 May 1904, 494–99.

Campisi, Paul J. "Ethnic Family Patterns: The Italian Family in the United States." *American Journal of Sociology* 52 (1948): 443–49.

Carsi, Edward. "Italian Immigrants and Their Children." *Annals of the American Academy of Political and Social Sciences* 223 (September 1942): 100–106.

# Select Bibliography

Cordasco, Francesco, and Eugene Bacchioni. *The Italians: Social Background of an American Group.* Clifton, N.J.: A. M. Kelley, 1974.

Dunne, Edmund M. "Memoirs of 'Zi Pre.' " *American Ecclesiastical Review* 49 (August 1913): 192–203.

Gans, Herbert J. *The Urban Villagers: Group and Class in the Life of Italian Americans.* Glencoe, N.Y.: Free Press of Glencoe, 1962.

Ianni, Francis A. J. "The Italo-American Teen-Ager." *Annals of the American Academy of Political and Social Sciences* 338 (November 1961): 70–78.

Kelley, Florence. "Italians in Chicago." *Bulletin of the Department of Labor,* (United States Bureau of Labor) 2 (1897): 691–727.

Landesco, John. *Organized Crime in Chicago.* Chicago: Illinois Association for Criminal Justice, 1929.

———. "Crime and the Failure of Institutions in Chicago's Immigrant Areas." *Journal of the American Institute of Criminal Law and Criminology* 23 (July-August 1932): 238–48.

———. "The Life History of a Member of the '42 Gang.' " *Journal of Criminal Law and Criminology* 24 (March 1933): 967–80.

Nelli, Humbert S. "The Italian Padrone System in the United States." *Labor History* 5 (Spring 1964): 153–67.

———. "The Role of the 'Colonial Press' in the Italian-American Community of Chicago." Ph.D. dissertation, University of Chicago, 1965.

———. "Italians in Urban America: A Study in Ethnic Adjustment." *International Migration Review* 1 (1967): 38–55.

———. *Italians in Chicago, 1880–1930.* New York: Oxford University Press, 1970.

Prindiville, Kate G. "Italy in Chicago." *Catholic World* 76 (July 1903): 452–61.

Sanders, James W. *The Education of an Urban Minority: Catholics in Chicago, 1833–1965.* New York: Oxford University Press, 1977.

Schiavo, Giovanni E. *The Italians in Chicago: A Study in Americanization.* Chicago: Italian American Publishing Company, 1928.

Sorrentino, Anthony. *Organizing against Crime: Re-developing the Neighborhood.* New York: Human Sciences Press, 1977.

Tomasi, Silvano M., and Madeline H. Engel, eds. *The Italian Experience in the United States.* New York: Center for Migration Studies, 1970.

Vecoli, Rudolph J. "Chicago's Italians prior to World War I: A Study of Their Social and Economic Adjustment." Ph.D. dissertation, University of Wisconsin, 1963.

———. "Contadini in Chicago: A Critique of the Uprooted." *Journal of American History* 51 (December 1964): 404–17.

———. "Prelates and Peasants: Italian Immigrants and the Catholic Church." *Journal of Social History* 2 (Spring 1969): 217–68.

Walsh, John P. "The Catholic Church in Chicago and the Problems of Urban Society, 1893–1915." Ph.D. dissertation, University of Chicago, 1948.

Whyte, William F. "Social Organization in the Slums." *American Sociological Review* 8 (February 1943): 37–39.

———. *Street Corner Society: The Social Structure of an Italian Slum.* Chicago: University of Chicago Press, 1958.

Wright, Carroll D. *The Italians in Chicago.* Washington, D.C.: United States Printing Office, 1896.

## Greeks

Abbott, Grace. "Study of Greeks in Chicago." *American Journal of Sociology* 15 (November 1909): 379–93.

Barrows, Edith C. "The Greek Play at Hull House." *Commons* 19 (January 1904): 6–10.

Burgess, Thomas. *Greeks in America.* Boston: Sherman, French and Company, 1913.

Kopan, Andrew T. "Greek Survival in Chicago: The Role of Ethnic Education, 1890–1980." In Peter d'A. Jones and Melvin G. Holli, eds., *Ethnic Chicago.* Grand Rapids, Mich.: William B. Erdmans Publishing Company, 1981.

Kourvetaris, George A. *First and Second Generation Greeks in Chicago.* Athens, 1971.

Steiner, Edward A. *On the Trail of the Immigrant.* New York: F. H. Revell Company, 1906.

Xenides, J. P. *The Greeks in America.* New York: George H. Doran Company, 1922.

## General Sources

Abel, Emily K. "Middle-Class Culture for the Urban Poor: The Educational Thought of Samuel Barnett." *Social Service Review* 82 (1978): 596–620.

## Felix Adler

Adler, Felix. *An Ethical Philosophy of Life.* New York: D. Appleton and Company, 1920.

———, ed., *Fiftieth Anniversary of the Ethical Movement, 1876–1926.* New York: D. Appleton and Company, 1926.

Bridges, Horace J., ed. *Aspects of Ethical Religion.* New York: American Ethical Union, 1926.

Friess, Horace L. *Felix Adler and Ethical Culture.* New York: Columbia University Press, 1981.

Kraut, Benny. *From Reform Judaism to Ethical Culture: The Religious Evolution of Felix Adler.* Cincinnati: Hebrew Union College Press, 1979.

Neumann, Henry. *Spokesmen for Ethical Religion.* Boston: Beacon Press, 1951.

Radest, Howard B. *Toward Common Ground: The Story of the Ethical Societies in the United States.* New York: Friederich Unger Publishing Company, 1969.

Baker, Ray S. "Hull House and the Ward Boss." *Outlook,* 28 March 1898, 769–71.

Banfield, Edward C., and James Q. Wilson. *City Politics.* Cambridge: Harvard University Press, 1966.

Becker, Dorothy G. "Social Welfare Leaders as Spokesmen for the Poor." *Social Case Work* 49 (February 1968): 82–89.

Beckner, Edward. *A History of Labor Legislation in Illinois.* Chicago: University of Chicago Press, 1929.

Benson, C. A. "Social Settlement Theatre: Hull House and Karamu House." Ph.D. dissertation, University of Wisconsin, 1965.

Bourne, Randolph S. "Trans-National America." In Carl Resek, ed., *War and the Intellectuals: Essays by Randolph S. Bourne, 1915–1919,* 107–23. New York: Harper and Row Publishers, 1964.

———. "The Jew and Trans-National America." In Carl Resek, ed., *War and the Intellectuals: Essays by Randolph S. Bourne, 1915–1919,* 124–33. New York: Harper and Row Publishers, 1964.

## Select Bibliography

Bridges, Horace J. *On Becoming an American.* Boston: Marshall Jones Company, 1918.

Buroker, Robert L. "From Voluntary Association to Welfare State: The Illinois 'Immigrants' Protective League,' 1908–1926." *Journal of American History* 18 (December 1971): 643–60.

Carlson, Robert A. *The Quest for Conformity: Americanization through Education.* New York: J. Wiley, 1975.

Caughey, Mary B. "A History of the Settlement House Theaters in the United States." Master's dissertation, University of Louisiana, 1927.

Conway, Jill. "Jane Addams: An American Heroine." *Daedalus* 93 (Spring 1964): 761–80.

Davis, Allen F. "Jane Addams vs. the Ward Boss." *Journal of the Illinois State Historical Society* 53 (Autumn 1960): 247–65.

———. "The Women's Trade Union League: Origins and Organization." *Labor History* 5 (Winter 1964): 3–17.

———. *Spearheads for Reform: The Social Settlements and the Progressive Movement, 1890–1914.* New York: Oxford University Press, 1967.

———. *American Heroine: The Life and Legend of Jane Addams.* London: Oxford University Press, 1973.

Davis, Allen F., and Mary L. McCree, eds. *Eighty Years at Hull House.* Chicago: Quadrangle Books, 1969.

De'Ath, Colin E., and Peter Padbury. "Brokers and the Social Ecology of Minority Groups." In George L. Hicks and Philip E. Leis, eds., *Ethnic Encounters,* 181–200. North Scituate, Mass.: Duxbury Press, 1977.

### John Dewey

Dewey, John. "The School as Social Center." In National Education Association, *Journal of Proceedings and Addresses* (1902), 373–83.

———. "Interpretation of Savage Mind." *Psychological Review* 9 (May 1902): 217–30.

———. "Pluralism." In Dagobert D. Runes, ed., *Dictionary of Philosophy and Psychology.* New York: Philosophical Library, 1902.

———. *The School and Society.* Chicago: University of Chicago Press, 1915.

———. *Schools of Tomorrow.* New York: E. P. Dutton and Company, 1915.

———. "Nationalizing Education." In National Education Association, *Journal of Proceedings and Addresses* (1916), 183–89.

———. *Democracy and Education.* New York: Macmillan Company, 1916.

———. "Universal Service as Education." *New Republic,* 22 and 29 April 1916, 309–10, 334–35.

———. "The Principle of Nationality." *Menorah Journal* 3 (October 1917): 203–8.

———. "Autocracy under Cover." *New Republic,* 24 August 1918, 103–6.

———. "Conditions among the Poles in the United States." In Confidential Report. Washington, D.C.: United States Government Printing Office, 1918.

Archambault, Reginald D., *John Dewey on Education: Selected Writings.* New York: Random House, 1964.

———, ed. *John Dewey on Education.* New York: Random House, 1966.

Eisele, J. Christopher. "John Dewey and the Immigrants." *History of Education Quarterly* 15 (Spring 1975): 67–86.

Feinberg, Walter. "Progressive Education and Social Planning." *Teachers College Record* 73 (May 1972): 485–505.

Franklin, Barry. "Essays Review 3: Education for Social Control." *History of Education Quarterly* 14 (Spring 1974).

Hook, Sidney. "The Snare of Definitions." *Humanist* 31 (September-October 1971): 10–11.

Karier, Clarence J. "Liberal Ideology and the Quest for Orderly Change." In Clarence J. Karier, et al., *Roots of Crisis: American Education in the Twentieth Century*, 84–107. Chicago: Rand McNally, 1973.

Katz, Michael B. "Review of Roots of Crisis." *Harvard Educational Review* 43 (Fall 1973): 440–41.

Katz, Michael. *Class, Bureaucracy, and Schools.* New York: Proeger, 1971.

Lawson, Douglas E., and Arthur E. Lean, eds. *John Dewey and the World View.* Carbondale: Southern Illinois University Press, 1964.

Peters, Richard S., ed. *John Dewey Reconsidered.* London: Routledge and Kegan Paul, 1977.

Ratner, Joseph, ed. *John Dewey, Characters, and Events: Popular Essays in Social and Political Philosophy.* New York: Holt and Company, 1929.

————. *Intelligence in the Modern World: John Dewey's Philosophy.* New York: Modern Library, 1939.

Zerby, Charles L. "John Dewey and the Polish Question: A Response to the Revisionist Historians." *History of Education Quarterly* 15 (Spring 1975): 17–30.

Drachsler, Julius. *Democracy and Assimilation: The Blending of Immigrant Heritage in America.* New York: Macmillan Company, 1920.

Farrell, John C. *Beloved Lady: A History of Jane Addams' Ideals on Reform and Peace.* Baltimore: Johns Hopkins University Press, 1967.

Glazer, Nathan. "Immigrant Groups and American Culture." *Yale Review* 48 (1958/59): 382–97.

————. "Ethnic Groups in America: From National Culture to Ideology." In Morris Berger et al., *Freedom and Control in Modern Society*, 158–73. New York: Octagon Books, 1964.

Gleason, Philip. "The Melting Pot: Symbol of Fusion or Confusion." *American Quarterly* 16 (1964): 20–46.

Gordon, Milton M. "Assimilation in America: Theory and Reality." *Daedalus* 90 (1961): 263–85.

————. *Assimilation in American Life: The Role of Race, Religion, and National Origins.* New York: Oxford University Press, 1964.

Hapgood, Norman. "The Future of the Jews in America." *Harper's Weekly*, November 1915, 511–12.

Hartmann, Edward G. *The Movement to Americanize the Immigrant.* New York: Columbia University Press, 1948.

Hays, Samuel P. "The Politics of Reform in Municipal Government in the Progressive Era." *Pacific Northwest Quarterly* 55 (October 1964): 157–69.

Herrick, Mary J. *The Chicago Schools: A Social and Political History.* Beverly Hills, Calif.: Sage Publications, 1971.

Higham, John. *Strangers in the Land: Patterns of American Nativism, 1860–1925.* New Brunswick, N.J.: Rutgers University Press, 1955.

Select Bibliography

_____. *Send These to Me: Jews and Other Immigrants in Urban America.* New York: Atheneum, 1975.

_____, ed. *Ethnic Leadership in America.* Baltimore: Johns Hopkins University Press, 1978.

Hill, Lewis W. *The People of Chicago: Census Data on Foreign-born, Foreign Stock, and Race, 1837–1970.* Chicago: Department of Development and Planning of the City of Chicago, 1976.

Hollinger, David A. "Ethnic Diversity, Cosmopolitanism, and the Emergence of the American Liberal Intelligentsia." *American Quarterly* 28 (May 1975): 133–51.

Horowitz, Helen L. "Varieties of Cultural Experience in Jane Addams' Chicago." *History of Education Quarterly* 14 (Spring 1974): 69–86.

## William James

James, William, *The Philosophy of William James, Selected from His Chief Works.* New York: Modern Library, n.d.

_____. *Talk to Teachers on Psychology: And to Students on Some of Life's Ideals.* New York: H. Holt, 1900.

Miller, Larry C. "William James and Twentieth-Century Ethnic Thought." *American Quarterly* 31 (1979): 533–55.

Johnston, Michael. *Political Corruption and Public Policy in America.* Monterey, Calif.: Brooks/Cole Company, 1982.

Johnston, Ruth. "The Influence of the Ethnic Association on the Assimilation of Its Immigrants." *International Migration Quarterly Review* 5 (1967): 147–211.

Jones, Howard M. *The Age of Energy: Varieties of American Experience, 1865–1915.* New York: Viking Press, 1971.

## Horace M. Kallen

Kallen, Horace M. "Nationality and the Hyphenated American." *Menorah Journal* 1 (April 1915): 79–85.

_____. *Culture and Democracy.* New York: Boni and Liveright, 1924.

_____. *Judaism at Bay: Essays toward the Adjustment of Judaism to Modernity.* New York: Bloch Publishing Company, 1932.

_____. "National Solidarity and the Jewish Minority." *Annals of the American Academy of Political and Social Sciences* 223 (September 1942): 17–28.

_____. *The Education of Free Men: An Essay toward a Philosophy of Education.* New York: Farrar, Straus and Company, 1949.

_____. "Democracy and the Melting Pot." In Benjamin M. Ziegler, ed., *Immigration*, 25–29. Boston: D. C. Heath, 1953.

_____. "Democracy versus the Melting Pot." In Benjamin M. Ziegler, ed., *Immigration*, 29–35. Boston: D.C. Heath, 1953.

_____. *Cultural Pluralism and the American Idea.* Philadelphia: University of Pennsylvania Press, 1956.

Hook, Sidney, and Milton R. Knovitz, eds. *Freedom and Experience: Essays Presented to Horace M. Kallen.* New York: Cornell University Press, 1947.

Janowsky, Oscar, ed. *The American Jew: A Composite Portrait.* New York: Harper, 1942.

Marrow, Alfred J., ed. *What I Believe and Why—Maybe.* New York: Horizon Press, 1971.

245

Ratner, Sidney, ed. *Vision and Action: Essays in Honor of Horace M. Kallen on His Seventieth Birthday.* New Brunswick, N.J.: Rutgers University Press, 1954.

Karier, Clarence J., et al. *Roots of Crisis: American Education in the Twentieth Century.* Chicago: Rand McNally, 1973.

Katz, Harriet. "Workers' Education or Education for the Worker?" *Social Service Review* 82 (1978): 265–74.

Kogut, Alvin. "The Settlements and Ethnicity: 1840–1914." *Social Work* 17 (May 1972): 22–31.

Kohn, Hans. *American Nationalism: An Interpretative Essay.* New York: Macmillan Company, 1957.

Krug, Mark M. *The Melting of the Ethnics: Education of the Immigrants, 1880–1914.* Bloomington, Ind.: Phi Delta Educational Foundation, 1976.

Lawless, D. J. "Attitudes of Leaders of Immigrant and Ethnic Societies in Vancouver towards Integration into Canadian Life." *International Migration Quarterly Review* 2 (1964): 201–11.

Lee, Joseph. "Assimilation and Nationality." *Survey,* January 1908, 1453–55.

Leonard, Henry B. "The Immigrants' Protective League of Chicago, 1908–1921." *Journal of the Illinois State Historical Society* 66 (Autumn 1973): 271–84.

Levine, Daniel. *Varieties of Reform Thought.* Madison: State Historical Society of Wisconsin, 1964.

————. *Jane Addams and the Liberal Tradition.* Madison: State Historical Society of Wisconsin, 1971.

Linn, James W. *Jane Addams: A Biography.* New York: D. Appleton-Century Company, 1935.

Loth, David G. *Swope of General Electric: The Story of Gerard Swope and General Electric in American Business.* New York: Simon and Schuster, 1958.

McBride, Paul. *Cultural Clash: Immigrants and Reformers, 1880–1920.* San Francisco: R. and Research Associates, 1975.

McCree, Mary L. "The First Year of Hull House, 1889–1890: Letters by Jane Addams and Ellen G. Starr." *Chicago History* (Fall 1970): 101–14.

Mann, Arthur. *The One and the Many: Reflections on the American Identity.* Chicago: University of Chicago Press, 1979.

May, Henry F. *The End of American Innocence: A Study of the First Years of Our Own Time, 1912–1917.* Oxford: Oxford University Press, 1959.

Mayo-Smith, Richmond. *Emigration and Immigration: A Study in Social Science.* New York: C. Scribner's Sons, 1890.

## George Herbert Mead

Mead, George Herbert. Review of *The Newer Ideal of Peace* by Jane Addams. *American Journal of Sociology* 13 (1907): 121–28.

————. "On the Educational Situation in the Chicago Public Schools." *City Club Bulletin* 1 (1907/8): 131–38.

————. "The Social Settlement: Its Basis and Function." *University of Chicago Record* 12 (1908): 108–10.

————. "Remarks on Labor Night." *City Club Bulletin* 5 (1912): 214–15.

————. Review of *Truancy and Non-attendance in the Chicago Public Schools* by Edith Abbott and Sophonisba P. Breckinridge." *Survey* 38 (1917): 365–70.

_____. "National Mindedness and International Mindedness." *International Journal of Ethics* 39 (1929): 385–407.

Barry, Robert M. "A Man and a City: George Herbert Mead in Chicago." In Michael Novak, ed., *American Philosophy and the Future*, 173–92. New York, 1968.

Miller, Herbert A. *The School and the Immigrant*. Cleveland: Survey Committee of the Cleveland Foundation, 1916.

_____. "The Rising of National Individualism." *American Journal of Sociology* 19 (1914): 592–605.

Philpot, Thomas L. *The Slum and the Ghetto: Neighborhood Deterioration and Middle-Class Reform, Chicago, 1880–1930*. New York: Oxford University Press, 1978.

Quandt, Jean B. *From the Small Town to the Great Community: The Social Thought of Progressive Intellectuals*. New Brunswick, N.J.: Rutgers University Press, 1970.

Ripley, William Z. "Races in the United States." *Atlantic Monthly*, December 1908, 745–59.

Rousmaniere, John P. "Cultural Hybrid in the Slums: The College Woman and the Settlement House, 1889–1894," *American Quarterly* 22 (1970): 45–66.

Sanders, James W. *The Education of an Urban Minority: Catholics in Chicago, 1833–1965*. New York: Oxford University Press, 1977.

Scott, Anne F. "Saint Jane and the Ward Boss." *American Heritage* 12 (December 1960).

Shumsky, Neil L. "Zangwill's *The Melting Pot:* Ethnic Tensions on Stage." *American Quarterly* 27 (1975): 29–41.

Sloan, Douglas. "Cultural Uplift and Social Reform in Nineteenth-Century Urban America." *History of Education Quarterly* 19 (Fall 1979): 361–72.

Solomon, Barbara M. *Ancestors and Immigrants: A Changing New England Tradition*. Chicago: University of Chicago Press, 1956.

Stein, Maurice R. *The Eclipse of Community: An Interpretation of American Studies*. Princeton, N.J.: Princeton University Press, 1961.

Stevens, Edward W., Jr. "Social Centers, Politics, and Social Efficiency in the Progressive Era." *History of Education Quarterly* 12 (Spring 1972): 16–33.

Szasz, Ferenc M. "The Stress on Character and Service in Progressive America." *Mid-America* 63 (October 1981): 145–54.

Thomas, John L. "The New Immigration and Cultural Pluralism." *American Catholic Sociological Review* 15 (December 1954): 310–22.

## William I. Thomas

Thomas, William I. "Standpoint for the Interpretation of Savage Society." *American Journal of Sociology* 15 (September 1909): 145–63.

_____. "Race Psychology: Standpoint and Questionnaire, with Particular Reference to the Immigrant and the Negro." *American Journal of Sociology* 17 (1912): 725–75.

_____. "The Prussian-Polish Situation: An Experiment in Assimilation." *American Journal of Sociology* 19 (1914): 624–39.

Janowitz, Morris, ed. *William I. Thomas on Social Organization and Social Personality*. Chicago: University of Chicago Press, 1966.

Park, Robert E., and Herbert A. Miller, eds. *Old World Traits Transplanted.* Chicago: University of Chicago Press, 1925.

Thrasher, Frederick M. *The Gang: A Study of 1,313 Gangs in Chicago.* Chicago: University of Chicago Press, 1927.

Tims, Margaret. *Jane Addams of Hull House, 1860–1935.* New York: Fawcett Publications, 1961.

Trueblood, Marilyn A. "The Melting Pot and Ethnic Revitalization." In George L. Hicks and Philip E. Leis, eds., *Ethnic Encounters,* 153–67. North Scituate, Mass.: Duxbury Press, 1977.

Warner, William, and Leo Srole. *The Social Systems of American Ethnic Groups.* New Haven: Yale University Press, 1945.

Weiss, Bernard J. *American Education and the European Immigrant, 1840–1940.* Chicago: University of Illinois Press, 1982.

White, George C. "Social Settlements and Immigrant Neighbors." *Social Service Review* 33 (1959): 55–66.

White, Morton and Lucia. *The Intellectual versus the City.* Cambridge: Harvard University Press, 1962.

Wise, Winifred E. *Jane Addams of Hull House: A Biography.* New York: Harcourt, Brace and Company, 1935.

Wringley, Julia. *Class Politics and Public Schools, Chicago, 1900–1950.* New Brunswick, N.J.: Rutgers University Press, 1985.

### Ella Flagg Young

Young, Ella Flagg. *Isolation in the School.* Chicago: University of Chicago Press, 1900.

———. "Modern Languages in High Schools." *Journal of Education,* 5 December 1912, 597.

———. "The Secular Free Schools." In National Education Association, *Proceedings* (1916), 63–68.

———. "American Education and the Inner Life." In National Education Association, *Proceedings* (1917), 99–103.

Smith, Joan K. "The Influence of Ella Flagg Young on John Dewey's Educational Thought." *Review Journal of Philosophy and Social Science* 2 (1977): 143–54.

Zangwill, Israel. *The Principle of Nationalities.* London: Watts, 1917.

# INDEX

# Index

Jews, German, 50, 74, 81, 83, 86, 90, 92, 114–15
Joint Committee on Americanization, 170
Joint Committee on the Education and Naturalization of Foreign-Born Adults, 178
Judson, Harry Pratt, 59

Kallen, Horace M., 4, 123, 147–51, 153–55, 159–60, 174–75, 184
Kelley, Florence, 94
Krug, Mark, 8
Kunz, Stanley H., 66
Kyriakopolos, George, 107

Labor Museum, 41, 46
Lambros, Peter S., 107, 133
Landsmanshaften, 28, 36, 42, 82, 87
LaSalle Political Club, 93
Lazar, Ben-Zion, 85
Liberal Progressives, 7, 11, 18–19, 27, 29–30, 48, 57, 60–66, 69–70, 76, 92, 123–37, 141, 147, 151–52, 156–57, 161, 165, 169–74, 176–77, 179–84
Like-mindedness, 2, 14, 152, 153, 177, 181
Lincoln, Abraham, 144, 163
Lipsky, Harry A., 90, 92–93, 130
Lower classes, 19–20, 61

McCormick, Alexander A., 64
MacDowell, Mary E., 7
Mack, Julian W., 18, 64, 93, 155–56
Madison Street Settlement, 171
Madonna Settlement, 99–100, 118
Marks Nathan Jewish Orphan Home, 81, 91
Mastro-Valerio, Alessandro, 42, 97–98, 100, 102, 115
Mazzini, Giuseppe, 97, 144
Mead, George Herbert, 7, 64
Middle class (native-born), 17–21, 68–70, 75, 120, 137, 153
Miller, Herbert A., 7, 53
Moscowitz, Henry, 171
Moses Montefiore School, 82
Municipal Voters' League (Chicago), 66, 70–71, 100
Mutual benefit societies, 36, 42, 82, 95, 100, 107, 124

Nagel, Charles, 18
National Committee of One Hundred, 177

National Conference of Charities and Correction (after 1917, National Conference of Social Work), 26
National Education Association, 55, 58, 69
National fraternal organizations, 28, 42–43, 73, 89–90
Nativists, 40
New World, 98, 99
Nirgin, Jaroslav V., 137
Northwestern University Settlement, 6

Order of Knights of Zion (formerly, Chicago Zionist Society), 83–85, 88–89

Padrones (ethnic bosses), 39, 64, 65, 100, 124–27
Pan Arcadian Federation, 105
Park, Robert E., 7, 136, 174
Parochial schools (bilingual), 35, 37, 38, 40, 50–55, 69, 98–99, 105, 116, 132, 135
Peer group society, 120
Pegeas, Leon, 105–6
Poale Zion, 93
Poles, 31, 44, 49, 55, 58, 69, 113, 137, 154, 163
Polish National Alliance, 72–73, 135–36
Powers, John, 66, 71, 98, 100, 102
Progressive movement, 1, 13
Progressives, 38, 59, 65
Public schools, 49, 51–60, 69, 132

qehilah, 35, 81

Robine, Jane E., 154
Roman Empire, 141, 154–56, 183
Rosenwald, Julius, 86, 92
Ross, Edward, 7
Rudowitz affair, 91–93
Russians, 43, 163

Salopoulos, Nicholas, 107
Schwartz, Charles, 178
Settlement house movement, 1, 22–23, 34, 165
Sissman, Peter, 93
Smulski, John F., 66
Social assimilation, 171, 173
Sons of Italy, 95
South End House, 4
Starr, Ellen G., 100

251